SHELLEY

SHELLEY

Poet and Legislator of the World

EDITED BY

Betty T. Bennett
and
Stuart Curran

THE JOHNS HOPKINS UNIVERSITY PRESS
Baltimore and London

This book has been brought to publication with the generous assistance of the
Carl and Lily Pforzheimer Foundation, Inc.

© 1996 The Johns Hopkins University Press
Chapter 8, "The Transgressive Double Standard: Shelleyan Utopianism and
Feminist Social History," © 1996 Annette Wheeler Cafarelli
All rights reserved. Published 1996
Printed in the United States of America on acid-free paper
05 04 03 02 01 00 99 98 97 96   5 4 3 2 1

THE JOHNS HOPKINS UNIVERSITY PRESS
2715 North Charles Street
Baltimore, Maryland 21218-4319
The Johns Hopkins Press Ltd., London

Library of Congress Cataloging-in-Publication Data will be found at the end of
the book.
A catalog record for this book is available from the British Library.

ISBN 0-8018-5175-0
ISBN 0-8018-5176-9 (pbk.)

Contents

Preface

The year 1992 marked the 200th anniversary of the birth of Percy Bysshe Shelley (1792–1822): poet, philosopher, political visionary, and cultural reformer. In celebration, the Keats-Shelley Association of America, with support from the National Endowment for the Humanities and the Carl and Lily Pforzheimer Foundation, sponsored a large international conference to consider multiple aspects of his art and thought. Among the specific concerns the conference addressed were the sources of Shelley's internationalism; his conception of the poet as legislator of the world; his actual legacy within the nationalist reform struggles of the nineteenth century and in passive resistance movements in the twentieth century; his recent emergence as a forerunner of poststructuralist philosophy and linguistics; the effect of the new textual scholarship (in particular the publication of the notebooks and manuscripts in facsimile); the diversity of his impact on various cultures (American, British, European, Asian); and the enduring importance of his poetry on a world scale.

Such a wide-ranging international conference was especially appropriate for a writer who was fluent in seven languages (who translated from six) and who, after the Enlightenment model, conceived of himself as a citizen of the world. It was also timely. The liberalization of eastern Europe, according to a script Shelley himself might have written, offered the first opportunity in the memory of almost all Shelley students for a free exchange of American and western European scholars with their counterparts in the east, many of whom had labored in isolation for years. This was also an opportunity to open a doorway to the newer scholarship now appearing in Asia. The conference drew participants from every part of the United States, from Canada, Britain, and South Africa, and from France, Italy, the united Germany, Finland, Greece, Hungary, Romania, Russia, Syria, India, and Japan.

This was the first time that a major international conference on Shelley had been assembled. Its purpose was not to homogenize the diverse cultural perspectives and traditions thus assembled, but rather to foster a spirited exchange among them. On the one hand, there was a fruitful examination of the ways in which Shelley's legacy has altered in time or has been reinvested. On the other hand, as useful as is such a consolidation of the past, it was equally important, as the abundance and intellectual vitality of current publication on Shelley indicates, to nourish the breadth of new perspectives that will carry Shelley's influence into a third century.

In particular, the conference focused on how much in recent years the motive force driving Shelley scholarship has been coming from different, virtually opposite, conceptions of his writings and thought. There is the libertarian Shelley who celebrates the progress of liberty as a human birthright and discerns the psychological and social responsibilities involved in ensuring its continuance. This is unquestionably the poet in a still potent role as "unacknowledged legislator of the world." There is, however, Shelley the confirmed skeptic who sees all words as metaphors, all systems as fictions, all truths as relative because ultimately unknowable. This deregulative thinker has been rediscovered as a precursor of modern poststructuralist/deconstructive linguistics and philosophy and of the indeterminacy of modern physics. There are likewise other alternative conceptions that invited a fresh exploration: between the British and North American Shelley, or between the Shelley of the English-speaking world and the figure translated into so many diverse cultures and contexts. Although such multiple interests necessarily took the conference participants in many different directions, at its center was constituted a remarkably coherent series of statements about the Shelley who speaks in a public capacity to a contemporary audience. Those statements form the twenty-three chapters of this book.

The editors have gathered them into four sections. The first five chapters concern themselves with the nature of the poet's cultural role as Shelley defined it, and with how specific cultural and political contexts of the later

Enlightenment help both to frame Shelley's writings in historical terms and to spur his attempts at superseding what he construed as the failed visions of the past. The second set of chapters focus directly on Shelley's own passionate political engagements, inquiring into their roots in his culture, their resonances on a world plane, and their impact on their time and later in the nineteenth century. In the third section are gathered voices literally from around the world, who represent both how Shelley conceived of a global politics and the ways in which his conceptions have influenced particular developments in various cultures or have stood as humane watchwords against repressions of all stripes. The authors of the fourth section ask how Shelley himself looked to the future, as well as how his discourse can be sifted or adjusted to respond to the dilemmas, recast imperatives, and paradigm shifts of a later age.

Shelley's very resilience across the transmutations of time is, of course, the fundamental *raison d'être* for this volume. It is, then, at once fitting to his memory and a harbinger of his future consequence that this assemblage of estimable scholar-critics can, in twenty-three prismatic reflections, so lucidly recast his presence into coherent wholeness and across such a diversity of historical epochs and cultures. The aim of the bicentennial conference and of the essays gathered into this volume is to establish a new plateau in our perception of Shelley as a poet and cultural thinker on the world stage.

It is with great pleasure that we acknowledge a number of colleagues whose special contributions have played key roles in the realization of this volume. William T. Buice, III, President of the Keats-Shelley Association of America, gave this project his always dependable and gracious support. Donald H. Reiman and Doucet D. Fischer were stellar in their handling of many of the details of bringing our conferees together. Joseph A. Wittreich has our special thanks for arranging our use of facilities in the Graduate School and University Center of the City University of New York. So, too, the New York Public Library kindly served as the site for some of our meetings. We wish also to acknowledge the American University and the University of Pennsylvania for the myriad ways in which they have given the co-editors their support over many years. Finally, Susan H. Hertz has been a mainstay as we tackled the challenges of shaping our impressive mass of disks and documents into an ongoing commemoration of the life and art of Percy Bysshe Shelley.

Abbreviations

We have adopted *Shelley's Poetry and Prose*, ed. Donald H. Reiman and Sharon B. Powers, 3rd ed. rev. (New York: W. W. Norton, 1981) as a standard for references to works by Shelley quoted in this volume. Occasionally, authors will refer to other Shelley texts not included in that edition. For other poetry, we have referred to the Oxford Standard Authors edition of *The Complete Poetical Works of Shelley*, ed. Thomas Hutchinson (1905); rev. G. B. Martthews (1970), cited as *OSA*. Citations for other prose works are keyed to the Julian Edition of *The Complete Works of Percy Bysshe Shelley*, ed. Roger Ingpen and Walter E. Peck, 10 volumes (London: Ernest Benn, 1926–30). For correspondence, references are to *The Letters of Percy Bysshe Shelley*, ed. Frederick L. Jones (Oxford: Clarendon Press, 1956)—cited as *PBSL*—and *The Letters of Mary Wollstonecraft Shelley*, ed. Betty T. Bennett (Baltimore: The Johns Hopkins University Press, 1980–88), cited as *MWSL*. Byron's poetry is quoted from *The Complete Poetical Works of Lord Byron*, ed. Jerome J. McGann (Oxford: Clarendon Press, 1980–93) and his familiar prose from *Byron's Letters and Journals*, ed. Leslie Marchand (Cambridge: Harvard University Press, 1972–94), cited as *BLJ*.

Contributors

MEENA ALEXANDER'S work includes *Women in Romanticism: Mary Wollstonecraft, Dorothy Wordsworth, Mary Shelley* (1989) and the novel *Nampally Road,* which has a chapter entitled "Wordsworth in Hyderabad." *The Shock of Arrival,* a collection of her essays and poems, is forthcoming. She is Professor of English and Women's Studies at Hunter College and the Graduate Center, the City University of New York.

ANDREW BENNETT is Lecturer in English at the University of Bristol. He is the author of *Keats, Narrative and Audience: The Posthumous life of Writing* (1994), editor of *Readers and Reading* (1995), and coauthor, with Nicholas Royle, of *Elizabeth Bowen and the Dissolution of the Novel: Still Lives* (1995) and *An Introduction to Literature, Criticism and Theory: Key Critical Concepts* (1995).

BETTY T. BENNETT is Dean of the College of Arts and Sciences and Professor of Literature at the American University, Washington, D.C. She is editor of *The Letters of Mary Wollstonecraft Shelley* (three volumes, 1980, 1983, 1988), and the *Selected Letters of Mary Wollstonecraft Shelley* (1995), coeditor of *The Mary Shelley Reader* (1990), and author of *Mary Diana Dods: A Gentleman and a Scholar* (1991, revised ed. 1994). Dr. Bennett is currently working on a biography of Mary Wollstonecraft Shelley.

LINDA BRIGHAM teaches in the Department of English of Kansas State University. She has published on Wordsworth and Shelley and has forthcoming a study on the relationship between monetary policy and poetic practice during the Regency. She is also embarking on a study of logic, technology, and literature from Romantic poetics to contemporary robotics.

MARILYN BUTLER is Rector of Exeter College, University of Oxford. Her numerous books include studies of Maria Edgeworth, Jane Austen, and Thomas Love Peacock, as well as *Romantics, Rebels and Reactionaries.* She is coeditor (with Janet Todd) of *The Works of Mary Wollstonecraft* and has also edited Mary Shelley's *Frankenstein* and Maria Edgeworth's *Castle Rackrent* and *Ennui.*

ANNETTE WHEELER CAFARELLI is Associate Professor of English and Comparative Literature at Columbia University. She is the author of *Prose in the Age of Poets: Romanticism and Biographical Narrative* and the forthcoming *The Female Machiavel: Women and the Formation of Romanticism.*

STUART CURRAN teaches English and Comparative Literature at the University of Pennsylvania and has written extensively on Shelley and on British Romanticism. He is the editor of *The Cambridge Companion to British Romanticism* (1993) and *The Poems of Charlotte Smith* (1993) and has editions of Mary Shelley's *Frankenstein* (a CD-ROM) and *Valperga* forthcoming.

P. M. S. DAWSON is Lecturer at the University of Manchester and the author of *The Unacknowledged Legislator: Shelley and Politics* (1980). He is associate editor on the Oxford English Texts edition of the complete poems of John Clare, the next volume of which (*The Shepherds Calendar*) is in press. His current research is on the development of Clare's poetry and the aesthetics of the modern graphic novel.

MICHAEL ERKELENZ is Lecturer in English at the University of Toronto. He wrote his doctoral dissertation on Shelley at Oxford University. He has published in Garland Press's series *The Bodleian Shelley Manuscripts* and is currently working on a study of Shelley's uses of Greek literary genres.

NEIL FRAISTAT is Professor of English at the University of Maryland, College Park. His publications include *The Poem and the Book* (University of

North Carolina Press, 1985), *Poems in Their Place* (University of North Carolina Press, 1986), and *The "Prometheus Unbound" Notebooks* (Garland, 1991). He is working on a study of the transmission and reception of Shelley's texts and is coediting with Donald H. Reiman *The Complete Poetry of Percy Bysshe Shelley* (Johns Hopkins University Press) and the second edition of the Norton Critical *Shelley's Poetry and Prose.*

TERENCE ALLAN HOAGWOOD's books include *Skepticism and Ideology: Shelley's Political Prose and Its Philosophical Context from Bacon to Marx* (1988), *Politics, Philosophy and the Production of Romantic Texts* (in press), and several editions including Mary Hays's *The Victim of Prejudice* (1990), Charlotte Smith's *Beachy Head, With Other Poems* (1993), and Mary Robinson's *Sappho and Phaon* (in press).

HORST HÖHNE is Professor Emeritus of English at the University of Rostock in the former German Democratic Republic. A translator of Shelley's poetry into German, he was for many years editor of *Zeitschrift für Anglistik und Amerikanistik.*

LILLA MARIA CRISAFULLI JONES, Associate Professor of English at the University of Bologna, Italy, and Director of its Center for Studies in Romanticism, is also the editor of the interdisciplinary journal "La Questione Romantica." She has written extensively on Shelley and is interested as well in the impact on him and on English Romanticism generally of the writings of William Godwin and Mary Wollstonecraft.

STEVEN E. JONES is Associate Professor of English at Loyola University Chicago. Author of *Shelley's Satire: Violence, Exhortation and Authority* (1994) and editor of two volumes in the *Bodleian Shelley Manuscripts* series, he is also the editor of the *Keats-Shelley Journal* and working on a study of satire and Romanticism.

E. DOUKA KABITOGLOU is Professor of English and Comparative Literature at the Aristotle University of Thessaloniki, Greece. She has published extensively in Romanticism and is the author of *Plato and the English Romantics: Dialogoi* (1990) and editor of *Logomachia: Forms of Opposition in English Language/Literature* (1994). Her research interests, apart from Romantic poetry and poetics, include philosophy, women poets, and feminist criticism.

WILLIAM KEACH teaches in the English Department at Brown University and is the author of *Shelley's Style* (Methuen, 1984). He is currently working on an edition of Coleridge's poems for the Penguin English Poets series and a book about politics and language in British Romantic writing.

GARY KELLY is Professor and Head of the English Department at Keele University in England. He has published books on the English Jacobin novel, British Romantic fiction, Mary Wollstonecraft, and women writers of the Revolution and Romantic Periods. He is general editor of *Longman's History of Women's Writing in English*.

MARK KIPPERMAN has taught at Princeton University and is currently Associate Professor of English at Northern Illinois University. He is the author of *Beyond Enchantment: German Idealism and English Romantic Poetry* (University of Pennsylvania Press, 1986) as well as articles on Shelley and Byron. He is currently working on a book on Byron and Shelley's utopianism in its historical context.

GREG KUCICH is Associate Professor of English at the University of Notre Dame. His publications include *Keats, Shelley, and Romantic Spenserianism* (Penn State Press, 1991) and a series of recent articles on the intersections of gender, historiography, and drama in Romantic era writing. He is currently working on a book-length study of the politics and gendering of Romantic literary historiography. He is also coeditor of *Nineteenth-Century Contexts: An Interdisciplinary Journal*.

ARKADY PLOTNITSKY is the author of *In the Shadow of Hegel: Complementarity, History, and the Unconscious* (1993), *Reconfigurations: Critical Theory and General Economy* (1993), and *Complementarity: Anti-Epistemology after Bohr and Derrida* (1994). His forthcoming study of Shelley is called *Physis, Nous, Eros: Shelley and Scientific Modernity*.

TILOTTAMA RAJAN is Professor of English and Director of the Centre for the Study of Theory and Criticism at the University of Western Ontario. She is the author of *Dark Interpreter: The Discourse of Romanticism* 1980), *The Supplement of Reading: Figures of Understanding in Romantic Theory and Practice* (1990), and coeditor of *Intersections: Nineteenth-Century Philosophy and Contemporary Theory* (1994). She is currently working on a book on the persistence of phenomenology in contemporary theory, as well as on a study of Romantic narrative.

DONALD H. REIMAN has since 1965 been editor of *Shelley and his Circle,* under the auspices of the Pforzheimer Foundation. He has also coedited *Shelley's Poetry and Prose* for Norton, initiated and edited or coedited eight volumes in *The Bodleian Shelley Manuscripts* and *Manuscripts of the Younger Romantics,* and is currently coediting *The Complete Poetry of Percy Bysshe Shelley* for Johns Hopkins University Press, which also published his latest book, *The Study of Modern Manuscripts: Public, Confidential, and Private* (1993).

BOUTHAINA SHAABAN is Professor of English Literature in the English Department of Damascus University, Syria. She received her M.A. and Ph.D. in English literature from Warwick University, England, writing her dissertation on Shelley's influence on the Chartist poets. She is currently the executive editor of *Foreign Literature Quarterly,* published by The Arab Writers Union, Syria. She has published *Both Right and Left Handed: Arab Women Talk about Themselves* (Indiana University Press, 1991), *Poetry and Politics* (Dar Talas, Damascus, 1993) and articles in the *Keats-Shelley Memorial Bulletin* and the *Keats-Shelley Journal,* as well as numerous articles in both English and Arabic on Arab women's literature. She is currently working on a book on Arab Women Novelists, to be published by Indiana University Press.

ALAN WEINBERG is Senior Lecturer in the Department of English of the University of South Africa in Pretoria. His numerous writings on Shelley include *Shelley's Italian Experience* (1991).

KAREN A. WEISMAN teaches in the Department of English at the University of Toronto. She is the author of *Imageless Truths: Shelley's Poetic Fictions* (1994), as well as articles on Romanticism and on contemporary literature and theory. She is currently working on the construction of Romanticism in contemporary culture.

CULTURAL AND
POLITICAL
CONTEXTS

I

I

Shelley and the Human Condition

Donald H. Reiman

1

TWO CENTURIES have passed since the leaders of the French Revolution experimented with their "rational reform" of social institutions and practices, ranging from the calendar to the church; a century and a half have gone by since the Reform Bills of 1832–33 heralded the more moderate changes in British society that led to the increasing influence of Utilitarian ideals throughout Europe. Later, powered by the ideology of Marx and Engels, these programs spread the doctrine of "the greatest good for the greatest number." But as implemented by totalitarian systems, this ideology often treated people as statistics rather than as human beings, and many of the programs imagined by the *philosophes* and later European reformers have now either collapsed or proved themselves ineffectual, in both industrial and underdeveloped countries. Even such timid American and British utilitarian variants of the Marxist dream as the public school and social welfare systems have seemed to many of their constituents inadequate to their self-appointed tasks. Students of the humanities may now, therefore, wish to reconsider the ideals of the first writers emerging from the aftermath of the French Revolution in order to discover whether their views on the failures of that more explosive experiment in human engineering can help us correct the course that Western societies have followed for the past 160 years.

I

Percy Bysshe Shelley was in many ways a child of the Enlightenment. Though he criticized the abuses of the French Revolution, he never totally repudiated the revolution itself, believing that the static condition of power and privilege that had preceded it in France and the reaction that succeeded it throughout the Europe of Metternich's Holy Alliance were worse alternatives than even the chaos and bloodshed during the early days of the revolution. Like Godwin, he held that "anarchy is better than despotism—for this reason—that the former is for a season & that the latter is eternal."[1] He also believed that the revolution, in spite of its perversion and defeat, brought some improvements, as is evident from the opening section of *A Philosophical View of Reform:*

> The Revolution in France overthrew the hierarchy, the aristocracy, and the monarchy, and the whole of that peculiarly insolent and oppressive system on which they were based. But as it only partially extinguished those passions which are the spirit of these forms, a reaction took place which has restored in a certain limited degree the old system. In a degree, indeed, exceedingly limited, and stript of all their antient terrors; the lion of the Monarchy of France with his teeth drawn and his claws pared, now sits maintaining the formal state of a most imperfect and insecure dominion. . . . reversing the proverbial expression of Shakespeare, it may be that the good the revolutionists did lives after them, their ills are interred with their bones. . . . France occupies in this respect the same situation as was occupied by England at the restoration of Charles the 2nd.[2]

Yet for Shelley this image of a French monarchy tamed was only a way station toward a more glorious future. At the end of act 3 of *Prometheus Unbound,* in his greatest statement of the positive goal of human social aspirations, Shelley writes of a humanity totally freed from the spirit as well as the tyranny of the old order:

> The loathesome mask has fallen, the man remains
> Sceptreless, free, uncircumscribed—but man:
> Equal, unclassed, tribeless and nationless,
> Exempt from awe, worship, degree,—the King
> Over himself; just, gentle, wise—but man:
> Passionless? no—yet free from guilt or pain
> Which were, for his will made, or suffered them.   (3.4.193–99)

Human beings become socialized within small groups, whether in extended kinship groups (as in the early days of human development), in local habitational communities—in villages and small towns, in stable neighborhoods or ethnic and religious communities within larger cities, or in the nuclear family that has become the norm in Western industrial societies. Those individuals who grow up in an impersonal situation, such as an institution, where there is no real love and affection, and those who live on the streets in amorphous groups, in which all must fend for themselves without trusting their companions, often have difficulty developing communal feelings and may become sociopaths, willing and able to destroy anyone who gets in their way. Such dysfunctional social groups descend into a Hobbesian state of de-nature in which life becomes truly nasty, brutish, and short. Can Shelley's ideal of a mankind "unclassed, tribeless and nationless, / Exempt from awe, worship, degree" become a model for a viable and humane social order in our time?

Shelley, we must remember, had himself grown up enjoying all the benefits of having been taught positive values and could take the communality of his origins for granted. Unlike Dickens, he had lived a life of privilege in a small, personal, and relatively prosperous agricultural community in which all the socializing supports had been firmly in place for generations. As heir to one of the richest landowners in the district, he had received more than his share of personal attention and positive reinforcement. Even though he seems to have felt a lack of affection from one or both of his parents, he had no occasion to doubt either the stability of the society around him or his own personal worthiness. In his experience, common laboring people, given adequate finances to support their families, would raise socialized children, most of whom would, in due course, follow the example of their parents as responsible members of a mutually supportive community. Among both the rural gentry and the students at Eton and Oxford he encountered a degree of social cohesion and uniformity of thought that no longer inheres in the experience of most of us in the twentieth century and that—if we can believe the testimony of Fielding, Wordsworth, and Dickens—was probably uncharacteristic of London during their times as well. After the ossifying forces of reaction had smothered the incipient fires of a French-inspired revolution in England, Shelley grew up in a community free from the fear of social chaos. For him, therefore, the greatest threat to human welfare lay in being bound so tightly within mundane, limited traditions and values that one might lose sight of the hope for improvement represented by what he calls in *A Defence of Poetry* the imaginative "records of the best and happiest moments of the happiest and best minds."[3]

Shelley, long a disciple of Godwin's writings, was a philosophical anarchist rather than a socialist. Knowing the depths of evil to which human beings were capable of sinking, he favored a moderate amount of societal policing to keep the strong from preying on the weak. What he would have thought of the ideals of a state that took decisions and responsibilities away from individuals and turned them over to experts and bureaucrats we can only guess, since no such state existed in the Europe of his day. But his belief in self-rule would seem to lead in the opposite direction. As he came to realize, self-will could be an evil, but a *self* directed toward the good of others and willing to limit its own actions so as not to infringe on their rights would seem to have been his ideal during his last years. Thus his ideal figures appear, even in the dark vision of the fragmentary "The Triumph of Life," as Socrates and Jesus—they who confronted the full power of social injustice and who chose martyrdom over either flight or violent resistance. At last aware of the dangers of trying to make his feelings and will a measure of the world's good, he came to see himself, as he portrayed the Maniac in "Julian and Maddalo," as one who would rather bear and forbear than injure, one who chose to suffer rather than inflict suffering.

II

When Shelley contemplated social and political changes that would be beneficial, he advocated the abolition of monarchy, the nobility, and other distinctions in title and rank. He favored the enforcement of a more nearly equal economic distribution by shifting the burden of taxation away from commodity taxes that weighed down the poor and toward greater taxation of income and accumulated property, perhaps with a cap on the highest income that anyone would be allowed to receive in a single year. He also advocated the abolition of state-supported religious institutions. Ultimately, he foresaw a democracy that would give each person one vote in the political process, but this was to be achieved over a series of stages, as a growing economic equality gave the poorer classes a stake in avoiding violent revolution and as improved education gave them a clearer sense of their own interests, so that they would resist manipulation by demagogues. We must start, then, by distinguishing Shelley's idealized statements of ultimate goals—

what he calls "beautiful idealisms of moral excellence"—from his advocacy of practical steps toward those reforms. In each of his programmatic political statements, Shelley takes into account the weakness of human nature and the gradations by which it must adjust to drastic change. Thus, in his early *Address to the Irish People,* he urged Ireland's Catholics to avoid those stereotypical weaknesses to which he assumed they were prone: "I wish you, O Irishmen, to be as careful and thoughtful of your interests as are your real friends. Do not drink, do not play [i.e., gamble], do not spend any idle time, do not take every thing that other people say for granted—there are numbers who will tell you lies to make their own fortunes.... Think, read, and talk; let your own condition and that of your wives and children, fill your minds; disclaim all manner of alliance with violence, meet together if you will, but do not meet in a mob."[4]

He expressed himself willing to accept first the steps toward reform backed by popular opinion, even if these efforts did little to ameliorate the social problems he wished ultimately to eliminate entirely through radical reform. While in Dublin in 1812, he also published *Proposals for an Association of . . . Philanthropists,* which was aimed at better-educated Irish readers. On the question of Catholic Emancipation, he wrote, "It is my opinion that the claims of the Catholic inhabitants of Ireland, if gained to-morrow, would in a very small degree, aggrandize their liberty and happiness. . . . I am happy however, at the near approach of this emancipation, ... because it is a sign of benefits approaching, a prophet of good about to come; . . . . it is the fore-ground of a picture, in the dimness of whose distance, I behold the lion lay down with the lamb, and the infant play with the basilisk."[5]

Such images of the harmony between lion and lamb, between child and deadly serpent, recur in Shelley's poetry and prose at least through late 1819, when he completed *Prometheus Unbound.* And if he employed less explicit images of beatitude during his final two and a half years of life, he nevertheless continued to remind people that "The world's great age" could begin anew. But he also intimated that, unless "love and reason" could expand their role in human relationships, the cycle of social reformation would be followed by renewed social decay and by the return of "hate and death." The final chorus of *Hellas* is, like many passages in Shelley's poetry, an instance of very successful mythmaking by a man whose Academic Skepticism precluded him from predicting that the evil he saw in the world around him could ever overcome the good of which he dreamed. At the same time, that chorus also bears a warning for those who might imagine that any victory by virtue would be irreversible.

III

The question remains: What did Shelley, in fact, believe about human nature? If a renovation would free men and women from the power of tyrants and abolish exploitative social structures, could—and would—human beings attain a paradisiacal condition, "Far from passion, pain, and guilt"? Shelley's clearest answer to this question appears, I submit, neither in *Prometheus Unbound* and Shelley's other "ideal" poems nor in *The Cenci,* which Shelley called "a sad reality" but which, though based on historical fact, presents the world (as many commentators have noted) as a dark shadow or specter of the ideal poems.[6] In *The Cenci*—as in "The Triumph of Life," the fragment that Shelley left on his desk when he sailed from Lerici to Livorno to welcome Leigh Hunt to Italy—evil itself is idealized into forms at least as pure as it had been in Shelley's early Gothic novels. Let us turn, instead, to a poem composed during the same period in which he was writing *Prometheus Unbound,* but one that he shaped as a realistic debate between himself and Byron upon the nature and destiny of man.

"Julian and Maddalo" opens with the surrogates of the two poets riding on the Lido of Venice, then an uninhabited sand dune on the edge of the Adriatic. The first dozen lines of the poem depict the waste and deserted nature of the place:

> a bare strand
> Of hillocks, heaped from ever-shifting sand,
> Matted with thistles and amphibious weeds,
> Such as from earth's embrace the salt ooze breeds,
> Is this;—an uninhabitable sea-side
> Which the lone fisher, when his nets are dried,
> Abandons; and no other object breaks
> The waste, but one dwarf tree and some few stakes
> Broken and unrepaired. (lines 3–11)

Though the scene describes an actual encounter between Shelley and Byron during their first meeting in Venice, the poetic function of describing this inhospitable setting of "boundless" "waste and solitary places" that Julian loves is to arouse the human mind to challenge Nature's essential Otherness: the vast emptiness of the world's "desert places" forces humanity to encounter Nature as sublimely indifferent to—and ultimately destructive of—all human hopes. Like the awe-filled scene before Mont Blanc and its terrifying glaciers, the desolate seaside has "a voice . . . not understood / By all, but which the wise [can] ... interpret," the "great ... make felt," and the "good ... deeply feel": it, too, declares, "Power dwells apart in its tranquillity / Remote, serene, and inaccessible." But, as a consequence of this confrontation with the inimical forces of natural Necessity, the adverting mind is made more fully aware of the preciousness of the communion of human beings with one another:

> I love all waste
> And solitary places; where we taste
> The pleasure of believing what we see
> Is boundless, as we wish our souls to be:
> . . . .
>   yet more
> Than all, with a remembered friend I love
> To ride as then I rode;
> . . . .
> So, as we rode, we talked; and the swift thought,
> Winging itself with laughter, lingered not,
> But flew from brain to brain,—such glee was ours—
> Charged with light memories of remembered hours,
> None slow enough for sadness: till we came
> Homeward, which always makes the spirit tame.   (lines 14–33)

In such other poems and fragments as "The Retrospect," "Letter to Maria Gisborne," and "The Boat on the Serchio," the intellectual communion of friends who are bound together by multiple sympathies that fuse the various meanings of the complex English word *love* becomes the ideal toward which all social amelioration must tend. In his fragmentary essay "On Love," written at Bagni di Lucca in July 1818, Shelley declares:

> Love ... is that powerful attraction towards all that we conceive or fear or hope beyond ourselves when we find within our own thoughts the chasm of an insufficient void and seek to awaken in all things that are, a community with what we experience within ourselves. If we reason, we would be understood; if we imagine, we would that the airy children of our brain were born anew within another's; if we feel, we would that another's nerves should vibrate to our own, ... that lips of motionless ice should not reply to lips quivering and burning with the heart's best blood.[7]

But Shelley's conception of love underwent significant change during the last years of his life. By August 1819, when he completed "Julian and

Maddalo" and sent it to Leigh Hunt, he had lost whatever hope he had once entertained that it was possible to find this kind of ideal response from any single person. There in the Maniac, whom Maddalo takes Julian to see, Shelley portrays his own all-too-human feelings of disappointment over a love turned sour. Not only had the Maniac's mate met his lips with "lips of motionless ice," but she had even expressed the wish, "with many a bare broad word," that she had never seen him, never embraced him: wished "That, like some maniac monk, [he] had torn out / The nerves of manhood by their bleeding root / With [his] own quivering fingers." This she said to a man so sensitive that he empathizes with the sufferings of people he has never even met—a man who is "as a nerve o'er which do creep / The else unfelt oppressions of this earth" (lines 420–50 passim).

By early 1821, Shelley continued to declare love the summum bonum; he no longer, however, defined love as a response from others to *his* nature, but rather as a pursuit and celebration of the good that he saw in others. As he wrote in *A Defence of Poetry,* "The great secret of morals is Love; or a going out of our own nature, and an identification of ourselves with the beautiful which exists in thought, action, or person, not our own" (487). In a later lyric (446–47), he expresses the same ideal more Platonically:

> I can give not what men call love,
> But wilt thou accept not
> The worship the heart lifts above
> And the Heavens reject not,—
> The desire of the moth for the star,
> Of the night for the morrow,
> The devotion to something afar
> From the sphere of our sorrow?

IV

Why did Shelley's conception of love change so dramatically from that in his essay of 1818, in which the other is required to sympathize and respond to the nature of the self, to one in which the self seeks to emulate and attain the superior qualities of the other? Why did the self, in other words, give up its pretensions as a teacher to become a pupil again? Intervening between July 1818 and the spring of 1821 were some obviously traumatic biographical events, including the deaths of the Shelleys' two children, Clara and William, and Mary Shelley's resulting depression, which drove an emotional wedge between her and Shelley. There may have been another tragic event surrounding the birth of the child in Naples whom Shelley registered as his and Mary Shelley's under the name Elena Adelaide Shelley—perhaps the death or even the suicide of the child's real mother.[8]

Whatever be the truth about this last case, the accumulated wreckage of destruction and unhappiness left in the wake of Shelley's attempts to implement his notion that the self was, or should be, the measure of the good ultimately forced him to reassess both his past actions and his ideals. Besides the suicides of Harriet Shelley, Fanny Imlay, and perhaps the mother of his Neapolitan child—and the premature deaths of his children Clara, William, and Elena Adelaide Shelley—the poet must have reflected on a series of alienations from his own family and close early friends, including his estrangement from his mother, his sister Elizabeth, and his cousins the Groves; from Elizabeth Hitchener and Harriet de Boinville and her circle; and from his sometime mentors Robert Southey and William Godwin. He had also witnessed the emotional turmoil that had afflicted Mary Shelley and her stepsiblings Charles and Claire Clairmont, partly as a result of their discipleship to him. Shelley eventually came to at least two conclusions: his own judgment about what was good for others was hardly infallible, and actions modeled on an absolute ideal could not be introduced into the quotidian world without the risk of serious and, perhaps, tragic consequences.

Exactly

The behavior of the three main protagonists in "Julian and Maddalo" reveals his developing view that human beings, even when freed from the shackles of external political tyranny, will not necessarily be able to rule the empires of themselves. Julian, though sympathizing with the Maniac and imagining ways in which he could "by patience find / An entrance to the caverns of his mind," and thus "reclaim him from his dark estate," nevertheless—urged by his affairs—leaves Venice the next day (lines 565–83). Maddalo, the cynic who has a low opinion of human nature and is judged in the preface as being too proud to take a lead in the renovation of his country, is the person who both ministers to the Maniac's needs and raises a daughter who is "a wonder of the earth . . . Like one of Shakespeare's women" (lines 590–92). But all ultimately fail: the Maniac apparently either by his hypersensitivity or by the undeserved behavior of his beloved; Julian by his mercurial nature or the pressures of his personal affairs; and Maddalo by his self-imposed isolation, for by the end of the poem, he—much like the wayward youthful poet in *Alastor*—is wandering "far away / Among the mountains of Armenia" (lines 586–87).

Thus, as early as the summer of 1819, Shelley had pulled back from the hopes expressed in *Queen Mab* and his Irish tracts that the lion might really lie down with the lamb, or that human beings, if freed from their external restraints, could recreate Eden in their personal lives. Even without giving any undue weight to the darkness of such poems as *The Cenci* and "The Triumph of Life," we can, perhaps, agree with C. S. Lewis, who wrote:

> It is simply not true to say that Shelley conceives the human soul as a naturally innocent and divinely beautiful creature, interfered with by external tyrants. On the contrary no other heathen writer comes nearer to stating and driving home the doctrine of original sin. . . .
>
> When Shelley looks at and condemns the oppressor he does so with the full consciousness that he also is a man just like that: the evil is within as well as without; all are wicked.[9]

Yet Shelley, sensing both that the social world was hostile to the development of the individual and that individuals were incapable of consistently living up to the moral imperatives to which they subscribed, still regarded it as "the province of the poet to attach himself to those ideas which exalt and ennoble humanity."[10] In the same way, he worked for social reform even though he foresaw that each period of social progress would be followed by a reflux of decay that would sweep away the advances so painfully achieved. The traumas of Byron's childhood imposed on him a sense of his own guilt and unworthiness, and only a career of literary successes and warm friendships enabled Byron to work through his problems to the point at which he was as skeptical about the outer world as he was about himself.[11] Shelley, who began with an exalted sense of his own worth and wisdom, eventually came to understand that he shared human limitations after he and those he loved had been too often buffeted by intractable realities. As all artists preach most of the time against their own particular weaknesses, Shelley urges men to pull back from attempts to impose their will on others. In the third act of *Prometheus Unbound,* he presents as a rule of political life the ideal that the Promethean ruler must always govern by example, never by coercion. Plato's ideal of a philosopher-king has been replaced by the ideal of a hermit-artist who creates or reinforces "beautiful idealisms of moral excellence" through the emulation of which human individuals can learn to rule the chaos of will and emotion. Prometheus, his ideal of "the highest perfection of moral and intellectual nature," and Asia, the Spirit of Intellectual Beauty that supports human aspirations toward perfection in the metaphysical universe, withdraw from the presence of mankind and rule humanity by neither precept nor coercion. They retreat to a cave where they will be visited by "lovely apparitions" upon which their minds shall cast "The gathered rays which are reality" and create "the progeny immortal / Of Painting, Sculpture and rapt Poesy / And arts, though unimagined, yet to be" (3.3.49–56). Even in the millennium, human beings lack the capacity to gaze on the deep truth and must content themselves with this mediated vision.

Shelley's view of the human condition is, ultimately, an existential one. Though lost in a state of mystery and doubt, moral individuals must decide, in commitments of faith, to live in such a way that if the universe fails to provide their lives with meaning—if there is no way within the frail and fading spheres of the visible cosmos to endow with immortality the Good, the True, and the Beautiful that they have created—it will be an injustice. Human beings—isolated, ignorant, and limited as they are—nevertheless provide the universe with its greatest example of moral courage: Recognizing the possibility that they may be both ephemeral and helpless and that their existence may be totally meaningless, they continue to imagine an ideal order and refuse to stop struggling to bring it into being for themselves and their posterity.

Eternity and the Ruins of Time: Shelley and the Construction of Cultural History

Greg Kucich

2

THE MOST compelling developments in recent Shelley studies have arisen largely from our increasing attentiveness to the indeterminate contraries at the heart of Shelley's poetic and philosophical procedures—the central topic of important recent works by Terence Hoagwood, Jerrold Hogle, and most of those critics included in the latest collection of essays on Shelley, G. Kim Blank's *The New Shelley*.[1] Blank representatively prioritizes the poststructuralist linguistic and philosophical emphases of these new studies; yet he also suggests the importance of extending our knowledge of Shelley's "dialectical constructs" to their points of relation with his material, historical contexts.[2]

One of the most provocative areas where we might explore such an intersection of dialectical and historical context lies in Shelley's intensive efforts to construct a poetic identity based on his sense of equal, if not superior, relation to the giants of literary tradition. That maneuver, expressed most dramatically in the "high comparison" with Aeschylus, Milton, Dante, and Shakespeare that legitimizes Shelley's own creative election in the preface of *Prometheus Unbound* (133), was shared by most of the major Romantic poets. Such monumental enterprises ultimately left most of them, as Keats felt in his embattled life-and-death struggle with Milton, deeply divided—confident at times about their transformations of the past, yet also suspicious of their success and, consequently, of their own highest claims to creative election. Shelley, for all his unique optimism about creative possibility, was no exception, asserting the high revisionary independence of mature works like *Prometheus Unbound*—which are not, as he puts it, "an imitation of anything" (*PBSL* 2:219)—while acknowledging that what he calls "the baffling models of antiquity" could push him near the brink of "despair[ing] of producing any thing original" (*PBSL* 2:22). Conflicting expressions of this sort have occasioned considerable dispute about Shelley's response to his predecessors and the larger ambivalence conditioning Romanticism's overall relation with the literary past. Rather than leaping to any Bloomian conclusions about Shelley's encounter with the Covering Cherub of poetic tradition, however, I would prefer to emphasize the persisting contrariety of his engagement with the past and its important role in shaping a creative consciousness grounded in the kind of duality that we are now finding central to his modes of being and writing.

We may come to appreciate more fully this relation between Shelley's historical consciousness and his mental indeterminacy if we trace his divided sense of the past to his strategies of historical invention. Such an investigation will move us away from strictly psychoanalytic readings of literary influence, which tend to posit literary tradition as a transhistorical, preordained monument passively received by Shelley and the Romantics, to demonstrate, instead, how the Romantics' procedures for constructing what Lawrence Lipking calls a "usable past" actually helped condition their divided idea of literary tradition and the related dualities of mind that govern Shelley's poetics.[3]

In the preface to *Prometheus Unbound,* Shelley defines his ultimate intellectual "purpose" as the construction of "a systematical history of what appears to me to be the genuine elements of human society" (135). That project, supported by his lifelong, voracious readings in a staggering range of historical contexts, actually preoccupied him throughout his poetic career, from his delineation of "The Past, the Present, & the Future" in *Queen Mab* (*PBSL* 1:324), to his "Vision of the Nineteenth Century" in *The Revolt of Islam* (*OSA* 31), through his millennial scenarios in *Prometheus Unbound,* to his vision of political progress in *Hellas.* Shelley scholars have recognized the central significance of his historiographical inclinations ever since Kenneth Cameron claimed, several decades ago, that "the main inspirational force in Shelley's work ... is his theory of historical evolution."[4] Although Cameron's assertion has been widely credited, and several individual studies have followed up on its implications, many basic contradictions in Shelley's historical procedures and their relation to his overall creative project have never been satisfactorily explained, prompting Stuart Curran to declare in a fairly recent review of Shelley scholarship that "The notion . . . of history in Shelley would profit from greater attention."[5] We may especially profit from an investigation of Shelley's recurrent tendency to juxtapose conflicting progressive and retrograde narrative strategies in his various formulations of cultural history—the idealized apocalyptic narratives in the later acts of *Prometheus Unbound,* for instance, versus the Furies' bitter record of historical degeneration. To investigate the origins of these competing narrative procedures would be to reach a fuller understanding of the interplay among Shelley's historical practices, his divided attitude toward literary tradition, and his dialectical cast of mind. I carry out such an inquiry by suggesting how the basic conflicts in Shelley's historical method derive from his broad engagement with the narrative strategies of eighteenth- and nineteenth-century social, political, artistic, and natural historiography.

Shelley was aware all along of the importance of fashioning a "usable past" rather than being controlled by, as he puts it, the "slow victory of the spirit of the past over that of the present" (*PBSL* 2:358). It is the "privilege" of "poets," he claims on more than one occasion, to mold "historical materials" into what he calls "idealized history" (*PBSL* 2:408 497). To mold those crude materials into a progressive history of cultural development became, in fact, an important mechanism for Shelley to authorize his own creative election as a poet whose very situation at the apex of literary history enables him to fulfill that central Romantic aspiration of transforming the achievements of the past. Shelley's concern with the problematics of such historical invention, however, was also a constant, beginning early in his career and developing with increasing complexity into a major shaping force in his poetry and critical prose. The experience of historical construction in *Queen Mab* immediately sensitized him to fundamental contradictions in his procedures, for the poem's contrast between the eternal ideals of an imagined future state and the ruins of time depicted in the bulk of its narrative highlights two competing strategies of historical narration—an ideal historical progression toward millennial completion versus a material account of actual human misery that documents, at best, a recurring cycle of the same dull round of suffering and, at worst, a retrograde descent into ever-deepening patterns of tyranny, injustice, and oppression.

This divided historical consciousness informs Shelley's earliest commitment to a full course of historical studies, advised by Godwin late in 1812. When Godwin urged him to study "History . . . in its most comprehensive sense" as a detailed "record [of] all that man has done," Shelley immediately committed himself to the project and ordered a list of historical works by such writers as Gibbon, Hume, Southey, Herodotus, Plutarch, and Thucydides (*PBSL* 1:340–42). Yet he viewed the "history" recounted in these works as nothing but a sustained "record of crimes & miseries," the study of which felt "hateful and disgusting to my very soul" (*PBSL* 1:340). And his reluctant application to such a loathful field of realities left him "hanker[ing]," at the same time, for the ideality of "metaphysical works" (*PBSL* 1:340). These divided inclinations to eternal and time-bound history would continue to inform Shelley's various and increasingly complicated efforts at historical invention, creating a sustained pattern of contrary narratives of historical progress and decline that is perhaps best encapsulated in one of his later imaginative reconstructions of Classical history. Consider, he writes to John Gisborne, that

> if the Athenians had, acquiring Sicily held the balance between Rome & Carthage, sent garrisons to the Greek colonies in the south of Italy, Rome might have been all that its intellectual condition entitled it to be, a tributary not the conqueror of Greece. . . . Who knows whether under the steady progress which philosophy & social institutions would have made . . . whether the Christian Religion would have arisen, or the barbarians have overwhelmed the wrecks of civilization which had survived the conquests & tyranny of the Romans.—What then should we have been? As it is . . . we are stuffed full of prejudices. . . . Our imagination & understanding are alike subjected to rules the most absurd: So much for . . . the Greeks (*PBSL* 2:156).

So much, Shelley might have added, for any certainty about that imagined "steady progress" of cultural development that would help legitimize his own creative aspirations.

Those critics attentive to Shelley's historical procedures have for some time recognized these intrinsic patterns of contrariety, but questions about their causes, the degree to which Shelley resolves them, and their relation to his overall idea of literary tradition have never been easy to settle. William Campbell, for instance, argues that Shelley alternately depicts historical culture progressing forward toward an eventual millennium and degenerating from an early state of superior excellence. To Campbell, these deviating narratives of progress and decline manifest a fundamental confusion and disappointment in Shelley's efforts to invent a "usable past."[6] What may seem like wavering and confusion on Shelley's part, however, may be understood more clearly if we situate the problematics of his cultural historicism within the broader narrative contraries of social, political, economic, and natural historiography in the eighteenth and early nineteenth centuries.

Shelley was always sensitive to the important distinctions among different kinds of history, such as the contrast between what he called "the history of men," or civilization, and "the history of titles," or political brutality (7:226). Yet it was more common for him to stress the interrelations of historical disciplines, especially the connections between literary and sociopolitical history. In the preface to *The Revolt of Islam,* for instance, he attributes a current retrogression in England's literary history to the "infectious gloom" cast over the culture's imagination by Malthus's gloomy history of society and population (OSA 34). Shelley would have learned to make such connections from the basic procedures of literary historiography that were developed in Britain toward the end of the eighteenth century. Following the publication of Thomas Warton's partial history of English poetry (1774–81), the project of building up a thorough account of Britain's literary development occupied most of the major and many of the minor writers of the late eighteenth and early nineteenth centuries, including such diverse figures as Southey, Campbell, Hunt, Wordsworth, Coleridge, and Hazlitt, as well as lesser-known historians and editors like Henry Headley, Alexander Chalmers, Percival Stockdale, and Nathan Drake. In fashioning a national literary record, these writers relied heavily on Warton and other eighteenth-century literary historians, such as Edward Young, William Duff, and Oliver Goldsmith. More specifically, they tended to follow the interdisciplinary approach to historiography that controls most eighteenth-century literary history. Such a "synchronism," as James Granger terms it in his 1769 *Biographical History of England,* bears most significantly on Romantic literary historiography, and on Shelley's particular historical procedures, in its incorporation of the broad, often conflicting narrative strategies of general eighteenth-century meditations on the past.[7]

One of the controlling narrative structures of these works entails the shaping of historical movement within a linear framework of progress and decline. This strategy issued generally from the intensive and ongoing debates about cultural improvement and degeneration that so preoccupied such giants of historiography as Bacon, Hume, and Gibbon in England, and Rousseau, Condorcet, Volney, Kant, Schiller, and Hegel on the continent. The gripping question taken up with endlessly creative variation by all these writers turns on the central issue of whether human society moves through time along a linear track of progress or regression. The very structuring of these narratives along such lines is itself informed, as René Wellek has argued, by scientific models of biological evolution and theological paradigms of Christian apocalyptic history.[8] Most important for literary historians of both the eighteenth and nineteenth centuries was the tendency in these narrative models to conflate the lines of progress and decline as essential components of a single pattern of contrary motion. To champion either the Prolific or the Devouring energies of this narrative was thus to embrace or at least acknowledge the pressure of its contrary.

If we keep in mind the models of contrariety that inform these master narratives, we may find them not simply delineating a contest between the ancients and the moderns—a direct opposition between the retrograde scenario of Gibbon's history of Rome and the optimistic patterns of Walpole's version of the steady "improvements in arts and sciences"[9]—but rather articulating complex theories of perpetual tension between the two extremes. Hume, for instance, argues in his *History of England* for a progressive refinement in British arts and government at the same time that he finds the arts and sciences subject to an inexorable process of decline. He characterizes this paradox in terms of an ongoing tension between "progress" and "decline," emphasizing the "contrary direction" toward which all human activity coalesces.[10] Goldsmith, in one of the most provocative formulations of such a doubling "direction," employs a scientific metaphor to conceptualize the warfare of contraries that he finds driving all human and elemental motion. "The heavenly bodies of our system," he concludes, are "acted upon by two opposing powers; namely, by that of *attraction;* which draws them toward the sun; and that of *impulsion,* which drives them straight forward into the great void of space; they pursue a track between these contrary directions."[11] With eighteenth-century narrators of social and scientific history thus mapping out such a trajectory of competing motions, it should not be surprising to find the period's more specialized literary histories, many of them composed or centrally influenced by these very authors of general history, describing a similar nexus of "contrary directions."

Among the multiplicity of competing, often contradictory, narratives of cultural development in eighteenth-century British literary historiography, such writers as Young, Duff, Goldsmith, Percy, Johnson, and Warton all tend to shape their narratives along linear tracks that swerve in "contrary directions." Warton presents the most complex and influential version of this contrary narrative pattern. Throughout the lengthy course of his rambling history of English poetry, he makes impassioned claims for the linear "progress of our national poetry, from a rude origin and obscure beginnings, to its perfection in a polished age."[12] So important was it for Warton to affirm the progressive structure of this history that, shortly after its completion, he repudiated the authenticity of the Rowley poems on the grounds that to locate such polished productions in the early stage of Britain's history could undermine his entire narrative of "the great lines of the history of poetry." "If it should at last be decided," he warns, "that these poems were really written so early as the reign of king Edward the fourth, the entire system that has hitherto been framed concerning the progression of poetical composition, and every theory that has been established on the gradual improvement of taste, style, and language, will be shaken and disarranged."[13] The depth of Warton's concern suggests the extent to which such constructions of progressive narratives, and the Romantic variations that followed them, could serve to authorize the elect identities of contemporary poets. Yet the uneasiness that registers in Warton's apprehensions about the overthrow of his "entire system" also reveals the openness of such linear histories to the contrary narrative of decline. Indeed, despite his commitment to "the great lines of the history of poetry," Warton recurrently qualifies his progressive narrative with contradictory insinuations that "the golden age of English poetry" has passed with the fading of the Elizabethans.[14]

Warton's history was reprinted, extended, and adapted throughout the early decades of the nineteenth century, and many of the Romantics found themselves incorporating and intensifying its narrative equivocations, along with those of the earlier eighteenth-century models that it subsumes. As their sense of creative mission became increasingly dependent on their conviction of successfully renewing earlier poetic traditions, they predictably turned to the eighteenth-century formulations of linear progress, adapting many of the specific scientific and theological metaphors that inform those narratives. They were encouraged in this inclination by the persistence of such progressive narrative strategies in new sociopolitical histories by such contemporary writers as Paine, Godwin, Drake, and John Dunlop. Yet just as the perfectibility argument of Godwin invited the counterclaims of Malthus, so the linear narratives of Romantic literary history became implicated in the "contrary directions" earlier traversed by Warton and his predecessors. The cases of Nathan Drake and Robert Southey are particularly apposite.

In 1804 Drake constructed a strenuous argument somewhat like Warton's for the steady improvement of British poetry up to the present era. "I hope to be able to shew," Drake announces his intention, "that so far from our poetical genius having degenerated, a cluster of names may be formed during the lapse of less than half a century, which perhaps, with the exception of a single individual, the unrivalled Shakespeare, will rise superior, not only to the phalanx Mr. Headley has arranged, but to the entire previous body of our poetry, should it be mustered in opposition to the product of the period we have assigned."[15] The reference to Henry Headley reveals how such linear narratives remained grounded in a history of "contrary directions," for several years earlier, Headley had presented such a narrative in precisely the opposite terms: "If we seriously and impartially examine the cluster of poetic names that shone . . . in the space of ninety-one years from the accession of Elizabeth inclusively, to the restoration of Charles the second, and compare them with those who have respectively flourished from that time to this, a period of an hundred and thirty-eight years, we shall find the phalanx of older classics but little affected by a comparison with the more modern muster-roll."[16] The extent to which the counternarratives of Drake and Headley share a common structural foundation is demonstrated most graphically in the way Drake reproduces the basic paradigm while only changing the names in Headley's tabular illustration of British poetic history (figures 1 and 2). To thus frame one linear narrative in the exact structures of its antithesis is to reduplicate the dynamics of contrariety that drives British literary history throughout the eighteenth century.

The persisting drama of such contrary narratives of cultural history is perhaps most poignantly rendered in Southey's dialogue *Sir Thomas More: or, Colloquies on the Progress and Prospects of Society* (1829). In the wistful self-irony of these colloquies, a passionate young proponent of "general improvement" in politics and literature, reminiscent of the idealistic young Southey, finds his enthusiastic narratives of "certain progress" repeatedly qualified by the ghost of Sir Thomas More, who resurfaces expressly to "disturb the comfortable opinion[s]" of the living with unyielding assertions, like the qualifying echoes in Warton's *History*, of the encroaching disintegration of "every thing which has hitherto been held sacred" in literature and government.[17] The relentless dialectic of this encounter, elaborated over two volumes of intensive colloquy, suggests how thoroughly the procedures of narrative contrari-

ELIZABETH began to reign in 1558.

Epic Poets.	Philosophical &Metaphysical	Dramatic.	Hiſtorical.
Spencer, Milton, Davenant.	Sir J. Davis, Phin. Fletcher, Giles Fletcher, H. More.	G. Gaſcoyne, Shakſpeare, Maſſinger, Jonſon, Beaumont & Fletcher, Shirley.	Niccols, Sackville, Daniel, Drayton, May, J. Beaumont.

Satyrical.	Paſtoral.	Amatory, & Miſcellaneous.	Tranſlators.
Hall, Marſton, Rowlands, Donne.	Warner, Drayton, Browne, Fairfax.	Raleigh, Drummond, Marlowe, Cowley, Carew, Corbet, King, Habington, Cartwright, Randolph, Suckling.	Fairfax, Sandys, Craſhawe.

FIGURE I   Tabular illustration of the history of British poetry from Henry
Headley's *Select Beauties of Ancient English Poetry* (1787).

ety had come to condition the Romantics' sense of their own creative project in terms of a divided relation to the literary past.

The extent of Shelley's immersion in the conflicting paradigms of eighteenth- and nineteenth-century historiography may be gauged by his lifelong preoccupation with many of those writers who emphatically confronted and articulated the "contrary directions" of historical process—such as Hume, Gibbon, Burke, Paine, Godwin, and Malthus. In fact, their impact on his developing historical consciousness was significant enough for

---

Epic.	Dramatic.	Lyric.	Descriptive.
Ossian.	Hoadley.	Gray.	Cowper.
Hole.	Moore.	Mason.	Hurdis.
Cumberland	Mason.	Warton J.	Gisborne.
Southey.	Walpole.	Warton T.	Bidlake.
	Home.	Sayers.	Sotheby.
	Murphy.	Hole.	Burges.
	Colman.	Richards.	Bloomfield.
	Cumberland.	Coleridge.	
	Jephson.	Sargent.	
	Sheridan.	Whitehouse.	
	Chatterton.		

Didactic.	Satyric.	Miscellaneous.	Translators.
Mason.	Churchill.	Goldsmith.	Warton J.
Hayley.	Anstey,	Beattie.	Colman.
Downman.	Wolcot,	Hayley.	Mickle.
Polwhele.	Gifford,	Barbauld.	Potter.
Darwin.	The Author of	Burns.	Hoole.
	The Pursuits	Langhorne.	Jones Sir W.
	of Literature.	Cawthorne.	Boyd.
		Penrose.	Polwhele.
		Scott.	Cowper.
		Pratt.	Beresford.
		Williams Helen.	Brooke.
		Smith Charlotte.	Boscawen.
		Bowles.	Carlysle.
		Seward.	Sotheby.
		Pye.	
		Rogers.	
		Radcliffe.	
		Maurice.	
		Polwhele.	
		Campbell.	

FIGURE 2　Tabular illustration of the history of British poetry from Nathan Drake's *Literary Hours* (1804).

him to extend one of their basic metaphors of progress and decline—that of germination and biological evolution—for many of his own most memorable characterizations of cultural development in *A Defence of Poetry*. His resulting tendency to conceptualize the past in these terms of linear contrariety was reinforced by his specific readings in several works of natural, literary, and sociopolitical history that give particularly strong emphasis to the "contrary directions" of history's movement through time—Condorcet's *Sketch for a Historical Picture of the Progress of the Human Mind,* Cuvier's *Essay on the Theory of the Earth,* Volney's *Ruins of Empire,* and Malthus's *An Essay on the Principle of Population.* Malthus's theory of human history as an "oscillation" or "vibration" between endlessly repetitive cycles of population growth and decline may have had the most profound influence on Shelley's thinking about historical contraries. For much as he despised the reactionary political implications of Malthus's argument—the doctrines, he claimed, of a "eunuch" and a "tyrant," the "apostle of the rich" (7:32; *PBSL* 2:261)— he must have recognized in Malthus's central characterization of historical process as a dynamic of "retrograde and progressive movements" one of the most striking encapsulations ever of the narrative contrariety that informs historical writing throughout the eighteenth and early nineteenth centuries.[18]

To recognize Shelley's ongoing engagement with this background is to understand more fully why his own constructions of cultural history so frequently result in competing linear narratives of progression and decline. We may see this pattern of relations most strikingly played out in one of Shelley's most elaborate poetic constructions of cultural history, *Prometheus Unbound,* which confronts Malthus in its preface and then proceeds to offer no less than four, in Stuart Curran's count, contrasting versions of progressive and retrograde history.[19] It should come as little surprise, considering the extent to which such narrative swerves conditioned the Romantics' sense of relation to their great poetic forebears, that we should find Shelley, in the preface to *Prometheus Unbound,* alternately expressing a strong confidence about his "high comparison" to the giants of literary tradition and a recurrent defensiveness about the lack of originality in his works. Conceptualizing his highest creative aspirations in such divided terms becomes increasingly customary for Shelley as his engagement with the contrary models of literary history proceeds and deepens in complexity. Whereas he can feel "incite[d]" by "great ancestors" in *The Cenci* to "do that for our own age which they have done for theirs" (241), he can also acknowledge in *Hellas* that the "very fragments" of his ancestors' "faultless productions" could seem to enforce "the despair of modern art" (409). If we recognize how Shelley's historiographical procedures thus help shape a creative consciousness deeply aware of its own dualisms and intently focused on the contrariety that drives all experience, we may more fully discern the historical contexts for the philosophical and linguistic indeterminacy that controls so much of his art.

It would be a mistake, however, to assume that Shelley simply reduplicates the narrative contrasts of his historiographical predecessors or that, in the end, he succumbs to a domineering past. Not only was his own sense of creative election at stake, but the negative political implications of historical contrariety threatened to subvert his passionate commitment to shaping a sustained vision of social reform, for the persisting retrograde motion in such a paradigm of history's "contrary directions" could seem to defer endlessly that triumph of the forces of liberty over despotism that he always considered one of the principal directives of historical process. Moreover, Malthus had indicated (most dismally in Shelley's opinion) that historical "oscillations" always enforce the prosperity of the elite while subjecting the lower classes to repetitive cycles of woe. If Shelley participates in the master narratives of linear contrariety that he inherits from his predecessors, he also finds it imperative to cancel the cycles of fallen history—as in act 4 of *Prometheus Unbound*—transforming their reactionary and inhibitive tendencies into a new historical dynamic that can ultimately empower rather than disable his own creative and political enterprises.

His revisionary method entails not so much a repudiation of the retrogressive structures in his historical models but rather a readjustment or redemption of their overall pattern of contrariety. Simply to champion linear progress over decline would be to remain locked within the conflicting and ultimately repressive paradigm of linear structure. Instead, Shelley seeks to refashion the linear conflicts of history's master narratives into a wavelike or cyclical pattern of contrariety that offers a more inspiring vision of cultural and political process. Here he draws upon what is redeemable in the very historical models he was seeking to transform. Condorcet and Godwin had modified their optimism about perfectibility, for instance, by arguing that human society progresses in wavelike developments, with frequent lapses into barbarism giving way to fresh cultural advances in an inexorable, though frequently interrupted, process of improvement. "The way in which general errors are insinuated amongst peoples and are propagated, transmitted, and perpetuated," Condorcet concludes, "is all part of the historical picture of the progress of the human mind."[20] Shelley gives that very "picture" sustained poetic expression in the Zoroastrian narrative of error and progress that controls *The Revolt of Islam*—an undulating movement of gain impeded by loss that he characterizes in the following description of the aftermath of the French Revolution: "There is a reflux in the tide of human things which bears the shipwrecked hopes of men into a secure haven after the storms are past. Methinks, those who now live have survived an age of despair" (*OSA* 33) Such a "reflux," as opposed to the endless warfare of linear contraries, controls Shelley's most substantial narrative of political history, *A Philosophical View of Reform,* in which the "human race" is shown persistently recovering from episodes of tyranny "to begin anew its difficult and obscure career of producing, according to the forms of society, the greatest portion of good" (7:19).

In the same essay, Shelley expands this new paradigm of contrary development by transforming the destructive and disconnected cycles of catastrophic change in natural histories like Cuvier's into a redemptive pattern of cyclical progression. Not only does history repeatedly spring forward from lapses into despotism, he argues, but those swings forward subsume and improve upon the achievements of earlier advances. Every great social breakthrough is thus "partial and imperfect" (7:6), with its strengths incorporated and its errors corrected by the next cycle of reform. Hence Classical Athens, its democratic innovations limited by its practices of slavery and sexual inequality, was the "predecessor" and "image" of the improved political systems of Renaissance Italy and Commonwealth England. Their social innovations, still impaired by the wars of religion, then helped stimulate the outbursts of more advanced European revolutions around the turn of the nineteenth century. Thus "what the Greeks were" became, through the corrective mediation of the Italian and English Republicans, the "influence and inspiration" of what "we are" in a narrative of cyclical progression that enables Shelley to commend what "we are" rather than lamenting—as he does in that other, self-disparaging comparison with Greek excellence—what we "should have been" (7:6, 226). Moreover, by linking these cycles of political reform with concomitant patterns of artistic renewal (an argument he develops more extensively in *A Defence of Poetry*), Shelley fashions the groundwork for a cultural history that authorizes his confidence in his own age's "high comparison" to both the political and poetic triumphs of antiquity. It is such an integrated redemption of history's linear contraries that enables him to voice, in the passage he later incorporates into the rousing conclusion of *A Defence of Poetry,* his most sanguine argument yet for the present age's renovation of the past: "The literature of England, an energetic development of which has ever followed or preceded a great and free development of the national will, has arisen, as it were, from a new birth" (7:19).

Much as Shelley now appears to have completed his formulation of a truly "usable past" in this version of what Earl Wasserman has called "a cyclically repetitive history,"[21] it is actually at this very moment, while composing *A Philosophical View of Reform,* that he laments that sad falling off from the ideal history of Greece he would have liked to uphold. Such a surprising contradiction may be understood if we consider the persisting linear structures in his narrative of cyclical progression. For all his efforts to transform linear contraries into redeemed wavelike or cyclical ones, he continues to rely on a narrative structure of sequential, chronological development—from Athens, to Italy, to England. That procedure implicates his historicism, as it had for so many writers before him, in the type of regressive linear structure informing his nostalgic vision of decline from Greece's superlative achievements. This problem recurs in the expanded preface to *Prometheus Unbound,* which helps explain the continuing alteration between infernal and apocalyptic historical narratives in that work. It is not until the composition of *A Defence of Poetry,* Shelley's most complex refashioning of cultural process, that he substantially transforms the linear structures of history into a more redemptive form of contrariety.

That step forward partly derives from a most unexpected inspiration: Malthus's essay on population. Despite his hatred of Malthus's politics, Shelley could still acknowledge that "Malthus is a very clever man, & the world would be a great gainer if it would seriously take his lessons into consideration." Moreover, Shelley was considering those lessons himself just as he began composing *A Defence of Poetry,* contemplating what he calls "Malthusian doctrines" and Godwin's reply to them in the very letter that informs Peacock of his intention to begin the *Defence* (*PBSL* 2:261). That curious juxtaposition suggests that on some level he conceived of the *Defence* as his own reply to or, we might venture to say, redemption of Malthus's "clever" lessons. What probably struck him as redeemable in Malthus's historicism is its tendency to integrate the forces of progress and decline in a thoroughly interdependent pattern of contraries that can actually be seen to transcend linear oppositions. Although Malthus offers one of the most vivid scenarios ever of linear progress and decline in his population theory, he also shows how those forces trigger each other, joining together in an antithetical union rather than moving as complete polar opposites in the typical pattern of historical contrariety. The expansion of population is the principal cause of its decline, and vice versa. Another way of comprehending this marriage of contraries is to see that the approach to perfection, or eternity, depends on a lapse into the ruins of time. Shorn of its reactionary political implications and its predominant emphasis on repetitive cycles of degeneration, such a doctrine could suggest to Shelley a way of conceptualizing eternity and time as perpetually interconnected contraries rather than the opposing endpoints of a linear continuum of history.

That is precisely how he characterizes the dynamics of cultural development in *A Defence of Poetry*. The great poets of history, he now argues, do not so much follow a sequential progress toward ultimate perfection as mutually inspire one another to apprehend the rhythms of eternity within the limits of their different time-bound historical contexts. The "eternal poets," as Shelley describes them, "imagine and express" the "indestructible order" of things, the "eternal, the infinite, and the one" in a shared process of visionary insight (482–83). Hence the "immortal compositions" of poetic history may be recognized not as graduated steps toward a perfected vision at the end of time, but rather as interconnected "episodes to that great poem which all poets, like the cooperating thoughts of one great mind, have built up since the beginning of the world" (493). Each episode of that transhistorical "great poem," however, takes living form within the "temporary dress," or the material errors of specific historical moments (487). Even Dante and Milton had to "walk through eternity enveloped and disguised" in "the mask and the mantle" of the "distorted" superstitions of their time (498). Indeed, Shelley adds, the limiting "alloy of costume" and "habit" are "necessary to temper" the "planetary music" of visionary ideals "for mortal ears" (487). Time therefore becomes not the enemy but the agent of eternity, the cooperating vehicle through which the "great poem" of history acquires form.

Such a beneficial marriage of contraries releases cultural history from the restrictions of linear or horizontal structure and situates it within a vertical cycle of mutually connected divinations. Fallen history's procedures of linear negations thus become redeemed in what Shelley calls "just history" (485) and its episodic pattern of true contraries. What does progress successively in Shelley's redemptive paradigm is the ongoing purification of those error-ridden forms in which eternity forever veils itself. The modern poet may thus be seen to innovate or improve on the material form of his predecessors, ever discovering new and purer time-bound applications of their eternal visions while also participating in a transhistorical cycle of shared insight that works outside the restrictive linear tracks of conventional history.

This most sophisticated form of Shelley's historical inventions enabled him to view himself, at last, as a partner in the enterprise of his illustrious forebears, one who instinctively assumed and modified the material lineaments of their eternal truths like a chameleon, as he put it, who absorbs and transforms the colors of what it feeds upon (*PBSL* 2:308). It would be reductive, however, to assume that such a development eliminated the contrariety at the heart of Shelley's sense of creative identity. For in coming to conceptualize the history of human experience in terms of a regenerative contrary process, he actually reinforced and redeemed that dialectical consciousness that had always been rooted in his earlier sense of historical contraries. He must have recognized, moreover, how his own historical constructions fell subject to the same temporal errors that limited the vision of his predecessors. If those inventions could give him an ecstatic spirit of companionship with the eternal poets of *Adonais,* their limits are also apparent in the subdued qualifications of cultural renewal at the end of *Hellas.* But rather than lament such oscillations between ideal and material history, Shelley could now view them as part of an eternal process of historical contrariety that both authorizes and empowers the modes of indeterminacy that we have come to rank among his most enduring strengths.

Literary Art and Political Justice: Shelley, Godwin, and Mary Hays

Terence Allan Hoagwood

3

SHELLEY'S MAJOR poems represent a dialectical theory that, like works by William Godwin and Mary Hays, is developed from arguments expressed by the *philosophes* and the *ideologistes*. Thinking about ideology combines with political pressures in the 1790s and again in the post-Waterloo years to move social and political philosophy into symbolic forms. Poetry is politicized in a hermeneutic way: The interpretive operation that is induced by the figural mode of symbolic fiction is taken into the fiction as its subject and theme. The theory of representation that is a political theory in Godwin's *Political Justice* becomes both an aesthetic form and a political contention in the symbolic figurations of novels, including Hays's *The Victim of Prejudice,* and also in Shelley's major poems.

Epipsychidion, Adonais, and *Hellas* take as their subject, and deliver as their contention, historical understanding and not historical events. The disjunctions in tone and narrative within individual poems, like the disparate points of view within the lyrical drama, represent multiplicity and change among mental frames. Understood as collective rather than individual varieties, and placed within a frame of historical time, these multiplicities of mental frames relativize the authority of beliefs and thus exhibit critically the fictionality of political forms of authority.

In France and England alike, the conjunctural pressure of political events submerges social and political philosophy in safely figural forms. Condorcet died in prison; Joseph Johnson, who published Hays's *The Victim of Prejudice* in 1799 and who was imprisoned in the same year (for publishing a supposedly seditious work by Gilbert Wakefield), also published a translation of Condorcet's great last work, written in prison, in 1795. Holbach wrote highly subversive treatises under the ancien régime; he smuggled his manuscripts to Holland, where they were printed as books, which were then smuggled back into France. He maintained anonymity and confusion about the authorship of his works: One edition of his *Système de la nature* is ascribed on the title page to Mirabaud; his *Christianity Unveiled* is sometimes attributed to Boulanger.[1]

In 1793, as *Political Justice* was being published, Thomas Muir and Thomas Palmer were sentenced to deportation on charges of sedition. In the same year, the Seditious Publications Act was passed. In 1794 twelve persons, including Thomas Holcroft and John Thelwall, were indicted on charges of treason; Godwin knew most of the indicted people personally. In 1795, the Treasonable and Seditious Practices Act and the Unlawful Assemblies Act were passed. Godwin wrote in protest of all these proceedings.[2] Godwin was also concerned for his political and personal safety: He wrote to Thelwall, who was imprisoned in the Tower, saying that he feared "to expose myself to the caprice of persons who . . . have . . . seized a despotical power into their hands."[3] In the same month in which these trials took place, he also published his novel *Caleb Williams*. The sequence is recurrent and important: Political suppression and persecution grow severe, and radical polemics attacking the suppression are moved into figural form.

An excellent but unjustly neglected writer whose work illustrates this pattern as tellingly as Godwin's or Shelley's is Mary Hays, who had met Godwin at the house of Joseph Johnson in 1791. Hays had read Mary Wollstonecraft's *A Vindication of the Rights of Woman* when it was first published in 1792, and an important intellectual friendship ensued among the three writers. In 1796 and 1797, Hays published a series of articles in the *Monthly Magazine* on the philosophy of Helvetius and more largely on the power of social forces to determine human lives and minds. Her epistolary novel *Memoirs of Emma Courtney* (1796) is a critique of social conventions, including especially sentimental fictions of romantic love and the power of such fictions to enslave and destroy women. In 1798, she published (anonymously) *An Appeal to the Men of Great Britain in Behalf of Women,* which presents arguments about the power of ideology in sustaining sexual inequality. In 1799, she published (under her own name) *The Victim of Prejudice,* in which the trope of writing models the inscription of social codes and the economic oppression of women is figured in a narrative of imprisonment. There is no evidence that Shelley knew Hays, or that he was self-consciously indebted to her work. Similarities in their artistic and polemical works reveal something much more important than personal influence: With Wollstonecraft and Godwin, Hays and Shelley participate in the elaboration of a theory of ideology from the *philosophes,* and they participate too in the submergence of that social and historical theory in aesthetic forms.[4]

In an essay of 1793, Hays writes that "of all bondage, mental bondage is surely the most fatal"; patriarchal "despotism . . . has enslaved the female mind."[5] In 1794, Godwin advised Hays to put her arguments about the condition of women and the power of custom and prejudice in the form of fiction; *Memoirs of Emma Courtney* does exactly that, and more effectively still *The Victim of Prejudice* represents the impoverishment of women, rape, imprisonment, violence, and the ideological structures that are correlative with these forms of suppression.

A more complex issue arises when these works, outwardly coerced into the form of submergence, take in that submergence as a theme. Hays's novels induce a hermeneutic operation, narrate acts of interpretation and the consequences of those acts, and also require a transcoding of themselves, as fictive signs of the actual times; the fictional signifiers are signs of "things as they are" (to quote the title of Godwin's novel known conventionally as *Caleb Williams*). That submergence becomes a theme of the fictions. This hermeneutic theme is a repetition in the contentions of verbal art of the material condition of suppression under which the art is produced.

The dialectical linkage of mental and material structures is a common theme among the circle of radical thinkers to which Hays belonged: Wollstonecraft writes that the imperfect governments in Europe "have arisen from this simple circumstance, that the constitution was settled in the dark days of ignorance when the minds of men were shackled by the grossest prejudices."[6] Holbach had argued that whole classes of society had first become enslaved precisely when ruling classes learned to exploit "ignorance" and "prejudice."[7] Godwin argues that "the opinions of men [are,] for the most part, under the absolute control of political institution."[8]

In the *Appeal,* Hays argues forcibly that "the world ever has been, and still is, more guided by custom and prejudice, than by principle" (128). Custom, prejudice, and opinion are not merely mental things, because they arise in material conditions: "all opinions degrading to women, are grounded on the rude ideas of savage nations" (131). Furthermore, systems of ideas produce material effects: "the cultivation of the minds and morals of women, is considered as the one thing needful ... the foundation, upon which any solid hopes of future improvement may be placed;—or any thing really beautiful can be raised" (204). In a letter of 1820, Shelley repeats Hays's point: "The system of society as it exists at present must be overthrown from the foundations with all its superstructure of maxims & of forms before we shall find anything but dissapointment [*sic*] in our intercourse with any but a few select spirits" (*PBSL* 2:191).

In Hays's *The Victim of Prejudice,* characters singly and collectively act in ways that exhibit the social production of ideas and (in dialectical corollary) the power that those ideas then represent. There is no dualism of circumstances and sentiment, of real and ideal; the structures of sentiment and of mentality are themselves social formations. Shelley's poems—for example *Prometheus Unbound* and *Hellas*—share this theme with Hays's novel: the thematizing of the hermeneutic operation as a political act within the outwardly safe and symbolic figurations of the literary art. The works come to be about the interpretive operations that they embody and require. Their political meanings include the contention that the institutions of social life and power also rest upon fictions that require such acts of interpretation.

From Newton (in terms of physical science) and Locke (in terms of philosophy of mind), Condillac developed a philosophy of the *sensibilité physique:* all knowledge derives from physical sensation. For the *philosophes,* the importance of this contention was not metaphysical but political. The "legislator-philosopher" (a phrase from Helvétius that Shelley uses in *A Philosophical View of Reform* 1819–1820 [7:20]) can achieve a reformation of society by way of a total system of reeducation founded in a total environmental determinism.

Godwin writes that he has "slight estimation" for any ethics "which confines itself to ... the offices of private life"; he is, he says, concerned rather with "communities and nations."[9] For Godwin and Hays, as previously for Helvétius, the argument for environmental determinism is not an abstractly philosophical contention. Differing in this way from Condillac, who was interested chiefly in epistemology, Helvétius sought from the doctrine of the *sensibilité physique* a social and political program. The *power* of intellectual operations, therefore, is emphasized by the same philosophy that insists that intellectual operations are socially and materially *determined*. The relationship between thought forms and material and social determiners is dialectical.

"Perhaps government," Godwin writes, "insinuates itself into our personal dispositions, and insensibly communicates its own spirit to our private transactions." Godwin states what Shelley was to repeat in the *Defence of Poetry:* "Were not the inhabitants of ancient Greece and Rome indebted in some degree to their political liberties for their excellence in art, and . . . in the moral history of mankind? Are not the governments of modern Europe accountable for the slowness and inconstancy of its literary efforts?"[10] Political and artistic forms are identified in the ground of their being and in the reciprocity of their mutual determinations.

Godwin's notoriously misunderstood concept of perfectibility is also a repetition and transformation of French arguments: Cabanis argues tenaciously through twelve treatises (all of them gathered in his *Rapports du physique et du moral de l'homme*) that environmental determinism, dialectically understood, implies a human capacity to progress indefinitely. Cabanis was interested in evolutionary models of biological explanation, and he was also interested in a political theory of progress founded in the open-ended developmentalism that the theory of evolution implies.

In *Outlines of an Historical View of the Progress of the Human Mind,* Condorcet argues also from the materialism of the *sensibilité physique,* and he argues that the development of a society is subject to the same laws as the individual development of faculties. From historical determinism proceed "perpetual variations." Condorcet says that "no bounds have been fixed to the improvement of the human faculties . . . the perfectibility of man is absolutely indefinite."[11]

In the *Appeal,* Hays joins Wollstonecraft in the contention that to raise women from mental degradation is to release them from political and economic bondage as well. From this context of political philosophy, a historicist conception of humankind and human institutions emerges, and so does a hermeneutical philosophy whereby interpretation is seen as a vital political act. Like Shelley in the first chapter of *A Philosophical View of Reform,* Condorcet says that the historical form of conception is necessary for a philosophical understanding of political history.

Condorcet's *Outlines of an Historical View* divides human history into ten epochs—a period of hordes, a pastoral epoch, a period in which writing is developed, a period in which the human mind progresses in ancient Greece, a fifth in which the sciences progress until their decline in the Christian dark ages, an epoch that culminates in the restoration of learning after the Crusades, a revival of learning that includes the invention of the printing press, an epoch "to the Period when the Sciences and Philosophy threw off the Yoke of Authority" (178), a "Ninth Epoch: From the Time of Descartes, to the Formation of the French Republic" (224), and the tenth epoch, "Future Progress of Mankind" (316).

Condorcet explains how it is that historicism produces not advocacy but rather understanding of intellectual formations in a context of historical change: "from the general laws of the development of our faculties, certain prejudices must necessarily spring up in each stage of our progress, and extend their seductive influence beyond that stage." He explains the reactionary operations of ideology in this way: "men retain the errors of their infancy, their country, and the age in which they live, long after the truths necessary to the removal of those errors are acknowledged" (16). Referring in his *Essay on Christianity* to "national and religious predilections which render the multitude both deaf and blind" (7:243), Shelley follows Condorcet on this point. Major poems, including *Hellas,* which juxtaposes religions and thematizes their historical vanishing, are about that historicizing conception.

Here is one example of Godwin's pursuing the same point: "There is a degree of improvement real and visible in the world. This is particularly manifest, in the history of the civilized part of mankind, during the last three centuries. The taking of Constantinople by the Turks (1453) dispersed among European nations, the small fragment of learning, which was, at that time, shut up within the walls of this metropolis. The discovery of printing was nearly contemporary with that event. These two circumstances greatly favored the reformation of religion, which gave an irrecoverable shock to the empire of superstition and implicit obedience."[12] In *A Philosophical View of Reform,* Shelley almost precisely reproduces this historical account from Godwin (2:5ff.), an account also mirrored in Condorcet's historical explanations.

The issues involve political justice and also literary art. In the *Essay on Christianity,* Shelley explains some implications of this historicist theory regarding the rhetorical forms that contingency mandates for writers who would overthrow those reigning prejudices. He writes that "the established religion of the country in which I write renders it dangerous to subject oneself to the imputation of . . . abolishing old [gods] . . . the metaphysician and the moralist . . . may . . . receive something analogous to the bowl of hemlock for the reward of his labors" (6:241). In consequence Shelley prescribes for politically insurrectionary discourse a cloaked form: A revolutionary writer adjusts his language and his forms to their social and historical context and "secures the prejudices of his auditors"; Shelley notes that "all reformers have been compelled to practice this misrepresentation" (6:243).

The issues involve literary art, but also political justice. Not only rhetorical form, but also the content of understanding is determined by the historical idea. Shelley writes that, during the French Revolution, "the oppressed, having been rendered brutal, ignorant, servile and bloody by long slavery . . . arose and took a dreadful revenge on their oppressors." He explains the reciprocal determination of morality and material conditions: this pernicious desire for revenge "arose from the same source as their other miseries and errors and affords an additional proof of the necessity of that long-delayed change" (7:13), which is of course the democratic revolution. As Shelley says in a letter of the same year, both the foundations of society and the superstructure of ideational forms need to be overthrown (Shelley to Leigh Hunt, May 1, 1820, *PBSL* 2:191).

Among the *ideologistes,* the act of interpretation is positively advocated and equally positively politicized. The condition of being that historical materialism describes for human experience entails an exigency of interpretation: because mental, moral, political, and material things are produced by forces operating historically, they require exegesis. The meanings of mental and material things are the determining forces that produced them. To understand anything, therefore, is to perceive the determinants of its production. As Plotinus once said, "finding everything to be made up of materials and a shaping form, . . . one naturally asks whence comes the shaping form"; "produced is to producing principle as matter is to form."[13] In the philosophy of the *ideologistes* and later in Shelley's *A Philosophical View of Reform* and *Hellas,* the producing principle is history.

I suggest, therefore, that Marx makes a mistake in the *Theses on Feuerbach* when he characterizes the French materialists and after them Feuerbach as mechanistic in their explanatory model, in contrast to his own dialectical explanations. The *sensibilité physique* in the arguments of the *philosophes* did entail a dialectical activity of thought and thing, the conformations of mentality configuring and in that sense determining material formations. The *philosophes* did construct a model of activity, action, force, and production, in place of a model of static and passive machinery. This fact about the explanatory model of the *philosophes* is something that Marx is concerned to conceal or deny, but it is something that it will be valuable to recover, as it is centrally important for interpretation of the ideological argumentation of the French writers and the English—Godwin, Hays, Shelley—who carry on their line of argument.

Shelley quotes Holbach to illustrate the contention wherein historicity mandates a hermeneutic response to the social world: "Man's earliest theology made him at first fear and adore the very elements and material and gross objects. . . . their anxious imagination labors continuously to create for itself chimeras which plague them until their knowledge of nature disabuses them of the fantoms which they have always so vainly adored." The "educated person ceases to be superstitious."[14] Likewise in *Hellas*, Ahasuerus and Shelley alike disavow any belief in supernatural agency, and Shelley's own disavowal of Christianity, in his notes to that play, opens a critical distance on passages including the famous chorus "The world's great age begins anew" (lines 1060–1101). This chorus voices a reactionary desire that Shelley's historicism discredits; his play historicizes and therefore relativizes such illusions, assimilating Christianity with pagan and Mahometan myths. *Hellas* does not endorse any of these religions or their codes of superstitious abstraction. The operation of the Greek chorus's ideological framework, like the operation of Mahmud's interpretive scheme, is shown to be constructed of socially and temporally relative thought-forms. The play is about the succession of belief systems, and not the credibility of any of them; the succession disallows the credibility. As Doris Lessing has said, "the merest glance at history would have told them . . . that their certitudes were temporary."[15]

The conceptual content of that passage in *Hellas* is an argument for the political act of interpretation; cognition does not stop at the ingestion of a signifying form but proceeds by way of historical dialectic to a construction of the "producing principle" that is its meaning. In Shelley's quotation from Holbach, the example is the myth of deity; in *Hellas*, examples include the Greek Christians's ideologically determined desire for the stability of eternity in the face of historical change. The desire to evade and to deny historical change, under the form of superstition and idealist delusion, is treated critically in the play, as a product of historical forces.

For Shelley and for the *ideologistes*, interpretations arrive at both skepticism and a theory of evolution: in *Hellas*, as in Volney's *The Ruins*, "Worlds on worlds are rolling ever / From creation to decay" (lines 197–98). For these two contentions—skepticism and evolutionary theory—the form of the interpretive operation is a higher-order meaning. The largest contention of this school of political philosophy—which is the school of Holbach, Helvétius, Godwin, Hays, and Shelley—is the contention that cultural forms are products of cultural forces and that political progress depends upon the hermeneutic operation that discloses those cultural forces and their temporality.

Whatever the particular reference, therefore, that a Shelley poem or a Hays novel might make, whatever its contentions (about George III, or the Peterloo massacre, or property law, or rape), a higher-order level of meaning is advocacy of interpretation. Shelley's poems, like the poetry and drama and fiction of many of his contemporaries and predecessors in the radical movement in England, are designed to induce hermeneutic acts. They are in that way *about* the interpretive operations that they produce, and this sequence (I repeat) is a political act because of the dialectical theory of ideological forms in which it is grounded and toward whose goals it aims its interventions.

Shelley and the Constitution of
Political Authority

William Keach

4

O N E   W A Y to indicate the focus of this chapter might be to claim that
I want the word *constitution* in my title to be taken literally. But then
what a "literal" understanding of *constitution* means from a Shelleyan perspective is a question I mean to pursue. So all I can do at the outset is to make
clear that my title refers primarily to *the* constitution in a specific institutional
and political sense: to the English constitution and especially to the Constitution of the United States. My argument here is also intended to interrogate
the word *Legislator* in the title of this volume by asking about the relation in
Shelley's writing of the *legislative* to the *lexical* and the *legible*. The common
etymological root points, I believe, to aspects of a Shelleyan *logos* that are
quite elusive and complex and that are deserving of further analysis. Shelley's
own distinction between "law" or the legislative and "constitution" is
pertinent in this context, and I shall return to that distinction shortly.

　　This chapter revisits—and I hope advances—issues explored very impressively in the chapter in Jerrold Hogle's *Shelley's Process* called "The
Distribution of Transference: *A Philosophical View of Reform* and Its Satellites."
In a section of that chapter called "How the Language of Legality Can Free
People from the Law," Hogle offers an insightful account of why "law" is a
crucially important nexus in Shelley's thinking about the connection of
thought to language, since with law that connection is so inescapably a

function of social power and social practice in history. My concern is with an aspect of this broader problem—with "constitution" as a distinctive mode of "law," or rather as the assumed originary basis of "law."

The passage in Shelley that turned my interest to these matters comes early in *A Philosophical View of Reform,* as Shelley nears the end of his survey of the political philosophy of the Enlightenment: "The system of Government in the United States of America," he writes, "was the first practical illustration of the new philosophy" (*SC* 6:974). Shelley goes on to praise the American system of government through a series of negations that Timothy Webb and Paul Dawson would recognize as being consistent with their observations about Shelley's rhetoric of negativity: "It has no King. . . . It has no [aristocracy *canceled*] hereditary oligarchy. . . . It has no established Church. . . . It has no false representation." Then suddenly the rhetoric of the passage undergoes a positive transformation:

> Lastly, it has an institution by which it is honourably distinguished from all other gover[n]ment[s] which ever existed. It constitutionally acknowledges the progress of human improvement, and is framed under the limitation of the probability of more simple views of political science being rendered applicable to human life. There is a law by which the Constitution is [revised *canceled*] reserved for revision every ten years. Every other [legislator or institutor *canceled*] set of men who have assumed the office of legislating & framing institutions for future ages, with far less right to such an assumption than the founder[s] of the Am.[erican] Rep.[public] [assumed *canceled*] to them [-selves the idea that *canceled*] their work was the wisest & best that could possibly have been produced: these illustrious men looked upon the past history of [man *canceled*] their species, & saw that it was the history of his mistakes, and his sufferings arising from his mistakes[;] they observed the superiority of their own work to all the works which had preceded it, & they judged it probable that other political institutions would be discovered bearing the same relation to those they had established, which they bear to those which have preceded them. They provided therefore for the application of these contingent discoveries to the social state without the violence & misery attendant upon such change in less modest & more imperfect governments.[1]

For all its echoes of Paine and other familiar sources (Shelley follows Paine more closely than Godwin in his views of "constitution"), this praise of the U.S. Constitution is remarkable. Three points in particular carry major, and contradictory, implications for Shelley's thinking about political authority, language, and history. First, and most prominent in Shelley's praise, the U.S. Constitution is in principle self-revising and allows for its own supersession. Commentators have had to note, of course, that Shelley was in error about the Constitution's being reserved for revision every ten years—that he was probably thinking, as Donald Reiman says, of the provision in article 1 "for reapportionment of the House of Representatives after each decennial census" (*SC* 6:976n.) or perhaps of the discussion in the 1789 French National Assembly of a ten-year period for constitutional revision (Godwin refers derisively to this discussion in *Political Justice*[2]). Second, and entirely implicit in the passage I have quoted, though obviously of great importance to my argument, the U.S. Constitution is a written document, a collectively produced and ratified text. As such—and this is the third key point to make about the passage—the U.S. Constitution becomes in Shelley's view a performative utterance, or more precisely an illocutionary political act. The Austinian terms privilege speech over writing in ways that limit their usefulness in a discussion of "constitution," but the relation of signification to action that they foreground is relevant all the same. The words of the Preamble—"We the People of the United States . . . do ordain and establish this *Constitution*"—enact what they name. The Constitution as Shelley regards it is a historically innovative textual performance of the republican principles of political organization that the document sets forth, and that Shelley admires.

Most of these observations turn upon the assumption that the U.S. Constitution's status as a piece of writing is one of the things that enables Shelley to see it as "honorably distinguished" from all previous constitutions or bases of government. Paine's response in *The Rights of Man* to Burke's championing of the ancient English over the new French constitution is the critical point of reference here. Paine begins, tellingly, by making his confrontation with Burke a linguistic matter—a matter of verbal definition: "it will be first necessary to define what is meant by a *constitution*. It is not sufficient that we adopt the word; we must fix also a standard signification to it."[3] Paine continues in a way that is at once deeply influential on and at odds with Shelley's thinking: "A constitution is not a thing in name only, but in fact. It has not an ideal, but a real existence, and wherever it cannot be produced in a visible form, there is none. A constitution is a thing *antecedent* to government, and a government is only the creature of a constitution" (71). For Paine, a constitution's status as the origin of governmental authority is inseparable from its status as writing, both because it stands as material evidence of the fact that "*individuals themselves,* each in his own personal and sovereign right, *entered into a compact with each other* to produce a government," and because, as "the act ... of the people constituting a government," the constitution "is the body of elements, to which you can refer, and quote article by article" (70–71). Shelley accepts Paine's belief in the originary, foundational value of a real constitution. But in *A Philosophical View of Reform* he is much less explicit about the U.S. Constitution's textual existence. To understand why, we have only to imagine Shelley's resistance to Paine's assertion that "wherever it cannot be produced in a visible form, there is none." The materiality of writing and reading (*quoting,* Paine's word, involves both) converges with the constitution of political authority for Paine in a way that it never does for Shelley, whose preoccupation with constitutional self-revision as a process betokening an awareness of "the history of . . . mistakes" and "contingent discoveries" coincides with his more evasive acknowledgment of the Constitution's status as writing.

Dawson is basically right, then, when he says that "Shelley never echoes Paine's insistence that a valid constitution must be written," that "Shelley borrows [Paine's arguments in *Rights of Man*] for the negative purpose of showing that England does not have [a constitution], whatever Whig rhetoric may say."[4] Even this "negative purpose," it should be pointed out, sets Shelley at odds with Godwin, for whom Paine's critique of the traditional unwritten constitution "seems to be rather verbal than of essential moment."[5] Still, the relation of constitutional authority to writing is nonetheless at issue for Shelley, even in the very early political prose to which Dawson draws our attention. In his *Proposals for an Association of Philanthropists* of 1812, for instance, Shelley indeed echoes Paine with the formulation "Constitution is to government what government is to law" (Paine's version of this is that "A constitution . . . is to government, what the laws made afterwards by that government are to a court of judicature" [71]). Shelley then proceeds in a direction that generally follows *The Rights of Man* but deviates into entanglements that Paine, with his practical confidence in the "real existence" of a piece of writing that you can "quote article by article," never encounters. Shelley momentarily opens up a powerful new line of analysis by saying that "Constitution may . . . be defined to be, not merely something constituted for the benefit of any nation or class of people, but something constituted by themselves for their own benefit" (5:260). The possibility that the U.S. Constitution is "constituted for the benefit of" a specific "class of people"—not just of the "nation"—is a question to which Shelley never returns directly. He goes on, still following Paine, to argue that what England has is not in fact a constitution at all, but instead "a system whose spring of agency" the "very few" who control political power "represent as something secret, undiscoverable, and awful as the law of nature" (65). Shelley is of course contending with Burke here, and his doing so bears very complicatedly on his own subsequent characterizations of power. For the terms Shelley applies to the English constitution—"spring of agency," "secret, undiscoverable, and awful"—are exactly those that in "Mont Blanc" designate the power whose "secret springs" are ultimately located at the "Remote, serene, and inaccessible" summit of the great mountain, a mountain which is at once silent and endowed with a "mysterious tongue," with

> a voice . . . to repeal
> Large codes of fraud and woe; not understood
> By all, but which the wise, and great, and good
> Interpret, or make felt, or deeply feel.   (lines 80–83)

In the *Proposals* it is as part of his imaging a corrupt and undemocratic *representation* of real power (rather than because he "deeply admired the European literary *tradition*," as Dawson says[6]) that Shelley is rhetorically more involved with Burke than with Paine.

Shelley's opposition in the 1812 *Proposals* to Burke's defense of the ancient constitution leads him into additional tangles that are overtly rhetorical and linguistic. "I heard much of [the English constitution's] being a tree so long growing which to cut down is as bad as cutting down an oak where there are no more," Shelley writes (65), recalling one of Burke's favorite figures of the English constitution's "working after the pattern of nature."[7] "But the best way, on topics similar to these," Shelley continues, now in his best Lockean-Painite vein, "is to tell the plain truth, without the confusion and ornament of metaphor." We can predict what happens next in this passage: "I call expressions similar to these political cant, which, like the songs of *Rule, Britannia* and *God Save the King* are but abstracts of the caterpillar creed of courtiers, cut down to the taste and comprehension of a mob." Shelley attacks Burke's metaphor first by denouncing metaphor itself, then by brilliantly extending the metaphor so that the constitution-as-ancient-tree is attacked and corrupted by those caterpillar courtiers who demagogically exploit Burke's metaphor. In his effort to subvert the authority of the unwritten English constitution, Shelley has to undermine but also co-opt the authority of Burke's writing and of writing more generally. In the place of

Paine's pragmatic confidence in writing as the actualization and confirmation of political compact, we have Shelley's more elusive shifting between the unwritten and the written.

Both in his early pamphlets and in his later prose, Shelley suspends himself between Paine's belief that political authority can and must originate in an act of collective writing and reading and a belief that true authority, as a manifestation of power, derives from "secret springs," from remote and unknowable origins to which writing and reading can necessarily have only an imperfect, residual relationship. When Burke says, in passages that Pocock makes much of in his essay on "Burke and the Ancient Constitution," that the English have "a constitution whose sole authority is that it has existed time out of mind," and that such authority is yet grounded "in the constitution of the human mind,"[8] he articulates a conservative version of epistemological convictions that play a crucial role in Shelley's radically different, change-oriented and future-oriented politics. Late in *A Philosophical View of Reform* Shelley will even observe that "It has been acknowledged by the most approved writers on the English constitution ["on," not "of"] (which is in this instance merely declaratory of the superior decisions of eternal justice), that we posess a right of resistance," and therefore ultimately of "insurrection" (*SC* 6:1061). This is putting Burkean constitutional theory to Painite political uses. Shelley's emphasis on what he takes to be the "law for . . . revision" in the U.S. Constitution may be seen, from the perspective I am developing here, not simply as a utopian celebration of a principle of reform that can obviate the need for insurrection or violent revolution, but as the characteristic gesture of someone for whom the authority of any text derives from its potential for self-generating revision and amendment, for self-transformation.

The foregoing observations are importantly indebted to Hogle's reading of Shelley and law: He too writes of "self-revision," of law as optimally "self-reinterpreting" and "self-transformative." But his account differs from the one I offer here in two respects: It is unflaggingly celebratory of Shelley's writing about law and places less emphasis on what I see as contradictory and unresolved impulses, and it treats "constitution" as a variant of the category "law" and not, as I have been treating it, as a related but distinct category with its own special claims to originary authority. Consider, for example, Hogle's recasting and recontextualizing of the passage I quoted from late in *A Philosophical View of Reform* on the "right of resistance": "'In [such an] instance,' the notion of an underlying 'Constitution' might return to being what some 'approved writers,' Godwin in particular, think it once was and might be again.... It might become no more than an unstated assumption 'declaratory of the superior decisions of eternal justice,' an insistence that all negotiated decisions now and in the future aim at an equal allotment of resources and potentials among the different types of people."[9] Hogle constructs a Shelley less vulnerable than I think he is to the tensions between Painite and Godwinian, or Painite and Burkean, attitudes toward "constitution."

Hogle's account of Shelley's critique of law as an illusory "durability of those forms within which the oppressors entrench themselves" (*A Philosophical View*, SC 6:1058) is brilliant; it proceeds in part from a semiotics of socioeconomic power that understands law and paper money as parallel forms of "illegitimacy": "both [paper money] and law," Hogle observes, "are signs of what can only be signs (in law's case, signs of legislative action), and yet both types (especially laws) are set up by declarations, using the cover of the official edict, to be commands apparently uttered from an unimpeachable center of authority" (242). What "the reformer" must do, Hogle goes on to argue, is "to square off against law and its language" (243). This militantly forthright squaring off becomes a more irregular encounter in the next sentence, as Hogle acknowledges that the reformer has to attack law "within the language the law employs"—first, "by break[ing] down the construction of law into the layered acts that have produced its present language" and second, by inculcating "a new understanding of the mind-language relationship" that recognizes that "Laws . . . would not gain the power to make people regard them as historical and absolute did not thinking depend on and desire a sign-system to give it shape—and mistakenly assume that system, later, to be independent of what it shapes" (243–44). This all seems quite persuasive to me—both because it is true to a major strain in Shelley's own discourse and because it conceptualizes so clarifyingly thinking that is often more darkly articulated in Shelley's prose. The question remains, though, whether this account of Shelley's critique of law fully addresses what Shelley says about "constitution." As I indicated at the outset, I believe that there is work still to be done.

Let me turn, as an instance, to the fragment apparently written just after *A Philosophical View of Reform* and usually titled "A System of Government by Juries." Hogle's analysis of this text is politically very incisive:

It sees that "government," however rudimentary, begins when "masses of the product of labor are committed to the discretion of certain individuals for the purpose of executing [the product's] intentions, or interpreting its meaning." . . . That transfer is from the start a linguistic act giving the authority behind the product and the product itself (like a written text) into the hands of interpreters, allowing them both to determine its intentions and to take on the authority granted to "meaning's" true announcers. This initial move and its inequities are forgotten when the class structure begun by this delegating act turn[s] into seemingly "permanent forms which regulate the deliberation or the action of the whole," whether the resulting "state is democratical, or aristocratical, or despotic, or a combination of all these principles" (243).

Hogle's reading here carries powerful implications for, among other things, literary texts themselves as "product[s] of labor . . . committed to the discretion of certain individuals for the purpose of executing [the product's] intentions, or interpreting [their] meaning." A fresh reading of Shelley's claim that "Poets are the unacknowledged legislators of the world" needs to confront this account—Shelley's and Hogle's—of what actually happens in the transfer of intellectual labor through the product of that labor to those who execute its intentions and interpret its meaning. But what Hogle enables us to see here depends upon the blurring of a distinction that Shelley makes quite insistently at the beginning of *A System of Government by Juries*—a distinction between "the fundamental—that is, the permanent forms, which regulate the deliberation or the action of the whole" society and "the necessary or accidental" rules, "those that determine, *not* the forms according to which the deliberation or the action of the mass of the community is to be regulated, but the opinions or moral principles which are to govern the particular instances of such action or deliberation" (6:289). "These may be called," Shelley goes on, "with little violence to the popular acceptation of those terms, Constitution and Law: understanding by the former, the collection of those written institutions or traditions which determine the individuals who are to exercise, in a nation, the discretionary right" of state authority.

Now what needs to be emphasized is not Shelley's distinguishing so forcefully (if complicatedly, because of that crossing among the terms *fundamental, permanent,* and *necessary*) between "Constitution" and "Law"—or even the stress he places on "Constitution" as "those written institutions or traditions"—but instead his saying, at the beginning of the next paragraph, "To the former, or constitutional topics, this treatise has no direct reference." Hogle's commentary on *A System of Government by Juries* works effectively to show that for Shelley "law can be exposed as the mere 'collection of opinions' that it is, divorced from the natural origin it tries to give itself and unveiled as 'opinion' conceived 'for regulating political power' " (243). But by eliding the distinction between "law" and "constitution," Hogle stops short of showing how the "written institutions or traditions" that make up the latter establish "fundamental—that is, . . . permanent forms" that "deter-mine" (Shelley's word) the regulation of "political power." To put this another way, Hogle's elision of Shelley's distinction between "constitution" and "law" repeats, without sufficiently attending to, Shelley's own gesture of writing a treatise on government that "has no direct reference" to what that treatise defines as the most "fundamental," "permanent," and determinative manifestation of political authority.

My broader argumentative claim is that Shelley's remarks about "consti-tution" take us into questions about the origin of political power and authority, and about the manifestations of power and authority in acts of writing and reading and in texts, that are not entirely answerable in terms of what Shelley says about "law." Consider one further example from Hogle: "Law can be made to release [the notion that the governing classes are now required to return sovereignty to those who mortgaged it away] back into its free drift across meanings and classes" (245). I would argue that "law" and the reformist understanding of sovereignty Hogle sees it as implying could never *drift free* "across meanings and classes" unless, in Shelley's terms, the "permanent forms" expressed in a constitution determined that no mean-ings and no classes were privileged. And that kind of determined freedom, as I think Shelley sees, would have to be a matter of a collectively willed and chosen relation to historical necessity rather than of "drift." To return again to the language of "Mont Blanc," the "secret strength of things / Which governs thought"—and which "to the infinite dome / Of Heaven" is not "law" but "as a law"—is given meaning only through the necessarily con-strained articulations of "the human mind's imaginings."

I close with this return to Shelley's verse because I believe that the questions provoked by his comments on "constitution" have a powerful bearing on what he thinks about poems, as well as on what he thinks about institutionalized public documents (or rather, about other kinds of institu-tionalized public documents). We not only could but should connect the assumptions about constitutions as collectively produced and interpreted texts to the claim in the *Defence of Poetry* that all poetic "compositions" are "episodes to that great poem which all poets . . . have built up since the beginning of the world." We should use Shelley's understanding of the performative, illocutionary force of the written constitution—and of the petition, another mode of political discourse to which Shelley attaches great significance—to think politically about the illocutionary force of apostrophic, vocative rhetoric in "Ode to the West Wind," *Prometheus Unbound,* and *Epipsychidion.*

And we should, in taking up this line of critical work, keep in touch with Shelley's capacity for skeptical political comedy and parody. The word *constitution* appears just twice in Shelley's verse—both times in *Oedipus Tyrannus, or Swellfoot the Tyrant,* both times in speeches by Purganax. "Grant me your patience, Gentlemen and Boars," Purganax says in his address to the assembly in the Public Sty at the beginning of act 2: "Ye, by whose patience under public burthens / The glorious constitution of these sties / Subsists, and shall subsist" (*OSA* 11:14). Then in scene 2 Purganax, in the Temple of Famine, offers up a toast to "The glorious constitution of the Pigs!" (*OSA* 1:33) Shelley's gruesome satire, written in the immediate wake of *A Philosophical View of Reform,* reminds us that there is nothing essentially good (much less sacred) about existing constitutions except that some of them make explicit a principle of self-revision, and that political invocations of the glories of the constitution, as much as of the rule of law, should arouse our critical curiosity and resistance.

Shelley and the
Ideology of the Nation:
The Authority of the Poet

Mark Kipperman

5

I N A *New York Review of Books* article written in October 1991, at the
height of the first Yugoslav war, Michael Scammel argued for the cultural
leadership of Slovenia's great poets:

> If the mark of an independent people is to be found in its poets (as
> opposed to its armies), Slovenia qualifies handsomely. Its very identity as
> a modern nation was largely created a century and a half ago by the
> great France Prešeren. . . . In today's Slovenia, it is not at all fanciful to
> see Edvard Kocbek, Prešeren's worthy successor, as the spiritual and
> intellectual father of the drive for national independence and self-
> fulfillment.

Yet one would expect some substantial defense of Slovenia's political aspirations, some hint of the possibility of a democratic future evolving from the
poets' leadership. But after remarking that "If democracy is to have a chance
at all in this region, it may be thanks to folk memories of Mitteleuropa,"
Scammel offers only the following: "Slovenes love opera (and operettas).
They consume a great deal of coffee and cake with whipped cream. Their
favored musical instrument is the accordion, their national dance a form of
polka."[1] I do not in the least quarrel with Scammel's admiration for
Mitteleuropean democracy. But in the current embattled climate, such

romantic nationalism, such an idealization of local folkways, might well seem an evasion of the very historical and political forces that underlie the conflict and require the elaborate defense in the first place. The evasion in this critic's position is made possible by an unquestioned and largely sentimental assumption that a culturally led nationalism is in itself a sign of emergent democracy.

When we today speak of Romantic nationalism, we are less likely than the Romantics of the revolutionary era to be speaking of a progressive, or even a particularly democratic, movement. By 1930, Ortega y Gasset could write, "The principle of nationalities is, chronologically, one of the first symptoms of Romanticism. . . . In periods of consolidation, nationalism has a positive value, and is a lofty standard. But in Europe everything is more than consolidated, and nationalism is nothing but a mania."[2] The "Romantic" adjective applied to nationalism has come to refer to a particular ideology that would, on a model often attributed to the Romantics, naively associate national liberation movements by definition with political progressivism, democracy, and cultural liberality. The charge of naiveté comes from a modern sense that this necessary association of nationalism with democracy originates with Romantics like Shelley, whose cultural idealism kept them from seeing that nationalism is not always the creation of poets, that it may just as easily emerge from less liberal folkways. Indeed, the "national" languages poets speak are often creations of a literate elite, not the dialects of a heterogeneous folk. Nationalism can always appear "ideological" in this sense, that it is an imaginary creation of an elite who may overestimate their direct relevance to the mass historical forces involved in nation-building. But psychological forces and cultural factors are not irrrelevant to the evolving self-definition of a nationalist movement, particularly in the revolutionary period. Shelley was particularly self-conscious about this problem of audience and authority. I argue that he was far more alert to the complexities of nation-building and the role of artists in his era than most Romantic nationalists.

The single most important historical-political development of Shelley's era was the emergence of the modern nation-state. Not even the revanchist legitimism of the Congress of Vienna could much forestall the evolution of the new power centers, driven by rapid urban economic development, bourgeois investment in internal industries, and popular loyalty to a common culture and language. In Shelley's day, nationalism would seem a generally progressive force, particularly in a period of struggle between constitutionalism and monarchist legitimism or outright tyranny. To support a rising national culture was to contest the totalizing claims of empire, of the British-Austrian-Russian Holy Alliance.

Both Byron and Shelley, of course, were personally involved in these struggles in Italy and Greece, as were hundreds of other progressive European aristocrats. Many, including groups of philhellenes from Germany, France, and Italy, actually went to fight for the emerging Greek state. But, as historians like William St Clair point out, their notion of Greece was an idealization, and many returned home in despair at the savage tribal warfare carried on by a brutalized peasantry unschooled in the hellenism of their foreign-educated leaders.[3] Though aware of these discouraging realities, Shelley persistently aspired to such intellectual leadership, and for him the ancient Greek city-state was the clearest model for the new nations of a future Europe. Shelley's ideas about nationalism itself, taken broadly and in historical context, have not been much explored, though they form the ideological background for some of his most important political poems, including *Hellas,* "Ode to Liberty," and "The Mask of Anarchy." In the creative tension between a universal concept of human emancipation through a democratic state and the particular determinations of national language, culture, and history, Shelley defines relations among ideals, political systems—and the poet, who is uniquely placed to articulate these relations.

In the development of nationalism in the nineteenth century, language itself would become a political issue and a driving social force. One well-known historian of nationalism goes so far as to say, "it was the poet, the philologist, and the historian who created the nationalities."[4] Though in the revolutionary period this was not generally true—the French revolutionaries explicitly did *not* count speaking French as essential to citizenship—nevertheless, among the literate elites who often had the most to gain from nationalism, language was a powerful unifying and defining force.[5] In western and eastern Europe, linguistic traditions and modern regularization were fought over, resulting in whole new literary languages. In Italy, for example, the Tuscan dialect was gaining ascendancy and was a focus for national pride. The subject-citizen of the emergent republic stands in his most immediate social relation not to established authority but to language itself. The citizen who is "king over himself" is master of a language that persuades, defines, and rules. The nation evolves politically, socially, morally, by articulating itself. For Shelley—who was, after all, not a political thinker aiming at a narrow theory but rather a poet—the urgent issue was the role of poetry, of art generally, in defining and leading the nation. Neither philosophers nor kings nor social economists can so form the political, social, and moral language of a nation as can its poets. The national poet could at that time be seen as embodying contestatory localism and giving confidence and identity to an emergent liberal bourgeoisie.

Any discussion of Shelley's view of national cultures must begin with his extensive treatment, in prose and poetry, of ancient Greece. As Timothy Webb has put it, Shelley "looked towards Greece as a political model, an intimation of the ideal society," its art and literature providing "glimpses of an alternative society, radiant images of what man could be and of what he could achieve."[6] That this ideal might be realized in modern Greece itself was naturally an exciting prospect, particularly in 1821 when Shelley and Mary Shelley met Prince Mavrocordato, a leader of the rebellion that broke out that spring, in Pisa. Mary Shelley took daily Greek lessons from him, and her husband no doubt saw an opportunity to discourse on the possibilities for the future state: "Prince Mavrocordato in the evening," she noted, "A long metaphysical debate."[7]

Shelley's universalizing of Greek culture is well known: "We are all Greeks—our laws, our literature, our religion, our arts have their root in Greece" (preface to *Hellas*). By so defining an idealized past, Shelley is defining an idealized and distinctly European future, the broad liberal national spirit, especially as defined in the vocabulary of the Enlightenment, that underlay all European civilization: the spirit of free inquiry; the citizen as the legitimate center of judgment; persuasion in speech over rule by force; the freedom of the citizen over his or her body and the passions; the development of the arts as the formal embodiment of a people's whole experience of nature and all social intercourse. Following Sismondi, among others, Shelley saw the nation-state as a development of the ancient and medieval city-states of southern Europe, whose autonomy prefigured this greater European ideal.[8] The nation-state is the collective objectification of the autonomous citizen-subject. Shelley often speaks of self-empire: "Man who man would be, / Must rule the empire of himself" ("Sonnet: To the Republic of Benevoto"; see also *Prometheus Unbound* 3.4.196–97).

For many critics, this political ideal that informs so much of Shelley's utopian poetry is a kind of Romantic ideology, akin to Hegel's *Volksgeist*. In fact, Shelley's view of the nation was far richer, more complex, and more historically dynamic than the rather arid statist idealism of a Hegel. It is true that the urbane hellenism of a Shelley or a Byron carries with it an air of aristocratic idealization. But the Shelley circle needed to idealize the classical city-state in the post-Napoleonic era precisely because they sensed a crisis not only in politics but also in culture itself in their age of failed revolutions, imperial reaction, and struggling nations.

The present era for them was emerging from authoritarian monarchy and Christianity to a new liberality, egalitarianism, and harmony. But it was also a world of new class relations, of emergent bourgeois liberal nationalism, in which there was no clear role for their class. The new conditions under which art itself was produced, disseminated, and received implied that the artist would be far more than an arbiter of taste or an epic chronicler of established power. For Shelley and his circle—emerging politically from a waning Whig-aristocratic "friends of the people" notion of elite leadership—this new situation was both a challenge to their traditional authority and an opportunity for new definitions. Indeed, this debate over the new historical role of poetry and the poet is the exact occasion for Shelley's response to Peacock on the poet's central national importance, *A Defence of Poetry.*

For Shelley in that work, especially in its famous conclusion, the poet mediates between a revolutionary nationalism and a humanist universalism. In the revolutionary climate of the 1820s, these were not so ideologically dissonant as they may appear to us; and indeed the young author of the *Proposal for an Association of Philanthropists* (1812) had expected that the local bond would be the precursor to the global bond: No occasions "are more interesting to Philanthropy, than those which excite the benevolent passions, that generalize and expand private into public feelings, and make the hearts of individuals vibrate not merely for themselves, their families, and their friends, but for posterity, *for a people;* till their country becomes the world, and their family the sensitive creation" (5:253, italics in original).

Historians of nationalism would find this a fairly typical expression of early revolutionary hopes: for Hans Kohn, "nationalism in its beginning in the West appeared compatible with cosmopolitan convictions and with the general love of mankind." More recently, Eric Hobsbawm confirms that "it was accepted in theory that social evolution expanded the scale of human social units from family and tribe to county and canton, from the local to the regional, the national and eventually the global."[9] The Romantic hope Shelley expresses is the notion that such expansion is a product of progressively developing imagination.

But that word, *hope,* reflects a real ambivalence, both in Shelley's poetry and in his prose. Imagination does not "progress" on its own; its agency is language and its agent the poet, and here, in this question of agency, Shelley both resists idealist mystification and confronts the real contradictions of the elite artist's engagement in a revolutionary moment. The authority of Shelley's poet is his power over the words necessary to imagine a nation, to conceptualize its present in light of the past and the future, to probe the correspondence of the local to the universal. But words do not establish their own authority. What if the words are products of aristocratic presuppositions, obscured by unarticulated relations of power? What if the poet's language represents not the universal values of liberation but only the reactionary fantasies of an embattled elite facing the challenge of revolution? Though Shelley wanted to believe that an advanced culture would lead to a more liberal society, he often feared that the opposite was in fact the case, that great literature emerges only from an already liberated nation. He understood the force of Madame de Staël's distinction (in a work he read in 1815) between the social effectiveness of precise analytical prose and the pleasures of *belles lettres:* "Among the various achievements of the human mind, it is philosophical literature—eloquence and reason—that I regard as the true guarantee of liberty. . . . Poetry has more often been dedicated to the praise of despotic power than to its censure. The fine arts in general can sometimes contribute, by their very pleasures [*leurs jouissances*], to molding subjects as tyrants wish them."[10]

In *A Philosophical View of Reform* (1819–20), Shelley acknowledges that the literary leaders of the French Revolution trumpeted a fearsome prophecy:

> The oppressed, having been rendered brutal, ignorant, servile and bloody by long slavery, having had the intellectual thirst, excited in them by the progress of civilization, satiated from fountains of literature poisoned by the spirit and the form of monarchy, arose and took a dreadful revenge on their oppressors. (7:13)

In this extraordinary passage, Shelley recognizes the paradox that "Tyranny entrenches itself within the existing interests of the most refined citizens of a nation" (7:13)—not in their consciousness but in their "interests." Both the French people *and* their literary elites shared a common ideological structure, of which they could not be aware: "superficial, vain, with little imagination, and with passions as well as judgements cleaving to the external form of things. . . . Their institutions made them what they were" (7:14). How then can any poet claim to be a "legislator" of progressive good? This conflict appears in Shelley's text only a few pages later, in the first appearance of the famous manifesto that would conclude the *Defence:* "the most unfailing herald, or companion, or follower, of an universal employment of the sentiments of a nation to the production of beneficial change is poetry." In the multilayered contradictions of this famous paragraph, the poets "measure" or "sound" the "spirit of the age" and legislate for it; yet they *also* are unconscious "trumpets," "priests of an *unapprehended* inspiration." In fact, for the most part the *Philosophical View* argues that poets "herald" a more liberal nation only in the loosest sense, only in the sense that the rooster heralds but neither causes nor affects the dawn. The real concern of the essay, then, seems less with the political effectiveness of poets (which Shelley does not really try to clarify) than with the ways in which a liberal nation *guarantees* its own progress through its acceptance of a *range* of positive critical practices, which poetry *in these circumstances may become.* But in an illiberal nation it might not. The question here is not only the confusion over whether poets are active legislators or passive trumpets— heralds, companions, or followers; it is, far more troublingly, how imperfectly they can know whether what they are "compelled to serve" is indeed "the spirit of good."

There is probably, as James Chandler has recently remarked of this passage, no way to resolve its rich and revealing contradictions.[11] But the problem of the poet's effective and moral leadership continued to trouble Shelley. How could "the most refined citizens of a nation" claim to lead a movement— revolutionary bourgeois nationalism—aiming to overthrow the power implicated in maintaining the conditions of their refinement?

This issue of urgent moral and political contradictions, I would argue, led Shelley to redefine the problem (in the hope that the dilemmas were more apparent than real) as a conflict more of theory than of praxis. In the tumultuous years of revolution in Spain, Italy, and Greece (1820–21), Shelley wavers between political poetry suggesting vatic inspiration and political prose of idealism tempered by careful practical analysis. Perhaps one could not know the value of local events in advance of a kind of applied historiography, a meticulous attention to the movements of history and a sober measuring of the present and local against similar cultural and political processes and outcomes in the past. Perhaps one could measure step by step the moral need for and implications of revolutionary violence. Indeed, a literary elite might just find itself able in this way to justify its leadership and test the moral and practical value of its vision. This is exactly the prosaic method of the *Philosophical View,* its visionary summary of progressive European history leading to a practical deduction of the chances for nonviolent reform in England right now.

It is also the method of the "Ode to Liberty," written in the summer of 1820, as the Spanish revolution established constitutional government and Naples declared a constitution in defiance of Austria. Under these circumstances, one would expect a rallying cry, and some readers find one. The *Ode,* says Kenneth Cameron, "rolls with a magnificent, organlike crescendo through the central movement of the rise of liberty in the past to the final upsurge of its projection into the future."[12] But the text does not reflect such self-assurance. The poet does not clearly claim for himself—or even poets generally—any power to provoke change by trumpeting a prophecy. The traditional dialogic form of the ode, apparent here as the ebb and flow of social liberation, seems forced and awkward, the visionary flight alternating with a strained history lesson. The dream-vision frame of the poem seems especially uncertain, even by Romantic standards (or by comparison with, say, *Queen Mab*): as an abstract historical force, Liberty is an "all-creative" potential that visits Intellectual Beauty but unfathomably withdraws "to its abyss" leaving only an anxious feeling of sinking, drooping, fading, dying, drowning. It is never clear whether this creative power is a kind of Being that a poet might struggle to represent in mimetic form or whether it is a kind of Becoming that reveals itself only progressively through the collective activity of human history. Athens "arose," Rome "was": the verbs elide clear human agency. "England yet sleeps. . . . her chains are threads of gold, she need but smile / And they dissolve" (XIII). The poem's central stanzas are indeed a powerful call for revolutionary action. But of what kind? And by whom?

All this apparent nervousness might seem to be either stylistic weakness or the inevitable price of a Classicist aristocrat indulging in uncertain utopianism. But I think the nervousness reflects both a sense of timely urgency and the dilemmas for the poet expressed in Shelley's prose: the uncertain effectiveness of the poet's voice and the moral ambiguity of violence in a nationalist revolutionary cause. "O that the free would stamp the impious name / Of KING into the dust! or write it there" (xv). The verse recoils from the implicit violence of stamping out to suggest instead an act of writing that is really an erasure, "So that this blot upon the page of fame / Were as a serpent's path, which the light air / Erases." The "blot" on the page refers to kings themselves only mediately, through the word *king* and ultimately to the ideology of power sustained by a language that seems on the verge of self-erasure yet is also remarkably implicated in originating the oppression it serves: "Lift the victory-flashing sword, / And cut the snaky knots of this foul gordian word, / Which, weak itself as stubble, yet can bind / Into a mass, irrefragably firm, / The axes and the rods which awe mankind." The "stubble" image suggests the already-faded coal, the always-belated powerlessness of words. The surprise is that whole social systems may originate in the binding together of images, which themselves become the fasces of the powerful.

But are the *poet's* words equally powerful? The "swords" that cut through the serpentine mystifications of ideology are, of course, the mightier pens of the poets. Or are they mightier? If the weak—that is, secondary, conditioned—words gain power by being bound up with the tools of oppression, what guarantees both the power and the difference of the poet's sword? It would seem that the power lies in the apparent difference itself, the poet's nonviolent exposure or "critique" of ideology. Yet Shelley is never completely secure in his Enlightenment faith that ideology can be merely thought away, and it would be a mistake to ignore his sense (sometimes a fear) that history will be made decisively only in the world of action. Indeed, as the poem concludes (xviii), it is *Liberty* that is called upon to lead *Wisdom* out into the open. The stanza ends not with the self-erasure of writing in the dust but rather returns to stamping out, "Disdain not thou... To set thine armèd heel on this reluctant worm." This turn reflects the ambiguous imagery of language and power.

The next stanza again offers the "Shelleyan" hope of a nonideological language, a beacon that will show the truth as the unconcealed. But in its turn its language undermines its hope. "The wise," it is said, "from their bright minds" may "kindle / Such lamps within the dome of this dim world" that authority based on outmoded ideologies—"huge codes of fraud and woe" in "Mont Blanc"—will dissolve. Yet here the erasure does not merely dissolve; it reveals the truth obscured by ideology:

> O, that the words which make the thoughts obscure
> From which they spring, as clouds of glimmering dew
> From a white lake blot Heaven's blue portraiture,
> Were stript of their thin masks and various hue
> And frowns and smiles and splendours not their own,
> Till in the nakedness of false and true
> They stand before their Lord, each to receive its due!

The words obscure the lake's reflection as the mind is confused by ideology, by what Mary Shelley and the Shelley circle called "cant." But the clouds that obscure the lake arise from it. The "free" and the "wise" are exhorted to act; but what enables *their* words to be free, when words seem tainted at their origin? Shelley appeals to "the judgment-throne of [human thought's] own aweless soul" but also to a perhaps more reliable "Power unknown"—and the ambiguous referent of "their Lord" reflects an anxious reaching for some unconditioned origin that might transcend the local and determined.

These ambiguities reveal most clearly Shelley's awareness of the strange ideological power of language, which both necessitates poetic revision and leadership and always renders that authority problematic. Again, perhaps these uncertainties over language's political effectiveness might be more puzzling to theory than to a more prosaic and practical—in Althusser's sense "scientific"—analysis of local conditions in light of fully articulated general principles. Of the *Philosophical View,* Shelley wrote to the Gisbornes: "I have deserted the odorous gardens of literature to journey across the great sandy desert of Politics; not, you may imagine, without the hope of finding some enchanted paradise" (*PBSL* 2:150; November 6, 1819). I would conclude that Shelley was seeking a less decentered language in turning to political prose. The universalizing tendency and appeal of poetic or imaginative language may display or engage political complexities that cannot be clarified within the bounds of art. At the same time, the decentering ambiguities of Shelley's poetic style themselves may serve a political purpose, for they illustrate not just a lyric celebration of the labor of liberation. Such ambiguities also press home to the reader the dramatic urgency of making a historical choice within the limits of present understanding and demand that the reader become educated in the contrarieties of political action. This process must always be played out in the particulars of national language and custom. But the author of *Address to the Irish People* and *A Philosophical View of Reform* argues that some elements of national language and custom are covert tools of entrenched power whereas others are elements of an always unfinished universal struggle of people to transform social life for the common good. The fact that language mediates between the local-national and the universal allows it to be either a tool of mystification or of progressive education.

Shelley generally distrusted an oppressed people to sort out these dual roles of language for themselves. At the same time, a literary avant-garde in touch with the progressive elements of a national culture might just be able to do so, to demystify a dehumanizing ideology—despite the contradictions inherent in such a pedagogy, its demand for both autonomy and engagement. Shelley's hope here anticipates the more systematic debates among Marxists early in our century over ideology and aesthetic autonomy, realism and expressionism, nationalist "survivals" and universal emancipation. Bertolt Brecht, responding to what he thinks is Lukács's narrow view, calls for a "popular realism" that expresses well the contradictions Shelley tried to navigate:

> Popular means: intelligible to the broad masses, adopting enriching their forms of expression / assuming their standpoint, confirming and correcting it / representing the most progressive section of the people so that it can assume leadership. . . . Realistic means: discovering the causal complexes of society / unmasking the prevailing view of things as the view of those who are in power / writing from the standpoint of the class which offers the broadest solutions for the pressing difficulties in which human society is caught up / emphasizing the element of development / making possible the concrete, and making possible abstraction from it.[13]

POLITICAL
ENGAGEMENTS

II

Unacknowledged Legislation: The Genre and Function of Shelley's "Ode to Naples"

Michael Erkelenz

6

IN EARLY July 1820 an army of revolutionaries entered Naples and forced a constitution upon the reigning monarch of the Kingdom of the Two Sicilies. As it became increasingly clear that Austria was not about to tolerate political innovation in one of its client states, Shelley responded by writing the "Ode to Naples." On September 26, 1820, the eve of the Congress of Trappau, he published his ode in a Whig opposition newspaper, the *Morning Chronicle*. It was subsequently reprinted in the *Military Register and Weekly Gazette* on October 1 and again on October 8. Possibly because the ode was long thought to have remained unpublished in Shelley's lifetime,[1] it has always seemed more a self-dramatization of the kind Irene H. Chayes finds typical of the Romantic ode generally[2] than a fully public poem bent on exercising political persuasion. Regarding the "Ode to Naples" as self-drama, however, fails to consider adequately the nature of the genre in which Shelley wrote and the appropriateness of this genre as a response to the political crisis he addresses. The "Ode to Naples," I argue, is a Pindaric ode designed to win to the cause of the Neapolitan revolution the hearts and minds of a classically educated, political elite.

By "Pindaric ode" I mean to suggest not the English tradition of the greater ode deriving from Cowley but the practice of Pindar himself. Pindar influenced Shelley directly. Nowhere is this more apparent than in metrical matters. The "Ode to Naples" loosely imitates the metrically defined, triadic structure common to most of Pindar's odes. The basic building block of these odes is the triad: a group of three stanzas that observe the principle of "metrical responsion." The first stanza (called the "strophe") sets a metrical pattern that the second stanza (called the "antistrophe") repeats exactly and that the third stanza (called the "epode") then roughly imitates but lengthens. With a few exceptions, Pindar's odes consist of at least one such triad. In those that include more than one, the metrical patterns established by the strophe, antistrophe, and epode of the first triad are respectively followed by the strophes, antistrophes, and epodes of all the subsequent triads.

Shelley's ode consists of two triads. They are somewhat difficult to identify because Shelley innovates upon Pindar in significant ways. He assigns different metrical patterns to each triad. He doubles the antistrophes and the epodes so that each triad consists of five stanzas. In each triad, furthermore, he places the first part of the epode in a position prior to the strophe. And instead of arranging the triads successively, he alternates between them: not strophe, antistrophe, and epode, but strophe I, strophe II, antistrophe I, antistrophe II, and so on. Yet however much Shelley innovates upon Pindar, he also adheres to Pindaric practice in one crucial respect. He observes the principle of metrical responsion, or at least its English equivalent. In each triad, the strophe sets a pattern of stanza length, line length, and rhyme that the antistrophe imitates in each of its two parts and that the epode imitates but varies in each of *its* two parts. The triads, in short, may each consist of five stanzas, yet these stanzas "respond" to one another in such a way that the formal structure of each "triad" remains genuinely triadic. It is for this very reason that Shelley continues to identify his stanzas using the traditional Greek terms, "strophe," "antistrophe," and "epode."[3] Structurally, his is an ode in the tradition of Pindar himself, and not by any means in that of Cowley's irregulars.

One function of Shelley's adaptation of the Pindaric triad is to bring to the fore the suggestion of a public performance. Pindar's odes were, of course, performed publicly by a chorus who sang to musical accompaniment and danced around an altar sacred to the deity in whose festival Pindar was taking part. Their triadic form was intimately connected with the demands of the performance. The chorus delivered the strophe circling the altar in one direction, delivered the antistrophe circling in the opposite direction, and delivered the epode facing the altar at a standstill. Any reader coming to the "Ode to Naples" with knowledge of the relation between the literary triad and the choral performance of Greek odes must immediately see Shelley's adaptation of the triad as being more than strictly literary. Shelley wrote his ode as if it was to be sung and danced by a chorus: not, now, the usual unitary chorus of Pindar, but one divided into semichoruses. Semichorus I delivers the parts of the first triad and semichorus II, those of the second. One responds to the song and dance of the other (hence the alternation between triads), yet each sings to its own music and dances its own dance (hence the formal differences between the triads). The semichoruses combine to present Shelley's double vision of the Neapolitan revolution. The first sings of it as an event in history and the second as an event in the realm of the ideal. Although Shelley could not seriously have written his ode for an actual performance, he might have expected an informed reader to have imagined such a performance taking place—perhaps around the very "Bright altar" where, he says, "armed Victory" bloodlessly sacrificed tyranny to "Love" (lines 59–61).[4]

The point of the performance of Pindar's odes was, of course, to celebrate and evaluate publicly the victory of a contestant in an event at one of the festival games. The audience normally consisted of the athlete himself and the citizens of the city he represented. The athlete and, it should be noted, the city at large were praised and flattered for the victory achieved. Drawing on some myth or legend concerning the athlete's family or his city, Pindar characteristically presented the accomplishment of the athlete as renewing through time the divine or heroic virtues of the mythic past. The victory was a sign of continuing worthiness on the part of the athlete and his city, and of continuing favour on the part of the gods. This favour, however, was not to be taken for granted. The gods are intolerant of excessive pride, and in any event fortune is capricious. "Pindar," as Frank J. Nisetich observes, always "sees success against the background of failure and death."[5] As he praises and flatters, therefore, he also admonishes. The performance of Pindar's odes sought to reveal for a specific public the ancient heroic virtues manifested by a particular accomplishment and to exhort this public to remain true to such virtues.

Much the same can also be said for the "Ode to Naples" and the performance Shelley invites us to imagine. As Pindar's athlete and the city-state he represented won a victory at one of the games, Shelley's Naples triumphed in a political contest fought against tyranny. In the celebratory strophes of the ode, Shelley praises the Neapolitans precisely for renewing the virtues of a heroic past. He relies here not on the extended narrative of a single myth but on the kind of fleeting elliptical allusions for which Pindar is also well known. From strophe I:

> NAPLES! thou Heart of Men which ever pantest
> Naked beneath the lidless eye of heaven!
> Elysian city, which to calm enchantest
> The mutinous air and sea, which round thee, even
> As sleep round love, are driven!
> Metropolis of a ruined Paradise
> Long lost, late won, and yet but half regained!
> Bright altar of the bloodless sacrifice,
> Which armed Victory offers up unstained,
> To Love, the flower-enchained! (lines 52–61)

And from strophe II:

> Thou latest Giant Birth
> Which the Titanian Earth
> Clothes as with armour of impenetrable scale;—
> Last of the intercessors
> Against the proud Transgressors
> Who hide the lamp of love! (lines 66–71)

The coming of constitutional government has transformed Naples into the open expression of an age-old, but now normally repressed, human desire for freedom; into the ever sunny Elysian fields associated by both Homer and Virgil with nearby Misenum; into a mother-city ("metropolis") giving new birth to the ruined paradise of the ancient Greek colonies in southern Italy; and into an altar where the old Greek god of love is worshipped again. The revolution, in addition, has renewed the war anciently fought at the Phlegraean fields, a mythical place some ancients associated with the volcanic plain located just northwest of Naples. Naples is the latest in the line of Giants (volcanic eruptions) to take up arms on behalf of their Titanic brethren and battle the Olympians for a return to the golden age. Like Pindar's extended mythological narratives, Shelley's multiple epithets forge a link between present victory and past greatness. They combine to present the revolution as restoring to southern Italy nothing less than the government and culture of the ancient Greeks. The golden age when Pindar visited and celebrated Magna Graecia has come again. Shelley praises the revolution, as Pindar praises the athlete's victory, for renewing old virtues through time.

He also, however, follows Pindar in seeing success against a background of failure and death. As he reveals in his prayer in the final epode, his god "yield[s] or withhold[s]" (line 175) favor as capriciously as any in Pindar. Naples may have made a bloodless sacrifice of tyranny, but the war is only half won. The reactionary Austrians are at the door, and the achievement of the revolution will stand only if "Hope and Truth and Justice can avail" (lines 64, 114). History is not, of course, rife with examples of hope, truth, and justice availing. There is a pessimism in the "Ode to Naples" that the political situation of the city justifies fully but that also reflects the conventional pessimism of the odes of Pindar. Shelley, consequently, sets against his strophes of Pindaric praise antistrophes of Pindaric admonition.

These address not the perils of pride and complacency but the difficulties of staying the course in the face of external threat. The "Cimmerian Anarchs dare blaspheme / Freedom and [Naples]" (lines 77–78) and "from their hundred gates . . . / With hurried legions move" (lines 74–75). In the weeks following the revolution, the Neapolitans sent an embassy to Vienna in the hope of convincing Metternich to recognize the legitimacy of the new government. The embassy failed. Metternich refused to accept the argument that the political changes in Naples were really only evolutionary. He even refused to commit himself "on the attitude of Austria in the event that Ferdinand [King of Naples] should himself inform the [Austrian] emperor of the change in government."[6] By the time Shelley began writing his ode, the *Examiner* was reporting that "it is stated as 'certain that immediate orders have been issued to the commanders of the regiments, who are to proceed to Italy without delay.'"[7] The Russians subsequently persuaded the Austrians to hold back their army and deal with the crisis formally through the congress system. The invasion finally began in March of 1821. Shelley devotes his antistrophes to strengthening Neapolitan hopes and resolve: Iα and IIα argue mythologically and then allegorically that truth and justice can indeed succeed against tyrannical force, and Iβ and IIβ contend that Naples is inspiring the states of northern Italy as the revolution in Spain inspired it, that, in other words, Naples is not to stand alone much longer.[8] These are all reasons why Naples should not let its "high heart fail" (line 73) and abandon the revolution. Shelley's admonitions find no precise equivalent in Pindar, but like Pindar's they are concerned with sustaining the achievements of the victory—sustaining those values of the past that victory has renewed.

The "Ode to Naples" is not essentially a dramatization of Shelley's private hopes and fears for the revolution. It is, rather, one of the most deliberate and accomplished imitations of Pindar in the language. The revolution inspired Shelley to write a poem that at least pretends to be intended for choral performance before a public audience. Shelley seeks, on the one hand, to celebrate this public by revealing the deeper significance of the victory it accomplished. The coming of constitutional government to Naples and the rest of the kingdom has returned to southern Italy the glorious government and culture of its Greek past. On the other hand, Shelley seeks to bolster the resolve of this public in the face of external threat. He urges the Neapolitans to defend those ancient Greek values they have just rediscovered. The political crisis addressed by Shelley demanded a poetry of praise and admonition. It was ripe for Pindaric treatment.

In the "Ode to Naples," then, Shelley assumes the persona of a second Pindar celebrating again the victory achieved by a Greek polis in Italy. However, one crucial difference between Shelley and Pindar remains. Pindar wrote his odes for the audiences he actually addressed. Shelley apostrophizes the Neapolitans but writes for the reader of the *Morning Chronicle*. This reader, like all *readers* of Pindar, stands at a remove from the drama of praise and admonition. What he or she witnesses is in fact an elaborate fiction, the fiction that the ode was written to be sung and danced before the city of Naples. Had Shelley genuinely written for the Neapolitans, his intentions would have been plain. But what was the intention of writing for the British while pretending to apostrophize the Neapolitans? The answer lies in the nature of the poem's actual public and of the political crisis it treats.

First, the audience. There is really little need to inquire as to who in 1820 was or was not reading the *Morning Chronicle*. The ode itself identifies its intended public, one every bit as circumscribed as its ostensible audience. Shelley genuinely wrote the ode as if for the Neapolitans. Precisely as in Pindar's odes, the poem is full of fleeting allusions to history or myth that one might expect only a local to recognize. I have already discussed several such allusions made by Shelley in the celebratory strophes. When he calls Naples the "metropolis of a ruined Paradise," he simply assumes that his audience will know that he is referring to Magna Graecia. Or when he addresses Naples as a "Giant Birth," he expects his audience to know that the Giant wars were reputedly fought in that nearby volcanic plain identified by some as the Phlegraean fields. Such expectations apply everywhere in the poem— in the very first line, for instance, where Shelley describes himself standing within "the City disinterred." Although he lost his nerve somewhat and provided a footnote, the line itself depends on our knowledge that, before the ruins of Pompeii were identified, the locals referred to them as "la città."[9] The "Ode to Naples" presents the non-Neapolitan reader with difficulties almost identical to those for which Pindar is famous. It is important to realize that Shelley's ode recreates not the ancient experience of watching Pindar but the modern experience of reading him. Just as the reader of Pindar must grapple with the difficulties of an ode that reflects, among other things, the history and the mythology of a dead culture, the reader of the "Ode to Naples" must grapple with the difficulties of a poem reflecting the history and the mythology of a foreign culture. Shelley wrote for a reader capable of coping with these difficulties, someone rather like himself: an aristocrat who enjoyed the benefits of a classical education and who had perhaps traveled to Naples on a grand tour or had at least read of such tours in books like the one Shelley carried with him, John Chetwode Eustace's *A Classical Tour of Italy*. This is, obviously, the very kind of reader whose views were likely to carry the most weight with the government of the day.

This is also the kind of reader likely to be enamored of the classical past, especially the classical past in southern Italy. At a time when travel to Greece was still a relatively perilous undertaking, the sites of Greek civilization in southern Italy were the most accessible anywhere. Much of the revivalist enthusiasm for Greek culture in late-eighteenth- and early-nineteenth-century Britain can be directly attributed to the treasure hunting and excavation that occurred in such places as Paestum, Pompeii, and Herculaneum. As John Buxton has written, "the findings of the archaeologists were not concealed in excavation reports in learned journals addressed to fellow-scholars; they were exhibited in sumptuous, illustrated folios to which leading members of society had been invited to subscribe."[10] These folios, along with such travel accounts as Eustace's and such books on Greek culture as Johan Joachim Winckelmann's *History of Ancient Art* (Winckelmann visited Pompeii but never Greece), publicized southern Italy's Greek past. Northern Italy was Latin; southern Italy, Greek. In his *Classical Tour*, Eustace doubts that "pure Latin ever was the vulgar language at Naples," and claims further that "at present there are more Greek words intermingled with the common dialect than are to be found in any other part of Italy." He even claims that "some villages [in the region] are known still to retain the Greek language, and are even said to speak it with more purity than the modern Greeks themselves; . . . a presumptive argument that their manners and blood may have hitherto been but little adulterated."[11] The reader for whom Shelley wrote subscribed to "sumptuous, illustrated folios" of Greek treasures and excavations and greeted such incredible claims as Eustace's with enthusiasm.

Second, the political crisis. To arrive at an adequate understanding of the purpose of the "Ode to Naples," it is necessary to appreciate the role Britain played in events surrounding the revolution. The revolution confronted the British government with a potentially embarrassing difficulty. Following the defeat of Napoleon, Britain had, of course, entered into an alliance with those autocratic states on the continent that were determined never again to allow revolution to compromise political stability in Europe. When revolution broke out in Naples, Castlereagh "held that Italy lay within Austria's sphere of influence, and that consequently Austrian policy in that quarter must be supported—albeit discreetly."[12] The necessity for discretion resided in the fact that the Neapolitans were asking for nothing more than the mode of government that Britain itself already enjoyed. The allied powers may have feared the recurrence of a "French" revolution, but the model that the Neapolitans appeared to be following was British. They sought to establish a constitutional monarchy, not a republic, and, what is more, they pursued their aims bloodlessly. They merely petitioned the monarch, who, at least publicly, granted the petition willingly and swore allegiance to the constitution. Here was a reenactment of 1688. Indeed, the immediate trigger of events in Naples was what Leigh Hunt in the *Examiner* called "the Glorious Spanish Revolution."[13] Earlier in 1820, Spanish liberals had forced a constitution upon *their* monarch. The British government took the view that Spain lay within *its* sphere of influence, and Castlereagh himself intervened on behalf of the Spanish to ensure that the other Allies did not interfere.[14] Naples adopted the very constitution drawn up by the Spanish, and actually had hopes of receiving British support.[15] Here then was the British government's predicament: Out of considerations of realpolitik it supported Austrian plans for intervention, but in doing so it was denying the Neapolitans what it allowed not only the Spanish but the citizens of Britain itself. As one historian has written, "the danger to Britain [i.e., the British government] was that she might have to declare herself openly either for or against constitutionalism."[16] At the heart of British policy was a lack of intellectual consistency and moral principle that invited attack.

Shelley's Pindaric treatment of the revolution responds precisely to this invitation. Admonishing the Neapolitans to stick to their intellectual guns in the face of an imminent Austrian invasion may seem rather quixotic. The point, however, is to distance Naples from the example of revolution set by France. The same applies to Shelley's celebration of Naples for disinterring the values of its Greek past. It is important to remember that the city-states of Magna Graecia were ruled by dynastic tyrants. An account of this rule included in a standard history of the ancient Greek world owned and read by Shelley is particularly informative. John Gillies, in his *History of Ancient Greece* (first published in 1786 and reprinted many times thereafter) describes the government of Magna Graecia, during the period of Pindar's life and visits, as restoring "the felicity of the heroic ages." Gillies attributes this restoration to the principles of government introduced to Italy by Pythagoras half a century before: "The philosophy, or rather the legislation, of this extraordinary man reformed and improved the manners and policy of Magna Graecia, and contributed in an eminent degree, not only to the quiet and happiness, but to the industry, power, and splendour, of that celebrated country." Pythagoras, more specifically, taught the Italian Greeks the value of moderation: "Pythagoras was deeply persuaded, that the happiness of nations depends chiefly on the government under which they live; and the experience of his own times, and of his own island in particular, might teach him the dangerous tendency of democratic turbulence on the one hand, and jealous tyranny on the other. He preferred, therefore, to all governments, a moderate aristocracy. . . . he was extremely averse to arbitrary power, whatever shape it might assume: and the main aim of his institution was, to prevent oppression in the magistrates and licentiousness in the people."[17]

Magna Graecia, under the sway of Pythagorean teaching, steered a middle course between the excesses of democracy on the one hand and of arbitrary tyranny on the other. The system of government responsible for the glories of Greek Italy was not all that different from the system by which modern Britain was governed. Indeed Gillies dedicates his book to George III, celebrating British government for exactly those qualities of moderation that he attributes to the rulers of Greek Italy: "To the King./Sir,/The History of Greece exposes the dangerous turbulence of Democracy, and arraigns the despotism of Tyrants. By describing incurable evils inherent in every form of Republican policy, it evinces the inestimable benefits, resulting to Liberty itself, from the lawful dominion of hereditary Kings, and the steady operation of well-regulated Monarchy. With singular propriety, therefore, the present Work may be respectfully offered to your Majesty, as Sovereign of the freest nation upon earth."[18] Shelley's claim that Naples has half regained the ruined paradise of Magna Graecia is implicitly an assertion of the moderate nature of the Neapolitan revolution. Naples, Shelley is saying, really has established not a militant republic but a mild, constitutional monarchy.

The central concern of the "Ode to Naples" is as much British hypocrisy as the revolution itself. In the final epode Shelley offers up a prayer for deliverance addressed to the "Great Spirit" (line 149) who from its "star, o'er

Ocean's western floor" (line 154) "rulest, and dost move / All things which live and are, within the Italian shore!" (lines 150–51). Shelley well knew that Britain was the ruling star of Italy, that the British had it within their power to preserve the revolution or see it smashed. The refrain with which he qualifies all his prophetic claims ("if Hope and Truth and Justice can avail") is easily misunderstood as merely expressing pessimism and despair. In fact it challenges smug complacency. At least since 1688 the British had considered themselves the leading lights of hope, truth, and justice. Shelley invites them to prove it. The "Ode to Naples" seeks to convince a politically powerful public well disposed toward things Greek that the Neapolitans have, in Gillies's terms, restored "the felicity of the heroic ages" and that it is incumbent upon Britain to preserve their victory.

Shelley was no monarchist, constitutional or otherwise. But he recognized in the Neapolitan revolution the founding of a relative freedom that, as such, demanded his allegiance. The Pindaric ode offered him the best poetic means of supporting the Neapolitans in the crisis facing them. Pindar's odes celebrate the conservative values of an aristocratic society. They aggrandize dynastic tyrants like Theron of Akragas and Hieron of Syracuse, praising them for embodying the virtues of the heroic past. In addressing the Neapolitans Pindaricly, Shelley sought to portray the revolution as merely restoring to Naples the political culture of places like Akragas and Syracuse. The Pindaric ode is essentially an aristocratic genre that Shelley employs to present the revolution in an aristocratic light.

The erroneous view that the "Ode to Naples" languished in some manuscript notebook until well after Shelley's death has done little for our understanding of the poem, or for Shelley's reputation as a political poet. The "Ode to Naples" unpublished carries too much an air of impotence about it. It becomes too easily read as an almost private meditation upon events frustratingly beyond the reach of the poet's influence. The historical facts are that Shelley could not have published his ode at a more politically opportune moment. The allies were just about to meet at Trappau to decide the fate of Naples, and the British public was just beginning to debate what position Britain should properly take. In this context, the ode cannot fail to be read as a fully public poem, and the function of its Pindaric genre becomes clear. Shelley was using a high-art form to influence an urgent political crisis. He was turning an aristocratic genre back upon the interest of the aristocrats. This Trojan horse tactic provides another view of what Shelley meant by "unacknowledged legislation."

From Avant-Garde to Vanguardism: The Shelleys' Romantic Feminism in *Laon and Cythna* and *Frankenstein*

Gary Kelly

7

FEMINISM OF and for the period now known as Romantic was a major theme in many of the diverse yet interrelated cultural and social movements of the time, including Utilitarianism, New Dissent, Evangelicalism, the provincial civic renaissance, professional science, humanitarianism, orientalism, and Romanticism. Although they drew on common intellectual sources, class ideology, and social critique and shared aims, methods, rhetoric, and fields of endeavor, they were also rivals for leadership of the cultural revolution that founded the modern state.[1] As such, they had to define themselves as an avant-garde—or a group with a particular ideology, including the conservative or reactionary, and evident claims to leadership—while avoiding mere vanguardism, or the pursuit of an avant-garde position for its own sake, a strategy that would have resulted in isolation from the majority of those they would lead.[2] Within this cultural revolution and at a particular moment in its development Percy Shelley and Mary Shelley enunciated similar yet different versions of Romantic feminism, in his poem *Laon and Cythna* and her novel *Frankenstein,* as part of their related yet distinct uses of literary discourse to construct a revolutionary cultural avant-garde. In doing so, they challenged certain aspects of the gendering of literary discourse in their time. Yet their reinscription of other aspects helps explain why his attempt ended in vanguardism, addressing only what Pierre Bourdieu calls the "restricted field of production" for "symbolic goods" such as literature, whereas hers succeeded in reaching the "large field of production," or wider "reading public," to become part of modern cultural mythology.[3]

The late-eighteenth- and early-nineteenth-century cultural revolution was conducted in the image and interests of the professional middle class and directed first against the institutions and culture of court monarchy and their supporters and emulators, from titled landed magnates through middle-class social climbers to plebeian dependents, and then increasingly against the lower classes, from rural laborers still immersed in customary culture to politicized urban artisans with their own versions of the middle- and upper-class social critiques. Certain figures were developed and used extensively by cultural revolutionaries, especially the subjective self and domestic "reality" and relations. Against what were treated as merely social categories of identity and practices of the self in the courtly and plebeian classes, the cultural revolutionaries projected an authentic, complex, inward, pre- or extrasocial identity to serve the emergent professional middle-class discourse of merit. Against the family as a property trust in the landed class and a production unit in the lower class and petty bourgeoisie, the cultural revolutionaries figured family as a network of intersubjectivities bridging "natural" differences of gender and age. Against friendship as a social, political, and economic alliance within a mercantilist, patronage-dominated economy and state or in a plebeian culture of mere sociability, the cultural revolutionaries figured friendship as an extension of domestic intersubjectivity beyond the family. Against the merely social and illusory world of courtly display and plebeian emulation thereof, the cultural revolutionaries figured a world of domestic and quotidian "reality." Against what was seen as the attenuated heroic culture of a courtly and aristocratic "modern chivalry," the cultural revolutionaries figured a heroism of domestic and civic life. From this brief account it will be clear that the Shelleys' work participated in the cultural revolutionary social critique, though as a radical form of it.

The Shelleys did of course practice cultural revolution in their private lives and among a changing set of fellow travelers, but their principal field of public action, literature, was also central to cultural revolutionary practice. Given the dispersal of the professional middle class throughout the country and their relative lack of social and institutional gathering places not already dominated by gentry and aristocracy, their cultural revolution was of necessity largely carried out through writing and print. But print was an increasingly commercialized form of cultural consumption and thus itself a field of struggle among emulation of court culture through the fashion system, "contamination" by plebeian and lower-middle-class culture through commercialism, and "reform" of the discursive order in the interests of one faction or another of cultural revolutionaries. Questions of "authenticity" in cultural production became more pressing, partly with the renewed ideology of the subject within the discourse of merit, but also with what was seen anxiously as "the rise of the reading public," a major factor in supplanting domination of culture by the courtly patronage system. The distinction between originality and novelty became more important as cultural revolutionaries alternated between aiming for a wide readership to intervene more effectively in cultural politics and asserting self-validation through manifestly avant-garde strategies, thereby risking incomprehension and rejection by the reading public and isolation in mere vanguardism. Here, too, the Shelleys and many in their circle preferred more radical forms of writing cultural revolution, ones that risked vanguardist isolation, while desiring the kind of readership and, presumably, ideological and cultural influence enjoyed by occasional fellow travelers such as Byron.

In part it was the Shelleys' dedication to a certain kind of feminism in their private lives and their writing that distinguished them from Byron and risked their slipping from the avant-garde into vanguardism. By the time they wrote, the condition of women and the figure of woman had long been major topics in the cultural revolutionaries' social critique; for centuries woman had been a figure for the ideological and cultural vulnerability of every class to seduction from above or contamination from below, largely because women were subordinated in every class and had less to lose in going over to class rivals. Professional middle-class cultural revolutionaries converted this "weakness" into a strength by constructing woman as the repository of their self-assigned "virtues." The seclusion of women in the domestic sphere was transformed from a defensive to an offensive social practice by having woman preside over the scene of subjectivity and the domestic affections as a counter to and refuge from a merely public and political sphere dominated by the social other and supposed to be irredeemably divided, conflicted, and temporal.[4]

This privileging of domestic woman was disseminated in the later eighteenth century through the feminized culture and literature of Sensibility that emanated—paradoxical though it may seem—from Enlightenment discourses that were male-dominated and seen at the time as masculine in nature, including epistemology, historiography, social anthropology, political economy, and science. The French Revolution revealed to British cultural revolutionaries the political potential of Enlightenment and Sensibility, provoked a crisis in the cultural revolution, and resulted in a reconstruction of that revolution's central figures. First to emerge was a revolutionary feminism, in which Mary Shelley's mother was the leading (but not the only) voice, arguing that the figure of woman constructed by both the British cultural revolution and the French political revolution was in fact a version of courtly woman and thus a threat to professional middle-class revolution on both sides of the channel. Revolutionary feminists, whether men or women, condemned marriage as practiced by the landed classes as oppressing women and domesticating courtly vice, and they argued that only by extending intellectual, moral (including erotic), domestic, vocational, and even civil rights to women of the upper and middle classes would the revolutions avoid self-vitiation and thus defeat by upper and lower class rivals. Among the contemporary works dealing with these themes were Catharine Macaulay Graham's *Letters on Education* (1790), Thomas Holcroft's *Anna St. Ives* (1792), Mary Wollstonecraft's *A Vindication of the Rights of Woman* (1792) and *The Wrongs of Woman; or, Maria* (1798), Mary Hays's *Memoirs of Emma Courtney* (1796) and *An Appeal to the Men of Great Britain in Behalf of Women* (1798), and Robert Bage's *Hermsprong; or, Man As He Is Not* (1796).

Many revolutionary sympathizers in Britain and France, especially the circles around Mary Shelley's mother and father, attempted to practice this feminism in their private lives, disregarding the legal forms of marriage and conventions of sexual chastity, condemning sexuality as mere power relation in court culture and mere physical urge in plebeian culture, and promoting an avant-garde amorousness based on mutuality of desire as an expression of unique and authentic subjectivity "above" mere social constraints.[5] This was the feminism that the Shelleys and their circle partly revived, thereby acquiring infamy, for counterrevolutionaries in both the 1790s and the revolutionary aftermath treated such conduct as evidence that "French principles" were a cover for the dissemination of decadent court culture throughout society, facilitating the eruption of the "naturally" subaltern into the political domain.[6]

Not only was gender an issue in the revolution debate, but the revolution itself became gendered therein. Before the revolution, cultural revolutionaries represented court government and culture as male-dominated but effeminate, and especially in Gothic fiction and drama figured themselves as women oppressed or menaced by more powerful males. This economy of representation was carried into the revolution debate. Helen Maria Williams's series of *Letters* from France, widely read in Britain and an influence on many Romantic writers, including the Shelleys, characterizes the early, Girondin-led stage of the revolution in terms of feminine and domestic "virtues," the succeeding Jacobin Revolution as a brutally masculine and vulgar recurrence of courtly oppression, the Directory as a flawed renewal of the good, feminine revolution, Napoleon's regime as a slide back into merely masculine and courtly political culture, and the Restoration as yet another attempt to found the state on public virtues originating in and nourished by feminized domesticity.[7]

Furthermore, this representation of the revolution enabled gendering of the international struggle between Napoleonic France and Britain and thus gave new force to domestic woman as a figure for cultural revolution. Such work expressed major reorientations in the cultural revolution from as early as the mid-1790s: withdrawal from political confrontation; retreat from coalition with politicized artisans; engagement in a critical dialectic with "enlightened" gentry culture; remasculinization of prerevolutionary feminized culture; increased emphasis on social and cultural mediation; invention of tradition and a national identity, culture, history, and destiny (largely by appropriating popular culture); comprehensive programs for social control of the lower orders; and of course aestheticizing the political. These moves were accelerated by increasing and widespread class friction, episodes of defection such as the naval mutinies of 1797, threats of imperial disintegration such as the Irish rebellion of 1798, and the transformation of counterrevolutionary war against France into a global struggle of national and imperial self-defense. The final defeat of Napoleon only revealed more clearly Britain's growing crisis in social relations, national unity, and imperial administration. The postwar European settlement could neither palliate the crisis at home nor ensure imperial security abroad, as the next two decades would show. The Shelleys and their circle of course took an intense personal and political interest in these developments, at least in part because of their implications for the place of gender in the cultural revolution.

For in the revolutionary aftermath many cultural revolutionaries reemphasized woman as social mediator and reproducer of the national character and culture, by extension of her domestic character. But this emphasis coincided with increasing remasculinization of culture, counterfeminism, restriction of women's intellectual and vocational opportunities and social and public life, and repression of their erotic and physical identity.[8] Most cultural revolutionaries wanted to avoid what now seemed the dangerous vanguardism of the 1790s, but without mitigating either their critique of court culture or their expropriation of plebeian culture.[9] Thus prerevolutionary feminisms were reconstructed to help maintain these tasks; promote the mediatory guise of the cultural revolution; assist the invention of a national community transcending differences of class, race, region, and gender; create a common focus for differing factions of cultural revolutionaries; and foster the coalition of professional middle class and gentry that would dominate British society, culture, and politics through the nineteenth and into the twentieth century.[10] In this revised feminism, woman became more the upper-class "lady," though domesticated and purged of courtly traits and distant from any contamination by the "vulgar," thereby revealing how cultural revolutionaries now felt more threatened by plebeian culture than by courtization. Revolutionary feminism was among the movements that had been left in vanguardist isolation in the mid-1790s. It had been suppressed or subsumed by the end of the decade, and in the revolutionary aftermath there were few who openly asserted its claims or practiced its avant-garde sexuality and conjugality.[11]

Mary Shelley and Percy Shelley and others in their circle were among the few. In the years immediately after the fall of Napoleon, the Shelleys, like many others,[12] worked on major postrevolutionary versions of the French Revolution, published in 1817–18 as *Laon and Cythna/ The Revolt of Islam* and *Frankenstein; or, The Modern Prometheus*. Whatever else these works may mean and be, they are particular expressions of a major theme of the revolutionary aftermath—the creation of social and national unity infused with the new domesticity and founded on the Romantic feminist version of woman.

Feminist themes in *Frankenstein* have been much discussed in recent criticism. One critic has called *The Revolt of Islam* "the most powerful feminist poem in the language" and another has argued that it "can be read . . . as Shelley's 'feminist' manifesto," expressing "his conviction that the repression of femininity" since ancient Greece "has affected mankind's total relation to reality—no less than the relationships of individual men and women to each other."[13] Both novel and poem draw on common intellectual sources, including Godwinian political justice and necessitarianism and the Enlightenment materialist epistemology that informed them, as well as the growing body of French Revolutionary historians, from Helen Maria Williams to Lady Morgan, and the Enlightenment historiography of the rise and fall of civilizations that informed their work. Both Shelleys exploit a common literary inheritance from the revolution and its aftermath, including the appropriations of romance and sublime epic traditions in classic English literature (especially Spenser and Milton), the English Jacobin novel, the Gothic romance, and the work of English Romantic poets, especially Wordsworth's *The Recluse,* Coleridge's "Rime of the Ancient Mariner," and Byron's *Childe Harold's Pilgrimage* and Greek romances. Finally, both *Laon and Cythna* and *Frankenstein* were written, as Michael Scrivener puts it, not "for the followers of Cobbett or Wooler," but "to arouse the leisure-class liberals to lead a radical social transformation."[14] To serve this common end, both *Laon and Cythna* and *Frankenstein* use similar structural elements in a similar compositional structure.

Most obviously, they use similar narrative structures. Both are mediated narratives, having individual tales set within larger narrative frames. In *Laon and Cythna,* Cythna tells her adventures to her brother-lover, and he tells his to the figure of the poet in the poem. In *Frankenstein* the daemon tells his adventures to his creator, who tells his to Walton, who writes all to his sister Margaret. Both works also use retrospective narration, in which a narrator tells his or her story from the viewpoint of understanding produced by the events and personal experience narrated. This is the pattern of English Jacobin novels such as William Godwin's *Things As They Are; or, The Adventures of Caleb Williams* (1794), Mary Hays's *Memoirs of Emma Courtney,* and Mary Wollstonecraft's *The Wrongs of Woman; or, Maria* (1798). Here personal experience of oppression produces a politicized awareness that oppression is systemic and "necessary," and not merely local, individual, or fortuitous. These novels deal with the upshot of such politicization in various ways, ranging from the romantic comedy convention of social reintegration, through the Sentimental topos of subjective frustration and social marginalization, to protorevolutionary confrontation, uncertain of success. Thus narration of this experience becomes a scene of revolutionary instruction, appropriating the late-eighteenth-century novel of education to what Godwin and others called the "spread of truth" from individual to individual in a nonviolent revolution, an act of mediation rather than enforcement, a moment of self-expression empowered naturally by the force of authentic subjectivity to transform that of another, and a figure for the work to be done by the English Jacobin text intervening in an actual and violent revolutionary situation.

Such revolution by reading rather than the barricades is obviously of and for intellectuals as the self-appointed avant-garde of the professional middle class, with their endearing and desperate confidence in the power of print—their own domain of practice. This extrapublic revolution is enabled by feminized practices of the "domestic affections," including romantic friendship and the bond of mentor and pupil, and conducted in face-to-face or epistolary privacy and embodied in the novel, forms conventionally gendered feminine. Set against the revolution and its aftermath, such communication represents either a feminine alternative to or feminization of the conventionally masculine domain of politics, in both cases preserving certain conventional gender differences while reordering the hierarchical relation between them. Both *Laon and Cythna* and *Frankenstein* continue to exploit these implications for the revolutionary aftermath.

In both *Laon and Cythna* and *Frankenstein* these effects of mediated narration mesh with use of the romance journey, as appropriated from Renaissance verse romance and the eighteenth-century picaresque novel and repoliticized by the English Jacobin novelists, especially in the form of "adventures of flight and pursuit."[15] In both English Jacobin and Romantic texts, experience of exile and return becomes telling narrative, illustrating the divided, conflicted, and relative character of the public, political sphere in contrast to the supposedly authentic domain of domesticated subjectivity. The pattern also dramatizes the marginalization of subjectivity and domesticity under the old hegemonic order while demonstrating that they should be central, forming the basis for state re-formation. The excursion also has the potential to disillusion, however, especially in Romantic texts, producing not only critical awareness of "things as they are" but dejection at the extent of corruption, injustice, and oppression.

The ambivalence registers the critical relation of Romantic to English Jacobin discourse and is evident in the revolutionary and revolutionizing journeys of both *Laon and Cythna* and *Frankenstein*. *Frankenstein* seems closer to Romantic pessimism, with Walton's Enlightenment quest for useful scientific discovery beyond the margins of civilization and the known world, Frankenstein's similar quest in the realm of darkness and death, the daemon's escape from subjection to his maker's desire and pursuit of him beyond the margins of the human and social in the alpine and arctic sublime, and the flight of Safie and the de Lacys from state-sanctioned and "oriental" suppression of authentic subjectivity and domesticity as romantic love and filial piety.[16]

Laon and Cythna desperately redirects English Jacobin optimism, with the quest of the figure of the poet for useful discovery in sublime realms beyond human society after revolutionary disappointment, Laon's narrative of heroic revolutionary quest and experience in the vitiated world of the "golden City," his account of the erotic-conjugal refuge in nature with his sister-lover after revolutionary defeat, and Cythna's similar but enforced journey of political discovery in the decadently oriental prison of Othman's court seraglio and her consequent dissemination of her brother's revolutionary vision to the subject peoples. Quietist domesticity and imaginative revolutionizing seem unsatisfactory alternatives to heroic revolutionary endeavor.

In both *Laon and Cythna* and *Frankenstein* such postrevolutionary ambivalences are figured in contrasting topographies of the social and sublime, on the one hand worlds of social difference and conflict and on the other authentic, restorative, sublime worlds of domesticity, nature, and supernature. This typology of settings parallels that in certain factual, historical representations of the revolution that the Shelleys knew, including those of Helen Maria Williams and Louver de Couvray. In both *Laon and Cythna* and *Frankenstein,* fantastic realities relativize the merely human and social, and the grotesque defamiliarizes crimes committed in the name of revolution or repression and made banal during the 1790s by revolutionary transgression and violence; in both works, description of sublime, "actual" nature is used to mediate between horrific social and historical realities and sublime visionary worlds, thus providing a path from unrevolutionized to revolutionized "realities." One aftereffect of revolutionary utopianism, however, was the recognition of sublime and fantastic realities as substitutes for, displacements of, or covert recodings of revolutionary projects, to be welcomed as affirmations of the revolutionary impulse or condemned, like the revolution itself, as impractical, unrealistic, and unrealizable and an unwitting acknowledgment of any revolutionary project's incompatibility with "reality." In this respect both *Laon and Cythna* and *Frankenstein* identify themselves as participants in postrevolutionary culture.

The postrevolutionary ambivalence of *Laon and Cythna* and *Frankenstein* toward revolutionary possibility is further darkened by their use of romantic irony, especially in conjunction with evidently visionary realities. The incommensurability of revolutionary aspiration and achievement was a commonplace of the revolution debate and its aftermath, seemingly proven by history and attested by numerous revolutionary biographies and autobiographies. In the case of revolutionary feminism there was of course the notorious fate of Mary Wollstonecraft, leaving her public reputation as a testament to the seeming impracticality of her project, leaving Romantic feminism with a burden of "respectability," and leaving her daughter motherless. In *Laon and Cythna* the political visions of the brother and sister revolutionaries are realized only briefly before despotism and its attendant social evils and divisions are reimposed on humanity. In *Frankenstein* the scientific visions of Walton and Frankenstein and the social vision of the daemon are thwarted by human and material nature.

In both *Laon and Cythna* and *Frankenstein* this impasse between revolutionary aspiration and "reality" is broken, rather than resolved, by the transcendence of the material and social. One such transcendence was through death, especially the Romantic revision of "Revolutionary death"—heroization of the subjective and especially the domestic in the face of revolutionary terror.[17] Such transcendence of revolutionary contradiction and violence was celebrated in Helen Maria Williams's *Letters* from France and other accounts, became a common move in postrevolutionary literature, and was variously judged to be a proper recognition of revolution's futility, a wise redirection of political action, a craven retreat from political engagement, or a canny aestheticization of politics. A related form of transcendence is the unleashing of subjectivity, a manifesting of self-plenitude in the face of a world unfit for or unable to accommodate the revolutionary subject. Strategies of apparent self-denial, including stoicism and suicide, in fact heroize and glamorize the subjective self, thereby enabling the bourgeoisie to retain domination of revolutionary discourse, especially when such domination seemed about to pass to a plebeian revolution.[18]

Thus whatever the outcome of the revolution might be, in the short or long term it is always already transcended by self-plenitude; it is always already and "really" a professional middle-class cultural revolution, whatever its political, institutional, or ethical embodiment might be at any time. History is relativized by subjectivity; revolutionary history is only valid insofar as it accommodates the already revolutionized subject. At the same time, literary representations, fictional or not, of self-plenitude and transcendence in the face of revolutionary failure served to validate the political authority of the writer because only someone of commensurate self-plenitude could, presumably, represent that of another. Writing the revolutionized subject not only transcends the merely historical revolution, it is one of the few authentic forms of revolutionary action. Writing the revolutionized subject constitutes a claim to be the revolutionary avant-garde and incorporates the implied reader in it, whatever direction the revolution itself may take.

Revolutionary transcendence takes a related form found not only in *Laon and Cythna* and *Frankenstein* but everywhere in Romantic culture—mythologizing as sublimation or rejection of history. The subtitle of *Frankenstein— the Modern Prometheus*—not only invokes a figure for romantic irony appropriated from classical culture but would suggest two historical figures then deemed "Promethean"—Rousseau, the revolution's adopted father, and Napoleon, the revolution's self-professed embodiment. But whereas "Prometheus" suggests myth, "modern" suggests history, and "modern Prometheus" suggests either a fall from myth into history or a repetition in history of the ambiguous heroic act that initiated human culture and history as division, conflict, and oppression. Frankenstein's botched repetition of the Enlightenment and revolutionary philosophers' project to create a "new man" suggests the futility of that project and of history as revolutionary process. The alternative seems to be death or a transcendence in life by retreat to the lyrical immediacy of the domestic, the quotidian, the familiar and familial—in short, the feminine. A similar pattern may be discerned in *Laon and Cythna*. Disillusioned by revolutionary history, the figure of the poet is edified by the narrative of Laon, an obvious parallel to Prometheus, whose gift to humanity of revolutionary fire also produces both good and ill, and who both retreats from revolutionary failure to conjugality and ascends from revolutionary martyrdom to the sublime.

In these ways both *Laon and Cythna* and *Frankenstein* seem designed narratively, thematically, and formally to exemplify a revolutionary avant-garde consciousness working not only within Romantic discourse but more particularly within and for Romantic feminism's discourse of subjectivity and domesticity as a critique of both the courtly and the plebeian. Furthermore, both texts cross conventional discursive boundaries of gender: *Laon and Cythna* advances major arguments and deploys major figures from feminized revolutionary discourse and may, as Laura Claridge says of *Alastor*, even be seen as "very close to creating an *écriture féminine*."[19] *Frankenstein* incorporates, however critically, elements that would be seen as masculine, including science, the sublime, and the grotesque, and it has the tone, style, and argumentative form associated with the novels of Mary Shelley's father, to whom, of course, it is dedicated.

Many readers, then and since, have assumed that such a text could only have been written by a man, or with a man's help.[20] Such transgression of gender convention in discourse would in itself advertise these texts as formally avant-garde and, in view of the highly politicized nature of literary form at that time, thematically avant-garde as well. Paradoxically, however, such implication depends on the author's identity being known; *Frankenstein* was published anonymously and its authorship was known to the Shelleys' circle, raising the possibility that the work is, at least in part, a coterie novel, like their friend Thomas Love Peacock's *Headlong Hall* (1816) and *Melincourt* (1817). *Laon and Cythna* is a deliberately "difficult" text, suggesting that it too is partly a coterie work. Whether the coterie is taken to be the actual Shelley circle or a notional group of readers individually isolated yet united by the capacity to grasp these transgressive (thus avant-garde) texts, the problem of merely preaching to the converted, of sliding from avant-garde to vanguardism, remains. More serious still, in aiming to recreate their readers as an avant-garde partly by transgressing gendered boundaries of discourse, *Laon and Cythna* and *Frankenstein* reconstitute gender difference formally and thematically and within Romantic culture as class-based critique and class property, in ways still alive today.

Most obviously, *Frankenstein* is a novel, a form still considered in the late 1810s a "women's" genre, despite the masculinization of such eighteenth-century novel forms as the epistolary and the politicization of such masculine forms as the picaresque by the English Jacobins during the 1790s and the remasculinization of postrevolutionary women novelists' achievements by Walter Scott in the mid-1810s. In contrast, *Laon and Cythna* is an epic romance in verse, a form practiced in the early nineteenth century with considerable commercial and critical success by many men but few women. Moreover, the novel was still widely regarded as subliterary and merely commercial entertainment, whereas the verse epic was potentially a "noble" and sublime genre supposedly by authors and for readers who were classically educated and intellectually trained, therefore probably male. The serious long poem was also becoming the form par excellence of literature as such, the writing-for-itself that centered and ordered not only literary discourse, or written verbal art, but also the entire discursive order of writing and print. Then as now, verse stood to prose as a "higher" stage of reflexive work on "ordinary" language. These differences are heightened by the fact that *Laon and Cythna* and *Frankenstein* were responses to the same postrevolutionary moment by two writers of revolutionary inheritance, united in body and law, and inhabiting the same avant-garde political-cultural space.

Within that space *Laon and Cythna* also uses certain thematic and formal traits to set itself apart from and above *Frankenstein* as a text of "excess."

Although both texts employ "poetic" language and are more figural than representational as part of their emphasis on the power of eloquence and expressivity in the "spread of truth," the poem not surprisingly deploys a greater variety of such language and gives it greater prominence in the compositional structure. The foregrounding of the beautiful and sensuous in *Laon and Cythna* also accords with the poem's emphasis on contrasting experiences of the erotic and the grotesque. Although both texts describe a central love relationship between actual or spiritual brother and sister, the poem's treatment of the erotic goes far beyond anything in the novel.[21] The same is true of the poem's treatment of the grotesque in describing counter-revolutionary war, as contrasted with the novel's description of Frankenstein's ghoulish science. The poem contrasts erotic conjugality with political violence, desire with horror, whereas the novel contrasts familial domesticity with transgressive inquiry and despotic oppression. *Frankenstein* is more in line with the rational and restrained Gothic of Ann Radcliffe, *Laon and Cythna,* with the extravagant Gothic of Lewis's *The Monk* and Percy Shelley's own novels *Zastrozzi* and *St. Irvyne.* Similarly, *Laon and Cythna* deals more overtly with, and with a wider range of, political subjects than *Frankenstein. Laon and Cythna,* like others of its author's political poems, is notable for its use of invective, an intensity of political expression characteristic of the heyday of the French Revolution and founded on the Sentimental rhetoric of expressivity: the polemical argument is supposed to be validated by the felt intensity of its expression. By contrast, counterrevolutionaries tended to rely more on traditionally genteel forms of satire or "wit." In *Frankenstein* invective is used only to express the protagonist's or the daemon's frustration with his circumstances.

The poem's feminism is likewise more overt and closer to that of the 1790s, openly restating the revolutionary feminist critique of courtly woman, though leaving this critique in an uneasy tension with the poem's postrevolutionary insistence on mediation. The novel, on the other hand, suppresses revolutionary feminist critique for postrevolutionary critique of the destruction brought on domesticity and feminized culture by the transgressive and male revolutionary impulse. *Frankenstein's* plot concludes more like that of Godwin's *Things As They Are,* in withdrawal from confrontation to domesticity, though not without heroizing revolutionary adventure. *Laon and Cythna,* in contrast, abandons political confrontation for poetic transcendence, or the kind of consciousness that the author has shown himself to possess by virtue of the texture of his text.

Such differences also help to account for the varying fates of these texts. *Laon and Cythna* was withdrawn, revised, and quickly republished as *The Revolt of Islam,* with certain political and erotic elements toned down because its publisher feared prosecution on political and moral grounds and its author wished to avoid unnecessarily alienating the reading public whose consciousness his poem was to revolutionize.[22] *Frankenstein* was not significantly revised until the 1831 Bentley's Standard Novels edition, to tone down passages viewed as potentially "indelicate" or politically abrasive, though the novel's recognition as a "standard," or classic, was also a consideration, especially after Scott's achievement had inspired greater acceptance of the genre in the emergent institution of national literature. Then, too, because of her personal circumstances, Mary Shelley stood in greater need of literary (indeed any) respectability in 1831 than she had in 1818. Most important, *Frankenstein* has enjoyed a far wider readership than *Laon and Cythna,* in its time and since, revealing the source of contemporary anxiety over the novel as a channel of ideological communication able to reach a readership larger, socially broader, apparently less intellectually trained, and thus presumed to be less politically qualified than the readership for poetry. Certainly Percy Shelley made it clear that *Laon and Cythna,* unlike *Queen Mab,* his previous long political poem, was designed for an intellectual, artistic, and political avant-garde. Implicitly, the poem was also designed to manifest its author's qualifications to lead such an avant-garde as the acknowledged legislator of the world. In the postrevolutionary moment of 1817–18 there were both new opportunities for such a role and increasing competition to claim it. *Laon and Cythna* is designed thematically and formally to put its author ahead of this competition, at the risk of leaving him isolated in mere vanguardism. Central to the poem's design on the cultural-political avant-garde is its restatement of revolutionary feminists' critique of courtly woman and transgressive sexuality and conjugality. But as the scandal of Lady Caroline Lamb's novel *Glenarvon* had shown in 1816, such avant-garde self-positioning either was not available to a woman or, if it were insisted upon, was immediately rendered ineffective.

Thus the similarities and differences between *Laon and Cythna* and *Frankenstein* may be attributed to the converging aims but different situations of Percy and Mary Shelley within Romanticism as a postrevolutionary avant-garde culture that was still gendered. Romantic feminism, like Bluestocking and Sentimental feminism before it, Evangelical feminism contemporary with it, and Victorian "woman's mission" feminism after it, did construct woman as the unacknowledged legislator of the world in her domestic roles, their extensions into local society, and their shaping of the "national" character and destiny. By the early nineteenth century the professional middle-class cultural revolution may have been composed of groups of "romantics, rebels, and reactionaries,"[23] but these diverse and differing groups were rivals for leadership of what was still a revolutionary class. As long as it continued to be so, Romantic feminism and Romantic discourse continued to be "progressive" and avant-garde in the sense of aiming to lead the offensive against what was represented as an entrenched hegemonic order. When this revolutionary class itself became hegemonic, it took on a defensive character in the face of class rivals, especially from below, and its cultural revolution became permanent as the sign of its legitimacy to itself and others, leaving new avant-gardes to struggle for leadership and risk vanguardism, down to the present day.

The Transgressive Double Standard: Shelleyan Utopianism and Feminist Social History

Annette Wheeler Cafarelli

8

THIS CHAPTER investigates some of the dissonances between utopian polemical discourse and the realities of the sexual double standard for women in the late eighteenth and early nineteenth centuries. Rather than being concerned with arriving at any specific conclusions about Shelley—or the various grievances and triangulations of the Pisan circle—the objective of this study is to explore the social context surrounding Romantic depictions of unmarried mothers and Romantic antimatrimonial and free love speculation. In reconstituting this larger intellectual milieu, I shall be concentrating on extraliterary texts, and in so doing I hope to imply some ways in which we can establish a feminist social history of the era and more accurately analyze the tacit social implications in the Romantic depiction of sexual liberty, prostitution, and illegitimacy.

THE ILLUSION OF COMMUNITY ENFORCEMENT OF PATERNAL RESPONSIBILITY

I begin by locating the rise of antimatrimonial discourse within a larger social context: the deterioration of the conventional family unit in the late eighteenth century. I suggest that the interest of such writers as Godwin,

Wollstonecraft, and Shelley in questions of marriage and offspring was precipitated by the gigantic and unprecedented increase in prenuptial conceptions that began in the 1760s and accelerated from the 1780s to midcentury—the most visible manifestation of a variety of unfavorable social conditions affecting the status of women.

Within this dramatic increase in illegitimate births—the overt sign of female sexual transgression—were some consensual unions arising from increased leniency toward premarital sexuality. Sexual relations could begin at betrothal, and it was not uncommon for the bride to be pregnant at marriage. That only a quarter of these births seem to have been subsequently legitimated by marriage of the parents, however, indicates the rise of the more serious consequence of prenuptial conception—the widespread increase in desertion, whether from a man of the same class repudiating his promises or a man of higher class seducing, say, a maidservant, by coercion or false promises.[1]

The crucial distinction between prenuptial conception and illegitimacy arises with fathers defying customs and evading child support; as standards enforced by families broke down with increased geographical mobility, there was less pressure for men to marry and less community protection of single women. Modern commentators have sometimes nostalgized a preindustrial golden age of collective household labor and community enforcement of paternal responsibility; in truth, there was plenty of drudgery for women laborers before industrialization and plenty of desertion and scorn for women left with the evidence of sexual transgression. The publisher James Lackington recollected how he successfully eluded a shotgun marriage in 1760; Robert Burns decried the parish censure of his unwed fatherhood in the 1780s; and the radical Samuel Bamford remarked of child support mandated by his parish in the early 1800s, "I never could have made up my mind to become the husband of the one I had thus injured." The degree of pressure necessary to achieve a connubial resolution is suggested in James Woodforde's account of a marriage he performed in 1787: "the Man being in Custody, the Woman being with Child by him. The Man was a long time before he could be prevailed on to marry her when in the Church Yard; and at the Altar behaved very unbecoming."[2]

The major burden of dismantled moral codes fell upon women, and the group most vulnerable to illegitimacy was the domestic servant class—the most ubiquitous example of the working-class, independent woman. Connected with the rising illegitimacy rates were the economic and social repercussions of enclosure and farm engrossment, which forced many daughters to work in service or outfarming away from home parish protection and avenging parents and, at the same time, put them at the mercy of the inadequate relief allowances and social isolation that were the lot of single women, leading many to calculate the relative benefits and risks of pregnancy in a bid for acquiring adequate economic maintenance and a home.[3] Despite contemporary denunciations of the immorality of factory life, there seems to have been no statistical differentiation in moral conduct.[4] Those modern historians who have argued that deterioration of the family resulted from centralization of labor into factories in the early nineteenth century have, in their complacent affirmation of the merits of family life, failed to take into account the prior displacement of unmarried females, a breakdown of family structure already evinced in illegitimacy rates.[5] But what was undeniably becoming more visible in the cities was the increased supply of prostitutes from the rural and urban ranks of discarded mistresses, pregnancies that destroyed marriageability, community outcasts, and the economically desperate.[6]

PARLIAMENTARY DISCOURSE

The prostitute—like the illegitimate child—was the visible brand of lost chastity, and it is illuminating to see that the aristocratic discourse of adultery connected the two. If the breakdown of social standards was most felt by working-class women, it was most prominently ventilated in that forum of aristocratic polemics, the parliamentary debate.

In practice, the era's divorce- and adultery-prevention measures pertained only to the wealthiest citizens, who could afford the parliamentary petitions that alone permitted remarriage (private separations were the most that could be arranged for the middle classes). But the vocabulary of the debates established a specific articulation of the issues involving the fallen women who transgressed outside marriage.[7] Although the debates alluded to Christian moral rehabilitation of the woman taken in adultery and pondered whether "the new morality" (as Lord Grenville put it)[8] was even worse than that during the era of Charles II, their chief focus was a male-centered concern with the influence of adultery on the wronged husband. Historically, of course, only a half-dozen of the approximately two hundred divorces granted between the end of the seventeenth century and the middle of the nineteenth (until the divorce reform act of 1857) were initiated by women. The related civil lawsuits, the notorious crim. con. cases (actions of damages for criminal conversation), were based on the presumption that a husband could claim damages for trespass (owning no property, the wife had no such claim upon a husband's paramour).[9]

Protection of this nuptial property chiefly concerned calibrating possible punishments for adulteresses (adulterers do not figure in the debates) and their genetically unrelated offspring. Lengthy parliamentary debates considered the criminalization of adultery to prevent the woman from marrying her seducer. Lord Eldon (later to deny Shelley custody of the children from his first marriage) claimed that "the most enormous crime in this country" could be prevented by prohibiting such marriages; Sir Ralph Milbanke (future father-in-law of Byron) thought it too punitive "to cast a frail, unprotected woman on the mercy of the world, and to shut her out from all decent society." What it came down to was whether, as the Bishop of Durham deplored, she should be allowed to "patch up her reputation by marrying her paramour" or whether, as the Earl of Moira contended, it was "adding mockery to cruelty" to tell her to go marry someone else.[10]

Just as the stigma of sexual transgression fell chiefly upon women, the stigma of illegitimacy was entailed chiefly upon female children. Lord Mulgrave observed that bastardy was of little consequence to male children, but that female bastards "have to struggle with every disadvantage from their rank in life."[11] Only one mitigating argument rang out against total condemnation of the adulteresses: should the fallen wives be forbidden to marry their "seducers" (she never initiates, she is misled) they would have no recourse but prostitution. The Duke of Clarence's assertion was largely accepted (he himself was midway through a twenty-year illicit relation with the actress Dorothy Jordan): wives "when fallen from their respectable situations, were in a manner expelled from society and deprived of the usual resorts for obtaining a livelihood. They could not work as menial servants; they were not instructed in any line of business: they could not beg. And what other line of providing the means of life was left open to them, but abandoning themselves to prostitution?"[12] The reductive sexual vocabulary of the era posited only two extremes for women: chastity or transgression, devoted wife or prostitute.

THE GODWINIAN PHILOSOPHY OF REFORM

Such were the social underpinnings of the middle-class radical discourse that William Godwin's *Enquiry Concerning Political Justice* (1793) almost single-handedly shaped with its language of monopoly, property, and cohabitation.[13] His doctrine of marriage as a form of property was central to serious community experiments such as those of the Owenites and Shakers. In terms of popular politics, however, the fascination of Godwin's argument about marriage ("It is absurd to expect the inclinations and wishes of two human beings to coincide, through any long period of time") resided in the question of constancy and divorce. Therein serious social reformers were out-numbered by hungry politicians who appropriated Godwin's ideology as a philosophical rationale for sexual browsing, without proposing any program for reforming the social stigma, property rights, and domestic responsibilities of women.

Godwin is strangely oblivious to the impact of his ideal state on women when he says that "the abolition of the present system of marriage appears to involve no evils." His economic rhetoric of wives as property fails to address the limited number of occupations permissible for women. And even as he denounces marriage as fostering "by despotic and artificial means . . . my possession of a woman," he ratifies a male-initiated culture in asserting, "It is a question of some moment, whether the intercourse of the sexes . . . would be promiscuous, or whether each man would select for himself a partner, to whom he will adhere, as long as that adherence shall continue to be the choice of both parties." A question of some moment indeed, for women, given the realities of contraception. For Godwin, the responsibilities of "propagation" and childrearing will simply be "regulated by the dictates of reason and duty;" and like subsequent marital speculators he naively assumes that dissolution will be mutually agreed upon: "no ties ought to be imposed upon either party, preventing them from quitting the attachment, whenever their judgment directs them to quit it." Curiously, the most radical agenda, his position on illegitimacy ("it will be a question of no importance to know who is the parent of each individual child") was removed in the revised third edition of 1798 commonly read today.[14]

Godwin's marriage to Wollstonecraft the year before was doubtlessly connected with his revision of his theories. His 1798 biography of her proclaimed the equality of their relationship ("one sex did not take the priority") and emphasized their mutual agreement: "We did not marry." But he also acknowledged that they were activated, as he said, "partly from similar, and partly from different motives": hers from a heart "withered by desertion" and his from "many years" of "well-grounded . . . apprehension." Becoming pregnant, "she was unwilling . . . to incur . . . exclusion from . . .

society," and they married. Many who had socialized with her as Mrs. Imlay, however, including Elizabeth Inchbald and Sarah Siddons, shunned her after her actual marriage, an irony that did not escape Godwin: "while she was . . . an unmarried mother; she was fit society. . . . The moment she acknowledged herself a wife . . . the case was altered." Inchbald later wrote Amelia Opie, calling Godwin "a terrific example for all conjugal biography; but he has marked out that path which may be avoided, and so is himself a sacrifice for the good of others." It is worth remembering that the popular backlash against Wollstonecraft arose not from her writings but from Godwin's *Memoirs,* which one commentator called "a convenient manual of speculative debauchery" and another indexed under the word *Prostitution, "See* Mary Wollstonecraft."[15]

SINGLE MOTHERHOOD

The realities of single motherhood were more arduous than utopian speculation indicated. Given the hostility to women who had not been able to obtain the legitimating male protection that society dictated, it is not surprising so many transgressive women gravitated to the Godwin-Shelley circles, where they could socialize freely without the stigmas that, for example, led newly acquired wives and daughters-in-law of old friends to refuse contact, and likewise made it difficult for the public to accept the reality that Mary Shelley had ever been married, preferring instead the image of Byron and Shelley throwing dice for the paternity of Allegra.[16]

Confronted with the realities of single parenting, Godwin himself was eager to secure a stepmother for the children, and after two unsuccessful proposals, to writer Harriet Lee and to Maria Reveley (Gisborne), he married Mary Jane Vial Clairmont, apparently, like Wollstonecraft, after she became pregnant. Mrs. Clairmont was in fact traveling under a nom de guerre, as Mrs. Mary (Wollstonecraft) Imlay had been, and it appears she may have herself been illegitimate along with her two children. Commendably consistent to principle, she and Godwin together managed five children from four different fathers.[17] Mary Shelley herself was to travel as a Mrs. Shelley while pregnant before marriage,[18] and her stepsister Claire Clairmont temporarily resided as Mrs. Clairmont during her pregnancy—not, unfortunately, as Mrs. Byron. It was Claire Clairmont, finally, who retained the most radicalized vision of single parenting, telling Mary Shelley in the 1830s that she pitied those who "had the misfortune to be born after the marriage of [their] parents" and calling for an allegiance among transgressive women: "I am always glad when a new member comes to join the ranks. . . . I want all the women married or single to amuse themselves courageously and get divorced or cut by society and if they would all do so, the question of cutting would be at an end." Claire Clairmont was ever to champion unwed parenthood—the source of her own, her mother's, and her daughter's birth—and refused to euphemize her past with a fabricated marriage.[19]

The Godwins were relieved to get Mary Shelley wed after her elopement. Godwin cynically wrote his brother, "You will wonder, I daresay, how a girl without a penny of fortune should meet with so good a match." But the 1817 letter of relief ("Her husband is the eldest son of Sir Timothy Shelley. . . . So that, according to the vulgar ideas of the world, she is well married") was considerably different from his original panic in 1814 ("a married man, has run away with my daughter. . . . he had the madness to disclose his plans to me, & to ask my consent"). It was clear that the other daughters of the Godwin ménage were going to have difficulty, and certainly such hypergamic marriages were rare under any circumstances. Godwin never forgave Shelley for ruining Claire Clairmont's prospects, and Fanny Imlay was kept away lest her chances be ruined too. His wife, knowing well the difficulties of a surreptitious past, had pursued the eloping daughters, hoping "to prevent a stigma from being fastened on their characters"; Godwin was not without self-reproach in this: "we are divided in this particular between justification & . . . the entire suppression of all knowledge of the affair."[20]

Somewhat incongruously for an anarchist family, it appears the Godwins actively investigated the likelihood of a parliamentary petition; in 1816 Mary Shelley's stepmother took Henry Crabb Robinson aside at tea to discuss the "practicability of obtaining the divorce of Mr. Shelley from his wife, who, Mrs. Godwin says, was guilty of adultery before Mr. Shelley ran off with Mr. Godwin's daughter." Interestingly, Robinson reported that the children unanimously approved of Mary Shelley's action. They had learned their lessons well—after returning from the elopement, the journals of Mary Shelley and Claire Clairmont show them canvassing Wollstonecraft's and Godwin's writings for affirmation. Robinson noted, however, that "Mrs. Godwin says not only that Godwin quite reprobates the act, but that none of his writings 'authorise' it. And when I pointed out to her expressions in *Political Justice* she declared her ignorance of them and says that certainly Godwin had forgotten them."[21]

It would have been uncomfortable to remember that Shelley had intro-duced himself to Godwin by confessing, "I did not truly *think & feel* ... until I read Political Justice," and that after he eloped with Mary Shelley and Claire Clairmont, Harriet Shelley declared: "Mr. Shelley has become profli-gate and sensual, owing entirely to Godwin's 'Political Justice.' The very great evil that book has done is not to be told. The false doctrines therein contained have poisoned many a young and virtuous mind."[22] Ironically, Godwin's complaint about Shelley's "impious" act "of seducing her, playing the traitor to me and deserting his wife" invoked the same language the Westbrooks later used in accusing Shelley of adhering to Godwin, the author of "*impious & seditious* writings."[23] Ironically, also, the Godwin connection may have been the only reason why Byron had any interest in meeting either Mary Shelley or Claire Clairmont. Polidori later wrote that Shelley "keeps the two daughters of Godwin who practise his theories."[24]

In the early letters, Shelley felt obliged to justify repeatedly to Godwin, Byron, and others his decision to succumb to the convention of marriage in order to ameliorate the burden of public opprobrium women unequally bear—an argument he seems to have gotten from his friend Thomas Jeffer-son Hogg. There were other influences on Shelley's antimatrimonialism, notably the preface to James Lawrence's novel *The Empire of the Nairs* (1811), whence he appropriated the term "superstition" to refer to chastity and the marriage ceremony.[25] The preface (condensed from an essay Lawrence wrote in 1793) may have been a response to Godwin, but its purported investiga-tion of polyandry essentially depicts a male utopian paradise of sexual opportunities bereft of any concrete ideas for instituting social reform. The book depicts a society without marriage in which women are honored for their prolific motherhood, oblivious to the fact that contemporary women were burdened by the lack of adequate reproductive control.[26]

Despite Shelley's enthusiasm for the book, it is not surprising that female response to the *Nairs* was cool (he had Mary Shelley, Claire Clairmont, and Harriet Shelley read it)—about as cool as Shelley's to Amelia Opie's *Adeline Mowbray* (1805), which Harriet sent him in 1811.[27] Opie's inverse view of antimatrimonialism shows how the burden of unlegitimated marriage falls upon women and children; reappropriating the Godwinian phrase "things as they are," her novel shows its antimatrimonialists recanting under the force of public custom just before they expire. Indeed, the disjuncture between male and female marital agendas is rather interestingly illuminated in Thomas Love Peacock's parodic novel *Nightmare Abbey* (1818): The Wollstonecraftian

Stella dismays the Shelleyan free-love hero by announcing that her anti-matrimonialism is monogamous.

QUEEN MAB: THE POLITICS OF PROSTITUTION

Shelley wrote Lawrence in 1812 to say that Lawrence's book "succeeded in making me a perfect convert . . . I then retained no doubts of the evils of marriage,—Mrs. Wollstonecraft reasons too well for that; but I had been dull enough not to perceive the greatest argument against it, until developed in the 'Nairs,' viz., prostitution both *legal* and *illegal*."[28] As incorrect as the letter is on Wollstonecraft's ideological goals, it reveals the thoughts that lay behind the "Even love is sold" footnote to *Queen Mab,* on which I shall focus here.

As with Godwin, practical experience altered Shelley's outlook on the nature of matrimonial politics and other issues. Both Mary Shelley and Thomas Medwin wondered whether he would have included the poem in his collected works; at the time of its piracy in 1821, Shelley claimed that he hardly remembered the poem.[29] But examination of *Queen Mab* sheds light on the collision of the naive idealism of 1813 and the realities he encountered later in life. In any case, I think we should regard Shelley's views, like Godwin's, as well intentioned, but as nevertheless sharing the blindness to gender-based issues that bedeviled the sexual ideology of the men of the era.

The understanding behind the "Even love is sold" note is fundamentally Godwin's equation of marriage with property,[30] infused with the inspired libertarian discourse of the early Romantic poets. The language of social revolution is carried to the rhetoric of love: "its very essence is liberty," its enforcement in marriage "intolerable tyranny," "servitude," a "system of constraint," and the "usurpation of the right of private judgment."

Shelley follows Godwin's reasoning. Constancy is nothing virtuous in itself (indeed he bolsters the Godwinian argument against monopolization by vindicating it as the right to free "enquiry").[31] Like Godwin, he evades the question of the duration of the union, asking, "How long then ought the sexual connection to last?" and answering, "This is a subject which it is perhaps premature to discuss." And like other post-Godwinian male radicals, Shelley's emphasis is on facilitating dissolution of marriage, rather than on the female radical agenda of property rights within marriage and educational and labor opportunities. As with Godwin, matters will simply sort themselves out: "from the abolition of marriage, the fit and natural arrangement of sexual connection would result."

More problematic, however, is the poem's treatment of prostitution, the undernote we have heard all along in an era that reductively used the term *gallantry* as a euphemism for male libertinism and the term *prostitution* as the accusatory equivalent for unchaste women.[32] The poem's analysis of prostitution hinges on the declaration "Prostitution is the legitimate offspring of marriage and its accompanying errors. Women, for no other crime than having followed the dictates of a natural appetite, are driven with fury from the comforts and sympathies of society." As with the parliamentary debates, adultery and prostitution are conflated. But what is the precise connection between prostitution and indissoluble marriage? Will cultural acceptance of multiple relationships and branding women with less infamy prevent prostitution? Herein lies the troubling error of the age: assuming that prostitution is simply the consequence of female sexual desires, rather than regarding the economic imperatives behind it.

Although Shelley elicits sympathy for the life of misery, disease, and social ostracism ("Theirs is the right of persecution, hers the duty of endurance"), he actually masks the more direct causes of prostitution: assault, desertion, seduction, illegitimacy, and poverty. Indeed, in personifying both the persecutor and the victim as female—"Society avenges herself on the criminals of her own creation"—the text implicitly assists in removing the blame from men.

Curiously, Shelley's strategy is to deflect pity onto men as the chief cultural victims: "Young men, excluded by the fanatical idea of chastity from the society of modest and accomplished women, associate with these vicious and miserable beings, destroying . . . exquisite and delicate sensibilities . . . annihilating all genuine passion . . . debasing that to a selfish feeling." Shelley's sensitive young men are compelled by society to consort with prostitutes; though in real terms, gallants were not excluded from modest and uncorrupted society, merely deterred from prenuptial sexual liaisons. Shelley's young men are not indicted for perpetuating prostitution, and there is no articulation of the fact that the miserable and diseased women to whom they resort were made so by other young men.

As Wollstonecraft pointed out in her *Vindication of the Rights of Woman* (1792), "Necessity never makes prostitution the business of men's lives; though numberless are the women who are thus rendered systematically vicious."[33] With his character of the "Magdalene" Ann in his *Confessions of an English Opium Eater* (1821), De Quincey was to be one of the first male Romantics to elicit sympathy for the prostitute as a cultural victim of men rather than as a purveyor of vice. Yet Shelley's earlier strategy is certainly less judgmental than the Victorian redemptive evangelicism of such artworks as William Holman Hunt's "Awakening," the Henry Mayhew and William Acton anatomizations of prostitution, or the scapegoating Contagious Diseases Acts of the 1860s, attitudes that dominated the spiritual and scientific response of the later nineteenth century.

MALE AND FEMALE RADICAL AGENDAS

The issues surrounding Shelley's particular liaisons are too well known to need summarizing here. Whatever we may think of Shelley's marriages, it becomes clear that, in contrast to Byron, for example, Shelley, like Godwin, upheld his ethical responsibility to children of free love or antimatrimonial unions. Leigh Hunt was one of many who testified to Shelley's integrity, explaining how Shelley refuted "that extraordinary privilege to indulge one sex at the expense of the other," vowed to live by Godwin's *Political Justice* and Milton's doctrine of divorce, and shocked a village ballroom by dancing with a woman who been shamed by the reputation of having once been seduced ("probably," Hunt says, "by some well-dressed gentleman in the room, who thought himself entitled nevertheless to the conversation of the most flourishing ladies present").[34]

It is clear that Shelley above all loved the language of rebellion (Harriet Shelley was held in "prison"; "her father has persecuted her in a most horrible way, & endeavours to compel her to go to school. She asked my advice: resistance was the answer").[35] His ecstatic writings catalyzed others who had never met him. The Owenite socialist Anna Wheeler closed a letter to Robert Owen by quoting Shelley's declaration, "Can man be free if woman be a slave?"[36] and although Owen never met Shelley, when he visited a spiritualist medium in later years, he seems to have greeted the spirit of the poet with the words "my old friend Shelley." Medwin attended an Owenite meeting with Lawrence and found *Queen Mab* and the *Empire of the Nairs* on sale; when he introduced himself as a friend of Shelley's, Owen "made a long panegyric on him, and taking up one of the *Queen Mabs* from the table, read . . . the following passage: 'How long ought the sexual connection to last?'"[37]

Thomas Poole observed that the planners of the Pantisocracy scheme of 1794, Coleridge and Southey, were not sure what to do with Godwin's matrimonial policy and noted that their chief problems had to do with the position of women: "the regulations relating to the females strike them as the most difficult."[38] Although Owen linked the rise of private property with marriage and sought to alleviate women's domestic "drudgery" and child-rearing through collectivism, women historians have come to distinguish the female Owenite agenda from the male: Whereas men popularized free love and divorce reform to solve the risks of perpetual marriage, women were more concerned with rights within marriage, educational equality, and destigmatizing female transgressors. Lack of control over reproduction was a crucial factor shaping the female radical view. It is interesting that, in the female utopian schemes of bluestocking novels written by women, such as Sarah Scott's *Millenium Hall* (1762) and Mary Walker Hamilton's *Munster Village* (1778), and in Shakerism itself, led by Anna Lee, utopian communities were connected with celibacy.[39]

Incongruities exist within the Romantic era and indeed within any era, and we can only measure any gesture of radicalism or social reform within its historically relative context. But it is also clear—and not only from the Romantic male-centered discourse on illegitimacy, divorce, and prostitution—that female and male radical priorities have not always coincided—although male radicals have tended to assume the correspondence of women's inter-ests. Simple assessments, however, are not easy to make.

The dissonance of male and female political agendas is evident in the history of suffrage reform. Despite the interest of Wollstonecraft and Ben-thamite radicals in female suffrage, Shelley's opposition to the female vote as "somewhat immature" in the *Philosophical View of Reform* (1819),[40] voiced the unreadiness argument that beleaguered suffrage activists until the twentieth century. The London Working Men's Association similarly allowed the dis-course of universal suffrage to lapse into the more expedient male suffrage; indeed, within early-nineteenth-century industrial reform there was consid-erable male unionist hostility to women, and their attempt to remove the cheaper female labor pool from the skilled trades often masqueraded as concern for affirming the home.[41]

Let us take another example. While Shelley's "Discourse on the Manners of the Ancients Relative to the Subject of Love" (circa 1818) places him in the vanguard of male feminist thought (denouncing the "degraded" state of women in Greek and Roman culture, "educated as slaves" and relegated to "inferiority"), his 1813 letter to Godwin on the subject of Classical educa-tion illustrates the conflict between male theories and female praxis. It was rebellious for Shelley as a man to denounce the emphasis on ancient learning as "a literary despotism . . . intended to shut out from real knowledge . . . all who . . . will not support the established systems of politics, religion &

morals";[42] but the fact that Mary Shelley, Claire Clairmont, and Harriet Shelley took advantage of the opportunity to learn Latin from him reflected the widespread intellectual feminist goal of acquiring Classical learning to overcome the traditional exclusion of women from high literary discourse.

The ideological contradictions of antimatrimonialism surround the radical publisher William Clark[e], who was prosecuted by the Society for the Suppression of Vice and subsequently jailed for reissuing *Queen Mab* in 1821 (preempting Shelley's own attempt to suppress the edition). That summer he seems to have also published a *Reply to the Anti-Matrimonial Hypothesis ... as laid down in* Queen Mab, which pointed out that Shelley's system failed to protect women from desertion in old age and distress, that affections are unlikely to subside simultaneously, and that Shelley considered women only as "the mere instrument of male gratification—the passive and unconsulted medium of his transports." The gender of the author is unclear, but viewed from a feminist perspective it echoes the radical critique of the sexual double standard put forth by female radicals in the late eighteenth century. Observing that "the evils of prostitution ... spring, in a great measure, from the want of laws, which *man* has neglected to frame, lest his gratifications should be limited," the pamphlet calls for "punishment of seduction" and requiring men to support the women who, after being discarded, have no way of finding employment once branded with illegitimate offspring: "it is considered *disgraceful* for a *gentleman* to degrade himself by a marriage with a poor, fond, deluded woman. . . . A small sum paid to the parish compensates for the crime, and annihilates the necessity of feeling. It is ONLY an illegitimate child. . . . What becomes of the mother, is a matter of still less consideration with the seducer. She is old enough to work. The parish does not insist upon a maintenance for her."[43]

MIDDLE-CLASS FALLEN WOMEN

Although most male radical commentators failed to perceive that prostitution and nuptiality trends were connected with economic disenfranchisement, radical women writers directly addressed the politics of seduction. It is not surprising to find fallen women suggesting the most concrete plans for remedying the transgressive double standard. Long before male radicals argued against desecration of female character, Laetitia Pilkington proclaimed in her 1748 *Memoirs*, "Is it not monstrous, that our seducers should be our accusers?" The unpublished *Female Protector* (1800) suggested making seduction a criminal offence. Wollstonecraft's *Vindication* (1792) repeatedly declared that laws should compel men to maintain women they seduced.[44]

These women were not deluded by the rhetoric of "natural protectors." Women radicals in the 1790s pointed with concern to the demographic trends that meant many women would be unable to wed.[45] As a result, feminist intellectuals increasingly directed their concerns to the limited job opportunities for women. As early as 1787, Wollstonecraft, in her *Thoughts on the Education of Daughters,* worried about the problem that many middle-class women were "genteelly educated" but left without a fortune and "must frequently remain single." She analyzed the consequences in her *Vindication,* when the "helpless" unmarried sister is viewed "with averted looks as an intruder," cast out "into joyless solitude," or reduced to "humiliating" occupations: "the few employments open to women . . . are menial." As Clara Reeve's *Plans of Education* (1792) put it, "there are very few trades for women; the men have usurped two-thirds of those that used to belong to them; the remainder are over-stocked." The following year Mary Hays declared in her *Letters and Essays* that women who "do not chance to marry (and this is not a marrying age) have scarce any other resources than in servitude or prostitution" and added that trades such as women's clothing, "which ought to be appropriated only to women," have been "entirely engrossed by men." Mary Ann Radcliffe, in *The Female Advocate* (1799), also saw prostitution as the consequence of inadequate forms of employment and "men usurping females' occupations." Perhaps the most radical document of the era, the anonymous *Appeal to the Men of Great Britain* (1798), asserted that men monopolized the traditionally female jobs and urged the potential of women in nontraditional occupations such as ministers and lawyers. Even the more traditionalist Priscilla Wakefield, in her *Reflections on the Present Condition of the Female Sex* the same year, said men had taken over and were paid better for jobs that should be reserved for women, and argued that middle-class women should not suffer social stigma for seeking work, because "there is nothing so inimical to the preservation of her virtue as the state of poverty." Things were no better in 1818, when Mary Brunton wrote, "These hard times compel so many women to celibacy, that I should think it no bad speculation to educate a few for respectable old maids." With her usual trenchancy, Jane Austen meditated in 1817, "Single Women have a dreadful propensity for being poor."[46]

Women who tried to espouse a sexual ideology resembling that of Romantic men, however, found themselves economically and socially marginalized; they paid a high price for demanding equality, and there were far greater punishments for female freethinkers than for male. Indeed, the middle-class fallen woman was an immensely radicalizing force. The women surrounding Shelley provide an interesting chronicle of the economic and social realities for women of the era who challenged conventional assumptions about female transgression.

Like other legally separated wives, Harriet Shelley was condemned to a life of loneliness or to the furtive amours that branded her as having "descended the steps of prostitution." Elizabeth Hitchener, who joined the "glorious cause" Shelley described, found her retreat to schoolteaching blocked until she laundered her past on the continent with a brief marriage. Claire Clairmont, whose intense commitment to independence made her a true daughter of Wollstonecraft, supported herself for over twenty years as a companion, governess, and day teacher. Like Wollstonecraft, she adhered to feminist theories of education ("my pupil should be left at liberty as much as possible . . . her own reason should be the prompter of her actions"), but she too found governessing a "life which lies stagnant from inactivity." Her situation was worse than Wollstonecraft's: Hounded by her unwed motherhood and her Godwinian past ("issued from the very den of freethinkers"), she was forced to change employers each time her reputation became known—an experience Medwin recounted using the words of Queen Mab: "theirs is the right of persecution—hers the duty of endurance." Experiencing a life of slander herself, Claire Clairmont came to sympathize with the traduced Harriet Shelley, defending her from tales about being the prostitute of a stableman.[47]

Unlike that of her stepsister, Mary Shelley's experience of hardship was long postponed, as she moved from the girlhood shelter of her father's household to the protection of a freethinking noble scion. She was eager to have Claire Clairmont's natural child removed from her house as soon as possible lest it injure her own precarious reputation—without realizing that, had Shelley died in his illness of 1815 or had Harriet Shelley induced him to return, she would have been in the same position as Claire Clairmont. Mary Shelley's stepmother worried, "everybody tells [Harriet Shelley] that love affairs last but a little time and her husband will be sure to return to her. . . . That is indeed but too true and what a gloomy prospect it opens to us."[48] Mary Shelley's radicalization, however, only occurred after she was left a widow, when she realized the isolation and circumscribed life of a woman without a male protector. Frustrated in her attempts to secure a settlement from Shelley's family and faced with the difficulty of supporting herself, she came to understand the position of Claire Clairmont and joined the un-successful attempt of Lady Mount Cashell, who had been Wollstonecraft's favorite student, to persuade Byron to provide Claire Clairmont with an annuity.[49] Her own shock at Byron's recommendation that she give her boy away to his male relations compelled her to reconfront the recommendations she had given Claire Clairmont about Allegra, and the rumors she had to combat upon returning home to England made her solicitous to protect Claire Clairmont's reputation from the scandal sheets at Byron's death.

Shelley, too, came to hard realizations in the course of his life. It must have been infuriating to have had to defend his morality to Byron in order to secure Claire Clairmont's visitation rights with Allegra ("I smiled at your protest about what you consider my creed. On the contrary, I think a regard to chastity is quite necessary, as things are, to a young female—that is, to her happiness—and at any time a good habit").[50] Likewise, he had to instruct his solicitor P. W. Longdill to propose a highly conventionalized (and gendered) plan of instruction in the attempt to gain educational custody of his children after Harriet's demise.[51]

It is disturbing to realize that as hard as their lives were, Claire Clairmont and Mary Shelley were in fact insulated from the full brunt of the transgres-sive double standard solely by Shelley's intercession. As tragic as her pleading letters to Byron are to read, Claire Clairmont's interests in Allegra were protected to the extent they were only by Byron's nominal concern with how he appeared to Shelley. She was in this sense protected, unlike the chambermaids on whom Byron "fell like a thunderbolt,"[52] or Margherita Cogni, who was trivialized to posterity as "the fornarina." The other side of the class-based implications of seduction, however, shielded the transgressive behavior of aristocrats such as Lady Mount Cashell, Lady Melbourne (aunt of Byron's wife), and Countess Guiccioli, whose second husband would introduce her as "Ma femme, ancienne maîtresse de Byron."[53] Only when Lady Caroline Lamb exceeded the farthest bounds of public propriety was she censured (characteristic of the era, she was ostracized while her husband conducted his liaison and went on to be Queen Victoria's prime minister).

It is also worth noting that not every middle-class woman was as heroic in her endeavors as Claire Clairmont or Mary Shelley. Jane Williams and Byron's supposed natural daughter Medora accepted support from a series of male "protectors" rather than forging their independence. But for both Claire Clairmont and Mary Shelley, it was the memory of Shelley's undaunted optimism that they credited in this uphill struggle—not his systems, but his inspiriting exhortation to action.

This is to say that mooring Shelley's utopian ideals in the context of practical schemes of reform, as I have done in this chapter, does not mean that we want *no* better bread than is made of wheat. Perhaps the concept most helpful in understanding Shelley's idealizations and his gift of inspiring others is the statement of his early biographer Edward Dowden, who in 1886 wrote that Shelley believed it was "a poet's duty to sustain the hopes and aspirations of men in their movement of advance, and at the same time to endeavour to hold their passions in check by presenting high ideals, and showing that the better life of society is not to be won out of the air."[54] This may in fact be the key importance of Shelley within contemporary reform movements: He was no demagogue—but he had, and has, the gift of inspiring others.

Shelley Left and Right:
The Rhetorics of the Early
Textual Editions

Neil Fraistat

9

UNQUESTIONABLY, of the 170 years that have passed since Shelley's
death, the two most crucial years for establishing his texts, textualizing
his life, and securing his reputation were 1824 and 1839, the years of Mary
Shelley's truly monumental editions. But any account of these authoritative
editions becomes complicated by the fact that they had their dark cultural
doubles, their evil twins, so to speak, in the unauthorized, "illegitimate,"
pirated editions of Shelley that proliferated between 1821 and 1840. Here I
pursue specific ways in which the authorized and illegitimate Shelleys so
reproduced might be said to be in cultural dialogue with each other.

As a start, let us think of the textual edition as a type of prosopopoeia, a
giving of face and figure that is always—whatever else it may be—inevitably
a defacement and disfiguration, a culturally specific form of what Paul de
Man has helped us to see as "monumentalized" discourse.[1] The materiality
of that discourse might then be conceived in terms of Jerome McGann's
distinction between a book's bibliographical codes—which include such
material details as the page format, paper, typefaces, price, advertising mech-

This chapter is an earlier version of the author's "Illegitimate Shelley: Radical Piracy and the
Textual Edition as Cultural Performance," *Publications of the Modern Language Association of America*
110 (May 1994):409–23. Reprinted by permission of the copyright owner, The Modern Language
Association of America.

anisms, and distribution venues—and its linguistic codes, which include not only all of the linguistic text of the poems as such but also what Gérard Genette has termed the set of surrounding "paratexts": "prefaces, dedications, . . . advertisements, footnotes, and the like."[2] Shelley's textual body, so to speak, could then be located within the "laced network" (13) of linguistic and bibliographical codes that ultimately comprise each edition's own monumentalized discourse. That discourse might itself be thought of as a rhetoric of Shelley, a cultural performance locating the textual space of the edition within the particularized social space of its production and reception. For the purposes of this chapter, I examine both Mary Shelley's 1824 edition of *Posthumous Poems* and William Benbow's piracy of that volume in 1826 as such cultural performances, considering the rhetoric of Shelley each produces as both a product of and a participant in a larger set of social discourses.

Mary Shelley's editorial efforts must be understood as cultural performances in the broadest sense of the term. The etherialized, disembodied, and virtually depoliticized poet to emerge from her textual editions was the corporate product of an entire cultural apparatus: sponsored by a nascent set of middle-class Victorian ideological positions, propagated by the publishing and reviewing institutions, undergirded as well as undercut by copyright law, mediated by the workings of the marketplace, and challenged by competing appropriations of Shelley.

Taking its impetus from a tendency in Shelley's own self-representations, both in his poetry and in his life, to slight the body for the mind or the spirit, the etherializing and disembodying of Shelley was, in fact, a project fostered by most of the Shelley circle, and also, importantly, by John Stuart Mill, F. D. Maurice, and the Cambridge Apostles—in particular Hallam and Tennyson. It took the form of various sorts of reductive readings of Shelley and his poetry: the reduction to sensation, the reduction to the lyric moment, the reduction to spirituality, the reduction to beauty. The master trope of these reductions was "purity" and its product was "pure poetry." Shelley thus became at once a signifier of "pure poetry" and a means by which pure poetry could be argued for as a cultural standard of England's national literature.

Mary Shelley's first entrance into the marketplace as an editor came in 1824, with the publication of *Posthumous Poems of Percy Bysshe Shelley,* a volume designed, as she explained to Leigh Hunt, as "a specimen of how . . . [Shelley] could write without shocking any one" (*MWSL* 1:397)[3] Her desire for a shockproof Shelley was especially conditioned by two moments in the early 1820s that played major roles in further polarizing the already polarized rhetoric through which Shelley was received: the reviews prompted by the pirating of *Queen Mab* in 1821, not to mention the trial of William Clark for pirating it; and the controversy in the obituary notices in 1822 over the significance of Shelley's life and work. In both instances, the vehement attacks from the political right worked, sometimes literally, to demonize Shelley, as the following quotation from the *Literary Gazette's* review of *Queen Mab* (May 19, 1821) illustrates well: "We declare against receiving our social impulses from a destroyer of every social virtue; our moral creed, from an incestuous wretch; or our religion, from an atheist, who denied God, and reviled the purest institutes of human philosophy and divine ordination, did such a demon exist."[4] Out to show that the "demon" existed only as an ideological illusion of right-wing critics, Mary Shelley followed the rhetorical tracks of Shelley's defenders on the left who were quick to fix a halo in place. Paratext and text work hand in hand in *Posthumous Poems* to produce a powerful rhetoric of Shelley, the master tropes of which are "unearthliness" and "elevation"—that is to say, purity inscribed by upper-class status, the rhetoric of high culture.

These tropes are most explicitly developed in the paratext of the volume, with its opening epigraph from Petrarch, which crossdresses a description of Laura to become one of Shelley that, as translated by Robert Durling, reads "In noble blood a humble and quiet life, / with a high intellect a / pure heart, the fruit of age in the flower of youth, and with / thoughtful aspect a happy soul."[5] The preface reenacts the rhetoric of the epigraph in its brief biographical sketch of Shelley's "unearthly and elevated" nature.[6] Rather than scanting the fact that Shelley was a devoted political reformer, the preface uses this fact to explain Shelley's notoriety: "like other illustrious reformers, [he] was pursued by hatred and calumny" (iv). This same strategy had already been employed in Horace Smith's obituary for Shelley in the *Paris Monthly Review* for August 1822, which, after anointing Shelley as the new Lycidas, comments, "yet never was there a name associated with more black, poisonous, and bitter calumny than his," a fact it explains by stating that Shelley "had the misfortune to entertain, from his very earliest youth, opinions, both in religion and politics, diametrically opposed to established systems."[7] But whereas Smith concedes that he does not intend to "exculpate Mr. Shelley from the charge of sometimes adopting crude and rash opinions" (32), there is little rash and nothing crude about the Shelley of *Posthumous Poems*. After dealing with Shelley's politics in only the most general frame of reference, the preface uses a class-coded language of sensibility to stress his refinement, describing in the process his ill health, his elegant scholarship, and his extraordinary emotional responsiveness both to nature and to others.

Perhaps the most crucial decision Mary Shelley made about the volume was to defer trying to publish Shelley's complete works, which would have prompted all of the by-now-familiar complaints and resistances, in favor of an edition of primarily posthumous works selected to show how Shelley could "write without shocking any one." As finally published, *Posthumous Poems* contained thirteen poems that had already gone out of print, five translations, and sixty-five formerly unpublished poems. Approximately one-quarter of the unpublished poems consisted of fragments, most of which were no longer than one or two stanzas, and several no more than two lines. Unlike Shelley's most ideologically contestatory poems—all of which were suppressed from the volume—these brief, nonnarrative fragments were politically safe, irreducibly poetic, and calculated to foreground Shelley as a writer of lyrics in whose work, as the preface explains, "more than [in] any other poet of the present day, every line and word . . . is instinct with peculiar beauty" (VIII). Mary Shelley's judgment in printing these fragments and such poems as "Stanzas, Written in Dejection, near Naples," "Song, on a Faded Violet," "When passion's trance," and "To Night" was rewarded by the enthusiasm of readers and reviewers, the latter quoting these lyrics at length.[8]

C. H. Reynell printed *Posthumous Poems* handsomely in octavo format on fine wove paper with wide margins for John Hunt and Henry L. Hunt, who published the book at the not inexpensive price of fifteen shillings. In its material production, its price, and its selection of poems, the book's bibliographical codes made clear what was already implicit in its linguistic codes: that it was designed for consumption by the middling and upper classes—certainly not the working class and artisan readers who were eagerly consuming inexpensive pirated editions of *Queen Mab*. Indeed, the volume succeeded in making Shelley accessible and acceptable to more of its targeted readers than he had ever reached in his lifetime. Within two months of its publication, over three hundred copies had been sold. Once put into social circulation by *Posthumous Poems,* the lyrics of the volume took on a cultural life of their own, so to speak, and were reproduced in articles, anthologies, musical settings, and critical discussions; quotations from the lyrics appeared as epigraphs to chapters in novels and to short fiction.[9] In this way, Mary Shelley successfully monumentalized Shelley as, in the words of her preface, "a bright vision, whose radiant track, left behind in the memory, is worth all the realities that society can afford" (iv). The pure poet of the lyric moment took textual form.

This text-based rhetoric of Shelley might have quickly become more complicated if Mary Shelley had been able to pursue her original plan, which was to follow the publication of *Posthumous Poems* immediately, first with an edition of Shelley's prose and then with a complete edition of the poetry, in which "any thing too shocking" for *Posthumous Poems* could finally be included. There were, however, to be no further authorized editions of Shelley's poetry for fifteen years, and Mary Shelley was even forced to recall all of the unsold volumes of *Posthumous Poems* itself some two months after publication, because—as is well known—Sir Timothy Shelley, upon whom she depended for financial support, forced her to promise not to bring Shelley's name before the public again during Sir Timothy's lifetime.[10]

Consequently, the rhetoric of Shelley fostered by the production and reception of *Posthumous Poems* took firm root in the developing middle-class culture. But this impression was not uncontested, both because of the culture's prior reception of Shelley and because, given the workings of copyright law and the marketplace, a number of literary pirates rushed in where authorized textual reproductions of Shelley could tread no more. Between 1822 and 1841 there were at least twenty-six pirated editions of Shelley's poetry, nine among which were of *Queen Mab* alone.[11] These piracies were primarily the work of radical pressmen, some of whom—including Richard Carlile—defiantly produced inexpensive pamphlets on birth control for sale to the lower classes, while others—including William Benbow and John Ascham—published obscene and pornographic literature.[12] "Pure poetry" found strange bedfellows here.

One might even say that, somewhat like Prometheus meeting the phantasm of Jupiter, Mary Shelley's 1824 *Posthumous Poems of Percy Bysshe Shelley* met its textualized other, also called up from the underworld, when in 1826 William Benbow pirated virtually the entire volume for his own edition, *Miscellaneous and Posthumous Poems of Percy Bysshe Shelley.* With the exception of the translations, Benbow printed all of the texts in *Posthumous Poems* as they had been arranged by Mary Shelley, simply adding at the opening and close of his edition eight more texts: the four poems of the *Rosalind and Helen* volume; "A Vision of the Sea," "The Sensitive Plant," and "To a Sky-Lark" from the *Prometheus Unbound* volume; and "Lines, Written on Hearing the Death of Napoleon," the lyric accompanying *Hellas.*

Benbow's paratext retains Mary Shelley's footnotes and the untranslated epigraphs to poems such as *Alastor* but, significantly, omits her epigraph from Petrarch and her biographical sketch of Shelley. There is, in fact, no prefatory material at all to contextualize Shelley's texts for the reader; that part of the volume's performance is consigned to its bibliographical codes. In place of the large octavo format of *Posthumous Poems,* with its fine print and wide margins, Benbow's edition is a much smaller duodecimo, with inexpensive wove paper and narrow margins, whose print is in the generic fonts characteristic of inexpensive books and pamphlets published in London at the time. Priced at five shillings, sixpence, Benbow's volume cost nearly two-thirds less than *Posthumous Poems.* Moreover, in place of the authorizing name of Mary Shelley, the title page of *Miscellaneous and Posthumous Poems* carried only the name of William Benbow, printer and bookseller, who, along with William Hone and Carlile, was one of the three most notorious radical pirates of the day. Thus the material form of the edition itself, as well as its venue of distribution, announce the book's appropriation of Shelley into a network of production and distribution that provided its own distinct cultural context from which to read the poet.[13]

The cultural space for radical literary piracy was, in effect, created by Lord Eldon's landmark decision in *Southey* v. *Sherwood* that Robert Southey could not stop the embarrassing piracy of *Wat Tyler* because "a person cannot recover in damages for a work which is, in its nature, calculated to do injury to the public."[14] In other words, the status as property of a literary work depended upon its propriety as determined by the courts, not on what might seem to be a natural relation between the author as producer and the fruits of his or her work.[15] Politically or religiously subversive work thus could not be claimed as legal property, a principle intended to punish authors and publishers who overstepped the line, as when it was first deployed by Lord Chief Justice Eyre in 1791 against Joseph Priestly, who wanted to sue for damages done to his manuscripts by a Church and King mob. But as Eldon himself recognized in *Murray* v. *Benbow,* this principle "opens a door for . . . wide dissemination" of works "calculated to produce mischievous effects."[16]

And mischief there was. A brief return to the reviewer for the *Literary Gazette,* whom we last left foaming at the mouth over *Queen Mab,* will illustrate the point. For this reviewer, Shelley's demonic tendencies were all the more threatening because they were embodied in "a book of so blasphemous a nature, as to have no claim to the protection of copy-right; it may be published by Scoundrels at all prices, to destroy the moral feeling of every class of the community" (305). Shelley's work, in short, was both morally and legally out of control. Too subversive to qualify as property over which Shelley could claim ownership, it could be reproduced by "Scoundrels" inexpensively enough to circulate freely throughout the social system, becoming, in the words of our reviewer, "dangerous to the ignorant and weak, hateful to the lovers of social felicity, and an enemy to all that is valuable in life, or hopeful in eternity" (306).

Benbow, an ultraradical who styled himself a publisher for the "ignorant and weak," seized on pirating as a form of proto–class warfare: "The enormous high price of books has long prevented the humble in place and purse from acquiring information, and we are not sorry to see the 'gates of knowledge' opened so that all ranks may enter therein for a mere trifle," he wrote in the *Rambler's Magazine* for March 1822.[17] Originally a shoemaker from the Manchester area, Benbow began his career as a literary pirate in 1821, with the financial backing of the by-now-notorious ultraradical George Cannon (a.k.a. "Erasmus Perkins")—a career beginning with a surreptitious piracy of *Queen Mab* in 1821, the so-called "New York edition," and ending in 1827 with a piracy of *The Cenci*.[18]

During this time, most, though not all, of Benbow's publications implicitly attacked the ideological underpinnings of church and state. Many were overtly political, like the several pro-Caroline pamphlets he authored and his compilation *Crimes of the Clergy* (1823); some were pornographic, like *The Confessions of Julia Johnstone* (1826), or the soft-core *Rambler's Magazine* he edited and published, which featured, along with literary and dramatic gossip and criticism, erotic verse and pictures. In response to attacks in *Blackwood's* and the *Quarterly* that his literary piracies were doing injury "to the lower orders of society," he proudly claimed in the *Rambler's Magazine* for September 1822 that his piracies "all tend to unmask those systems of corruption and hypocrisy which the *Quarterly* and *Blackwood* so devoutly adore."[19] Benbow, in short, was attacking "Old Corruption" with a vengeance.

In 1826, the year Benbow pirated *Posthumous Poems* and planned on being the first publisher ever to produce a complete poetical works of Shelley, Robert Southey described Benbow's second shop, "The Byron's Head," as "one of those preparatory schools for the brothel and gallows; where obscenity, sedition, and blasphemy are retailed in drams for the vulgar."[20] Thus connected to the radical underground and retailed among obscenity, sedition, and blasphemy in inexpensive editions for working-class and artisan readers, Shelley's poetry in general—but especially *Queen Mab*—gained or regained its most transgressive implications. As reproduced by low publishers primarily for "vulgar" readers, then, the unauthorized or illegitimate Shelley took textual form as an earthbound body with a vengeance, circulating through the culture as a signifier of certain kinds of culturally prohibited knowledge and behavior. The "purity" of Shelley's poetry, if not of poetry itself, was thereby reinterrogated by the radical counterrhetoric of the early pirated textual editions.

Although the repressed in Shelley and his works might thereby be seen as staging a return, the extent to which Shelley's works—and, in particular, the shockproof Shelley of *Posthumous Poems*—could also resist the rhetoric of radicalism itself should not be underestimated, as the fate in the marketplace of Benbow's attempt to appropriate that collection in *Miscellaneous and Posthumous Poems* suggests. Writing in the *Metropolitan Quarterly Magazine* for September 1826, in an essay on Shelley upon which I have not seen previous critical comment, Derwent Coleridge states, "A surreptitious edition of Shelley's works has lately been attempted in cheap numbers, but the sale has not been sufficient to induce the publisher, (Mr. Benbow) to proceed with it."[21] Coleridge attributes the failure of Benbow's edition to the fact that Shelley's works "have no charm for the ignorant or half-informed [as] is proved by their narrow sale, notwithstanding all the arts of low and venal publishers. They are indeed addressed to the highest order of readers, to whom the nature both of the thoughts and the diction confines them, much more effectually than a learned or even a technical language" (195).

Whether or not Coleridge accurately accounts for the financial failure of Benbow's edition, his claim that the linguistic codes of *Posthumous Poems* successfully resisted appropriation by the bibliographical codes of the piracy invites us to reimagine the differences in the rhetoric of Shelley produced by the early textual editions as functions of a cultural semiotic in which "high" and "low" are terms as crucial as "left" or "right." Considered from the bottom up, in light of Gareth Stedman Jones's argument that for radicalism "the dividing line between classes was not that between employer and employed, but that between the represented and the unrepresented," the piracy of Shelley, an aristocrat writing against aristocracy, can be seen as one means for radicals to gain a purchase on the system of representation itself, a way in which low culture could attempt to appropriate high culture so as to come to know itself better as a public—and, ultimately, as a class.[22]

Jon Klancher has observed that "Radical discourse was not as much 'expressed' by a nascent working class as it formed the latter's ideological and interpretive map. Yet, like an atlas in which one map overlaps another . . . the boundaries between middle-class and working-class discourses were not immobile lines but strategic, shifting latitudes of force" (103). Few others of his day would have been more aware of these shifting boundaries or the need for radical discourse to provide the working-class with such an interpretive map than William Benbow, himself a shoemaker become an artisan intellectual, a man socially dislocated from his own class who nonetheless still attempted to identify himself with it. Dislocated in many ways from *his* own class during his lifetime, Shelley became as monumentalized text a figure of tremendous mobility, simultaneously underwriting and undercutting both the rhetoric of "purity" and the rhetoric of "radicalism." As reproduced in both high and low cultural registers in the mid-1820s, he becomes a telling sign for what Klancher calls "the very separation of publics and the deeper division of class it designates" (102). This separation in reading publics and classes, this "wound of a fracture"[23] in the social semiotics of late Georgian England, is almost uncannily reflected in the self-contending rhetorics of, and the cultural performance enacted by, William Benbow's piracy of *Posthumous Poems*.

Shelley and the Chartists

Bouthaina Shaaban

10

ONLY A FEW years after Shelley's death and with the rise of Socialist political movements in the Britain of the 1830s, literary journals began to show a changed perspective toward Shelley's works and philosophy. Despite their political differences, the Owenites, the Chartists, and the Christian Democrats seemed to agree that Shelley's poetry and thought needed to be reevaluated. The extent of Shelley's presence in the main organs of these movements will require further years of study and analysis.[1] The common elements that instigated a new attitude toward Shelley's poetry and philosophy seemed to stem from three major arguments:

1. Shelley's poetry had suffered from politically motivated misinterpretations.

2. His reputation had suffered from an unfair distortion of facts related to his personal life.

3. The question of his atheism required fair and serious consideration.

In the *New Moral World* (1835–45), some twenty-one items on Shelley were published, including five on *Prometheus Unbound*.[2] Shelley's poetry was generally approached as that of a long-neglected genius. The *Athenaeum*'s early review of Shelley's "The Mask of Anarchy" sums up the attitude of a whole generation toward Shelley: "GENIUS, though it may be for a time unhonoured, must eventually have its triumph on—it may live friendless, and lay down a wearied spirit in a welcome grave—but the hour of its glory must come, when all living men shall acknowledge it, and all succeeding generations join in one loud song of exultation and praise."[3] Leaving out Leigh Hunt's writings on Shelley, which were rightly acknowledged as the most significant efforts to introduce Shelley to later radical movements, this was one of the pioneering reviews in the new era of Shelley criticism.

Yet, as the century entered its fourth decade, it was the Chartists who expressed a special affinity toward Shelley both as a poet and as a political philosopher. In the *Northern Star* alone (1838–52), over fifty items on Shelley appeared. The *Chartist Circular* (1839–41) published eight lengthy articles on Shelley's poetry and politics. In the two Chartist papers edited by Ernest Charles Jones, *Notes to the People* (1851) and the *People's Paper* (1852–57), Shelley was awarded a very special place indeed. In the *People's Paper*, Jones introduces Shelley's poetry to his readers with the intention of shaping the poetical mind of the country; he announces, "We purpose opening to our readers a school of poetry, and for a while, withdrawing all original compositions, giving them those masterpieces of sentiment and expression, which may tend to elevate and form the poetical mind of the country. We commence with SHELLEY."[4]

Perhaps one reason for the special affinity the Chartists seemed to feel toward Shelley was that most of the Chartist leaders were themselves poets. Most of them felt that they were the future generations whom Shelley was engaged in addressing both in his poetry and in his political tracts. Many of the Chartist poets also suffered from the same dilemma that bewildered Shelley: the question of whether to seek immediate or future reform and their own indecision between their functions as poets and as political reformers. In one sense, Shelley was perceived by the Chartists as the martyr of their own cause, the cause of the working classes and free thought. H. Buxton Forman was one of the first to observe Shelley's influence on the working classes. In his *Vicissitudes of Shelley's* Queen Mab: *A Chapter in the History of Reform,* he observes that "the poem and its notes have played a considerable part in the growth of free thought in England and America, especially among the working classes."[5] Forman's judgment was later supported by George Bernard Shaw. All sources agree that he was one of the main inspirations for the Chartist movement, that there was always a Shelleyan vote though there was no way of counting it, and that *Queen Mab* was called the Chartist Bible.[6] Articles on him were written and his poems were published and advertised in all the major papers of the time, including the *New Moral World,* the *Northern Star,* the *National,* and the *Reasoner.* In the *Reasoner,* for example, Shelley's poems, particularly *Queen Mab* and "The Mask of Anarchy," were advertised along with Thomas Paine's works and Mary Wollstonecraft's *Vindication of the Rights of Woman* under the title "Books on Free Inquiry."[7]

The prevalence of Shelley's thought and political philosophy could be felt not only in the literary journals of the time but also in the lives and works of contemporary poets. Literary sources show that there was hardly any contemporary poet who had not read Shelley and either dedicated poems to him or echoed him in his compositions. Charles Kingsley's (1819–75) poem "Ode to the North-East Wind" (1859) is much better understood when compared to Shelley's "Ode to the West Wind." The same poem by Shelley finds an echo in "Winter will Follow" by Richard Watson Dixon (1833–1900). Shelley's "Ode to Life" echoes in "The Ode of Life" by Lewis Morris (1833–1907) as well as in *Studies of Sensation and Event, Poems by Ebenezer Jones* (1820–60), a volume admired by Browning and Rossetti.

Moreover, Sumner Jones, the elder brother of the poet Ebenezer Jones, describes his brother's first reaction to Shelley's poetry in this way: "A Little thick Duodecimo edition of Shelley's Poems was also obtained, and this had afterwards a magical effect upon him." A few pages further on, Sumner Jones is more specific regarding the impact that Shelley had on his brother's poetry and thought: "The poet of the 'Ode to Liberty,' from his station in the heaven of Fame, seemed also to his young enthusiasm to bend over him with a smile." Shelley was much with him at this time: He made allusions to Shelley even when writing argumentatively to M. Considerant on his plan for the "Conciliation of Society by the Organization of Labour," printed in 1839 in the *New Moral World* of Robert Owen. In a footnote to this remark, the editor prints that part of the letter to which Sumner Jones refers: "Who wrote the Revolt of Islam? Not Shelley! 'Tis the mighty utterance of a society whose eyes have just opened to the glory of truth, and she made him her priest. He was the lute; she the power of musi—he was but the prophet; she was the God."[8]

Both the argument of the letter and Sumner Jones's description of Shelley's status at the time as being "in the heaven of Fame" are indications of Shelley's popularity at the time. In fact Ebenezer Jones's poems, *Studies of Sensation and Event,* are dedicated to Shelley, but the dedication did not appear until the 1879 edition of the poems, nineteen years after the death of Ebenezer Jones. The dedication reads as follows:

To the Memory of
Shelley
Who died 8th July 1822
But who lives for ever
in the hearts and minds of poets
I inscribe this book
Not so much in reverence
For his perfection in art
As in love of the infinite Goodness
of his nature
In which partly for its essential beauty
And partly because it was human
It has often been given me to rejoice
With joy unspeakable and full of glory

Yet, like Shelley, Jones was a neglected genius. In a biographical note on Jones published in *Notes and Queries,* Dante G. Rossetti describes him as "a remarkable poet, who affords nearly the most striking instance of neglected genius in our modern school of poetry. I met him only once in my life, I believe in 1848, at which time he was about thirty. Some years after meeting Jones, I was much pleased to hear the great poet Robert Browning speak in warm terms of the merit of his work."[9] In another note about Jones, the Rev. T. Mardy Rees acknowledges the fact that Jones was introduced to Shelley early on in his life: "Ebenezer Jones was the third child and son of Robert Jones born at Canonbury Square, Islington, 20th January 1820.... All three were exceptionally brilliant and when they got hold of the works of Shelley and Carlyle they soon devoured them."[10]

Furthermore, the lives and works of such Chartist poets as Thomas Cooper and Ernest Charles Jones have many parallels in Shelley's life and work. Thomas Cooper's (1805–92) *Eight Letters to the Young Men of the Working Classes* echo in both tone and content Shelley's *Address to the Irish People.*[11] Also like Shelley, Cooper wrote inquiries into the nature of Deity.[12] Cooper's long poem *The Purgatory of Suicides* calls to mind two poems by Shelley: *Queen Mab* and "A Song to the Men of England." The Chartist poet and leader Ernest Charles Jones (1819–69) modeled himself on Shelley's example since childhood. It is not a coincidence, perhaps, that the pseudonym under which the first work by Jones appeared was Percy Vere.[13] As Jones's lectures, journals, and poems were to show later on, Shelley was ever present in his mind.

In his preface to *An Anthology of Chartist Literature,* Yuri V. Kovalev describes Jones as the most talented pupil and heir of Shelley: "Jones had a

magnificent feeling for, and mastery of, language. He succeeded in developing a style that conveyed a feeling of the epic grandeur of events, the titanic
power of a people in revolt. No other Chartist poet attained such a wealth of
rhythm, such variety and perfection in rhyme, so exact and acute a use of
words. The literary significance of Jones's work far transcends the limitations
of Chartist poetry. He was an outstanding English poet of the nineteenth
century, worthy of a place among the most talented pupils and heirs of
Byron, Shelley and Keats."[14]

Like Shelley, Jones was born to a well-to-do family with even royal
connections, but later he espoused the cause of the working classes and
identified totally with them. Although he reached a leadership level in the
movement, he was first and foremost admired as a man of intellect, as a man
of creative literary mind rather than as a politician. Kovalev considers Jones
the most important Chartist poet, and Martha Vicinus argues that Jones "was
particularly successful in embodying Chartist ideals and actions in his poetry."[15] Like Shelley, Jones was deeply aware of the political function of his
poetry. Only a few months after he joined the movement, on October 8,
1846, a strongly worded entry in his diary reads as follows: "I am pouring the
tide of my songs over England, forming the tone of the mighty mind of the
people."[16] For Ebenezer Jones, too, the poet can play a very significant role
through his poetry. In a poem called "Life," he writes

> OH! who said that life was a vanishing show!
> A cheat to humanity given
> How could he be poet, when poets, we know,
> Can change even hell into heaven[17]

Like Ebenezer Jones and Ernest Charles Jones, the Chartists shared with
Shelley his belief that poetry is "the first language of civilization—a nation's
history, a nation's literature, begins with it; and it puts the seal upon its records
and its glory. 'Let me write the ballads of a country, and who will may make
its laws,' was, indeed, a true sentiment—attesting alike the antiquity, the
power, and the perpetuity of poetry in the moral government of man."[18] In
the same vein, Ernest Charles Jones bears witness to another similar saying:
"'Give me a nation's songs, and I will give you the character of a nation's
people,'" is an old and valuable maxim; the people mould a poet, but a poet
directs a people." In his letters "To the Young Men of the Working Classes,"
the Chartist poet Thomas Cooper stresses to his audience the remarkable
influence that poets of the past—not least among them Byron and Shelley, of

course—exert on their lives: "Let no hard-minded scoffer persuade you that this would be the language of romance. True and worthy emotions, justified by reason, never deserve that censure. The realm of peerless Alfred,—the cradle-land of Shakespeare,—that earth made sacred by the ashes of Wickliffe and Latimer, by the blood of Hampden and Sydney,—the soil on which were reared Chaucer and Milton, Byron and Shelley,—where Bacon arose to remodel all human knowledge, Newton to span and gauge the circles and depths of the material universe, and Locke to form anew the science of the mind." Although Shelley's name is one of many in this letter, it is paid a special tribute in another. Recommending a reading list to his audience, Cooper impresses upon their minds the importance of Shelley's philosophy and its relevance to their lives and needs. Starting with Shakespeare, he goes on to suggest that, "next to Shakespeare, you cannot say that you are acquainted with the true standard of poetry unless you have companioned with the sublimity of Milton, the fervour of Byron, the feeling of Burns, the thought of Wordsworth, the beauty of Keats, the *prescience* of Shelley—for *his* hand awoke upon the lyre the first notes of the choral hymn of future ages: *We* understand but a part of his music: it remains for the world of enfranchised men to comprehend the whole."[19]

The Chartists concurred with Shelley that poets are the "unacknowledged legislators of the world," and they considered him one such legislator. Hence, the Chartist poet saw himself, in part at least, as the fulfillment of Shelley's hopes—the "future" object of his prescience. These were the two most fundamental bases of the affinity that the Chartists felt toward Shelley. Indeed, of all the Romantic poets, Shelley came closest to the Chartists in the emphasis he put on the political function of poetry. By transcending the poet's function and expanding it into the political sphere, Shelley presaged the Chartist habit; his dedication of much of his poetic production to the cause of future reform was greatly admired by the Chartists. What is more, Shelley prophesied the emancipation of man and "glimpsed the rising new sun, the sun of the proletarian revolution,"[20] and this constituted an obvious link between him and the Chartists. The difference, though, is that, apart from the political poems of 1819, Shelley tended to write epic poems that dealt with the broad and eternal fundamentals of reform, whereas the Chartists, though basing their arguments on the same political doctrines as Shelley, designed their compositions to initiate and, if possible, complete an immediate political change. Thus it is safe to say that the homogeneity between the political philosophy of Shelley and that of the Chartist poets fostered a forceful link between them which might not have otherwise existed.

The Chartist poets also seemed substantially to agree with Shelley that the principal function of poetry is to imbue its readers with faith and hope in a better future. "Keeping alive the flame of hope in the souls of the toiling" was one of the major tenets that the Chartists found most valuable in Shelley's poetry. The *Chartist Circular* stresses that Shelley is one of the poets who kept the torch of freedom alight: "Homer and Demosthenes in Greece, Cicero in Rome, the poets and martyrs of the middle ages, and, in later times, the voices of Burns, of Campbell, of Shelley, Byron, and Elliot have echoed through the universe, Liberty! and that cry has been continued, and will not cease to be heard till tyranny is no more."[21] Another article, headed "P. B. Shelley," to which Shelley's "Song to the Men of England" is appended, pays Shelley's poetry and principles a special tribute: "Among the few who have been called 'Poets of People,' assuredly the first and noblest name is that of Shelley. Born and educated an aristocrat, his noble and benevolent soul scorned such a connection—broke the many fetters which birth and education had cast around it, and *shone forth in its strength and beauty the foremost advocate of liberty to the despised people*" (my emphasis).[22] What should be noted here, however, is that Shelley's impact on the Chartists can be measured not only through articles written about him and items related to his poetry and philosophy that appeared in literary journals, but also through the echoes of his poetry and political philosophy that are pervasive in Chartist poetry.

As a poet, Jones read Shelley a long time before he joined the Chartist movement. As early as September 28, 1839 (only one year after his arrival in England from Berlin, where he had been born and raised), the entry in his diary reads thus: "Splendid day. I called on the Bells's. Wife Bells alone. Afterwards Mr. Bells came in. Then escorted them to Facet's library opposite the [? orrow] Road and back. I then sat in Kensington Gardens reading Shelley while they left me, and walked home over Nottinghill Square."[23] Later, after he joined the Chartist movement, his writings and speeches were never short of references to Shelley. For example, speaking of Gerald Massey's Democratic poems, Jones concludes, "In the name of Burns and Shelley, of Milton and Byron, we claim his talents for the People's Cause."[24] Again, in an introduction to his *Notes to the People* that he started immediately after his release from prison, Jones draws an implicit comparison between Shelley and himself: "Free citizens of the republic! my country has been called the 'Ark of freedom'—but, in yours I see its Ararat, and to you, at whose hands Shelley looked for vindication and immortality, a humbler bard now dedicates his work."[25] In fact, Jones can also recall Shelley's poetry on less serious types of occasions. His review of J. De Jean-Fraser, for instance, pays tribute to the memory of Shelley before it gets to Fraser's work: "It was on Sunday, and in the Sabbath of the year, the joyous, rich summer time. The day was calm and beautiful, like the remembrance of a solemn hymn; and the glowing air, full of silent harmony, reminded me of Shelley's lines: 'Music, when soft voices die, / Vibrate on the memory.'"[26]

It is no wonder, therefore, that contemporary reviewers of Jones's works were also reminded of Shelley. The *Observer* (August 11, 1855), in a review of Jones's *My Life,* is reminded of Shelley's *Rosalind and Helen:* "the poem is a production which reminds the critic in many places of Shelley's *Rosalind and Helen,* without reminding him at the same time of imitation, still less of plagiarism." The *Athenaeum* (May 24, 1856), in a review of Jones's *The Emperor's Vigil,* observes that "His conventionalisms are not of the 'puling brook' school, but rather savour of Shelley's democracy. He pictures a world ruled by ferocious kings and cruel priests, talks much of knouts, chains, and dungeons,—and looks upon thrones as raised upon the grave of martyrs." What is more, in a *Scrapbook of Newspaper Cuttings etc. on Ernest Jones,* I found what seem to be the first two pages of a book on Ernest Jones (which as far as I know was never written) by Eliana Twynam that was to be called *Ernest Jones: An Appreciation.* There is a table of contents sketching the themes of its nine chapters, "a list of poems quoted in full," and what seems to be the start of an introduction. Of particular interest are the epigraphs to this "book," taken from Jones's and Shelley's poetry. Immediately below the heading of the book and the name of the author we read

> No tears for him who ne'er gave rise to tears;
> His requiem be an Echo of his song
>
> Ernest Jones

followed by

> Till the Future dares
> Forget the past, his Fate and Fame shall be
> An Echo and a Light unto Eternity.
>
> Percy Bysshe Shelley

Moreover, on the opposite side of the page she writes, "After Shelley—the greatest poetical Genius this country or the world has ever known,—we socialists can truly claim Ernest Jones *the* poet who has accomplished *most* in the making of our movement. It is therefore our duty, as it is our delight to put before the public this sketch of his life with selections from his works."[27]

Jones's "The Poet's Prayer to the Evening Wind"[28] seems to echo in more than one respect Shelley's "Ode to the West Wind." Like Shelley, Jones's concern is the poet's function vis-à-vis that of the wind as a destroyer and a preserver. Shelley's poem begins by apostrophizing the wind as the power of life and death, then seeks identification of the poetic spirit with this power, and finally seems to achieve some sort of union between speaker and subject. Jones, on the other hand, with less sense of dramatic development, uses the wind and the poet interchangeably from the first stanza and, one suspects, reproduces a variation of Shelley's poem. The opening of Jones's poem is strikingly Shelleyan. Shelley starts his poem with "O WILD West Wind, thou breath of Autumn's being, / Thou, from whose unseen presence the leaves dead / Are driven, like ghosts from an enchanter fleeing" (1–3). Jones begins with "WILD rider of grey clouds, beneath whose breath / The stars dissolve in mist, or rain, or sleet" (1–2). There is a sense of intensity in Shelley's sentence that is lost in Jones's, mainly because of his use of the indecisive "or." Moreover, Shelley's long sentence seems packed with energy, as though nothing will ever stop it. Whereas Jones's line is held up by the punctuation at the end of the second line, Shelley's enjambment at the end of line 2 permits no such inertness. However, it is interesting to note how Jones spells out Shelley's metaphoric reference to the wind's unseen presence when he says, in the penultimate stanza, "So let me cull each isolated truth, / Where old bards left their thoughts' eternal youth— / Till man, while listening to the harp unseen, / Himself feels greater since the great has been" (31–34). The "harp unseen" here is no longer that of the wind; rather it is that of the "old bards." Jones's metaphor, "thoughts' eternal youth," acknowledges the everlasting influence of poets and is very deftly handled; the paradox of "eternal" skillfully describes something one thinks of as passing and temporary: youth. But whereas Shelley traces in the structure of his poem the process that demonstrates that the wind is a "Destroyer and Preserver," Jones seems to take the idea for granted: "Keeper of life, in ocean, earth and air, / That else would stagnate in a dull despair! / Dispeller of the mists! whose airy hand / Winnows the dead leaves from forest-band!" (9–12).

The role of the wind as destroyer and preserver in ocean, earth, and air, developed in three stanzas of Shelley's poem, is taken over by Jones and stated in one single line, and Shelley's plea to the wind to scatter his thoughts in the universe and bring about "a new birth" is echoed by Jones in his last stanza:

> sing my death-song, thou unequalled bard!
> And tear my ashes from the clay-cold urn
> To whirl them where the suns and planets burn,
> And shout aloud, in brotherhood of glee:
> "Like me to sing and to be loved like me!"   (36–40)

Yet Shelley's implicit comparison between the poet and the wind is made explicit and granted new dimensions in Jones's poem. Indeed, just as the wind is a "dispeller of mists" the poet is a dispeller of "fears, and cares and doubting vain; / Till hearts of men upon my impulse sail, / And falsehood's wrecked in truth's victorious gale!" (22–24). As the wind culls "scattered treasures of the land," the poet culls "each isolated truth." Jones, in fact, not only switches emphasis in his poem from the wind to the poet but also carries the idea further by stressing the political function of the poet:

> And while I live, oh! teach me still to be
> A bard, as thou, brave, fetterless, and free.
> Past cot and palace, to the weak and strong,
> Singing the same great bold unfearing song!   (25–28)

Jones's description of the bard here as "brave, fetterless, and free" and of his song as "great bold unfearing" highlights the explicit political dimension he gave to an idea that, though inspired by Shelley, was shaped and developed to make an impression on a more politically aware audience and to have a more direct political effect.

The echoes of Shelley's verse in Chartist poetry are too many to contain in this chapter, but a reference must be made to the impact that Shelley's "Song to the Men of England" (1819) had on many Chartist poets, as seen in two poems by Ernest Jones and Thomas Cooper. Shelley's "Song" seems to be the source and inspiration for Jones's "The Song of the Lower Classes."[29] Like Shelley, Jones highlights the idea that the poor people are the real producers of wealth, which their oppressors enjoy while they are left in want. Implicit in both poems is an attempt to urge the people to rise up, change their devastating conditions, and claim their rights. Notably, the first question put by Shelley—"MEN of England, wherefore plough / For the lords who lay ye low?" (1.1–2)—finds an echo in the opening line of Jones's poem: "We plough and sow—we're so very, very low." It is clear here that the key words in both quotations—plough and low—and the contents are the same. However, in the same question form, Shelley goes on: "Wherefore weave with toil and care / The rich robes your tyrants wear?" Jones raises the same point but not with the same gusto:

> We're low—we're low—we're very, very low,
> Yet from our fingers glide
> The silken flow—and the robes that glow
> Round the limbs of the sons of pride.
> And what we get—and what we give,
> We know, and we know our share:
> We're not too low the cloth to weave,
> But too low the cloth to wear!

The message conveyed in these lines is unmistakably one that Shelley's lines express: Although the people make the clothes, it is their tyrants who wear them. Moreover, the key words—*robes, weave,* and *wear*—are the same in both quotations. However, Shelley's persistent questioning corresponds to a feeling of wonder and amazement that, by underscoring the simple and obvious facts, is meant to shock those whom it informs, whereas Jones's statements demonstrate no such literary skill.

Although Thomas Cooper's poem *The Purgatory of Suicides* recalls Shelley's *Queen Mab*,[30] the first six stanzas of *The Purgatory* (which are supposed to versify Cooper's "Address to the Polters and Colliers" on strike at Hanley on August 15, 1842) are comparable not to *Queen Mab* but to his "Song to the Men of England." In their opening lines, both poets urge the workers to stop their work, which has been turned by their employers into an effective measure against their very rights. Shelley's opening rhetorical question— "MEN of England, wherefore plough / For the lords who lay ye low?"—is echoed in Cooper's "SLAVES, toil no more! Why delve, and moil, and pine, / To glut the tyrant—forgers of your chain?" (1.1.1–2).

In his poem, Shelley questions the wisdom of continued submission and objects to a situation in which the people must work only to serve, feed, and clothe their oppressors (5–10). Cooper attempts the same:

> Away!—the howl of wolves in sheep's disguise
> Why suffer ye to fill your ears?—their pride
> Why suffer ye to stalk before your eyes?
> Behold, in pomp, the purple prelate ride,
> And, on the beggar by his chariot's side
> Frown sullenly, although in rags and shame

> His brother cries for food! Up, swell the tide
> Of retribution, till ye end the game
> Long practised by sleek priests in old Religion's name   (1.5.1–9)

Cooper's imagery is expressive of a more fiercely oppressive and difficult reality—"the howl of wolves," "in rags and shame," and "his brother cries for food"—than we find in Shelley. On the other hand, in these very stanzas, Cooper, like Shelley in "The Masque of Anarchy," warns his audience against the impetuosity of violence. While acknowledging the grounds that might well give rise to feelings of vengeance, Shelley emphatically stresses that such feelings should be controlled: "Stand ye calm and resolute, / Like a forest close and mute, / With folded arms and looks which are / Weapons of unvanquished war" (79.1–4).

In the same way, in the sixth and last stanza of his versified speech, Cooper urges his audience to "Join but to fold your hands, and ye will foil / To utter helplessness,—yea, to the core / Strike both their craft with paler death!— Slaves, toil no more!" (1.6.7–9). Whether or not Cooper had Shelley's "folded arms" in mind while writing his "fold your hands," it is amply evident that his lines convey the central thought with which Shelley's lines are imbued.

I have in this chapter sought neither to establish direct influence nor provide a statistical account of literary parallels, but rather to demonstrate Shelley's ubiquitous presence in Chartist literature. His poetry was read and declaimed in political meetings, cited and studied in literary journals. To many Chartist poets, Shelley was the poet-prophet who prophesied the necessary ignition of their movement. During the Chartist period, for the first time in the history of Shelley criticism, the political aspects of his poetry were understood as he meant them to be understood, and his political views were granted the appreciation that had long been their due. Hence the Chartists were the first literary and political body to acknowledge "the unacknowledged legislator of the world."

SHELLEY AND
OTHER
CULTURES

III

"The Name of Freedom":
A Hermeneutic Reading of *Hellas*

E. Douka Kabitoglou

11

erzen men, o despoine, tou pantos kakou
phaneis alastor he kakos daimon pothen
Aeschylus, *The Persians,* 353–54[1]

THE TYRANNY of Greece over Shelley could not have been foreseen, if one were to judge from the young poet's early utterances on the
subject, and definitely not in the summer of 1812, when he was writing to
Godwin, "Before I was a republican—Athens appeared to me the model of
a government, but afterwards Athens bore in my mind the same relation to
perfection that Great Britain did to Athe[ns]" (*PBSL* 1:303). In late July, in
yet another letter to Godwin, after a brief reference to Athenian rule as
"oppressive & arbitrary,"[2] he passes from political to "literary despotism,"
launching an attack (very much in Plato's fashion) on the poets: "And what
do we learn from their poets?" He phrases a rhetorical question to Godwin,
to come up with a subversive answer: "as you yourself have acknowledged
somewhere 'they are fit for nothing but the perpetuation of the noxious race
of heroes in the world'" (*PBSL* 1:317). However, it was precisely through the
reading of Greek literature (and philosophy) in the years that intervened
between 1812 and 1818—most readily expressed in the avowal "I read the
Greek dramatists & Plato forever" (*PBSL* 2:364), and also through the

mutual intellectual stimulation and encouragement of Shelley's "Athenian" circle[3]—that the original criticism and suspicion toward things Greek was enlightened (or bedimmed), Shelley's attitude passing from rejection to acclamation via recognition of difference: "the manners & feelings of the Athenians—so different on many subjects from that of any other community that ever existed" (*PBSL* 2:20), From this point on, Shelley's ravishment with Greece and its productions follows an ascending ladder of rhapsodic exclamations, praising "the manners and feelings of those divine people, who, in their very errors, are the mirrors, as it were, in which all that is delicate and graceful contemplates itself" (*PBSL* 2:29). In a letter addressed to Peacock early in 1819, Shelley laments the self-destructive violence that brought about the downfall of Greece: "O, but for that series of wretched wars which terminated in the Roman conquest of the world, but for the Christian religion which put a finishing stroke to the antient system; but for those changes which conducted Athens to its ruin, to what an eminence might not humanity have arrived!" (*PBSL* 2:75).

It was in this mixed mood of exultation and regret that the news of the Greek war of independence reached Shelley, firing his imagination: "Greece has declared its freedom," he announced triumphantly to Claire Clairmont, expressing his deepest, if premature, conviction that "Greece will most certainly be free." His joy was tainted only by the unavoidable "knowledge of the blood that must be shed on this occasion," a thought quickly brushed aside at the prospect of the fulfillment of a deep longing: "What a delight it will be to visit Greece free" (*PBSL* 2:278). Yet news of the (inevitable) bloodshed that arrived from the site of war presented the descendants of "those glorious beings" to Shelley's eyes as "degraded by moral and political slavery to the practice of the basest vices it engenders—and that below the level of ordinary degradation" (*OSA* 447). As a result, his enthusiasm for the just cause—"Greece has risen in this moment to vindicate its freedom"— was spoiled by the cruelty of military practices. As he announced to Medwin two days later, admitting his reluctance to engage in activities that were of dubious integrity, "Massacres of the Turks have begun in various parts.—This is a sufficient objection to our Grecian project even if other circumstances would permit my being one of the party." Shelley's moral reservations, however, did not prevent him from dreaming: "There is nothing I so earnestly desired as to visit Greece; but the fates do not seem propitious to my desires" (*PBSL* 2:280). Ultimately, Shelley's "Grecian project" turned out to be one of not presence but representation, not praxis but *poesis:* "I am just finishing a dramatic poem called *Hellas* upon the contest now waging in Greece—a sort of imitation of the Persae of Aeschylus, full of lyrical poetry" (*PBSL* 2:363–64).

It is not accidental, I believe, that Shelley should have chosen the genre of Greek tragedy to body forth his vision of a regenerated Greece, since it was his conviction, proclaimed in the *Defence of Poetry,* that social perfection and dramatic excellence are correlative. Shelley praises drama as the highest expression of the creative faculty of Greece, which he sees as resisting evil practices and social corruption by enhancing the powers of imagination and pleasure, by alerting the "sensibility to the influence of the senses and the affections," while also enhancing "those thoughts which belong to the inner faculties of our nature" (494). If, as Shelley believes, "the connexion of poetry and social good is more observable in the drama than in whatever other form" (494), then the choice of the Aeschylean *Persians* as a prototype for *Hellas* (following the precedent of *Prometheus Unbound*) should not surprise us, since it would be the best example of Shelley's celebrated proposition that "Poets are the unacknowledged legislators of the world" (508). Or, as this statement appears in an earlier and expanded version, "Poets and philosophers are the unacknowledged legislators of the world" (*Julian* 7:20). In fact, it is in the equation of poetizing, philosophizing, and legislat-ing—the creative practices of poets, thinkers, and founders of state (as Heidegger puts it)—that, in Shelley's view, the historical difference between classical Greece and modernity is to be found: "The study of modern history is the study of kings, financiers, statesmen, and priests. The history of ancient Greece is the study of legislators, philosophers, and poets." (*Julian* 7: 226).[4]

But what did the term *legislator* mean for ancient Greece—how did it sound to a Greek ear? Plato's definition of a legislator as given in the *Cratylus* is not a maker of laws, as one would expect, but a "maker of names" (389a).[5] In the course of the discussion on the nature of language in the same dialogue, Socrates repeatedly contends that the "artist of names is called the legislator" (431e), because "naming is an art, and has artificers," who are none other than the legislators (428e–29a). So, by transferring the art of naming from linguists, or rhetoricians, to legislators, Plato sets the problem of the ultimate authority of language and its vital role in the formation of society and origination of history.

This founding role of language is also detected by Heidegger, who claims that although language is commonly used for communication and exchange of information, its primary and pristine function is to "name," an act that inaugurates the historical existence of man, when the "poet speaks the essential word," thus nominating "the existent as what it is." Such a hermeneutic dialogue between man and world can be achieved in a dual manner, as Heidegger affirms: (philosophical) thinking and (imaginative) poetizing: "The thinker utters Being. The poet names what is holy." So the thinker whose task is to proclaim being and the poet who has the mission to name the holy—both legislators in the platonic sense of the word—are the initiators of human historicity, since language is the essential prerequisite for man's constructing of a world. In that sense, for Heidegger (and Shelley) poetry's nominating function is sustained, in that it gives a "habitation and a name" to the opacity of natural forces and psychic powers to which man is subject, thus setting in motion the historical process: "Poetry is the foundation which supports history." History itself begins, Heidegger informs us, only when beings are drawn into an "unconcealment" initiated by the questioning of the very nature of being. This unconcealment or open region to which man comes as a historical entity is the space of "freedom," a freedom that is not the property of man but the essence of truth to which humans belong by virtue of history. The existence of historical man begins at the very moment when "the first thinker takes a questioning stand"—or when the first poet names freedom's possession of man—because "Man does not 'possess' freedom as a property. At best, the converse holds: freedom . . . possesses man."[6]

The thought and name of freedom were originally contemplated and uttered for both Heidegger and Shelley in the inaugural moment of history that coincides with ancient Greece. Because Shelley and Heidegger look upon Greek as a language that can speak being, they recognize it as the logos of freedom. To the extent that (Greek) language creates history, it also creates freedom by naming it, calling it into existence, disclosing it, retrieving it from ontological or semantic confusion or from speechlessness—an act (or verbum) that simultaneously transforms chaos into cosmos. Shelley's lifelong concern with freedom is constantly present in both his theoretical and his poetic work. In fact, I think that one would be quite justified in proposing that the binary opposition freedom/slavery is the axis on which is constructed his political, ethical, and metaphysical universe. There are two places, however, where Shelley attempts to give what we might call a genealogy of freedom—*The Revolt of Islam* of 1817 (that imaginary preview of the Greek revolution) and the "Ode to Liberty" of 1820. The historical moment when freedom literally comes into being coincides absolutely for Shelley with the awakening into consciousness of Greece. The "Ode to Liberty," after its diachronic representation of the vicissitudes of freedom across the whole of European history, ends by foregrounding the distance traversed from freedom's archaic call to the poet to the modern poet's desperate call to freedom:

> O Liberty! if such could be thy name
>   Wert thou disjointed from these, or they from thee:
> If thine or theirs were treasures to be bought
>   By blood or tears, have not the wise and free
>   Wept tears, and blood like tears?   (lines 266–70)

This call to freedom finds its historical justification for Shelley in the rising of modern Greece against Turkish tyranny, and its textual incarnation in his lyrical drama *Hellas,* in which he hopes that Greece can "again become / The fountain in the desert whence the earth / Shall drink of freedom" (*OSA*, Prologue, 137–39). The modeling of the poem on *The Persians* of Aeschylus not only explains its dramatic form but also shows the appropriate choice from the Greek tragic canon of a play based on a historical event rather than a mythical account, to house the "glorious contest now waging in Greece" (408), still in progress. Although Shelley seems to doubt the artistic value of his goat song, one can discern in the poem the tripartite structure of tragic myth as expounded by Aristotle in the *Poetics: peripeteia* (change in action), *anagnorisis* (change of mind), and *pathos* (suffering). By placing the setting of the drama in enemy territory, Shelley, like Aeschylus, adopts a methodological strategy that looks at the same from the perspective of the other. In the case of Aeschylus, this technique vindicates the construction of the tragic out of heroic materials. In Shelley's case, it operates both as a formal device and as a thematic element: Transformation of sameness into otherness lies at the core of this controversial compound that calls itself a lyrical drama and is the key event in both the dramatic and lyrical parts.[7]

The name of Freedom first enters the poem through the speech of Christ in the (discarded) prologue, charged with an aura of unrealized potentialities and being related to the pervasive ophidian imagery that clusters around Shelley's conception of the good:

> from Tyranny which arms
> Adverse miscreeds and emulous anarchies
> To stamp, as on a wingéd serpent's seed,
> Upon the name of Freedom.   (*OSA* 105–8)

"Freedom" reappears in the speech of Satan, who presents it as a freshwater spring overflowing from Greece (*OSA* 137–39) and associates it with "power," "pleasure," "glory," "science," and "security," which "On Freedom hang like fruit on the green tree" (*OSA* 158), an image reminiscent of "The Mask of Anarchy," in which "Science, Poetry, and Thought" are made the "lamps" of a freedom that is identified with "Justice," "Wisdom," "Peace," and "Love." In the opening scene of *Hellas,* introduced with a *parodos,* a choral song uttered by the group of Greek captive women, the presence of freedom strikes like "lightning"—which is in fact the dominant iconographic representation Shelley employs. Freedom "enlightens" in a total transvaluation of given assumptions and conditions, as for instance "sleep," whose "softness," "depth," "calmness," and "quietness" are suddenly revealed in its adverse character—"death" and "deadly," lulling and treacherous: When "Tyrants sleep, let Freedom wake" (line 29). Playing with the theme of appearance and reality, the chorus tosses about binary oppositions, giving hints of a chaotic condition that both preceded "the great morning of the world" (line 46) and the advent of freedom and also follows upon its withdrawal and oblivion.

The first *epeisodion* or dialogic part, in fact the whole of the drama as such, is concerned with the education in the ways of freedom of the protagonist, the Turkish sultan. When Mahmud opens his eyes, he seems to be trailing clouds of otherness from the world of sleep back into ordinary reality, ready to undertake a journey of discovery that will lead him to *anagnorisis.* His first utterance strangely echoes the confusion of opposites and the state of nondifferentiation introduced by the chorus: "One spark may mix in reconciling ruin / The conqueror and the conquered" (lines 119–20). The "mightier world of sleep" (to remember "Mont Blanc," line 55) hangs heavily on him, enticing him to a dangerous quest on the path of knowledge. Bored, tired, languid but intellectually restless, Mahmud leaves behind the security of the familiar world built on firmly defined oppositions to enter the perilous area of (philosophical) questioning and (imaginative) equivocalness—the freedom of thought, where the materialist despot becomes exposed to the menace of thinking and "being." Somehow duplicating the recollective process of Prometheus, Mahmud wants to remember "strange and secret and forgotten things," eager to pursue a regressive procedure that will reactivate buried memories. His temptation is to pass from action to introspection, to recollect, to move backwards into personal and collective history in a counterclockwise motion, searching the caverns of mind and "being," in line with Shelley's conviction that "If it were possible that a person should give a faithful history of his being, from the earliest period of his recollection, a picture would be presented such as the world has never contemplated before" (*Julian* 7:61). Mahmud's initiation into freedom begins when he undertakes the return journey in a (platonic?) *anamnesis* of the past.

The confrontation between the tyrant Mahmud and the philosopher Ahasuerus is an education in "error." "Philosophy," as Shelley enunciates in his essay "On Life," "destroys error, and the roots of error. It leaves, what is too often the duty of the reformer in political and ethical questions to leave, a vacancy. It reduces the mind to that freedom in which it would have acted, but for the misuse of words and signs, the instruments of its own creation. . . . Our whole life is thus an education of error" (477). Mahmud's "education" is literally a leading-out from "the tide of war" and into "the chrystalline sea / Of thought and its eternity" (*OSA* 697–699). Ahasuerus, who is not only an adept in "Greek and Frank philosophy" (line 742) but also a compendium of *all* philosophy (not to mention Shakespeare)—in that his teaching encompasses almost the whole spectrum of Western and Eastern theories, variations of anything from Platonism to (British) empiricism, (German) idealism, and Hinduism—entices him to the treacherous region of every (and any) philosophy, undermining the common sense of reality taken for granted by the unsuspecting realist, who ignores the fact that there are more things in heaven and earth than are dreamt of in his (non)philosophy. By presenting an immaterialistic view of the world as the product of subjectivity, denying the independent existence of phenomena, Ahasuerus shatters Mahmud's assumptions and convictions and thrusts him into the state of *aporia*. Ahasuerus in fact undertakes the dual Socratic role of the expert dialectician who simultaneously undermines the intellectual securities and presuppositions of his pupil through skepticism while exposing him to a vision of reality astonishingly different from that of the unthinking materialist.

The first instance of Mahmud's paradisiacal ignorance having been stung by the Greek serpent of philosophical wonder is indicated in an ontological experiment, so to speak: his playing around with the verb *to be*. In fact, the whole dialogue between the tyrant and the prophet is an exercise in inflection of the grammar of "being." Mahmud initiates the game by addressing his instructor with the words "I honour thee, and would be what thou art / Were I not what I am" (lines 751–52), subverting any firm sense of identity and throwing a questioning light on the relation between self and other or subject and object. Ahasuerus joins in with an allusion to hubris, the pride of individuals "Who would be what they may not, or would seem / That which they are not" (lines 765–66), gradually expanding from a psychological to a cosmic perspective, to the whole by which all beings "have been, are, or cease to be" (line 779), unveiling the hidden relation between "that which has been, or will be, to that / Which is—the absent to the present" (lines 794–96). As Mahmud is tricked onto the quicksand of philosophical relativity, "Wild—wilder thoughts convulse" his spirit (line 806), and "war" becomes internalized in his skull. The "hiss," "roar," "crush," and "shriek" that trouble his mind echo the chorus lines of the previous *stasimon* (as well as Prometheus's engagement with the Erinyes), indicating Mahmud's gradual subjection of imperial authority to the authorship of philosophy and poetry: "Thy words / Have power on me!—I see—" (lines 812–13).

The Turkish tyrant's painful process of "paedeutics" from ignorance of knowledge to knowledge of knowledge, through knowledge of ignorance, is an introduction into the realm of freedom, where he allows things to be what they are—the "letting be" or "let it come" (line 759) that characterizes man's exposure to the openness of being.[8] As Mahmud gradually discards selfhood, calculation, mastery over things and time—in short monarchy—Ahasuerus prepares for him (at his own request) the second phase of the rite of passage, the transition from the experience of philosophy to that of poetry, or the plunging into the mental condition called "free imagination" that dissolves the normal sense of reality. As Shelley has indicated in his notes to the poem, in staging Mahmud's encounter with otherness, he has entirely relinquished any supernatural agency—adopting instead, I would suggest, what Keats has called "negative capability" or what Coleridge nominates "the willing suspension of disbelief which constitutes poetic faith." Shelley has the cold realist, Mahmud, lured "to that state of mind in which ideas may be supposed to assume the force of sensations through the confusion of thought with the objects of thought, and the excess of passion animating the creations of imagination"(*OSA* 479, n6).[9] We must remember here that freedom in the exercise of imagination is one of the things for which Shelley envied the Greeks.

As the monarch Mahmud becomes subject to "Thought / Alone, and its quick elements, Will, Passion / Reason, Imagination" (lines 795–97), experiencing the eternity of thought in the Parmenidean sense ("Thinking and being are tautological"), the thinking of being that has nothing to do "with time or place or circumstance" (line 802), the conjoined forces of philosophy and poetry erupt into the space of history, transposing the realms of reality and dream. Mahmud, reenacting the scene of Prometheus's contact with the phantasm of Jupiter, is confronted by the phantom of Mahomet, "communing" with a "portion" of himself (lines 854–55), thus following the recollecting process to its ultimate extremity. With the total crumbling of the symbolic order that began with his subjection to dialectical *elenchos*, Mahmud ends by being drawn into the imaginary, into a "mighty trance" (line 914) from which he is totally reluctant to emerge—despising those "human voices [that] wake us and we drown." Inevitably, though, Mahmud is forced back into habitual consciousness (and history), wondering, like Keats in the "Ode to a Nightingale," whether it was all "a vision or a waking dream" (line 79), and carrying ambivalent intimations of mortality (as well as immortality) that have utterly exploded his categories of experience (and language), since "on all things surest, brightest, best" are cast "Doubt, insecurity, astonishment" (lines 790–91). Having exchanged "power" for "knowledge," and having gone through philosophical skepticism to a state of existential "freedom," Mahmud has gained insight into the fabrication of opposition, the games of power—and glory—that sustain the system and mechanism of subject/object, tyrant/slave, victory/defeat: "Victory? poor slaves!" (line 930).

Slavery as such, in its political and social aspects, is represented in the poem through the Greek captive women, whose singing of memory and desire spans the past and the future and evokes the name of freedom (in nature and history) in multiple ways, spellbound as they are by the very power of poetic imagery and the harmony and rhythm of lyric. It is in their songs that the permanence and eternity of (Greek) thought are contrasted with the mutability of history and time, conflict, decay, and corruption, and in their visionary flights that the millennial expectation of a return of the Golden Age is expressed. Amid a piling up of references to natural, social, political, and personal freedom, the chorus celebrates the intellectual freedom inaugurated by Greece, the liberation of thought from time, place, and circumstance:

> But Greece and her foundations are
> Built below the tide of war,
> Based on the chrystalline sea
> Of thought and its eternity;
> Her citizens, imperial spirits,

> Rule the present from the past,
> On all this world of men inherits
> Their seal is set—   (lines 696–703)

Unaware of (or indifferent to) the "hermeneutic" violation that they commit, in their support of "logocentrism," intending to substitute an intellectual imperialism in place of a political one, the chorus of Greek captive women (and Shelley?) seeks refuge in the detached serenity of Greek noetic constructs, removed from the "tide of [historical] war," ignorant (?) of the fact that the oldest surviving voice of the "peaceful" eternity of Greek thought, the Anaximander fragment, speaks of flux and "war," revenge and discord, conflict and antithesis—mental and cosmic strife: "But where things have their origin, there too their passing away occurs according to necessity; for they pay recompense and penalty to one another for their recklessness, according to firmly established time."[10] Similarly, Heraclitus, yet another ancestral voice "prophesying war," has proclaimed that "War is father of all and king of all; and some he has shown as gods, other as men; some he has made slaves, others free," the originary *polemos* that precedes and dominates all forms of existence, the struggle that divides but also joins. "One must realize," Heraclitus tells us in another fragment, "that war is shared and Conflict is Justice, and that all things come to pass (and are ordained?) in accordance with conflict." In fact, harmony and concord appear to be the other side of discord, not its elimination, since "The counter-thrust brings together, and from tones at variance comes perfect attunement, and all things come to pass through conflict."[11]

So, if we are to interpret the Greek captive women's ideas concerning the "origins" of Greek thought as essentially illusive, we should be expecting yet another "education" (in freedom) to take place in Shelley's lyrical drama that calls itself *Hellas.* If we open up to a hermeneutic (or deconstructive?) "dialogue" with the chorus, we soon come to realize the cracks that imperceptibly appear in those solid "foundations" of tranquil meditation and calm composure. The chorus's initiation entails not the sacrifice of selfhood, as in Mahmud's case, but a sacrifice of innocence in the recognition and acceptance of metaphysical, and physical, tension. Theirs is a passage from the Apollonian aesthetic vision of "chrystalline depths" of a "stainless sea" (line 490) to the essentially Dionysian, i.e., tragic, quality of human existence—in other words their enforcement to confront the problem of evil. Of course, "evil" is not such stuff as lyric songs are made of (especially in romantic dramas). But the reality of evil somehow projects itself as a "necessary" shadow upon the chorus's utopian vision.

The second choral song, "Worlds on worlds are rolling ever," probably gets its cue from Mahmud's reaction to a "shout within," that it bodes "Evil doubtless like all human sounds. / Let me converse with spirits" (lines 186–87), indicating the allocation of evil to the human rather than the supernatural world. In his notes to the song, Shelley affirms once more both his preoccupation, not to say obsession, with the presence of evil and the futility of hoping to solve it: "Let it not be supposed that I mean to dogmatise upon a subject, concerning which all men are equally ignorant, or that I think the Gordian knot of the origin of evil can be disentangled by that or any similar assertions" (*OSA* 478, n2). Although his remarks on the possibility of divine malevolence, which he considers "inexplicable and incredible," refer to the god of Christianity, in a manner tragically ironic, they are also pertinent to the "tragic theology"[12] of Greece. Shelley refuses to tackle the ontological "Gordian knot" of evil's origination, postponing the "true solution of the riddle" to a future state and leaving the matter at that, choosing instead "to attach himself to those ideas which exalt and ennoble humanity," such as the notion of freedom (as individual perfectibility, social progress, and political equality).

Yet, despite Shelley's separatist stance, "freedom" and "evil" seem to be inextricably linked, and their correlation is of course the crux of ethical science. One interesting instance of looking at this issue is to be found in the idealist philosophy of Shelley's contemporary, Schelling. Heidegger, in his extensive discussion on Schelling's *Essence of Human Freedom,* after an initial proposition that asserts the familiar Heideggerian postulate, "Man is at best the property of freedom," testifies that "human freedom is the faculty of good and evil," evil being defined as "the individual will gaining mastery over the universal will." So a metaphysics of evil becomes the foundation of an ethics of freedom, because "evil is a way of man's being free." Freedom as the function of good and evil is a reiterated motif in the essay, which explores the various aspects of the term, proposing its subdivision into categories, the basic distinction giving us, on the one hand, the idealistic concept of freedom as "self-determination in terms of one's own law of being," and on the other "true freedom," which is "found only where a choice is no longer possible and no longer necessary."[13] Such is what seems to me the tragic *hermeneia* of "freedom as an understanding of necessity," expressed by Aeschylus and the other Greek dramatic writers. Or, as Ricoeur puts it, "It is precisely the tragic myth which is the depository of the Ineluctible implied in the very exercise of freedom, and which awakens us to those fateful aspects which we are always stirring up and uncovering as we progress in maturity, autonomy, and the social engagement of freedom." "That is why tragedy has never finished dying," Ricoeur concludes; "Killed twice, by the philosophical Logos and by the Judeo-Christian Kerygma, it survived its double death."[14]

The final chorus of *Hellas* opens with the celebratory hymn to the (historical or metaphysical) rebirth of Greece: "The world's great age begins anew, / The golden years return" (lines 1060–61). The vision of a regenerated world bears close resemblance in terms of its imaginative representation to act 4 of *Prometheus Unbound*. Here again,

> The earth doth like a snake renew
> Her winter weeds outworn:
> Heaven smiles, and faiths and empires gleam,
> Like wrecks of a dissolving dream.   (lines 1062–65)

Subsequently, the description of natural transformation focuses on the Greek landscape, and the advent of the idyllic Golden Age makes itself apparent in a series of Arcadian scenes, in which the repeated use of comparatives denotes a vision of nature as perfectible: a "brighter Hellas," "waves serener far," a "new Peneus," "fairer Tempes," "Young Cyclads," "sunnier deep" (lines 1066–71). The song gains momentum, passing from nature to culture, applying the same principle of evolution and amelioration to the archetypal stories of Greece: a "loftier Argo," "Another Orpheus," a "new Ulysses" (lines 1073–76). Yet these seemingly positive references to the mythical age, which foreground the virtues of heroic adventure, erotic devotion, and patriotic fervor,[15] are unavoidably accompanied by a sinister resonance, as they carry an "other" or hidden side of evil practices: Argo's quest "prize" is not only the golden fleece but the murderess Medea; Orpheus is the transcendental singer who suffered dismemberment at the hands of humanity; Ulysses is also the crafty villain responsible for the destruction of Troy.

In the following stanza, uncontrolled and unredeemable tragedy, as well as ominous prophecy, momentarily burst into and violate the lyrical space:

> O, write no more the tale of Troy,
> If earth Death's scroll must be!
> Nor mix with Laian rage the joy

> Which dawns upon the free:
> Although a subtler Sphinx renew
> Riddles of death Thebes never knew.   (lines 1078–83)

In its regressive movement through time toward cultural origins, the Golden Age that is to be revived, the chorus takes an imaginative leap from history to myth, uncovering those primal scenes to be not Rousseauistic or romantic spots of primeval innocence but demonic stories of war, murder, destruction—tales of unavoidable and unmitigated violence depicting the evil at the heart of (human and divine) existence. The "painted veil" is quickly drawn, and the Greek captive women, closing their eyes to the repulsiveness of the tragic vision and rejecting recollection, turn again to teleology and the millennial expectations of historical evolution (appropriately "named" after an illusory and utopian past): "Another Athens shall arise" (line 1084).

But the abyss has opened, the reality of tragedy gaping beneath both historical "content" and lyrical "form." A last reference to "Saturn and Love," the reigning deities of the Golden Age, supposedly superior to all divinities of posterity—"Saturn and Love their long repose / Shall burst, more bright and good" (lines 1090–91)—conducts the chorus from romance to ritual, to the place of sacrificial offering: "Not gold, not blood, their altar dowers / But votive tears and symbol flowers" (lines 1094–95). The allusion is to the earlier reference in the poem to "Pity's altar," which stood in "sacred Athens," dedicated to the "unknown God" whose "broken shrine" should be worshipped with "Love for hate and tears for blood" (lines 733–37). But what about the known *alastores,* avenging spirits or "wicked" gods of tragedy, and the tragic themes of revenge, wrong, guilt, suffering, and death—the dying that is not an ordinary death but sacrifice, implied in the utterance immediately preceding this one (lines 729–32), and which, taken from the *Agamemnon* of Aeschylus, shows the danger and futility of ignoring the pervasive presence and inscrutable workings of the divine? The double negation of "Not gold, not blood" simply multiplies the force of the image that Shelley wishes to eliminate, adding negativity to radical evil and expounding all the rich and ambiguous complexity of the cluster gold/blood/tears that constitutes, I believe, the controlling metaphor of the poem. "Votive tears" can be as much signs of gratitude as instances of unrelieved despair, expressive of conditions of extremity and suffering. By a crucial (if unwilling) semantic transference, the chorus sees the two-in-one nature of blood—the dual, if terrifying, essence of violence, whereby "evil and the violent measures taken to combat evil are essentially the same"—in the function of ritual, which is to purify social aggressiveness and bloodshed through the blood shed in sacrifice. Such is the symbolization process— "symbol flowers" and all—that substitutes the *pharmakos,* the surrogate victim, as the "necessary" recipient of human malice. It is upon the sacrificial altar, it has been argued, that "the clock of history" was "set in motion, and the beginnings of a social life [were] plotted out."[16]

Confronted with such an *apocalypsis* of "the horror," of the tragic origins of history, that inevitably darkens any vision of a utopian Golden Age, the chorus's optimistic resistance totally collapses:

> Oh, cease! must hate and death return?
>   Cease! must men kill and die?
> Cease! drain not to its dregs the urn
>   Of bitter prophecy.
> The world is weary of the past,
> Oh, might it die or rest at last!   (lines 1096–101)

After such knowledge, what expectation? The chorus falls into a lyrical paroxysm in the tragic realization that regeneration is impossible, that there is no "second coming" of any Golden Age, except in the ultimate extinction of the past and the radical annihilation of the world as we know it. In such circumstances the urge of the semichorus, uttered shortly before, takes an ironic resonance:

> Let the tyrants rule the desart they have made—
>   Let the free possess the paradise they claim,
> Be the fortune of our fierce oppressors weighed
>   With our ruin, our resistance and our name!   (lines 1008–10)

These words add a new interpretation to that "name of freedom" which may after all be a mere sign without a referent, a signifier totally devoid of any type of a signified—let alone "paradise."

Before the lyric chorus of Greek captive women,[17] maddened by Dionysian *pathos,* turns into a tragic *thiasos* in maenadic possession, Shelley interrupts the action of his lyrical drama *in medias res.* With a masterful platonic gesture, reenacting the act of the statesman in the *Republic,* who exiled the tragic poets as dangerous to the social welfare, Shelley the legislator overrules Shelley the poet when the Hellenic tragic vision threatens his "beautiful idealisms of moral excellence" (135), his conviction that "man could be so perfectionized as to be able to expel evil from his own nature, and from the greater part of the creation" (*OSA* 271). As it is, the rest is silence. Because there is only one way the poem could have ended after it just stops with the prophecy "Saturn and Love their long repose / Shall burst, more bright and good"—"That twenty centuries of stony sleep / Were vexed to nightmare by a [glorious war], / And what rough beast, its hour come round at last, / Slouches towards [Athens] to be born?"[18]

Shelley's Impact on
Italian Literature

Lilla Maria Crisafulli Jones

12

IT IS important to stress the prodigious cultural and emotional impact of
Italy upon Shelley's work, an impact particularly evident in such works as
"Julian and Maddalo," *Prometheus Unbound, The Cenci,* and *A Defence of
Poetry.* Italy became, to a great extent, an essential reference around which
Shelley spun the refined wefts of his imagination—the place where he
fashioned most of his poetical visions and built his surprising utopias. Italy
was a forge that provided the occasion for an uninterrupted and secret
dialogue with Dante, Petrarch, Boccaccio, and Tasso, a fruitful dialogue that
led to the technical and formal experimentation familiar to readers of
Shelley's later work, with its extraordinary economy and conciseness and its
impressive clarity of images. Shelley, however, became in his turn an endless
source of confrontation and literary influence for many great Italian writers
of the nineteenth century: I am thinking here of De Bosis's devoutness, of
D'Annunzio's exaltation, of Carducci's sober admiration, and of Pascoli's
discovery of Shelley's *A Defence of Poetry.* But there is no doubt that, for a
long time, Byron's fame on the continent overshadowed that of Shelley. In
Italy this was even more evident. Both spent many years of their life in Italy,
where they wrote most of their work. Yet, unlike the many references to
Byron, hardly any contemporary Italian writer seems to have mentioned
Shelley, either during his lifetime or even during the first twenty years after

his death. One notable exception was the Italian patriot Lorenzo Damaso Pareto, who translated *Adonais* in 1830 before being forced to emigrate to France.

The critic Giacomo Zanella, in an article published in 1883 in the prestigious late-nineteenth-century literary magazine *Nuova Antologia,* noted the extraordinary popularity that preceded Byron's arrival in Italy and that increased during his stay on the peninsula.[1] A powerful myth was built around his figure—a myth that for a long time cast a shadow over Shelley, if what John O. Hayden observes in *The Romantics' Reviewers* is true: "Since the title 'Satanic' implies only moral considerations, there should be no difficulty in connecting Byron and Shelley with that title, since both published works which were subject to moral condemnation in an age during which literary criticism was concerned with moral issues."[2] To belong to what was called Byron's "Satanic circle" and at the same time not possess all the charm, the fame, and the charismatic power that Byron exhibited with beautiful arrogance gave Shelley a sense of unforgettable guilt. In 1834 in his *Vita di Lord Byron,* Giuseppe Nicolini briefly discusses Shelley, describing him to his readers as a minor figure, inevitably dwarfed by the giant image of a heroic Byron. Shelley becomes "the unfortunate friend of the great poet" (lo sventurato amico del grande poeta): a man of misfortune but also of little scruple, an atheist and deeply immoral.[3]

Italian critics must have been particularly sensitive to such moral considerations. One of the first Italians to consider Shelley's poetry was Giambattista Niccolini. In 1844, after having recognized in Shelley a powerful imagination and an astonishing dramatic talent, well expressed in *The Cenci* (of which he himself attempted a rewriting), Niccolini reproached Shelley for having belonged to the "Satanic School" and condemned his unorthodox views, which, Niccolini believed, had rightly led to Shelley's banishment from British society. The critic also interpreted the ideas expressed in *Prometheus Unbound* as a beautiful but impious attempt to free man not just from temporal tyrannical powers but especially from spiritual and fideistic ones. In this reading, Demogorgon's triumph over Jupiter signified the victory of pantheism over all other religious faiths. Niccolini ended his attack by declaring that Shelley's beliefs were very similar to the dangerous and censurable doctrine that Spinoza had practiced and preached, for which he was universally condemned.[4] Similar opinions were expressed by Saverio Baldacchi in 1844 in his innovative article "Della vita e delle opere di Percy Shelley." He described Shelley and Byron as great artists who were nevertheless limited by the lack of that sublime spiritual harmony that heaven alone can inspire and provide.[5] Condemnation of Shelley's choice of naturalism or pantheism over Christianity becomes more or less the refrain of the Italian criticism of Shelley.

Going back to Giacomo Zanella's article, we realize that he pointed out another important reason behind Byron's popularity and Shelley's anonymity in Italy: the former always participated in Italian social and political life; the latter seemed unable to do the same. The picture of Shelley that Zanella gives us and that predominated during the second half of the nineteenth century explains all. We see a Shelley averse to worldly life, a sort of hermit lost in his dreams, his vegetarianism, and wild landscapes, but always animated by a powerful spirit: "quella sua faccia infantile . . . come di una verginella . . . [con] grandi occhi limpidi e pensosi" (his infantile face like that of a young virgin, with clear and pensive eyes); "quel gracile corpo vestito strettamente di nero" (that graceful body always garbed in black); [but also] "uno spirito in aperta ribellione con tutte le leggi, che governavano l'umano consorzio" (a spirit in open rebellion against all the laws that govern human interchange) (417). From this picture we can clearly understand how Carducci coined the famous definition for the English poet as a "spirito di titano entro virginee forme" (a titan's spirit in a virginal form).

According to this tradition, Shelley's solitude and anonymity in Italy were basically of his own choosing and due to his disdain of wordly life and his dislike of mixing with local people or of acting as a "galante" during the "conversazioni." These refusals certainly did not go down very well with the Italian aristocratic "salotti" of the time, well attended by Byron. It is true, however, that the only company or friends accepted by Shelley, with a small number of important exceptions (Emilia Viviani, the "improvvisatore" Sgricci, Dottore Pacchiani, and the Guiccioli/Gamba families), were English, and this precisely at a time when Byron was avoiding the English, to the point of expressing critical views on English travelers. In 1817, in a letter from Venice to Thomas Moore, he says, "I wished to have gone to Rome; but at present it is pestilent with English. . . . A man is a fool who travels now in France or Italy, till this tribe of wretches is swept home again."[6]

Byron, then, actively participated in Italian society: from the "popolane di Venezia" to the "nobildonne di Pisa e Ravenna"; from the Carbonari patriots whom he helped on more than one occasion—he asked, for example, for the post of British consul in Ravenna for Pietro Gamba, who was persecuted by the local authorities[7]—to intellectuals and artists, such as

Vincenzo Monti or Pietro Giordani, whom he met. It was Monti who asked Byron, who by then had moved to Venice, to receive Pietro Giordani. Giordani was a powerful Italian intellectual, not so much as a writer but as a thinker and theorist. His influence was such that he tyrannized the literary criticism of the time by imposing Classicism as an indisputable rule of style. (In Milan the Romanticists and the Classicists had been at war during the opening years of the century, the two sides grouping around two literary magazines, *La Biblioteca d'Italia* and *Il Conciliatore,* the latter edited by Giovanni Berchet.) Giordani remained heavily involved in contemporary literature and politics, ending up in prison more than once for his political activity. He represented, therefore, a significant Italian mixture of Classicism and of patriotism, but what matters here is that he may have influenced Giacomo Leopardi and his reading of Shelley's work.

Pietro Giordani met Lord Byron in Venice in 1818, as he mentions in a letter to Gaetano Dodici on July 3. Giordani was admitted to Byron's circle, but with the specific promise not to speak of his work or make any mention of either Romanticism or the Romantics. Their conversations turned instead to politics. What is interesting to remember here is that two months after his meetings with Lord Byron, Giordani went to Recanati to spend two weeks of endless discussions on art, politics, and life with Leopardi. This would have been a good occasion to talk about Byron to Leopardi, and Giordani may also have mentioned Byron's friendship with Shelley, a new interest in the young Italian poet. In any case, Leopardi's well-cultivated family had a good knowledge of English; the family's library contained several books in that language. Zanella carries these suppositions further, suggesting that Leopardi may have been influenced by Shelley because of their common intellectual ground. Both Shelley and Leopardi derived many of their ideas, and therefore much of their poetry, from the reading of the ancient Greek philosophers as well as from Montaigne, Bacon, Locke, and the modern empiricists. Both were able to enrich the materialism of these philosophies with the splendid garments of their imagination. But whereas in Leopardi reason and rationality seemed to predominate, in the English poet fantasy and dreams gained most of the ground—to the point, observes Zanella, that his long poems display a dangerous imbalance between image and idea; after all, it is the harmony between fable and truth that produces the perfection of beauty in art. This perfection, says Zanella, was always achieved by Shelley in his short lyrics, whereas Leopardi's classic simplicity and his philological approach made it possible to express it in most of his poetry. Nevertheless, to his mind, Leopardi's "Canto alla Primavera" has very much in common with Shelley's "Hymn to Intellectual Beauty," as does his "Canto alla sua donna" with *Epipsychidion,* and "La Ginestra" with "Stanzas Written in Dejection, near Naples." To conclude this literary parallel, the Italian critic observes how both poets rejected their age, their contemporary world. Yet while Leopardi looked back to a past, forever lost, to find some intellectual comfort and soothe his pessimistic soul, Shelley fed himself and his poetry with the marvelous dreams of an impossible future. But for Zanella both died too early, without having known the beneficial effects of a religious faith.[8]

All nineteenth-century Italian critics recognized that although Italy may not have had much influence in terms of friendship or social circles, it did mean a lot for Shelley's imagination, which fed on Italian political hopes, on the country's architecture and archeology, and, above all, on its landscapes and exuberant nature, on the intense and dazzling light of its seas and rivers, on its skies and mountains. For example, Federico Olivero, a critic writing at the turn of the century, noted that Shelley received the wild beauty of Italian nature as a spontaneous gift of the earth, as a transparent mirror to his soul and a symbol of his own spirit.[9] Shelley's poetry becomes, then, a spiritual as well as a geographical voyage, all his poems showing signs of the bewitching presence of Italy. Poetry and reality, emotions and landscapes, are so tightly interwoven that they become one.

Returning to Shelley's relationship to Italian literature, we have noted how he was not particularly interested in contemporary writers. There is no mention of either Giordani or Monti, with the exception of two brief quotations in Mary's journal: on September 14, 1818, when she admits to be reading *Cajo Gracco* by Monti, and, on the following day, when she is reading his *Manfredi*.[10] Even Vittorio Alfieri apparently received little attention. Alfieri was mentioned by Shelley only a few times, although in fact one of the first of these was at a very early stage, in September 1816, when Shelley at Bishopsgate ordered some titles that included Alfieri's tragedies (*PBSL* 1: 433). The second mention, a short note to Mary from Padua, dated September 22, 1818, is somewhat more interesting. Shelley, who was at the time encouraging Mary to write a play on Charles I, asked his wife to bring to Venice some of her translation of Alfieri's *Mirra*. Alfieri would be mentioned again in a letter to Leigh Hunt, sent from Pisa in May 1820, in which Shelley discussed the unfavorable reception of *The Cenci* in Britain: "Bessy tells me that people reprobate the subject of my tragedy—let them abase Sophocles, Massinger, Voltaire & Alfieri in the same sentence, & I am content, & I maintain that my scenes are as delicate & free from offence as theirs" (*PBSL* 2: 200).

Alfieri's *Mirra,* which deals with the theme of Mirra's incestuous love for her father and ends with her declaration of guilt and suicide, reveals many important parallels with the plot of *The Cenci.* It was well known to Shelley not only because he was a passionate reader but also because he had many conversations with Byron, and there are numerous and important references to Alfieri in Byron's letters. They range from a simple mention to the point of Byron seeing himself as one of Alfieri's followers. But what may indicate a more precise interest is Byron's reaction to the rehearsal of *Mirra* that took place one night in Bologna in 1819. He describes his feelings in a letter to John Murray on August 12 and again on August 24.[11] In any case, Alfieri represented for Byron the perfect model of neoclassicism—open to passions but with an order and a decorum that revealed unknown emotions and intriguing characters—a Classicism, then, that marked the beginnings of modern tragedy. What was on Alfieri's stage was neither a pure dream nor a simple, superficial reality, but a striking and painful contrast in human psyches. This is where Alfieri's modernity can be identified, and it is also what marks Byron's and Shelley's interest in his work. This interest was stressed by Mary in her journal throughout the month of September 1818, when Alfieri became an important, almost constant, object of reading and translating.[12]

With Ugo Foscolo the relationship was an even more complex one. Shelley, for instance, did not seem to be interested in this Italian Romantic expatriate, although Foscolo's life shared many of the problems that the two English poets had had to face. Foscolo, largely ignored by the English intelligentsia, greatly admired Byron and suggested various new literary enterprises to him. Byron, however, may not have had the same enthusiasm. He seems not to have read the best of Foscolo's poems, such as "Dei Sepolcri," "le Grazie," or his "Sonetti," and in a letter to Murray he openly reproaches the Italian writer for possessing genius but not being capable of exploiting it. Nevertheless, as has recently been suggested by Alan Weinberg, Shelley might have been to some extent influenced by Foscolo's *Letters of Jacopo Ortis* when he wrote his "Lines Written among the Euganean Hills."[13]

Despite all this, Shelley did not really seem to be involved with Foscolo's literary activity, nor did Foscolo look with any interest at Shelley or at his poetry. For him, the English Romantic poet seemed to be still dazzled by the light of the great writers of the past, almost unable to see those who had followed. Dante, Petrarca, Tasso, and Ariosto remained Shelley's real concerns in an Italian cultural context in which he did not notice anything except death, slavery, and desolation. As Giovanni Caldana pointed out in an article in 1907, Tasso was the most recent Italian writer to arouse a real interest in Shelley.[14] There is no doubt that Tasso interested Shelley both for his adventurous and painful life and for his literary skill. In many ways Tasso represented the perfect figure of the poet: the sort of persecuted and tormented genius that he felt was very close to his own persona. Shelley read Tasso's works several times, as well as biographies of him in two different editions: *La Vita di Torquato Tasso* by Pietro Antonio Serassi (1785) and the better-known biography by Giovanni Battista Manso (1619). All this had a great influence on his thought, to the point that he felt the need to visit many of the places where Tasso had spent the most significant periods of his life.[15]

In terms of the reception of Shelley's own work, however, things changed dramatically toward the end of the nineteenth century, the golden age of a reawakened Italian literature. This was a period of interest for many reasons. The situation in Italy after unification seemed for a while to have extinguished all passions and aspirations. Yet these passions and aspirations were still present; rather than burning in the hearts of patriots, they were now consuming the souls of artists. Suddenly what had prejudiced Shelley's poetry in the eyes of the Italian literary establishment—that is to say, his political faith and his atheism—no longer existed. What was left and exalted were his aesthetics, his poetical theory. *A Defence of Poetry* was discussed and quoted so often and in such exciting terms that Emilio Cecchi and Benedetto Croce, writing some years later under the colder influx of modernism, approach it with the specific aim of reducing its revolutionary force. According to Cecchi, Shelley was unable to grasp the object ("difetta il senso dell'oggetto"), and his passions were disembodied, the burning of a perpetual dream. According to Croce, his poetry partially failed because of its redundance, imprecision, and prolixity: In *A Defence* Shelley's opinions did not give a concrete answer to the real meaning of poetry.[16] But such inhibitions did not prevent three of the great figures of Italian literature—Carducci, Pascoli, and D'Annunzio—from undertaking their own reappraisal of Shelley. These poets represented three fundamental stages in the development of our national literature.

Giosuè Carducci, through the independence of his thought, was able to mediate between the Classical tradition, deeply rooted in Italian literature and running without a real break from Petrarch to Leopardi, and the new aspirations toward irregular passions and wild beauty expressed by the post-Romantics or the so-called decadent writers. It is from this position of balance and understanding that in 1894 Carducci was able to express his disappointment at the way in which Shelley's poetry and ideals had been received in Italy: too late and too reductively. Shelley, says Carducci, paid for his unique combination of Classicism and idealism—an idealism, moreover, consisting of revolutionary content and altruism, a combination that was thus alien to the Italian literary tradition. Furthermore, being an academic, Carducci appealed to the sense of responsibility of those cultural centers that should have guaranteed the diffusion of Shelley's reputation among Italian readers, openly accusing public libraries and universities of having buried Shelley's work in oblivion.[17]

Carducci believed himself to have many things in common with the English poet: a socialist faith, the lack of a religious belief, and the deep conviction that poetry could not only speak to the heart but also have a great influence on the intellect and on the will of its readers. Numerous traces of Shelley's influence can be found in his poetical and critical work. For instance, he wrote to Shelley's memory the moving ode "Presso l'urna greca," in which, without hesitation, he defines the young dead man as a "poeta del liberato mondo" (poet of an unbound world), as if he really considered Shelley to be the trumpet of the prophecy that had awakened an enslaved Europe and announced the freedom that had at last been achieved. The poem "Alle fonti del Clitunno" also shows strong emotional echoes of Shelley's poetry. For Carducci, Shelley is an interesting mixture of idealism and Classicism, of objectivity and individualism, but he is also the poet of the natural world. Faced with nature, he becomes a chameleon changing from a modern Englishman into a sort of ancient German, or into a tribal Indian able to understand and decipher even the faintest signs of the universe. He is able to feel the oneness of the world and not be afraid, to make myths out of it in order to preserve its mystery and beauty and celebrate them in the highest and most intense religious feelings.[18]

The Italian poet discusses Shelley's love and benevolence, saying that they appear so powerful thanks to the extraordinary and peculiar idealism on which they are based, an idealism composed of objective understanding and true unselfishness, of D'Holbach's materialism and of the Enlightenment, and warmed by a high and limpid Spinozian humanism. Finally Carducci draws a daring parallel between Shelley and Goethe. Both, he says, show a tremendous objectivity of vision, but whereas in the German poet the intellect of the one and of the "I" prevails, in the English poet it is the whole and otherness that triumph. Whereas Goethe expressed in his work a sort of egotistical view of the world, basing his aesthetic vision on the spiritual as well as the existential experience of the self, of an inner "I," Shelley inherited from the Enlightenment a deep understanding of otherness and based his work upon the concepts of sympathy and benevolence.

When we come to talk of Shelley's influence on Giovanni Pascoli, we move onto more difficult and uncertain ground. Pascoli took part in the experimentation at the end of the century but belonged to the decadent movement in a very particular way. Eschewing the internationalism of De Bosis's literary magazine, *Il Convito,* and D'Annunzio's exotic and refined taste, Pascoli certainly did not pose as a pre-Raphaelite aesthete but instead expressed in his own way a deep need for change. Walter Binni noted this difference in his *Poetica del decadentismo,* observing how Pascoli represented a sort of indigenous decadence affiliated with a bourgeois and provincial tradition rather than with a European source. Pascoli was a follower of Virgil, the delicate singer of the countryside, and Pascoli's apparent lack of intellectualism or daring sensuality does not reduce the importance of his silent revolution against the old poetics.[19]

Pascoli's poetry brings to light the centrality of a myth he discusses in his literary manifesto *Fanciullino.* The myth is entirely personal and is based upon the idea of a Homeric primitive poet, a poet whose primitivism and essentiality recall those of a child. In both primitive poet and innocent child Pascoli recognizes himself and his own sensibility, able to enlarge and make great what is insignificant and reduce to an absolute simplicity what is magnificent. It is here in Pascoli's *Fanciullino* that, besides an obvious Wordsworthian echo, we perceive Shelley's influence. In fact, we gradually discover in this manifesto a particular role for the poet and his poetry, a poetry Pascoli defines as "pure" but that succeeds in sending forth a magic mysticism by which the child/poet is soon recognized as the only one able to discover the truth or to perceive the soul that animates the natural world. The poet's aim seems to be a return to the womb of mother nature from which he came. This return does not stop there but comes to mean an enrichment and an illumination; that is to say, an epiphanic metamorphosis that takes place within process, in nature herself. Despite the fact that Pascoli remains a "modern" in openly rejecting a moral end for poetry, eventually he says that "il poeta è ispiratore di costumi solo indirettamente, non volendolo" (the poet is the inspirer of customs, although he does not realize it), or, again, "Ora si trova a mano a mano che impoetico è ciò che la morale riconosce cattivo e ciò che l'estetica proclama brutto" (we gradually discover that unpoetical means whatever morality defines as bad and whatever aesthetics recognizes as ugly). We are facing, in a way, what Walter Binni calls "aesthetic moralism or moralistic aesthetics."[20]

At the end of the *Fanciullino* we read, "I veri poeti vivono nelle cose le quali per noi fecero essi" (the true poets live in all the things they made for us). Here Pascoli comes very close to Shelley's *Defence,* to his idea of a poet/legislator of mankind, although his proceeding and achievement are more cognitive than heroic and do not imply a dimension of action. Nevertheless his poet, like the Shelleyan poet, draws out from chaos and darkness a new harmony and teaches mankind how to speak. Again like Shelley's poet, Pascoli's Fanciullino must inspire humanity with that "pietas" and benevolence necessary for human beings to survive and not be dismayed by the infinite breath of the universe, by death, or by the terror of nothingness. Pascoli writes in his "I due Fuochi," "Tu poeta nel torbido universo t'affissi; / tu per noi lo scopri e chiudi / in lucida parola e dolce verso / si ch'opera è di te quel che l'uomo sente / fra l'ombre vane e gli spettri nudi." (You, poet, gaze at the turbid universe; / For us you discover and enclose it / in bright words and sweet verses / so that your work is what man perceives / among the vain shadows and the naked ghosts.) These lines point to the same miraculous overcoming through poetry and the poet.

Moreover, as has been recently demonstrated,[21] Shelley's poetry and technique may also have influenced Pascoli's own poetry. In both poets there is an abundant use of synesthesia and a very high degree of abstraction—the poetic images are enriched by allusions that appeal to a reader through the use of alliteration and assonance. A recurrent phonosymbolic language is confirmed in the frequent use of figures of speech, such as onomatopoeia: the "trilli" and "strilli" of the birds in many of Pascoli's poems recall the "shrill," "thrill," or "thrilling" of Shelley's "Ode to Naples" or "To a Skylark." Similarly one encounters lexical returns of abstract, aerial, or liquid terms that belong to such semantic areas as dream/wake, height/depth, eternity/temporality, flowing/staying, in which words and thoughts appear intimately linked to one another.

Finally, in addition to Pascoli's library, containing many books of American and English poetry, we should also remember the translation that the Italian poet made of Shelley's lyric "Time Long Past" to be included in the anthology *Sul limitare,* a translation that was the fruit of the collaboration between Pascoli and his friend Gabriele Briganti, an enthusiastic admirer of the English Romantics. In this respect Briganti says, "Poi continuò a parlarmi di letteratura inglese . . . soprattutto dello Shelley, di cui sentiva, oltre lo splendore alato delle immagini, il commosso anelito al bene." (Then he went on talking of English literature . . . and above all of Shelley, about whom he felt, besides the aerial splendor of his images, the moving yearning toward good.) In his turn Pascoli, writing to another friend, Manara Valgimigli, on August 17, 1898, says, "Se intanto hai trovato qualche cosa di bello o in versi o in prosa comunicamelo. Dì la stessa cosa al gentil Gabriele [Briganti]. Al quale dì pure, che mi prepari allo stesso modo qualche poesia breve dello Shelley. Quella l'ho tradotta, e ritmicamente è venuta bene. Solo qua e là strozzata. Ma tradurre veramente non si può. Il meglio è cercare di rendere, anche più che il senso, la suggestione del testo."[22] (Meanwhile, let me know if you have found something good in verse or in prose. Tell Gabriele [Briganti] to do the same. Tell him also to prepare in the same way some short poems by Shelley. I have translated the other one, and rhythmically it has come out well. A bit stifled here and there. But, really, to translate is impossible. The best thing is trying to restore not so much the meaning as the suggestiveness of the text.) Pascoli seems somehow to be struggling with this translation not only because he has evident problems with English but also because he feels a sort of threat, as if his own poetry could not be kept silent underneath the borrowed lines.

This brief analysis concludes with a discussion of the contribution of the most significant Italian artist of the end of the nineteenth century and the beginning of the twentieth, Gabriele D'Annunzio. It was first through the Milanese Scapigliatura movement and later Decadentism that Shelley came to be recognized in Italy as the great artist he was. The early nineteenth century had not entirely accepted him because of his belonging to the so-called "Satanic School." Conversely, the mid–nineteenth century had, following the Victorian interpretation, made him into a sort of spotless angel whose political tension was nevertheless also to be appreciated (and was in fact very much welcomed by the pre-Risorgimento and Risorgimento Italian patriots, who used Shelley's "Ode to Naples" as a sort of national anthem). The end of the century would instead turn him into a hero whose transgressions, whose living against the law, give him a new and fascinating halo. Shelley's pantheistic lyrics and spirit became a favorite among the Decadents, who were among the aesthetes of the fin de siècle. All saw in the Romantic poet a forerunner of their own poetical rapture and expectations.

The unmaterialistic mysticism that moves the Decadents was also seen as a moving force behind Shelley's poetry. They rejected what they viewed as social or moralistic in his poetry in favor of a desire for absoluteness and truth. If for the Classicists the poet was the expert on the human heart and for the Romantics he came to symbolize the heart itself, for the Decadents he was the consciousness of music, the mystery of mankind's interiority and its soul.[23] They began with an idea of poetry as the revelation of a mystery and, at the same time, as the assertion of a universal correspondence, of a sublime analogy to which we all belong and from which we all originate. While the poet acts as a hero and a superman, his poetry must sound like pure music. Music in fact becomes a central art because it tells without describing, reveals without teaching, reaches the mystery of the world and of the human consciousness without destroying it or making it banal. Music becomes knowledge, power, and will. Here the Decadents meet Shelley. Here D'Annunzio recognizes Shelley as a precious referent as much as a powerful lyricist and musician.

D'Annunzio's interest in Shelley began in 1892, when he was 29, on the centenary of the poet's birth. During the first Shelley centenary most of the Italian intelligentsia seemed busy celebrating the man who was by now famous as "il poeta del rinnovato mondo" as Carducci put it, or, following the epitaph, as the "cor cordium," which suddenly seemed also the best definition for the English Romantic poet. Articles, translations, and reviews all combine to suggest a general atmosphere of triumph. Magazines such as *La Nuova Antologia, Il Marzocco, Il Fanfulla della Domenica,* and *Il Giornale d'Italia* all contributed to it.[24]

The Decadent poets show an unusual predilection for Shelley, in whose poetry they perceive an endless, mysterious interaction between nature and beauty. D'Annunzio had pointed out in the literary magazine *Il Convito* that, in order to be perfect, a work of art does not have to imitate but rather to continue nature. The Decadents saw this creed embodied in Shelley as well as in Swinburne—their poetry being a rare, harmonious continuation of nature, not a simple reproduction but a making and a remaking of her intensest, most sublime colors and sounds: a poetry, in short, above all really able to capture and unveil the "secret of life."

It was D'Annunzio who celebrated Shelley in the most exalted way. In his "Commemorazione di Percy Bysshe Shelley," delivered in Naples in August 1892, he defines Shelley as the greatest English poet of the nineteenth century, a poet's poet, a heart of hearts. Nobody like him had ever been able to put into verse such immaterial and spiritual harmonies as did "this son of the Ocean"; his poetry would awake and bring again to life a voice buried and asleep in the universe. And even if his virtue is like those of the supreme masters of the past, nevertheless everything is new in him. Shelley's *Prometheus Unbound,* which D'Annunzio judges to be a work even greater than Goethe's *Faust,* is the most beautiful fruit of his art. It is an art in which the past is separated from death and is restored to the light of the future; where love and joy sing with beauty and make a chorus of voices in unison with nature. Shelley is really a "spirit-tongued" poet because all the shapes, colors, sounds, perfumes, and appearances of the universe, whether lasting or fleeting, all receive a voice in his poetry, a new and deeper life. In his poetry, then, everything lives, breathes, palpitates. There is no distance between nature and art; they have become one.[25] If Shelley is able to infuse his spirituality and sensuality into the natural world, nature, in turn, assimilates him, making him her own interpreter, a "spirit-tongued" poet, giving him the power to transform her sounds and colors into tangible words, into feelings, visions, and emotions.[26]

With D'Annunzio, and in general with all his followers, Shelley is transformed into a hero, a hero/poet or a poet/hero who becomes similar, in a daring parallel, to a Christ figure through his benevolence, his goodness, and the extraordinary intensity he was able to express. Shelley becomes for D'Annunzio a spiritual giant, always ready to overcome the eternal war between Ormuzd and Ahriman and to fight only for the principle of good and the source of light.[27] Here the Italian poet not only reaches the peak of his exalted celebration but also discloses his own poetic vision, the inner process of his aesthetics. The exchange between life and art, the making of art into *the* supreme value superseding morality or ideology, and the attendant vision of art as the only way open to salvation and revelation constitute in fact the central feature of the poetics of the Decadentists.

D'Annunzio, however, never forgot this early experience, and his reading of Shelley can be traced throughout his work. In 1902 D'Annunzio dedicated his ode "Anniversario Orfico P. B. Shelley VIII Luglio MDCCCXXII" to Shelley's tragic death. Again, in his *Trionfo della Morte,* Giorgio Aurispa, walking along the shore near the solitary southern village where he lives, remembers the poet's death by water and feels that death is in itself an allegory of the fusion between the body and the natural elements that Shelley had sung throughout his life. In a Shakespearean mood, he discovers in his soul an infinite desire to die and be transformed, by the mysterious communion with the sea, "into something rich and strange." Shelley's echoes will also be evident in *Il Piacere,* where quotations from the English poet are frequent and seem to occur when the atmosphere becomes rarefied and a spiritual dimension is established. Finally there is *Alcyone,* in which Shelley's poetry represents for D'Annunzio a sort of bridge between death and life, between the sensual and the spiritual, between a metaphysical tension and the materiality of the natural world.

It is no coincidence that Shelley's most powerful impact on Italian literature is to be found in the production of three of the greatest Italian poets. Whereas Italian critics of the nineteenth century and of the first half of the twentieth century were often unable to understand the full implications or the revolutionary nature of Shelley's work, Carducci, Pascoli, and D'Annunzio identified there a consistent source of inspiration. They were ready and able to exploit Shelley's view of the supremacy of poetry, the extreme musicality of his verse, his identification with nature, and his restless quest for liberty.

Shelley and the
Empire in the East

Marilyn Butler

13

S HELLEY'S NOTION of legislating for the world has its own history; so does his underlying assumption that the world needing (Western) legislation is largely Eastern. In sketching these histories I limit myself to two texts by other writers directly concerned with legislating the East, on which Shelley modeled his: Volney's *The Ruins* and Southey's *Thalaba the Destroyer.*

The legislators of the world were not figments of Shelley's imagination. The term for poets that he uses in *A Defence of Poetry* had a prior textual existence in the idealized legislators of France, whom Constantin Volney depicts in Chapter 19 of *The Ruins; or a Survey of the Revolutions of Empires* (1791). Volney's legislators convene a general assembly of the people of the world, a motley and innumerable crowd assembled in the open air, whom the French revolutionaries address "in the name of justice and peace":

> Inhabitants of the earth, . . . we were for a long time tormented with the same evils as you; we have enquired into their origin, and we have found them to be derived from violence and injustice. We perceived that there existed in the order of the universe, and in the physical constitution of man, eternal and immutable laws which waited only his observance to render him happy. O men of different climes, look to the heavens that give you light, to the earth that nourishes you! . . . Has not [the Power that directs their motions] hereby declared you to be all equal and free?

O nations! let us banish all tyranny and discord; let us form one society, one vast family; and since mankind are all constituted alike, let there henceforth exist but one law, that of nature; one code, that of reason; one throne, that of justice; one altar, that of union.[1]

Volney's book as a whole advances the universalist narrative of history that underwrites this address. He adapts Rousseau's argument in the *Second Discourse: On Inequality* (1752) that humanity suffered an early, evil revolution at the end of the pastoral phase of culture when, in order to till the ground, people had to claim to own it. From the principle of property followed the modern world's ills—greed, competitiveness, exploitation, war, and social inequality. Volney rewrites Rousseau's epochal shift in economics as a revolution within discourse. Leaders, he alleges in his historical resumé in chapter 22, learned to control nations by controlling thought. The master discourse that in early times achieved social control was religion.

This makes *The Ruins* a work of political theory, and a highly politicized history of "empire," or the mechanisms by which states have governed; formally it is fiction and fantasy; its paratext includes a thick corpus of notes. From the opening scene, in which a gigantic apparition manifests itself to a European traveler from among the tombs of Palmyra, we are in a dystopic landscape, Arabia deserta dotted with the ruins of the imperial cities of the ancient world, Nineveh and Babylon, Egypt and Rome. A similar wasteland, viewed under a gaze that takes in continents at a time, makes a powerful impact, dehumanized and chilling; others, including Shelley, follow Volney in making it *the* visionary landscape appropriate to revolutions, past and to come. In Shelley's longer poems at least, as Geoffrey Matthews memorably said, "Human society is always seen in a cosmic setting, and human history is inseparable from the history of stars and insects."[2]

Any claim to a world perspective entails diminishing or omitting something—for example, individual experience, the private sphere, cultural difference, or local attachments such as family, tribe, nation, or religion. The global terms of the legislators' address certainly work to undercut the ethnic diversity of the audience of the world's people, as Volney has just described it. Moreover, in what is supposed to be a political dialogue, it is essentially the French legislators who do the talking.

Volney was himself a deputy in the revolutionary French National Assembly; but he uses *legislators* more broadly, as a term for France's reforming intellectuals or ideologues of the 1790s. Of real-life politicians—servants of the unregenerate old regime rather than the new transcendent republic—he speaks unfavorably, as a "valueless fraction . . . priests, courtiers, public accountants, commanders of troops, in short the civil, military or religious agents of government."[3] Shelley follows this definition of oppressors as the agents of government in *Queen Mab,* his most Volneyan poem—"From kings, and priests, and statesmen, war arose," with the same implied corollary, that the time has come for this group to pay the price—"Let the axe / Strike at the root, the poison tree will fall" (4.80–83).

Volney was to prove useful to Shelley in offering him a powerful, proto-Foucauldian critique of discourse as yet another agency of existing power, one that includes but is not identical with religion. He is most Foucauldian in his historical resumé in chapter 22, where he tells the early history of religion as primitive natural science as well as poetry, until all the knowledges are appropriated by Moses, the first evil legislator to engross the mechanisms of power.[4] He is least Foucauldian in excepting himself, and the skeptical Enlightenment comparative religionists who furnish his notes, from an otherwise universal corruption of discourse through its penetration by state power. Volney writes as if unaware of or unimpressed by some recent currents in the West's discourse on the East, for example, the attempt from 1784 of Sir William Jones in India to understand traditional Hindu and Moslem law not as (Western-style) institutions of state but as customary, localized codes—by which, admittedly, the British could in future conveniently govern India. At least Jones found a place in the polis for real-life communities. For Volney there seem to be only two conditions, and these were successive rather than in dialogue: slavery to archaic, theocratic empire, or postrevolutionary enlightenment. The brutal rhetoric of *The Ruins* consigns the East to the old condition, while the Western intellectual spearheads the new.

Volney was a hardline ideologue, propounding a totalitarian vision as harsh and engrossed with power as the regimes it condemned. He took no interest in exploring the psychology of state functionaries, priests included: Were these teachers of an otherworldly ideology all hypocrites, and thus the state's willing tools, or were they unconscious dupes? Might some be remorseful, others the open allies of the people? Godwin was by comparison exceptionally subtle in creating his representative Burkean aristocrat, Falkland in *Caleb Williams* (1794), who is at times a genuine idealist, a victim as well as an agent of the system. By emphasizing only function, Volney deprives members of the first and second estates, France's traditional ruling classes, of the reader's sympathy; he prepares them as victims for slaughter; and the priests he anathematized soon were slaughtered in their hundreds. It must make us uncomfortable that Shelley resembles Volney rather than his father-in-law, the novelist Godwin, in adopting this nonpsychological, non-individualistic, but functional approach to character, for example, in his attack on kings in the last hundred lines of the fourth canto of *Queen Mab* and on God in the seventh canto, and his symbolic rendering of state power in the demonized figures of the Eastern Sultan and the Christian priest in the finale to *The Revolt of Islam*.

Having begun by whittling down the enemy to "the civil, military or religious agents of government," Volney in the second half of his book limits himself further. He thickens the case against priests specifically, with world-wide examples of their secrecy and manipulativeness probably assembled earlier in the 1780s, when infidel French mythography was particularly fashionable and (to be fair) less likely to lead immediately to bloodshed. Eclectic footnotes build up a cumulative argument, until the penultimate one demands that we adopt the term *magician* for all clergy in all cultures:

> What is a magician, in the sense in which the people understand the word? a man who by words and gestures pretends to act on supernatural beings, and compel them to descend at his call and obey his orders. . . . And when a Christian priest pretends to make God descend from heaven . . . what is all this but a trick of magic? Yes, the identity of the spirit of priests in every age and country is fully established! Every where it is the assumption of an exclusive privilege, the pretended faculty of moving at will the powers of nature; and this assumption is so direct a violation of the right of equality, that whenever the people shall regain their importance they will forever abolish this sacrilegious kind of nobility which has been the type and parent stock of the other species of nobility.[5]

Volney surely captured Shelley's attention, not as a historian or political philosopher, but as a popular rhetorician and master of the art of demonizing an opponent. His book has genuine literary flair and suggestiveness: It points the way to both oriental fantasy and paranoid Gothic as promising genres for political allegory in the decade to come (and in England especially both genres retain the Volneyan stamp for a whole generation, as late as Maturin's *Melmoth the Wanderer* of 1820). He is all the more effective a tactician for concentrating his case on the clergy, who for centuries had provided the local educators, moralists, and legislators with advice on personal matters. Even in relatively centralized and parliamentary (that is, secularized) Britain, the Bible and prayerbook constituted a code of social discipline far more closely meshed with most people's lives than law or constitution. What gives edge to Volney's work gives it to Shelley's too. He becomes one of Volney's new-style legislators, who is also an educator, when he makes "state religion" the central plank of his portrayal of the old regime in *Queen Mab, The Revolt of Islam, Prometheus Unbound, Hellas,* "The Witch of Atlas," and *The Cenci.*

The most outwardly Volneyan of Shelley's works, *Queen Mab* is also strongly indebted to Erasmus Darwin's *Botanic Garden* (1791) and Southey's *Thalaba the Destroyer* (1801), two of the most inventive English literary recensions of French Revolutionary ideology. The highly characteristic format these works all share aims at a semipopular market and especially at the new middle-class preoccupation with education within the home. Each has a narrative, made accessible by a high proportion of biblical material. The three English poems are all addressed to a young person, Darwin's and Shelley's to a girl. Through the addition of a paratext including tough, seemingly authoritative, and intellectually ambitious footnotes, family readers get for their money a book that works for several family members at once—a story, a serious textbook, even an anthology of materialist thinking, for the footnotes employ antireligious matter culled from natural science and infidel mythography. Twentieth-century critics have sometimes assumed that the footnotes could hardly have been read. Wrong: They constituted a motive for a new class of book buyer, and a further inducement for the piratical publishers Clark and Carlile, who from 1821 and 1822 made *Queen Mab* the most widely read and influential of Shelley's poems.[6]

Southey's original plan for *Thalaba the Destroyer* repeats Volney's description of the machinery of despotism. Southey's schoolboy project to write a poem about each of the world's great religions easily embraced Volneyan polemic. Not many adjustments needed to be made, in that Volney was writing in a recognizable if exaggerated eighteenth-century French-orientalist style, which already saw the Middle East as a semifeudal empire engaged with the supernatural in two characteristic forms: radiant but delusory visions of paradise, and horrific or sadistic black magic. Volney may be indebted, for example, to a striking political allegory, published in 1789, about an Eastern revolution: a collection adapted from Arabic sources by Denis Chavis and Jacques Cazotte as *Continuation des mille et une nuits* (1788–89) and translated into English as *Arabian Tales* by Robert Heron (1792).

Notwithstanding the date of writing, these oriental tales were an early contribution to the literature of counterrevolution. Chavis was an Arab-speaking Catholic priest from North Africa, Cazotte an active royalist, a writer of oriental and moral tales, and a member of a religious group, the Martinists, who believed in the existence of dual powers eternally at war. In the last and best story, "The History of Maugraby," Cazotte (the accepted principal author) builds an ancient North African story into a strange modern fantasy about the corruption of orthodox (Mohammedan) rulers by the powers of darkness. Meanwhile a story began to circulate that at this time Cazotte was prophesying the violent deaths of the French royal family and other leading figures at the hands of their political enemies. "The History of Maugraby" could itself be such a prophecy. Maugraby stands among other things for secularists and republicans in contemporary European states: He is a master magician who tricks his way into royal favor and thereby power, captures and bewitches the young, and ends by terrorizing the Eastern world from Tunis to Cathay from his cavernous stronghold, Domdaniel, "under the roots of the sea."[7]

Southey found the story in the summer of 1798 and by the following year was adapting it for use in most of the strictly Arabian scenes in his metrical romance. Maugraby's horrific underworld reappears in books 2 and 9 of *Thalaba,* his daylit garden of delight in the Atlas Mountains in books 6 and 7; Cazotte's plot, featuring one shape-shifting magician, emerges naturalized in books 3–6 as the hero's encounters with different wicked old men. If power takes diffused rather than state-centered form in *Thalaba* compared with Southey's other Eastern romance, *The Curse of Kehama,* that could owe something to its ideologically polarized nature in Volney and Cazotte.

In his pantisocratic years, Southey read Volney and Priestley's *History of the Corruptions of Christianity* (1782), and in poems, letters, and his Bristol lecture course of 1795 fulminated against state religion.[8] But he also continued to read widely (as his *Commonplace Books* prove), from Greenland to Peru, with the result that during the next two to three years he developed a quite un-Volneyan interest in local oral cultures, not visibly under centralized social control. Disillusion with the course of the French Revolution may have helped foster the new localism that Romanticists know from Coleridge's conversation poems; Southey's prolific verse of the same years explores particular historical communities and resumes an interest in British cultural diversity that already showed in his adolescence in the 1780s. From 1798 Southey produced two innovative types of short poem in considerable number: ballads on Gothic themes, set in contemporary as well as past times, and dialogic eclogues, in which the principal speakers are uneducated. Like the copious footnotes to *Thalaba,* these can retain Volneyan overtones: Bishop Hatto, in a ballad of 1799, burns the population in a barn, on the grounds that they are in time of famine "rats that consume the corn"—only to be eaten himself the following day by an irresistible tide of rats that gnaws its way into his fortress. It seems to be the popular psychological assumptions underlying the genre—guilt and a conviction of the certainty of punishment—that generate Southey's preoccupation. He begins to read past religious cultures, through artifacts, for their record of human feelings and concerns: fear of death and of the afterlife, burial customs, the treatment (sometimes ill-treatment) of the body before or after death.

At least a third of the footnotes to *Thalaba* illustrate Moslem beliefs, apocrypha, and popular superstitions, often providing Christian analogues. For the target aimed at in *Thalaba* is, in effect, *anyone's* medievalism—or, more precisely, the religiously sanctioned hegemonic state modeled on an idealized Christendom by Thomas Warton in his *History of English Literature,* 1100–1603 (1774–82) and by Burke in his *Reflections on the Revolution in France.* Southey collects yarns from eclectic sources—from early and recent travelers to modern newspaper reports—about graveyards, revenants, the use in forbidden magic of body parts and body fat, and vampirism, along with the method of exorcising it. This unexpected injection of social anthropology has ideological implications; it serves, for example, (1) to democratize both the Burkean and Volneyan account of *cultural discourse,* shifting its center from elite writing to oral tales and common practices; (2) to correct Volney's simplified view of institutional religion as largely political, or of popular religion as largely institutional; (3) to show that the West has no special access to enlightenment, religious truth, or indeed error, all of which recur in similar proportions anywhere; (4) to show that although cultures are porous, allowing stories to pass around, each story also emanates from somewhere—a unique climate, terrain, or culture (hardly Volney's "one law, that of nature").

Shelley grows up an admirer of Southey. He borrows for *Queen Mab* the much-criticized unrhymed stanza Southey developed for *Thalaba.* He copies the first line, "How beautiful is Night," for his own opening, "How wonderful is Death, / Death and his brother Sleep." He repeatedly uses for his visionary poetry Southey's fantastic oriental machinery of journeys by magic aerial car and unmanned boat—just as Mary Shelley borrows Thalaba's last purgatorial journey by dogsled for the closing sequence of *Frankenstein.* With *Alastor,* a poem concerned with all three so-called Lake poets as a group, echoes of Wordsworth and Coleridge occur at certain points, but the debt to *Thalaba* is structural and pervasive. The life journey of Shelley's hero takes him from the Gothic horrors of Domdaniel in book 2 of *Thalaba,* via the naturalistically realized desert scenes of books 3–5, past the loss of the Arab maiden (Thalaba's wife dies on her wedding night at the end of book 7), and her reappearance as an evil spirit (book 8), to the long journey into the wasteland, partly by boat, and the hero's eventual lonely death.

But although Shelley relishes Southey's oriental devices, indeed his polished *literary* use both of Arabian or Persian story and imagery and of European Renaissance romance, he is not at all attuned to his precursor's folkloric insights as a cultural and social historian. Immensely well read though Shelley is in 1790s radical high theory—by Condorcet, Volney, and Bichat in France, and Wollstonecraft, Godwin, and Darwin in England—he never adopts that decade's popular discourse, where the challenge came from below. Like other dabblers in the Gothic, Shelley could have profited from Southey's sociological and psychological approach to superstition.[9] Notionally Southey and Shelley do have one democratizing feature in common: their environmentalism, a fellow feeling with the lower species with which human beings share the world. Yet even here there are extraordinary differences of nuance and vocabulary between the two poets. The theme is more dominant in *Thalaba* than in any poem by Shelley, and the creatures Southey introduces as allies of his human characters—an old mare, a vulture, a locust, a pelican—tend to be humdrum or ugly, unlike Shelley's routinely graceful flora, his skylarks and eagles, the lamb that looks his human murderer in the face. Shelley's decorative animals (symbolic and heraldic, in the opening stanzas of "The Witch of Atlas") are literary props that dilute, rather than enforce, the French Revolutionary vision of a new transcendental republicanism. Coleridge expressed this far better to Francis Wrangham, in the exuberance of the pantisocratic year 1794: "I call even my Cat Sister in the fraternity of universal Nature. Owls I respect & Jack Asses I love: for Aldermen & Hogs, Bishops & Royston Crows I have not particular partiality—; they are my Cousins, however, at least by Courtesy."[10]

Southey writes in the same fraternal spirit when in *Thalaba* a bat, a toad, and a viper offer themselves as surrogate victims on a pyre the witches intend for the hero (9.30). Shelley understands the egalitarian import of the new life sciences, whereby mankind functions by principles of bodily organization shared with other animals: hence his vegetarianism. But he rejects the homespun vocabulary and cast of *Thalaba* when he writes on men in nature.

Nigel Leask argues in *British Romantic Writers and the East* that in *Prometheus Unbound* Shelley mitigates the Eurocentrism that is pervasive in his other Eastern poems; at last women, easterners, perhaps even Eastern religious traditions are allowed some degree of agency; the European male strapped to his rock cannot dictate what happens.[11] Yet even Prometheus remains, like Laon and like Byron's heroes in his Eastern tales, explicitly aristocratic, European, and male. The stuff of the nineteenth-century romantic hero, these protagonists emerge from the West's hereditary ruling caste to enforce liberation on an Eastern sphere of war.[12] They are, among other things, surrogates for a writer assuming the masterful Volneyan gaze. Meanwhile, those who are being led—the Eastern populace—are barely heard or seen in either poet. In the absence of those other voices, what we hear is the voice of the legislator.

"The Witch of Atlas" should be an exception. To be sure, this witty skeptical retelling of the history of ancient religion as, in effect, universal intellectual history, until in Egypt it is subsumed in state power, is among other things a creative retelling of Volney's history of the same topic in chapter 22 of *The Ruins*. But, as a journey over North Africa it is also a variant on the quest of the shepherd boy Thalaba. In fact, the poem is incurably sociable in its calling up of other texts. In describing how one religious culture must give way to the next, it follows the plot of Keats's *Hyperion* of the same year (1820). And, as the emanation of an entire people, the sum of successive generations' ways of constructing the world, the Witch resembles the manmade Creature in Mary Shelley's *Frankenstein* (1818) and Albion in Blake's *Jerusalem* (1820).

But, although representative of her culture, she is avowedly a "magician," and so distanced from humanity. Like Frankenstein's Creature, she changes, grows, becomes acculturated to a world passing from primitive to advanced. After her birth out of the elements of sun, sea, and earth, she is first defined by early Greek nature-religion (Silenus, Faunus, Pan, Priapus), next by its North African equivalents ("the rude kings of Pastoral Garamant") (line 130).[13] She sends away the charming, childlike creatures of this religious age in order to take on a more sophisticated but still early concept, that of the hermaphrodite, who reunites male and female in one body. By the middle of the poem the Witch must respond to the central concerns of personal religions—the belief in rewards and punishments according to individuals' moral deserts and the desire for personal immortality.

As a narrative, "The Witch of Atlas" belongs to the genre of invented tradition, particularly the invented cultural history of a specific region—an internally British, prerevolutionary genre with which *Thalaba* and *Jerusalem* are also aligned. So in one sense it is odd to find Mary Shelley complaining (according to the poem's opening lines) that "The Witch of Atlas" has no story. It echoes, after all, the story of stories, the Bible: but the Bible ironized and brilliantly contracted, in a commentary recalling Hume's *History of Natural Religion* (1757) and Priestley's *Corruptions of Christianity*. Each episode, or age, draws to its close when the Witch disappoints her worshippers by not merely denying but mocking the human desires they call on her to satisfy. These worshippers are realized for us only when the story arrives in historical time: They are the false, politicized religionists of ancient Egypt, ushering in Volney's Age of Empire, and ordinary domestic lovers, who could be alive today. With them she performs her perennial role as fantasist, tease, echo, like the oracular Demogorgon in *Prometheus Unbound:* "These were the pranks she played among the cities / Of mortal men" (lines 665–66).

Reworking his old ground, exceptionally persistent, Shelley continues to read idealism as ideology, matter as real but transient. With this difference: that in "The Witch of Atlas" he finds the idea of religion pleasant—on condition we view it as a product of human intelligence and imagination, aesthetic and internalized. Especially when the poem is compared with the other texts Shelley brings to mind, the costs of this modified interpretation prove considerable. Where in his earlier poetry the reading of religion seems overly didactic, totalizing, implicitly domineering, later it can become cold in a different sense. The new emphasis on its constructedness, and hence its provisional and ephemeral nature, functions to repress material reality.

Idealism in this poem is always frail, never efficacious. The human dead body, its mortality remorselessly exposed, magically remains as a motionless husk to mock the very sublimation the Witch represents: "And there the body lay, age after age, / Mute, breathing, beating, warm and undecaying" (lines 609–10). Contracting the scale of religion's operations, by comparison with Volney, Shelley in this poem comes near to denying the practical use of skepticism as well. Equally negative, even inhumanly so, is the handling here of death, interment, bereavement. At the personal level, among the common people Southey observed, religious customs and the care of the dead brought comfort. Those doctrines concerning the immortality of soul or body that for Shelley distinguish one religion from another lack the universal emotional meaning of Southey's topic, customary rites. Mary Shelley's resistance to her husband's poem, glossed by her as a question of story, may surely have stemmed from its repression, along with the facts of bodily decay, of grief at the loss of those we love best.

To legislate for the world, as Shelley seeks to do, is not, evidently, uncontentious. For some commentators on Shelley, including Matthew Arnold and T. S. Eliot, the interventionist side of Shelley was unacceptable for political reasons. Equally for political reasons, his crusading streak draws some twentieth-century admirers, who readily conflate his radicalism with our own. But radicalism and libertarianism, or in Shelley's day the revolutionary rhetoric of liberty and equality, can assume very different forms: They can evoke a world that is notionally free and equal (soft rhetoric), or they can propose to make such a world (hard rhetoric). Especially where India is the topic, British Romantic poetry displays these divergent tendencies in all their complexity. In this respect, if the differences between Shelley and the religiously orthodox or politically conventional are perhaps too obvious to yield new insights in this day and age, the differences between Shelley and fellow-radicals or fellow-colonialists are still unfolding.

Shelley's India:
Territory and Text,
Some Problems of
Decolonization

Meena Alexander

14

I NEVER KNEW autumn as a child. The line "O wild West Wind, thou breath of autumn's being" evokes for me the scents of the monsoon wind blowing in from the west, from the Indian Ocean and the Arabian Sea. For I first heard Shelley's poetry, fragments of his lyrics, recited to me when I was a child growing up in Kerala, on the southwest coast of India. Lines from "Ode to the West Wind" or others from "To a Skylark" seemed then to me to be Indian poems, part of the same world of utterance as the words of Tagore or Mahakavi Vallathol. And if there was a difference in the language that worked the textures of sound and sense—illuminating the images of wind, water, cloud, leaf, bird—then it was nothing particularly to be remarked on. For English then was braided in for me with Indian languages: Malayalam, my mother tongue, and others, including Tamil, Hindi, Marathi, and phrases of Bengali.

When I was a little older, I moved to North Africa with my parents. Arabic flowed all around. I was entrusted to a British tutor and realized with a sharp shock that she knew her language, her utterance was superior to mine. Carefully, with great patience, she made me unlearn the English I already knew and repeat words from a primer after her, over and over again. Her strict colonial pedagogy, in the Sudan, a country that had just received its independence from Britain, was reinforced by the British school to which

I was sent. Sometimes I felt as if a thick skin, an otherness, had covered over the poetry I loved, and I struggled in a dim, wordless way to return to a landscape of sense, a complex, interanimating realm of linguistic recognition that was starting to alter beyond my understanding.

It was years later that I realized the violence of the colonial language, its canonical burden, part and parcel of the territory of empire, had to be faced up to, spelled out. I had to reread poems like the "Ode to the West Wind" and *Prometheus Unbound,* tearing apart colonial territory and poetic text, then setting them side by side, in a postcolonial project of reading—both a bloodying of the waters and a clarification of what connects radical, Romantic epistemology to the contortions of British imperial power.

In 1821, the year in which Shelley was writing his *Defence of Poetry,* with its convoluted sense of the purity of poetic language, which precisely through its symbolic disconnection from events clarifies the "un-apprehended relations of things" (line 482), his compatriot Major General Sir John Malcolm, who was stationed in India, laid down a set of instructions for the British officers under his command. These instructions put great stress on language and its properties for enabling a just rule of the natives. The major general argued for the morality of "this great empire," the preservation of which it seemed to him depended on the natives being convinced of the necessary superiority of British rule: "Almost all who from knowledge and experience, have been capable of forming any judgement on the question, are agreed that our power in India then rested on the general opinion of the natives of our comparative superiority in good faith, wisdom, and strength to their own rulers."[1] British power in India then rested not merely on military force, but also on the ability to persuade. The study and codification of Indian languages upon which William Jones and others like Nathaniel Halhed and John Gilchrist embarked was implicitly part and parcel of this complex, often ambivalent system of colonial governance.

William Jones, the first president of the Asiatick Society of Bengal—the society was established in Calcutta in 1784—had already by 1771 published his *Grammar of the Persian Language.* Persian and Arabic were in those earlier years thought to be the language of accomplishment for a young Englishman fitted for rule of India: the Eastern equivalent, as it were, of Greek and Latin. By 1785 Jones was deeply immersed in the study of Sanskrit, and his desire to effect a true text—the irrefutable basis of knowledge of an Indian code (whether philosophical or legal)—worked hand in hand with his belief that the British future in India was to be connected to the majesty of the Classical

Roman past. In a work commissioned by the East India Company, the image of William Jones may be found cut in stone in Saint Paul's Cathedral; he is dressed in a toga, leaning on two volumes meant to represent the essence of ancient Indian law, the Code of Manu.

Bernard Cohn, the anthropologist and historian, has argued that the massive records of the East India Company, together with the detailed labor of the orientalists, represent a tribute in print and manuscript to the British Empire, the term *tribute* used here in the sense of a "payment by one ruler or nation to another." It seems to Cohn that "The conquest of India was a conquest of knowledge" and that orientalism "had the effect of converting Indian forms of knowledge into European objects."[2] Indeed, well before Edgar Quinet's *Genie des Religions* (1841), with its chapter on "The Oriental Renaissance," the powerful effects of orientalism had been felt. With its vision of a spiritualized East, a realm of pure knowledge superior to the vicissitudes of European history, a perfect foil was created for British military power. Clearly Jones's celebrated essay "On the Gods of Greece, Italy and India" or his "Hymn to Narayena," with its invocation of a "Spirit of Spirits, who through ev'ry part / Of space expanded and of endless time," was no threat to imperial rule.[3] As Edward Said argued in *Orientalism,* speaking specifically of Schlegel and Novalis, who urged a close study of the spiritual riches of India, "what mattered was not Asia so much as Asia's *use to* modern Europe."[4] Indeed, one could go further and argue that the renewal of the European spirit through access to the East for which Jones and others had hoped required the prior presence of an imperial force, one that could be taken for granted, absorbed by the fabricated spirituality of India.

Raymond Schwab points out that Quinet's handwritten notes allude to the English Romantic poets in cryptic if clearly comprehensible form: "England, Lake School, Coleridge, Shelley completely India."[5] How true, for William Jones's influence in his own time cannot be underestimated. In December 1812, as part of his copious reading project, Shelley ordered Jones's *Works* as well as Robertson's *Historical Disquisition Concerning the Knowledge which the Ancients had of India.* These two books he added to Moor's *Hindu Pantheon,* which he had previously ordered. A year and a half earlier, in the summer of 1811, Shelley spoke in a letter of "the Indian Camdeo, the god of mystic love," alluding perhaps to Jones's "Hymn to Camdeo." But surely just as critical to Shelley's vision of what India might be was Southey's *The Curse of Kehama,* which he describes as his favorite poem. It led him to Keswick, to "pay homage," as he put it, to Southey.

Indeed Shelley's sources are numerous and include Mountstuart Elphinstone, George Stanley Faber, and Sydney Owenson's novel *The Missionary: An Indian Tale,* which she published in 1811 *(PBSL* 1:101, 191).[6]

The fabricated East, whose shimmering fabric included the mythic, paradisiacal Cashmir of *Alastor* and the Hindu Kush mountains of *Prometheus Unbound,* permitted the poet a realm of ideality within which Romantic self-consciousness could unfold. Such textual elaborations, inconceivable without the territory of a well-translated East, allowed the Romantic image to blossom in that foundatory nothingness that Paul de Man has character- ized as critical to its ontology.[7] The paradox that Shelley's own poems, with their radical rewritings of gender and nationalism, were based on the intel- lectual productions of colonialism would not have been lost on him. Hence, I would argue, the painful disconnection he imposed on the world of the actual, so that power is split from bodily being, and the violence of the actual—poverty, despotism, the sexual enslavement of women, the impossible fulfillment of desire—must call forth the explosive symbol: "Graves," as he put it in his sonnet "England, 1819," "from which a glorious Phantom may / Burst to illumine our tempestuous day" (lines 13–14).

In 1819, before he could complete his great work *Prometheus Unbound,* Shelley was faced with the repressive force of the British government when unarmed civilians—men, women, and children agitating for parliamentary reform—were shot, wounded, and killed by British cavalry in what has come to be called the Peterloo Massacre. Shelley's rage and bitterness poured out in "The Mask of Anarchy," with its extraordinary vision of nonviolent resistance. It was a vision that had a powerful effect on Mohandas Karam- chand Gandhi when a century later he was locked in a fierce struggle against the repressions of the British Empire.

In 1899, as a young man in London, ready to explore the new morality of the world around him, Gandhi encountered the circle of vegetarians. His reading of Henry Salt's 1889 pamphlet, *A Plea for Vegetarianism,* in which the cruelty of flesh consumption was related to the claims of social justice, converted Gandhi to a doctrine for which his Hindu upbringing had well prepared him. It was in Salt's work that Gandhi first encountered Shelley's poetry, and his further study of the vegetarians—Howard Williams and Anna Kingsford—reinforced the bond. And it is in this context that we find Gandhi's first reference to the poet. In South Africa now, working as a lawyer, Gandhi writes on February 3, 1896, to the editor of the *Natal Examiner,* praising him for his support of the vegetarian cause and including a list of the great men he believes were vegetarians. These include the Buddha, Pythagoras, Plato, and Shelley. Jesus is added on at the very end.[8]

If this were all, one might have let it drop, writing off Gandhi's pleasure in Shelley as part of the eccentricity of a vegetarian vision, its meatless quest fit fulfillment of an ideality that flees the bodily realm. But the connection goes further. By 1906, at the genesis of *satyagraha,* which arose in the context of the nonviolent resistance to the Asiatic pass laws in South Africa, Gandhi defined the notion in the following way: "Truth (*Satya*) implies love, and firmness (*agraha*) engenders and therefore serves as a synonym for force."[9] Certainly by 1906 Gandhi knew of Shelley. Although the poet is not overtly mentioned in the company of Tolstoy, Thoreau, and the devotional texts the Gita and the Sermon on the Mount, as part of the inspiration for *satyagraha,* Shelley's radical political views and the nonviolence at the core of both "The Mask of Anarchy" and *Prometheus Unbound* had a deep effect on Gandhi and those he in turn inspired in the Indian nationalist struggle. Clearly, the vegetarians were not Shelley's only conduit into the radical nationalist circles of India.

By the 1820s, well before it was institutionalized in Britain itself, English literature had become established in the curriculum in British India.[10] The colonial underpinnings of this educational project were never masked. What was at stake was the moral uplift of the natives, the species of persuasion required for the perpetuation of British rule of which Major General Malcolm speaks. Indeed, just within the scope of Shelley's tragically foreshortened lifetime, one finds the literature of Shakespeare, Milton, Dryden, and Pope taught as part of the curriculum of institutions like Hindu College in Calcutta. This was the syllabus that the young poet Henry Derozio, with his fierce rationalism and anti-British sentiments, found himself teaching. The introduction of poetry into the literary curriculum worked in ways that could not have been foreseen, with the argument for the moral superiority of English culture—which rested in part on the appeal to universal sentiments of justice, mercy, and freedom, all of which were stressed—working itself out in ways rudely intolerant of imperial rule. Tom Paine was read by young Bengalis in the late 1820s, and the radical, freethinking doctrine developed into an overt call for Indian freedom, along lines drawn by the French Revolution. In the *Hindu Pioneer* of 1838 a graduate of Hindu College writes of "The violent means by which foreign supremacy has been established and the entire alienation of the people of the soil from any share in government," which can never be justified.[11] In the later years of British

174 / SHELLEY AND OTHER CULTURES

rule the Romantics were introduced into Indian universities: Wordsworth, Coleridge, Keats, Byron, and Shelley. The lyrics of Shelley were taught and have remained part of the set curriculum of Indian universities: "Ode to the West Wind," "To a Skylark," even the great elegy *Adonais*. But the radical, political poet, whose words would have been too disruptive of an imperial order that sought the careful importation of poetry into the colonies, was cauterized, cut away.

I wonder how many of my students at Delhi University or at the University of Hyderabad, where I taught in the late 1970s, had any idea that Gandhi, the father of the nation as he is commonly called, had recited key stanzas from "The Mask of Anarchy" at a critical juncture in his discussions on *satyagraha*. How would it have mattered to them? For part of the postcolonial effort has been to peel away the legacy of Gandhi's nonviolence, seeing in it a nationalism that has arisen as a precise counterpart to the colonial force in our history. To a generation facing the tumult of the postcolonial world, would Lord Macaulay's Minute of February 2, 1835, which crystallized the British intent in educating the natives, have touched a pressure point? "We must at present do our best to form a class who may be interpreters between us and the millions whom we govern; a class of persons Indian in blood and color, but English in taste, in opinions, in morals and intellect."[12] What has become of that imperial world, that lordly phantasm, now? The terrible self-division that it required of the colonial subject seeks elaboration here, at the tail end of the twentieth century, in figurations that a Frantz Fanon, with his radical if mutilated brilliance, could not have envisaged.

For Fanon, the objectness of the native is critical. Violently dehumanized by an occupying power, he must grip violence to restore himself from "thingness" to humanity. I use *he* advisedly, for nowhere in Fanon's major arguments on decolonization are women as subjects mentioned. For Gandhi, in sharp contrast, it is the humanity of the native that must be preserved, precisely through the abnegation of violence. In acts of *satyagraha* orchestrated against an oppressive colonial power, the living body—as it accepts violence, *lathi* blows, even gunshots—is transformed into a spiritual symbol. It is here that poetic text and the performance of *satyagraha* come together. Consider the crucial stanzas from "The Mask of Anarchy" in which Shelley invokes the ordinary people of England, who in their urgent quest for social justice must face much more than verbal blows:

> Stand ye calm and resolute
> Like a forest close and mute,

> With folded arms and looks which are
> Weapons of unvanquished war
> . . . .
> And if then the tyrants dare
> Let them ride among you there,
> Slash, and stab, and maim, and hew,—
> What they like, that let them do.   (lines 319–22, 340–43)

Their suffering will rise up, prophetic, "Eloquent, oracular," as the poet puts it, to "the Nation" (lines 360–62). What Benedict Anderson was to call "ghostly *national* imaginings" forge a pivot on which this mystic transubstantiation turns.[13] But there is more at work, for here as elsewhere in Shelley, the power of nonviolent suffering triggers a symbolic change so radical that materiality is vanquished, and imprisoning chains dissolve into gentle dew as the people metamorphose into paradisiacal "Lions after slumber" (line 151). The poem ends with the celebrated line, "Ye are many—they are few" (line 372), both a plea for popular resistance and a stoic acceptance of the price of nonviolent resistance.

Gandhi loved these lines from "The Mask of Anarchy," and he quoted them in 1938 at a crucial point in an argument to impress upon his Western listeners—a group of British missionaries who wanted to understand *satyagraha* and its connection to pacifism—the difficult spiritual discipline involved in the practice of nonviolence. "In my opinion," Gandhi argues, "non-violence is not passivity in any shape or form. Non-violence, as I understand it, is the activest force in the world." As the argument proceeds, and this is just prior to his invocation of Shelley, Gandhi's thought runs into some turbulence. He speaks of the Jews of Europe: They must love and pray for the Germans, rather than curse them. He turns to the Chinese: If the Japanese slaughter them with superior weapons of war, they must stand utterly still, resolute in their nonviolence. In support of his position, sensing perhaps the discomfort of his listeners, Gandhi quotes Shelley, who for him was the great poet of nonviolence.[14] And where else could one find such truth? After all, even in the Gita, Krishna must counsel Arjuna to the bloody war requisite to the working out of *dharma* (the moral law of the universe). We come closer now to the ways in which Gandhians read Shelley's heroic Prometheus, who by being "king over myself" (line 492), was able to establish a strict moral economy, converting suffering into true good.

Lines from *Prometheus Unbound* were quoted in the pages of Gandhi's periodical *Young India*. It was 1921, and within the nationalist movement the

176 / SHELLEY AND OTHER CULTURES

conditions of *swaraj* (self-rule) were being hotly debated. Gandhi spoke to the central platform of noncooperation with the British Raj. It was essential that students in large numbers should be mobilized for noncooperation: "Even if we cannot completely boycott schools and colleges, we must destroy their prestige. That prestige has almost gone and is daily decreasing. And we must do nothing . . . till they are nationalized and answer the requirements of the nation." The violence inherent in a colonial pedagogy could be resisted through active noncooperation. Later in the same issue of *Young India,* Gandhi alluded to the massacre in Jalianawalla Bagh: innocent civilians gunned down by British soldiers under the command of General Dyer. "Dyerism," wrote Gandhi, "has evoked a yearning after freedom as nothing else has." A student active in the noncooperation movement then contributed a piece arguing against the "intellectual asphyxia" of the government schools. "Real liberty, real freedom, real Swaraj," it seemed to this young man, could only come from the purification that suffering brings, the tribute of nonviolence. To buttress his argument, he cited "the immortal lines of Shelley," the entire last stanza of *Prometheus Unbound* spoken by Demogorgon now that "Conquest is dragged Captive through the Deep":

> To suffer woes which Hope thinks infinite;
> To forgive wrongs darker than Death or Night;
>   To defy Power which seems Omnipotent;
> To love, and bear; to hope, till Hope creates
> From its own wreck the thing it contemplates
> . . . .
> This is alone Life, Joy, Empire and Victory.   (4.570–74, 578)[15]

The movement through negativity underwritten by the Romantic epoch has flowered in radical form. The contortions of power have turned into textual fictions, words that blossom out of torment, rewriting the very meaning of empire for readers struggling a century later against British imperialism. But there are analogues to be drawn, and points at which the analogues break down, for the contortions of power are still with us, afflicting our reading, and poetic text and colonized territory exist in uneasy tension.

Just as Shelley could not conceive of his protagonist "unsaying his high language, and quailing before his successful and perfidious adversary" (preface, line 133), so the Gandhians who resisted the British in India held firm to their conception of noncooperation. The "high language" of the poetic text, however, was brought low, rendered performative in multiple acts of *satya-*

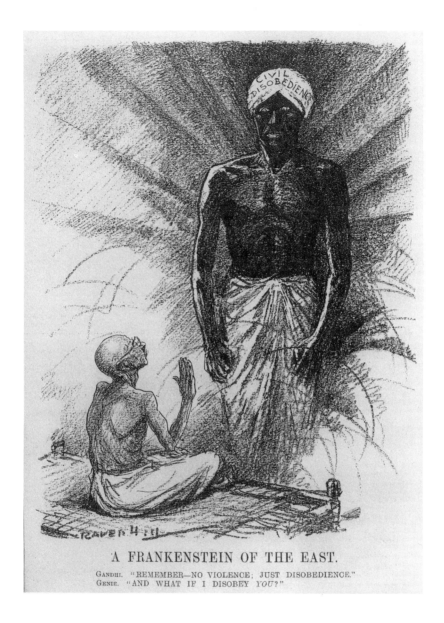

A FRANKENSTEIN OF THE EAST.

GANDHI. "REMEMBER—NO VIOLENCE; JUST DISOBEDIENCE."
GENIE. "AND WHAT IF I DISOBEY *YOU*?"

FIGURE 1   A 1930 *Punch* cartoon: Gandhi facing the monster of decolonization. Cartoon by Leonard Raven-Hill (1867–1943). Reproduced by permission of *Punch*.

graha. But for Gandhi, as for Shelley before him, such symbolic use of the body—textual in Shelley's rendition of Asia, territorial in terms of the recuperation that inspires a nationalist movement—required a shearing away of otherness, and a paradoxical absorption of the feminine into the projections of a masculine desire.

In its March 12, 1930, issue, *Punch* regaled its readers with an image of a massive black male dressed in "Eastern" garb (figure 1). On his turban were printed the words "CIVIL DISOBEDIENCE." Beneath him on a rope bed sat the tiny, bespectacled figure of Gandhi, hand raised as if in supplication. "A FRANKENSTEIN OF THE EAST," read the caption. Beneath, in smaller letters, ran two lines of a brief interchange: "Gandhi. 'Remember—no violence; just disobedience,'" to which this 1930s reworking of Mary Shelley's nameless monster replies, "And what if I disobey *you?*"

An anxious colonialism had found its perfect figuration, displacing onto the East—out of which the shining orientalist conceptions had once emerged—the brutality of power, spilled again into lines that masked gender inequalities. In incipient recognition of the bonds that hold together colonizer and colonized, Mary Shelley's vision of a material being resistant to its male creator's will to power is displaced onto a looming black figure who surges forward to threaten the pale creator Gandhi. The figuration of the body as the site of nonviolent resistance to the aberrations of the imperial will to power is contorted by the grotesque—made visible here by that semicomical phantasm, the monster of decolonization.

Shelley's Humane Concern and the Demise of Apartheid

Alan Weinberg

15

VOTERS BURY APARTHEID
Headline, front page, *Star* (Johannesburg), March 19, 1992

Today we have closed the book of Apartheid. That chapter is over.
F. W. De Klerk's victory speech,
Star, March 19, 1992

He said the result was in principle the farewell to Apartheid, but its real demise
depended on a change in thought patterns and institutions.
Report of Nelson Mandela's comment on the referendum results,
Star, March 19, 1992

GIVEN THAT Shelley, as poet and prophet, was committed to the total liberation of mankind from superimposed law and dogma, it might be assumed that he has much to say concerning a country like South Africa, which has decreed the most repressive racial legislation in the world since the period of fascist government in Europe. Over the years, I have been deeply impressed by the accuracy of Shelley's insights. His understanding, in particular, of the psychological determinants of the power struggle in society is unsurpassed by any writer I have come across, including the renowned analyst of colonial rule, Frantz Fanon. Shelley also anticipates the abhorrence felt toward colonialism in our century, since he regarded the treatment of the negro in the West Indian islands to be "the deepest stain upon civilized man" (*Julian* 7:19). It seems to me that if one were to attempt a validation of Shelley's thought, one could hardly do better than to apply it to the phenomenon of apartheid, South Africa's notorious system of government. Shelley's interpretation of history, as it relates to South Africa, is doubly prophetic: It offers the possibility of a "brighter Hellas" here in the subcontinent of Africa, while acknowledging that, in view of the persistence of evil and ignorance, the great promise of a "new South Africa" may not be fulfilled. In his lyric drama *Hellas*, Shelley foresees both the best and the worst of all possible futures:

> Another Athens shall arise,
>   And to remoter time
> Bequeath, like sunset to the skies,
>   The splendour of its prime,
> And leave, if nought so bright may live,
> All earth can take or Heaven can give.
> . . . .
> O cease! must hate and death return?
>   Cease! must men kill and die?
> Cease! drain not to its dregs the urn
>   Of bitter prophecy.
> The world is weary of the past,
> O might it die or rest at last!   (1084–89, 1096–1101)

Skeptically aware of the mutability of Athenian values in the cycles of history, Shelley calls for the cessation of war and misery even as he suggests that "hate and death return," that "men kill and die." This reluctant admission of the human being's destructive inclinations highlights the inevitability of strife. In South Africa, the process of reform has, in fact, been accompanied by unceasing violence, resulting in massacres of innocent men, women, and children.

Typically, Shelley's political and historical sense is given philosophical weight by reference to the idea of fate or necessity. In "Lines Written among the Euganean Hills," for example, the decline of Venice and Padua is presented within a perspective that accounts for the irrepressible laws of nature. At a crucial moment of reflection, the speaker laments, prophetically,

> Men must reap the things they sow,
> Force from force must ever flow—
> Or worse; but 'tis a bitter woe

> That love or reason cannot change
> The despot's rage, the slave's revenge. (231-35)

As manifested in these lines, the concept of necessity is the index of Shelley's assessment of reality and, for him, a direct pointer to the way things might be ordered, if only we scrupulously observed its workings and respected its power. Necessity cannot be argued away or "moralized," since it is not intrinsically "right" or "wrong" but simply "the way things happen to be." It expresses an impersonal form of strict justice untempered by mercy and unmitigated by extenuating circumstances. The premise upon which the concept of necessity is predicated is stated in the first line quoted above— "Men must reap the things they sow": "must" registers the imperative nature of a chain reaction that binds cause to effect, the actor to the outcome of the action. In accordance with this natural process (highlighted by the familiar imagery of reaping and sowing), human beings do not act with impunity; rather they bring upon themselves, "measure for measure," their own retribution. As the succeeding lines in the above extract indicate, the imposition of will, namely "force," to effect what we desire sets in motion the defense and hostility (force) of the antagonist. The repetition of "must" again emphasizes the operation of necessity. Force grows from force as inevitably and as naturally as a river flows from its source. Thus it is that the "despot's rage" elicits the "slave's revenge." Commenting in *A Philosophical View of Reform* on the uprisings of the peasantry during the Reformation, and of the negro slaves in the West Indian plantations, Shelley states that "power" is "so dear" that "the tyrants themselves neither then, nor now, nor ever, left or leave a path to freedom but through their own blood (*Julian* 7:6). Present, past, and future are scanned in terse and swiftly moving phrases, to highlight the inexorable process of necessity. Displacing a contradictory deity who, in pretence of good, willfully and inconsolably punishes human beings for their obstinate sins, necessity manifests itself in Shelley's writing as the "blind" and neutral power of nature to which events in the real world ought to be referred.

From the standpoint outlined above, it is clear that, for Shelley, the deplorable outcome of the French Revolution owed itself primarily to the intransigence of the aristocracy, which for centuries refused to yield power or privilege to the deprived masses, or to offer them the opportunity for enlightenment:

> The tyrants were, as usual, the aggressors. Then the oppressed, having
> been rendered brutal, ignorant, servile, and bloody by long slavery,

having had the intellectual thirst, excited in them by the progress of civilization, satiated from fountains of literature poisoned by the spirit and the form of monarchy, arose and took a dreadful revenge on their oppressors. (*Julian* 7:13)

Despite the appalling consequences of oppression, it gives some satisfaction to realize that the tyranny of inherited privilege is not everlasting or omnipotent. The aristocracy finally yielded to a power greater than itself, necessity. Instead of recoiling from the havoc the revolution unleashed, Shelley took note of the self-destructiveness of autocratic rule. If, as in the case of France, the despotism of the aristocracy was soon tragically replaced by the despotism of pseudo-Republican rule under Napoleon, this was because the tyranny of the ancien regime had willed only its own eradication, not the eradication of tyranny as such. Ideas of equality, fraternity, and liberty were slogans to people who sought power for themselves. Invariably the oppressed changed roles with the oppressor and the ceaseless struggle in history between the haves and the have-nots was sustained.

This seemingly repetitive cycle, which has the sanction of being determined by necessity itself, constitutes, one might say, the pattern of history. It is testimony to the broad scope of Shelley's argument that his interest in the political events of his time (specifically the liberation movements of the early nineteenth century) was grounded in the recognition of a universal historical process. Although accused, by F. R. Leavis, of having a "weak grasp upon the actual,"[2] Shelley proves to be a poet who unflinchingly faced up to the reality of life and refused to be comforted or appeased by easy rationalizations of the human condition. This sense of reality in Shelley seems to have been innate and to have been strengthened by his love of the Greeks.

As the starting point for his quest for liberation, Shelley acknowledged the impossibility of breaking a cycle that drew strength from extreme opposing forces. In "Lines Written among the Euganean Hills," he laments the inefficacy of either "love or reason" to put an end to the eternal opposition of those entrenched in power and those rendered powerless. "Love" is the quality that unites antagonists in the recognition of our common humanity, whereas "reason" promises to resolve conflict by argument, debate, and negotiation. Once the "despot's rage" or the "slave's revenge" is set in motion, there is little, if anything, to stop either. It was in consequence of the fact that the tyrant will not willingly relinquish power (since he enjoys its privileges) that Shelley turned his attention to the oppressed for some possibility of beneficial change. So long as they remain committed to a mere reversal of fortune, the exploited changing place with the exploiter, there is no hope of a genuine renewal. But if the oppressed were genuinely to liberate themselves from the quest for power and self-aggrandizement, then there would be hope. In *Prometheus Unbound,* Shelley explores the potential for liberation. He depicts the oppressed hero's recognition of the futility of hatred, revenge, and a fixed resistance to tyranny since they merely perpetuate conflict. In that acknowledgment, Prometheus breaks the polarity between himself and Jupiter and thus becomes the determiner of his own being, and his own liberation. He effectively negates the power of the oppressor, awesome as it is, and revitalizes the energies trapped by rigid oppositions. He brings into being, albeit with the aid of his consort Asia, a world free from externalized control, a world in which love can flourish and, indeed, rule as the inward principle of life in harmony with all the elements. Having been rendered redundant and insubstantial, Jupiter, the fabricated tyrant of human existence, is brought down and engulfed by Demogorgon, the primal power that activates the law of necessity (now under the guidance of love and not hate).

The hope embodied in the "unbinding" of Prometheus ("unbound," by its reference to "bondage," dramatizes the emancipation of mind and body from slavery) may be applied to the present situation in South Africa.[3] This country, in many respects, conforms to the picture of historical necessity enacted in the French Revolution, and which threatened to repeat itself in the England of Shelley's time. As was the case in France, South Africa has a minority privileged class that has ruled despotically over a deprived and, in many respects, destitute majority. Civil strife—in particular, government repression and the imminence of bloody insurrection—has characterized the country's history over the last forty years. As in Regency England, the liberals have called for reform, while the government and its white electorate, fearful of revolution, have taken refuge behind a barrage of security legislation. The latter have paid lip service to ideas of democracy while simultaneously strengthening or condoning state repression of dissident forces. Yet there are signs that the process of liberation that Shelley imagined might still become practicable in South Africa. The extreme polarization of minority government and the revolutionaries in exile has been broken, owing to the initial willingness of the exiles to pursue peaceful change when finally the situation seemed desperate. They were helped in this regard by a small band of rebels and philanthropists who, in Shelleyan style, led the way to change.[4] Both the rulers and most of the revolutionaries have officially renounced violence in favor of negotiation.

If the time has not yet come in South Africa for the triumph of "love" (and where on earth has it triumphed?), it remains to be said that, notwithstanding the persistence of apartheid in the minds of a good percentage of whites—and that persistence is in itself ominous—there is hope that reason might prevail. Not the least indication of optimism is the resounding victory of those in favor of reform in the national white referendum on March 17, 1992. This vote does not necessarily represent a complete rejection of apartheid: It does, however, reflect the admission of white South Africans that there is no real choice but to reform. The setting of a date for the first free elections in 1994 commits the white population to majority rule and a just dispensation.

This change has no precedent in South Africa. Over the last three hundred years, since the time when South Africa was colonized by the Dutch in 1652, the white settlers made little attempt to meet the demands of the indigenous peoples. War after war was fought to settle disputes over land, while gradually the blacks were deprived of almost everything they could call their own. Even their own sense of personal dignity was taken from them. Finally, in 1948, the system of apartheid was imposed on the entire population. From that moment onward, the polarization of black and white intensified. Increasingly the government resorted to repression, finally banning black opposition in 1963 and forcing many blacks to seek exile or asylum and to relinquish a policy of nonviolence that had characterized the African nationalist movement (as embodied in the ANC) since its inception in 1912.

In South Africa, the oppressor is usually identified with the Afrikaner and with the policy of apartheid. It is the Afrikaner who invented draconian laws to prevent the black South African from gaining any access to the power of the whites. However, it must be understood that the Afrikaner is the historical agent of a form of despotism already inherent in colonial rule itself.[5] This conception of colonialism follows the well-known position of Frantz Fanon in *The Wretched of the Earth*[6] (strongly endorsed by Jean Paul Sartre in the preface to that book). It is a position also shared by critics of apartheid, who, like Shelley, do not advocate Fanon's philosophy of violence. In J. M. Coetzee's view, the disparaging attitude of Europeans toward the Hottentot suggests that the white colonialist found it impossible to identify himself with the indigenous peoples of Southern Africa.[7] Apartheid is frequently linked to the values of Western civilization. On this point, Njabulo Ndebele writes that "for the majority of the oppressed, the experience of western civilization has largely been the experience of poverty, malnutrition, low wages, mine accidents, police raids, selective justice and a variety of other similar negations."[8]

A colonialist—one who partakes of the benefits of colonial rule—is inherently committed to the maintenance of his own supremacy, even if he pretends to believe in democratic values. This is the contradiction facing every white South African (and memorably recorded in Coetzee's novel *Waiting for the Barbarians*). The British in South Africa have, in large measure, been willing to exploit the advantages of white status while outwardly condemning the severities of racial discrimination. Interpreting Luke 4:18 in his *Essay on Christianity,* Shelley writes that because they were "too mean-spirited & too feeble in resolve to attempt the conquest of their own evil passions, and of the difficulties of the material world, men sought dominion over their fellow-men as an easy method to gain that apparent majesty and power which the instinct of their nature requires" (*Julian* 6:244). In Shelley's view, the inherent grandeur of the human species is displaced by the greed for an outward show of power and prestige. From this broad perspective, colonial rule, which by its very nature imposes itself on the host country, unjustly legitimizes the false distinctions already manifest in the home country. It is a rigidification of the hierarchical structures inherited from the past. If the impoverished laborer was regarded at home as an inferior human species, it was not difficult to relegate the negro to the status of primate and thus justify every form of ill treatment on that assumption. (The Nazis of course applied the same logic to the Jews.)[9]

Colonization is performed by those who, for the most part, did not originally belong to the privileged classes, but who act on their behalf, thus assuming their role. The dominion of aristocracy is replaced by that of the "merchant and the bureaucrat." Shelley calls this class of persons "a new aristocracy. . . . in whose employment there is nothing to exercise, even to their distortion, the more majestic faculties of the soul" (*Julian* 7:28). We are all settlers, writes Sartre to his fellow modern Europeans: "we must face that unexpected revelation, the strip-tease of our humanism. There you can see it, quite naked, and it's not a pretty sight."[10]

Possessed of superior force, the colonizers gradually assumed control over the native inhabitants. As in the United States and Australia, the aborigines (in this case the Bushmen and Hottentots), whose cultural sophistication now provokes the astonishment of social anthropologists, were almost completely exterminated.[11] Given the increasing insecurity of the whites, as their dependency on black labor grew, and as the numbers of the black population multiplied in the squalid townships adjoining the cities, it comes as little surprise that, eventually, the policy of apartheid crystallized. The more threatening a situation is, the more likely it is that defensive structures will be set up to forestall it. The dominion already enjoyed by the settlers was entrenched in a myriad of laws that reified the inferiority of the blacks. In South Africa, apartheid has been the justification for every kind of oppression. The irony is that an oppressor immediately loses his claim to superiority by succumbing to force, hatred, and insult to retain power.

It is paradoxical that the proponents of forced racial segregation (apartheid) have been avid churchgoers and dedicated to the Calvinist faith. Shelley's insight into the nature of institutionalized religion explains this phenomenon. The poet insisted that the authoritarian structure of the church and its theology flatly contradicts the humanist teachings of its celebrated founder: It confirms the inequalities in social life and justifies the maltreatment of those thought to be incurably pagan. In South Africa the church reinforced the racially based class system. The blacks were essentially heathen even if they were converted to the faith. They were barred from worship in the same church with their fellow Christians. The advocates of apartheid were, for a long time, successful in their application of its tenets because their society is fundamentally authoritarian. The individual is not expected to think for him- (or her-) self; rather he or she is expected to follow the edicts, customs, and ideologies established by parents and the elders and leaders of the community. They, in turn, derive their status from God, who is perceived as a figure of supreme authority. His law is fixed and definite and his decisions unrelenting.

The god so worshipped, though called Jesus Christ, has more in common with the autocratic and legalistic deity of Deuteronomy and Leviticus than the compassionate redeemer represented in the Gospels. Such a god, in Shelley's view, is a demon. Despotic rulers are not unaccustomed to citing scripture in their defense, because those chosen texts reflect a primitive authoritarian concept of the deity that (ironically) was meant to be superseded by the Christian theology. It was even possible for the architects of apartheid to identify the *trekboers* with the harassed Israelites of Exodus, though the former were escaping (so they thought) the influence of the black tribes and emancipated slaves and British, whereas the latter wandered out of slavery and into the desert for forty years. In *The Cenci*, the Count tyrannizes his family by enforcing the authority of the father who replicates, in the family, the paternalism of God the Father and the church hierarchy. Though the drama depicts a Catholic society, Shelley writes in *A Philosophical View of Reform* that, following the Reformation, religious practice "subsisted under all its forms . . . in the shape of intolerant and oppressive hierarchies" (*Julian* 7:7–8). It is this system that was imported to South Africa by the Dutch immigrants.

In *Prometheus Unbound,* the figure of Jupiter is an all-embracing conception of authoritarian rule. He is the demonized God of institutional life, misappropriating the power of necessity and torturing the creative spirit—imaged by the figure of Prometheus in chains. His rule is described, in another context in *Laon and Cythna,* as constituting "Faith, and Folly, Custom, and Hell, and mortal Melancholy" (*Laon and Cythna, OSA* 5.2185–86). This notably male emanation is not content to lord it over the minds of men and women. He promises rewards and privileges for submission to his authority. (In the South African context this has been called a "golden handshake": a handsome pension granted to placate a dignitary or civil servant who has embarrassed the governing forces and lost his post.) Failure to comply with Jupiter is answered by the menacing Furies, who, as agents of state oppression, terrorize the liberal Promethean spirit by mocking the Titan's efforts to serve humanity. Since they encourage false hope, prophets and martyrs have apparently made worse the lot of mankind. It is the threat of despair, and a warning to abide by the law and rigid authority. Religion, as represented by Jupiter, is used, paradoxically, to justify the failures and "sins" of mankind, and to secure the power of those whose principal motive is self-interest. In South Africa, the call to patriotism has exonerated every evil: It has been equated with a blind worship of the white, and more specifically Afrikaner, fatherland, and the exclusive service of the *volk*. The church has—up until very recently—unfailingly promoted the cult of the state. Nationalism in this guise is really an egotistical sectarian religion and is diametrically opposite to that quality of "disinterestedness" that, for Shelley, characterizes virtue (*Julian* 5:263) and that he identifies with the morality of Jesus and of Socrates.

Like Blake's Urizen, Jupiter assumes an air of moral rectitude, declaiming against man's obdurate spirit and lack of obedience:

>   alone
> The soul of man, like unextinguished fire,
> Yet burns towards Heaven with fierce reproach and doubt
> And lamentation and reluctant prayer,

Hurling up insurrection, which might make
Our antique empire insecure, though built
On eldest faith, and Hell's coeval, fear.   (3.1.4–10)

His punitive, prohibitive laws, which establish a censoring code to secure his empire, do all they can to repress the creative and rebellious instinct—even if, as Jupiter seems to acknowledge, they never quite succeed. Like the Puritans in Elizabethan England, the proponents of apartheid have been intimidated by a free, questioning press and by the freedom of artistic expression. The list of banned works has been portentous.[12] (People were banned from sight as readily as books.)

   Jupiter is the principle of nonbeing and is thus the enemy of life and the creative arts. Those who share in his rule gradually assume a severity usually associated with death. The stern aspect of white governmental figures in the postwar period was the loveless emblem of apartheid. Likewise, those on the receiving end of Jupiter's edicts have been robbed of their vitality and their sense of worth. Frantz Fanon has drawn attention to the devastating effects of colonialism on both the white and the black: "The disaster and the inhumanity of the white man lie in the fact that somewhere he has killed man."[13] Shelley, in his last work, makes a similar point with reference to those who become captive to the deathly figure that parades as life:

From every form the beauty slowly waned,

From every firmest limb and fairest face
The strength and freshness fell like dust, and left
The action and the shape without the grace

Of life.   ("The Triumph of Life," lines 519–23)

The loss of beauty corresponds to Shelley's depiction of the "foul shapes" that assume "many a name and many a form" and that he says, in *Prometheus Unbound*, "Were Jupiter, the tyrant of the world" (3.4.180–81, 183). The hearts of those who serve this demon are inevitably "broken by long hope" (185).

   If, under these conditions, what is called "life" is but "a painted veil," concealing and distorting reality, how is the "loathsome mask" of Jupiter to be "torn aside" (3.4.190–93)? How, in the case of South Africa, does the Promethean Age return and the reign of Jupiter end? This is a vexed question because Jupiter can hold sway even when the offensive laws that prohibit freedom of thought and movement are abolished. Modern Western democracies are still caught up in hierarchical and bureaucratic systems, and the worship of technology—as Shelley foresaw in *A Defence of Poetry*—increasingly threatens to inhibit the creative impulse, the very impulse that, he points out, inspired invention in the first place (502). Even racial prejudice is far from dead in the advanced countries, and their inhabitants are just as ready to conform to authority and to trends as they ever were. In South Africa, all the laws that have unjustly discriminated between white and black and forcefully kept them from associating with each other have been abrogated. This in itself has been, for some, an almost miraculous achievement. In the cities blacks are treated with more dignity than before, but the apartheid mentality is firmly in place and the psychological effects of apartheid have been devastating, depriving the majority of people of their self-esteem and stimulating violence and crime.[14] Writing in his *Philosophical View of Reform,* Shelley claims that the

> strongest argument, perhaps, for the necessity of Reform, is the inoperative and unconscious abjectness to which the purposes of a considerable mass of the people are reduced. They neither know nor care. . . . Unless the cause which renders them passive subjects instead of active citizens be removed, they will sink with accelerated gradations into that barbaric and unnatural civilization which destroys all the differences among men. (*Julian* 7:49–50)

The call for liberation is evoked by the very situation that has suppressed it. Shelley strongly advocated political reform in England at a time when it was undergoing a transition similar to that taking place in South Africa. He recognized that given the immense dissatisfaction of the majority of the English, the country could face either anarchy or despotism. His aim, in his writings, was to chart his course between the Scylla of the one and the Charybdis of the other (*A Defence of Poetry,* 501), always in the hope that society would learn to free itself from a dependence on legislative control.

Knowing that those in power would inevitably resist change, in *A Philosophical View of Reform* he encouraged civil disobedience and called for nonviolent protest at every level to ensure that the oppressors would "concede some limited portion of the rights of the people, and disgorge some morsels of their undigested prey." It is at this point that negotiation would begin. To make certain that reform, when it did come, might not be bloody and destroy the people's cause, Shelley advocated a policy of gradualism that is anything but revolutionary:

> It is better that we gain what we demand by a process of negotiation which would occupy twenty years, than that by communicating a sudden shock to the interests of those who are the depositories and dependents of power we should incur the calamity which their revenge might inflict upon us by giving the signal of civil war. (*Julian* 7:52)

In some measure the liberation process in South Africa, since the unbanning of left-wing political organizations in 1990, has run along lines similar to those Shelley recommends. The oppressors have indeed "disgorged some morsels" and seem to have reformed themselves in the process (as if conceding power were rewarded by a certain moral "feedback"). In reality, reform for the authorities is largely a matter of political expediency, since a full and honest recantation has never been attempted. Moreover, the white rulers, once so hostile to democratic principles, are now keen to promote them in order to protect their own interests and influence future policy. Many of the oppressed have shown considerable powers of endurance, given their demoralization, penury, and precarious existence. But, as the promise of a new South Africa begins to emerge, it is increasingly clear that the Shelleyan perspective is much broader than that of certain of the country's political leaders, intent as usual on securing a power base and on winning party support—in extreme instances, at the cost of fomenting further hostilities. As regards a new democratic order, Shelley did not believe that equality could ever be safeguarded institutionally, or be successfully imposed on the nation. In the commentary on Luke 4:18 in the "Essay on Christianity," he writes that the artificial "distinctions of property and power" will not be "abolished without substituting something equivalent in mischief to them, until all mankind shall acknowledge an entire community of rights" (*Julian* 6:245–46). It is on this account that the institution of a new democratic constitution in South Africa, however welcome, is no guarantee that genuine equality will prevail. The accent, in Shelley's thinking, is on the liberalization of the public mind from the burdens of the past and the outmoded ideologies that distort reality. This means that the psychology of apartheid—insofar as it has affected the mentality of all South Africans—has to be transcended if political reform is to succeed.

Because prejudices are deeply ingrained in the human psyche, it is not possible to be entirely optimistic about the future of South Africa. One cannot expect people who regard each other with deep suspicion, if not enmity, and who have an inherited sense of difference, suddenly to embrace each other across the racial divide. Not only, according to Fanon, do blacks in a colonial situation regard themselves as inferior to whites (having slavishly accepted the definition imposed upon them by their conquerors) but, in addition, whites have a deeply embedded cultural prejudice against the color black, which is associated with ugliness, ignorance, and even the devil himself.[15] There are also fierce divisions within the black and white communities that cause strife. Yet mutual love, together with a recognition of the autonomy and inviolability of each human being, constitutes the Shelleyan program for "universal benevolence" that, following the law of necessity, "should supersede the regulations of precedent and prescription, before these regulations can safely be abolished" (*Julian* 6:249). The communal practice of the early Christians did not work because "precedent and habit" soon "resumed their empire" (*Julian* 6:251). In "The Triumph of Life," Shelley focuses with even greater intensity on the subjection of mankind to mental conditioning. He seems to recognize the extreme difficulty of starting anew, of "destroy[ing] error, and the roots of error," of "leav[ing] . . . a vacancy," so "reduc[ing] the mind to that freedom in which it would have acted, but for the misuse of words and signs, the instruments of its own creation" ("On Life," 477).

If Shelley was himself distressed by the lack of human progress, it is not surprising that South Africans, contemplating life in a fevered climate of violence and intolerance, have been inclined to despair about the future. The positive results of the referendum, and the slow but significant progress in multiparty negotiations, have been undermined by factional fighting, extremist anarchy, and the perpetual threat of civil war by marginalized and desperate reactionary groups. Yet there is a sense in which lack of hope is self-indulgent and also counterproductive. It closes the door on the future and encourages a bitter end. The deepest inclination of Shelley's mind was in the opposite direction. This is revealed in a very touching manner in a letter to Maria Gisborne, written in October 1819, in the aftermath of the Peterloo massacre:

> Let us believe in a kind of optimism in which we are own gods. . . . it is best that we should think all this for the best even though it be not, because Hope, as Coleridge says is a solemn duty which we owe alike to ourselves & to the world. (*PBSL* 2:125)

The words of Creina Alcock in Rian Malan's *My Traitor's Heart* may serve as a South African's response to Shelley's philosophy of hope:

> I realized that love, even if it ends in defeat, gives you a kind of honor; but without love, you have no honor at all. I think that is what I had misunderstood all my life. Love is to enable you to transcend defeat. . . .
>
> To live anywhere in the world, you must know how to live in Africa. The only thing you can do is love, because it is the only thing that leaves light inside you, instead of the total, obliterating darkness.[16]

Shelley's Satire of Succession and Brecht's Anatomy of Regression: "The Mask of Anarchy" and *Der anachronistische Zug oder Freiheit und Democracy*

Steven E. Jones

16

IN 1947 BERTOLT BRECHT produced a ballad in imitation of Shelley's "The Mask of Anarchy," *Der anachronistische Zug oder Freiheit und Democracy.*[1] This imitation has a special value for students of Shelley: Because it was written by one of the twentieth century's most trenchant satirists, it can help us to see what is satiric in Shelley's ballad. In this chapter I use Brecht to read Shelley, to look briefly at the satiric strategies of "The Mask" in light of Brecht's very different satiric techniques in *Freiheit und Democracy.* But I also use Shelley to read Brecht, to illuminate the rhetoric and aims of the modern ballad from the perspective of Romantic satire. The historical gap separating England in 1819 from Germany in 1947 can provide critics of Shelley in the 1990s with a useful differential, a kind of distancing from the work of both poets. In this case, the comparison starts by viewing both as satirists. Brecht's satire attacks the pretensions to progress in postwar Germany as covering a kind of ideological black market, the selling of one worn-out system as the new world order. "The Mask of Anarchy" is a satire of succession that attempts to figure the people's intervention in the otherwise continuous descent of power. Whereas Shelley hopes for change through a radically redrawn succession, Brecht mocks the "new" as a mask for reaccession. The juxtaposition highlights the power and the limits of both satiric works.

We begin in Manchester, early August 1819, with the now-famous call for a meeting on parliamentary reform and (so the announcement in the *Manchester Observer* read), "to consider the propriety of the 'Unrepresented Inhabitants of Manchester' electing a Person to represent them in Parliament" (July 31, 1819). This proposal led to contingency plans for dispersing any such meeting, for fear it would turn into an assembly for electing illegal legislators, out-of-doors representatives.[2] The ultimate result, as is well known, was the Peterloo Massacre of August 16. As a campaigner for reform, and the son of an M.P. who was groomed for a career in Parliament, Shelley well understood that the movement was fundamentally about the question of representation. His immediate response to the violence at Peterloo was to write "The Mask of Anarchy," which openly calls for another meeting like the one just dispersed, a poem in which Shelley aims to "represent"—to stand in the place of and to speak for—the people.[3] Shelley seeks to act as an exiled, out-of-doors representative, to figure the predicament of the people in a way that will move them to intervene in events.

After its opening stanza, Shelley's ballad shifts to a "masque" or procession of Anarchy, a parade of disguised "Destructions" drawn from the composite allegorical tradition that includes everything from the Dance of Death to the political cartoons of Gillray and Cruikshank. Shelley implies ironically that Murder, Fraud, and Hypocrisy wear the masks of actual politicians— Castlereagh, Eldon, and Sidmouth—and that the underlying reality in each case is abstract evil, the living persons mere façades. They are led by Anarchy, a royal and sacred figure ("God and King and Law") at the center of the triumphal progress. This is a kind of antimasque run amok, as Stuart Curran has suggested, a collection of antithetical caricatures set in motion only in order to be overturned.[4]

"The Mask of Anarchy" aims to participate in a broad reformist discourse, one that gathers a medley of various popular conventions and forms, including—to name one especially relevant to a comparison with Brecht— theatrical pantomime. The English pantomime, at its peak in Shelley's day (the era of the famous clown Grimaldi), had inherited from the commedia dell'arte a two-part structure, with an abrupt shift from an opening allegory or fable to a contrasting raucous harlequinade.[5] This turn hinges upon a brief "transformation scene," in which a luminous "benevolent agent," usually an idealized feminine figure, strips away the characters' costumes and removes cartoonlike papier mâché masks (or "big heads") to reveal allegorical type-characters: Harlequin, Pantaloon, or Columbine.

Shelley's ballad turns on a "transformation scene" as well, an unmasking in which the "maid" Hope and a sublime "Shape" effect the violent (self-)destruction of the masque, and a transition to the famous song exhorting the men of England to "Rise like lions." Structurally, "The Mask of Anarchy" can be said to divide (though asymmetrically) into two major parts: the first part, twenty-one stanzas of the satiric masquerade, then, after a brief transition scene, the second part, fifty-five stanzas of exhortation.[6] The transition consists of fifteen stanzas of allegory—the poem's own dramatic transformation scene. Emerging from this scene, Hope walks "ankle-deep in blood," Anarchy lies dead, and his horse grinds "to dust" the rest of the procession. The satirical mode of the first part gives way to the exhortative mode of the final part, but only though a purgative representation of figurative violence. This may be Shelley's attempt to counter, rather than merely imitate, the real violence just experienced in Manchester, but its effects are ambivalent. Precisely what happens during the poem's transition is difficult to say; the transformation scene takes place as it were through a veil, or a theatrical scrim.

When Brecht came to imitate "The Mask of Anarchy" in 1947, he simply skipped the opening frame stanza, and dropped both the concluding exhortation and the apocalyptic transformation scene. His stripped-down ballad imitates only what he once translated as "*Der Maskenzug*"—the masque-procession proper; that is, it imitates the grotesquely satirical portion of Shelley's poem. Brecht opens with an image of tentative hope for change: "Frühling wurd's in deutschem Land. / über Asch und Trümmerwand" (Spring returned to Germany. / In the ruins you could see / Early green birch buds unfold / Graceful, tentative and bold.)[7] But this turns out to be a false frame for the rest of the poem, which actually depicts the grotesqueries of a Germany in ruins through imagery that could have come from a George Grosz cartoon of the 1920s (the last time Brecht was in Germany). The collapsed state is the site of a grisly parade celebrating the return of freedom and democracy. Those celebrating, however, are mostly reconstructed Nazis or collaborationists. Swastikas have been clumsily altered to resemble crosses and jackboots are still visible under new clothes. In late 1946 Brecht reportedly expressed tentative optimism about the future of Germany.[8] But the ballad, written less than a year later, shows only the slightest hint of this: It pictures "voters" of every stripe joining the column of the absurd. Passing through Munich, the marchers meet at Nazi headquarters six allegorical shades: Oppression, Plague, Fraud,

Stupidity, Murder, and Robbery (two of which marched through Shelley's ballad, as well):

> In six cars those six assorted
> Party members are transported
> While the crowd shouts: Now we'll see
> Freedom and Democracy.　　　　　　(lines 121–24, *Poems,* 413)

Brecht's poem ends not with a rousing popular song but with a chorus of rats, who crawl out of the rubble to join the pied-piper procession, squeaking "Freedom and Democracy!" It has been said that Brecht inverts Shelley's structure,[9] but it is probably more accurate to say that he truncates it—lopping off everything but the allegorical cartoon, and letting that speak ironically for itself.

Brecht's divergences from Shelley are not surprising, but calling attention to them highlights the cynicism and exhaustion of the modern satire, its deliberate resistance to effects of pathos and empathy in the wake of the war, its squeamish loss of faith in Romantic solutions of imagination, hope, and apocalypse. From Shelley's side, the comparison also serves to highlight what is most characteristic about "The Mask of Anarchy": its careful structure, the formal medley of satire and exhortation, and its emotional appeal to the people. Shelley's satire is meant to promote a succession of changing conceptual and material "realities"—the displacement of one by another. Brecht's is meant only to destabilize the current myth of an *achieved* succession, the triumph of "freedom" in only one (uncontested) sense of the term. But Brecht's demystification begins with a satiric technique also present in Shelley's opening masque: the highly formal, stylized conventions of caricature, which work by estranging the reader from its exaggerated targets. In this case the target is a tendentiously capitalist restoration.

Brecht's friend Walter Benjamin well understood the fundamentally satiric nature of his work, how it acts as a corrosive agent for exposing the underbelly of the status quo. In these terms, Benjamin argued, Brecht can be seen as a satirist in the tradition of Marx: "Marx, who was the first to undertake to bring back the relations between people from their debasement and obfuscation in capitalist economics into the light of criticism, became in so doing a teacher of satire, who was not far from being a master of it. Brecht was his pupil."[10] These remarks were made in the context of the famous controversy over "socialist realism," beginning in the late 1930s with a debate between Brecht and Georg Lukács over Brecht's alleged formalism.[11]

Brecht defended himself by calling on the example of Shelley—an effective rhetorical move, since Shelley had the political respect of Brecht's circle despite his Romantic "symbolism." In one 1938 essay, Brecht quotes at length from "The Mask of Anarchy" (in English with his own German translation), in order to argue that true realism does not rule out the use of allegory or symbol, because realism is not a matter of mimesis but of critical analysis.[12] To combat reification, Brecht argues, formal discontinuities and effects—even symbolism—might prove necessary. The point is to call attention to one's own formal representations, in keeping with his best-known dramatic theory: *Verfremdung,* or the "alienation" (or "estrangement") effect. The purpose of his kind of drama, according to Brecht, was to place the audience at a critical distance from the familiar structures of society through the use of stylized gestures and forms, parable, allegory, the breaking of dramatic frames, and—significantly in the present context—masks, like those of traditional Japanese theater or the commedia dell'arte. The ultimate effect should be liberation from dominant ideological structures, a kind of defamiliarization. As Brecht put it elsewhere, "To estrange is to historicize, that is, to consider people and events as historically conditioned and transitory."[13]

To a surprising degree, this debate focused on questions of genre. Brecht accused the realists of privileging the nineteenth-century novel, the mirror of society, and of ignoring what he saw as the "realistic" function of work by writers such as Cervantes, Swift, Grimmelshausen, and Voltaire—tellingly, all satirical writers.[14] It is in this context of satirical realism that he situates "The Mask of Anarchy"; for all its symbolism, he argues, the poem is actually quite "concrete" in its representations of freedom. *True* "realism," in Brecht's terms, works to expose the "causal nexus" (*Kausalkomplex*) of social relations, "to unmask the dominant viewpoint as the viewpoint of those in power"[15]—and Brecht astutely realized that this is one place where his theory overlapped with Shelley's. Benjamin reads Brecht as a realistic satirist; Brecht reads Shelley as a realist (and thus, in effect, a satirist); I take this cue to read Shelley as a satirist whose satire is aimed at exposing the causal nexus of reified social relations—though under the necessity of a historical context very different from Brecht's.

In September 1947, Brecht (then living in California) was called before the House Committee on Un-American Activities. He appeared on October 30 and left the country shortly thereafter; but, unable to enter the West German Zone, he was forced to settle temporarily in Zurich, returning to Berlin only in October 1948.[16] *Freiheit und Democracy* was published in the journal *Ost und West* that same month, but according to Brecht's *Arbeits-journal,* it had been written back in America, as early as March 1947.[17] The news Brecht received from Berlin at the time was bleak: Both sides of the partitioned city were suffering amidst the ruins. But the Western powers were working to rebuild capitalism, initiating "the economic miracle" with an influx of American dollars.[18] It is easy to see how, from Brecht's perspective, this must have seemed a regressive restoration of decadent capitalism. His ballad begins with the impossibility of even representing the future, as signaled by the cliché slogan that passes for a refrain.

Brecht's antinostalgia would seem in direct opposition to Shelley's rhetoric, which appeals to "The old laws of England" (line 331) to protect the inherited rights of her "sons." But like other nineteenth-century reformers, Shelley is actually attempting to exploit constitutional and traditional sanctions for the cause of radical change. By alluding to "The old laws," he is building on the legal doctrine of representation (the right of anyone—an heir, say—to stand in the place of another) to question the concept and ground of the succession itself. Legal theories of representation supported the idea of orderly succession, especially during the French Revolution and the Regency, when the issues of *royal* succession and popular representation came together in the arena of political conflict.[19]

Shelley's satire would enter this arena by calling on the people to intervene in history and redraft the charter (or redraw the stemma), suggesting that they have the sovereign right to represent themselves, to stand in the (usurped) place of the present rulers—starting with members of Parliament. This focus on the idea of succession as a site of contested meaning inevitably places a powerful rhetorical burden on the ballad's central symbol: the amorphous and ethereal "Shape," a figure of figuration or a symbol of the power of the mind to think by way of figurative representation itself:

> As flowers beneath May's footsteps waken
> As stars from Night's loose hair are shaken
> As waves arise when loud winds call
> Thoughts sprung where'er that step did fall.   (lines 122–25)

The most effective argument of "The Mask of Anarchy" takes place at the level of its own structure of transforming figures, a succession of images meant to prompt a rethinking of change and the intervention required to enact it. But Shelley was aware of the conflicts between continuity and change inherent in his chosen figure of succession. On the inside cover of one notebook he wrote, "the spring rebels not against winter but it succeeds it."[20]

When delicate spring tentatively returns to Germany in Brecht's ballad, it is primarily to mock, through *negative* correspondence, the touted rebirth in the social realm. Brecht's satire can be seen as a first step in the process of "estranging" his audience from a coercive reality. Shelley would say that the satiric mode in itself was unlikely to lead to liberation; his rhetorical dialectic culminates in exhortation, a deliberative mode (leading to action).

Shelley's medley, with its focus on representation and the semiotics of politics, argues a point that Brecht (embroiled as he was in theoretical debates) might well have found appealing: that to change the world, the point is, one must interpret it. But this is so much a part of many of our own Romantic assumptions (or wishes) about interpretation and the world that we scarcely notice it in Shelley. What is stranger, and potentially more unsettling for us, is Shelley's apparent faith in the power of poetic representation to induce radical reinterpretation.

Brecht was writing from within a particularly austere political context, and he might understandably have recoiled from certain features of "The Mask of Anarchy," perhaps most of all from its call on the people to bring about apocalyptic change through a putatively nonviolent assembly. For many readers of Shelley's poem that call still carries the disturbing hint of collective self-sacrifice. It is understandable that Brecht should swerve away from Shelley's sublime and violent transformation scene, with its pools of blood and its "Shape arrayed in mail" (line 110). These self-imposed ironic limitations of his imitation speak to our own need to temper and contextualize Shelley's Romanticism in the perspective of intervening history.

This provisional comparison is only intended to demonstrate that we cannot escape the necessity of reading Shelley through Brecht, or through the modern historical perspective of which Brecht is merely one representative. "The Mask of Anarchy" appears, from the vantage of the late twentieth century, to be a very strange document of sublime aspiration, the embodiment of a powerful desire and an ambivalent hope for imaginative transformation of minds—and reality. In this way it raises questions about Brecht's relative world-weariness and cynicism. But in the end we cannot help but take seriously, from the vantage point of our own historical moment, Brecht's skepticism toward Romantic transformation, and all myths of renewed continuity and succession—even when they seem to be brought about through interventions by the people.

Since November 1989 it has become increasingly clear that the term *reunification* oversimplifies what continues to be a complicated and unpredictable process, in Germany and in Europe as a whole. In May 1990 the graves of Brecht and his companion Helene Weigel were painted with anti-Semitic slogans, only one of a series of neofascist, nationalist, or xenophobic acts that have continued to trouble Germany and other countries (including the United States) in recent years. In 1990, George Steiner commented on the euphoric celebrations of reunification at the Berlin Wall: "Nothing in this circus would have surprised Bert Brecht."[21] I would add: The arena was ripe for Brecht's kind of skeptical satire. These days we would do well to read our Shelley alongside Brecht—who learned to satirize from both Marx and Shelley—because the historical differentials thus brought to light may call into question any supposedly triumphal and completed succession, especially one that would claim to mark the end of history rather than another eddy in its complex, conflictual process.

Shelley's "Socialism" Revisited

Horst Höhne

17

THE TITLE of this chapter is, of course, meant to be provocative. The word *socialism* had to be put in quotation marks; Shelley certainly never used the term or touched upon its implications, and nobody now could call him a socialist according to the modern definition of the word even in its broadest connotation. Yet what I first thought of when trying to find a topic relating to the general subject of the poet as legislator was even more daring: something like "Shelley's Responsibility for the Failure of Socialism" or "The Failure of Would-Be Socialists to Listen to Shelley." One could also have asked, "Was socialism altogether a romantic idea bound to come to nothing in the real world?" Or, more seriously, "Is there something in Shelley's poetry and prose worth revisiting in political terms after the triumphant victory of the market society over several generations of an endeavor to build an alternative society that turned out to be the very opposite of what had seemed to be a feasible idea?"

Socialism is now a dirty word in my nation, and the names of Marx and Engels have been or are being speedily wiped out in the cities and towns of their home country. Along with this, there is a state of mental lethargy and despair among innumerable scholars, writers, and artists in the so-called Neue Deutsche Länder that reminds one of Shelley's description in the preface to *The Revolt of Islam* of the situation of writers in England after the

Napoleonic Wars: "gloom and misanthropy have become the characteristics of the age in which we live, the solace of a disappointment that unconsciously finds relief only in the wilful exaggeration of its own despair." I hasten to add that the historical parallel implied in the quotation is far from exact, for a careful analysis of the contemporary scene in the still-different parts of the united Germany—and, for that matter, the countries of eastern Europe—would produce more differentiated results. Yet as a vague feeling it holds a most peculiar element of truth. However, this is not the topic I have in mind.

As we all know, Shelley's politics in his reform poetry as well as in what he called the "beautiful idealism[s] of moral excellence" of his more sublime poems went far beyond liberal reformism, and, as many scholars have shown, there is no basic contradiction between both kinds of verse. I would even assert that it is particularly in his highest achievements in poetic excellence that he is the most radical in the true sense of the word, more so than in his prose pamphlets, where he tends to be impeded by the shortcomings of abstract language (as William Keach has shown in his remarkable book on *Shelley's Style*[1]), and where he is often overcautious and circumspect for political reasons. When, in the third act of *Prometheus Unbound*, he has the Spirit of the Hour sum up the results of the Titan's liberation, we meet with a valid definition of utopian man/woman and society in poetic terms:

> The painted veil, by those who were, called life,
> Which mimicked, as with colours idly spread,
> All men believed and hoped, is torn aside—
> The loathsome mask has fallen, the man remains
> Sceptreless, free, uncircumscribed—but man:
> Equal, unclassed, tribeless and nationless,
> Exempt from awe, worship, degree,—the King
> Over himself; just, gentle, wise—but man:
> Passionless? no—yet free from guilt or pain
> Which were, for his will made, or suffered them,
> Nor yet exempt, though ruling them like slaves,
> From chance and death and mutability,
> The clogs of that which else might oversoar
> The loftiest star of unascended Heaven
> Pinnacled dim in the intense inane.   (3.4.190–204)

If this concept of social uptopia is interpreted to be merely mental liberation, it is complemented by the profoundly earthly, material structure of the lyrical drama in which Prometheus's origin, home, and responsibility are with the forces of the real world, his mother earth, his brethren, and the subterranean power of Demogorgon, in community with the figurations of the cosmos. Of course, Shelley's social alignment with the working people of England is made explicit by his reform poetry and prose.

At a time when the first vague ideas of socialism in England had started growing, it was not unusual that the working-class movements of Shelley's age and the liberal and radical intellectuals of succeeding generations would appropriate his work as the expression and confirmation of their own theories. We know of his high rank among the Chartists and the Owenite socialists, by whom Shelley's *Queen Mab* was seen as something of a bible, as Thomas Medwin, his cousin and former classmate, reported. Newman Ivy White, reflecting on Medwin's remark in his biography, went to some length in assigning to Shelley a role in the history of socialism: "Shelley was indeed the patron saint of their periodical literature. . . . If, as has been claimed, Robert Owen was the founder of British socialism, it is possible for modern socialism to claim Shelley as a sort of grandfather."[2] From here it does not seem too far a stretch to trace Shelley's early heritage to the founders of so-called scientific socialism, Marx and Engels. Young Friedrich Engels, who was the son of a Westphalian merchant and had to resign his career as a poet to support his father's firm in Manchester, in the early 1840s sent elegantly written reports on the state of England to German papers. He referred to the growth of a working-class literary culture in Britain and made the point that there, contrary to middle-class practice, the poetry of Shelley and Byron was read in unexpurgated editions. Engels became so enthusiastic about Shelley that he started translating him and even harbored ambitious plans for publishing a collected edition in German. These, however, came to nothing because of a rival project. In his remarks on Byron and Shelley he referred to "der geniale prophetische Shelley, und Byron mit seiner sinnlichen Glut und seiner bittern Satire der bestehenden Gesellschaft" (the ingenious prophetic Shelley and Byron, with his sensuous fire and his bitter satire on existing society).[3] Among other poems, he translated "The Sensitive Plant" and parts of *Queen Mab,* which he particularly liked because of its drive toward the emancipation of women. His translation of the line from *The Revolt of Islam,* "Can man be free if woman be a slave?" (*OSA* 1045), was to become a slogan of the German working-class movement.

Karl Marx—whose historical insights and social theory were to a high degree based on his vast knowledge of world literature and, more particularly, of Shakespeare and the English writers of the eighteenth and nineteenth centuries—preferred Shelley to Byron. There is still no confirmation of his famous estimate of the two poets, as it has come down to us through the words of his son-in-law Edward Aveling and his wife Eleanor:

> As Marx, who understood the poets as well as he understood the philosophers and economists, was wont to say: "The real difference between Byron and Shelley is this; those who understand them and love them rejoice that Byron died at thirty-six, because if he had lived he would have become a reactionary *bourgeois;* they grieve that Shelley died at twenty-nine, because he was essentially a revolutionist and he would always have been one of the advanced guard of socialism."[4]

These sound like carelessly rude remarks possibly snatched from private conversations, in which, as we know from Marx's letters, he can be shockingly sarcastic about people, even friends. But since Eleanor Aveling coauthored the paper, read in 1887 before the Shelley Society and later published in the German Social-Democratic *Neue Zeit,*[5] she seems to have confirmed the authenticity of her father's assertion. The harsh denunciation of Byron in favor of Shelley may be more understandable when we consider the sickening glorification of the "effeminate," "ethereal" Shelley on the part of German liberalists—when, for instance, Georg Herwegh could write lines like the following:

> Ein Elfengeist in einem Menschenleibe,
> Von der Natur Altar ein reiner Funken,
> Und drum für Englands Pöbelsinn die Scheibe.
> Ein Herz, vom süßen Duft des Himmels trunken,
> Verflucht vom Vater und geliebt vom Weibe,
> Zuletzt ein Stern im wilden Meer versunken.[6]

> (An elfin spirit in a human body,
> Of Nature's altar a pure spark,
> And thus the glowing brands for England's mob!
> A heart, from Heaven's sweet odor drunk,
> Cursed by his father and loved by his wife,
> At last a star sunk in the wild ocean.)

Or, worse even, Moritz Hartmann and Rudolf von Gottschall, the latter of whom wrote,

> Er war so sanft, von mädchenhafter Milde,
> Sein Aug' ein lindes Regenbogenlicht;

Ein Abendsonnenschein, der das Gefilde
Warm übertauend, durch die Wolken bricht.
Sein Herz so reich, auf Blüten hingebettet,
Die er zum Kranz der Menschheit liebend wand;
Ja, jede Blüten, von dem Sturm errettet,
Ein treu Asyl in seinem Busen fand.

In the further progress of the poem, Shelley becomes a nineteenth-century
Rousseau and ascends to heaven:

Ja, des Jahrhunderts Rousseau bist Du worden;
Dein Name, Shelley, glänzt in Gottes Buch!
Die Menschheit schenkt Dir ihre Ehrenorden,
Und Deinen Feinden schenkt sie ihren Fluch.[7]

(He was so gentle, of a maiden's kind,
His eye a soothing rainbow light,
An evening sunshine breaking through the clouds,
Shedding warm dew on pastoral fields.
His heart, so soft, on flowers had its bed,
Which lovingly he wreathed for humankind.
Yea, each blossom, salvaged from the storm,
A true asylum in his bosom found.
Yea, you the Rousseau of the century became,
Your name, oh Shelley, sparkles in God's book!
Mankind adores you with its honor-crown,
And to your enemies it flings its curse!)

Marx's reaction may even have been provoked by an opinion, widely held
in England as well as in Germany, that Shelley's early death was beneficial to him
and his readers since it prevented him from sinking farther down into the hells
of atheism and immorality. F. Gustav Kühne in 1838 had welcomed Shelley's
physical disintegration, for he had noticed traces of madness in his last poem:
"Er schrieb noch an dem Fragment gebliebenen 'Triumph des Lebens,' als
der Zufall, in Gestalt der stürmischen Wellen im Busen von Spezia, der
Notwendigkeit seiner Auflösung vorgriff und ihn in die Nacht der Tiefe
stürzte, aus der ein ewiges Auferstehen zu lichten Herrlichkeiten erfolgt."
(He was still engaged in writing his fragmentary "Triumph of Life," when
accident, in the shape of the stormy waves in the Bay of Spezia, anticipated
the necessity of his disintegration and plunged him into abysmal night, out
of which will come a resurrection to the glories of light.)[8] Thus, as it were,
Marx answered rudeness with rudeness, reversing the prevailing opinion.

But the question remains of how Marx and some of his companions could claim Shelley for socialism, in accordance with their ideas on the emancipation of the working classes as a prerequisite for the liberation and humanization of mankind in a revolutionary process of class struggle—a claim that, in any case, was not upheld by later Marxists. One of the reasons for what is certainly a grave misconception is the ongoing split between Shelley's outspokenly political ideas and his political and philosophical approach toward the emancipation of society through the emancipation of the individual. There is a parallel development in the approach toward Marx's own ideas even during his lifetime and the reception of Shelley and other Romantics during the latter part of the nineteenth century. In his early writing, particularly in the fascinating *Philosophisch-ökonomisches Manuskript,* the "Feuerbach-Thesen," and other anthropologically based studies, Marx had concentrated on the universal nature of the human being, whose individual identity he defined as the "ensemble" of social relations and the development of his senses in the course of civilization.[9] Reversing the Benthamite utilitarian principle of the greatest happiness for the greatest number as the ultimate goal of social organization, he had concluded that a classless society should be "ein Assoziation, worin die freie Entwicklung eines jeden die Bedingung für die freie Entwicklung aller ist."[10] But, as Engels had reason to emphasize repeatedly after Marx's death, the economic questions in the elaboration of their theory had gained a harmful dominance over the essentially philosophical and cultural problems, and he warned against undue simplifications.[11] Yet these nevertheless took place, and it was not only in the later Leninism that the original humanist content of Marx's vision became more and more distorted, until it came to stand for the dictatorship of the proletariat.

At the same time, with the advance of modernism and New Criticism, Romanticism was discouraged as the outgrowth of a self-searching subjectivism. Modern scientific methodology and a new technology combined with the overall antagonism between the worlds of capitalism and socialism after the Russian revolution. Under these conditions, a careful consideration of Shelley's position could not happen: His appropriations both by the New Critics and for symbolic and mythological interpretation were shunned as "bourgeois" formalism or mysticism. German socialists and even leftist writers did not take up the early endeavors by Marx and Engels, and Anatoly Lunacharsky and Walter Benjamin, who wrote significant works about the Romantics,[12] were disregarded.

In the 1930s, when the world economic crisis, large-scale unemployment, and the ascent of fascism and war produced a feeling of general doom, literary disputes among Marxists assumed a lethally dogmatic tone. In the Soviet Union—which, despite growing Stalinism, was still looked to as the fatherland of many German and other refugees—the ominous theory and practice of socialist realism were developed and rigidly enforced. Its main concept was a proliferation of naturalism in the interest of the Soviet state as the homeland of the international proletariat. Significantly, one of the elements of this kind of literary strategy was to be "revolutionary romanticism," which dreamed of the prospect of a bright socialist future, all the while being restricted by dogmatically held convictions about laws of social development that, in a deterministic process of history, led toward socialism.

This concept, which was advanced by Maxim Gorky, had its roots in the cult of Byron and the so-called revolutionary Romantics, including Shelley. They were completely separated from and contrasted to the first generation of Romantics, the Lake poets, who were condemned as downright reactionary. At that time Georg Lukács, who had taken refuge in the Soviet Union and who dominated the scene of politically loaded literary criticism, played a most pernicious role. Defending the rich humanist tradition of critical realism against what he considered morbid decadence in modern Western literature—including the work of the avant-garde (who often were socialists) and the "destruction of reason" in contemporary philosophy—he established a literary canon based on the mimetic art of Shakespeare, Goethe, Balzac, Tolstoy, and Thomas Mann. Experimentation, formal innovation, the exploration of myths, and the individual soul were to him anathema. Thus, along with the work of the modernists, the alleged irrationalism and subjectivism of the Romantics were to be rejected as ingredients of mental states leading to fascism.

Of course, there were reasons for suspicion of the old and new attacks on reason and social realism in Germany. German ideologues had adopted and misrepresented myths of Teutonic origin as instruments for "healing the sickness of the world."[13] In an aggressive, chauvinistic, antisemitic, and generally antiforeign spirit, a special kind of blood-and-soil irrationalism had been exploited in order to manipulate the German people. Therefore, "truth to life" in its external forms was to be the basis for literature in the interest of the socialist struggle for existence.

However, not everybody supported the Stalinist policy of dehumanization in the ruthless enforcement of streamlined socialist realism. Highly talented writers in the Soviet Union as well as in Western countries compromised or tried to circumvent the worst by opening up new venues to the overall concept of socialist realism. Bertolt Brecht and Anna Seghers, who lived as exiles in the West, took up the defense of avant-gardist and modernist writing in an attempt to include a wider and deeper understanding of realism. It was particularly Brecht, who in his shrewd ways had developed his own avant-gardism while tending toward Marxism and communism, who now made use of Shelley in order to overcome the obvious limitations of formalist dogmatism. In his famous article, "Weite und Vielfalt der realistischen Schreibweise," he argued in favor of Shelley's powerful symbolic style, and as a case in point he translated large passages from "The Mask of Anarchy."[14] He did not have a chance: The Stalinists prevailed, and when after the war the German Democratic Republic (GDR) was founded in 1949 Brecht himself fell under suspicion, though he was nonetheless given his famous theater, Am Schiffbauerdamm in East Berlin, where he performed miracles with his Berliner Ensemble.

Until the early 1960s there was an aggravating trend toward the exclusion of Romantic, together with modernist and avant-gardist, writing, now reinforced by the cold war, during which the two Germanys were separated by the most highly sensitive border between two hostile systems. Wilhelm Girnus, one of the exponents of cultural policy and for a time minister of higher education in the GDR, in 1953 published his edition of Goethe on art and literature, which was widely used as a textbook for the new socialist culture. Dealing with the dispute between the Classic and the Romantic as they pervaded the intellectual climate in the Age of Goethe, Girnus acted as legislator: "Goethe sagte die Wahrheit, wenn er das Klassische als das Gesunde und das Romantische als das Kranke bezeichnete. Es ist daher nur logisch, daß Hitler die Romantik als *das* Vorbild hinstellte." (Goethe told the truth when he defined the Classical as healthy and the Romantic as sick. It is thus logical that Hitler established the Romantic as *the* model.)[15] In a word, Romanticism was equated with fascism. Communication with the Romantics was only possible—in the case of the English writers—through the appropriation of the political ideas of Byron and Shelley (whereas Keats, of course, was to be avoided as representative of bourgeois "l'art pour l'art").

Reading and talking about such dangerous stupidity today, one tends to be shocked and even frightened, but it will take some time and much scholarly endeavor to carry out an objective assessment of what was happening in the world of socialism under the conditions then prevailing. In any case, the impetus for slow change, and valuable help, came, surprisingly enough, from the Soviet Union, even before the short-lived Khruschev thaw and the later Gorbachev glasnost. In the late 1950s dogmatically held theories of realism came under attack by scholars and writers who declined to follow the rigidity of the prescribed rules of life and literature. On the one side, there was the desperate attempt to identify epistemological materialism with a realism that in the course of world literature allegedly fought a permanent struggle against idealism and formalism (or decadence), until its final resolution in socialist realism as against modernism. On the other side, there were the exponents of a theory that claimed that there are other modes of writing—such as sentimentalism, Romanticism, or Classicism—that, though different from realism, also contributed to the "faithful reproduction of life" as mimetic arts reflecting realities of social and individual existence. Their difference was to be in styles of representation: metaphorical or symbolic language, fantastic hyperbolism, satirical exaggeration, grotesque distortion, and so on. Linguistic and stylistic studies by W. Winogradov and also the school of Russian formalism began to play a role, as they could point to the textual basis of significant change in imagery in Pushkin and other writers in the course of their literary development.[16]

The Maxim Gorky Institute of World Literature in Moscow held highly publicized conferences on these issues, and slowly a more differentiated view on ways of writing emerged. In this process studies in English Romanticism played a major role. It was Anna Arkadevna Elistratova in particular who pointed out that it was ridiculous to call the work of the English Romantics realistic because some of them were politically acceptable. In a polemic against the orthodox line, she angrily mocked the assertion that, for example, Byron's main literary value was seen in the fact that he had outgrown Romanticism, or that Shelley in *The Cenci* and his fragments of *Charles the First* had turned realist. "This kind of construct," she wrote, "is based on the naive idea that progressive art is invariably realistic and that in these cases Romanticism appears merely as a form of pseudonym or mask of realism."[17] In a truly great book, *Nasledie angliiskogo romantizma i sovremennost* (*The Heritage of English Romanticism and the Present*), published in 1960, she expounded her historically and linguistically based views on the "romantichesky khudoshestveni metod" (romantic mode of writing) and gave a well-informed introduction to the work of Blake, Wordsworth, Coleridge, Byron, Shelley, and Keats that was thereafter built upon by a whole school of Russian and other scholars and editors in the Soviet Union.[18] However, even though Elistratova tried to overcome the worst schematism of an identification between political, philosophical, and literary representation, she was still impeded by a deterministic view of the progression of literary evolution along teleological lines. "The explicit or implicit rejection of the method of Enlightenment realism on the part of the romantic writers, therefore," she concluded her argument, "at that age was historically progressive in its aesthetic aspects, even if they simultaneously opened the way for the intrusion of idealist tendencies in the arts." Thus, the romantic mode of writing was the expression of a "historically necessary phase of the development of artistic consciousness and of the recognition of the world at that phase."[19]

This, of course, was a compromise with the dominant idea of a politically based evolutionism in philosophical rather than literary terms. Nevertheless, studies in Romanticism could now gain a certain independence, and in the course of the 1960s, when I began my own studies in Blake, Shelley, and Keats, the demand by publishers to fill the enormous gap in revisiting the Romantics was overwhelming. This was reinforced by a general tendency on the part of writers and readers in the state of so-called true socialism to return to the mysteries of the German and English Romantics. There were two major reasons for this trend, which, significantly coincided with a new wave of women writing on a high level. Arguments couched in the language of the centrally regimented public media no longer satisfied the reading public. The realities of life in a deteriorating social situation under the misrule of an entrenched party leadership contradicted all the propagandist slogans of continuous progress; the new socialist personality proclaimed by endlessly repeated rhapsodism had long since deteriorated into mean, egotistical, and hypocritical time-serving.

The second reason for the return to the Romantics is one shared by all industrial societies: an increasing level of mechanization, commercialism, alienation, and loss of individual identity. Under these conditions, Romantic literature in the 1970s and 1980s could gain a new political dimension. If a way could be found to couple a socialist system of social security and welfare with a deep insight into the unlimited and unacknowledged work of the imagination, the search for individual identity, such an augmented system could perhaps become the foundation for a new, truly alternative society. This could be seen in Shelley, Blake, Keats, and the other English Romantics and even in the Germans: for instance, in Novalis, who had always been the butt of the criticism leveled by the straitlaced representatives of reason and materialism against mystic yearning and idealism. Even given its limitations, socialist society had provided the basic material and cultural conditions for a welfare state. There was shelter for everyone, free medical care, labor guaranteed as an essential human right, free education, artistic endeavor on all levels, sports and leisure facilities, inexpensive food and transportation, kindergartens and support for mothers, equal opportunities for women. But all that had been bought at the cost of a new utilitarianism, with the loss of individual decisionmaking. From beginning to end, individual life was to be subsumed under the control of the state, and it was the state that sought to channel the human desire to explore the world, to transcend the borders of an ever-so-well-organized social structure.

Is it too farfetched to compare the scenario I have outlined with the situation Shelley felt to be impending in Britain in 1818–19? The unrest of the masses in the GDR in the 1980s grew dangerous; the coercive measures of the state became harsher; a revolutionary situation was emerging. There was a fear of imminent bloodshed, of failure that would have unheard-of national and international repercussions. It was what Shelley had feared and what he had continually warned against. But what we should not forget in the assessment of his political and social writing is that he remained truly and unswervingly on the side of the people, as Mary reported. He was convinced that a new human society could achieve its growth only through the humanization of the individual self, in a long process of self-education, and his most severe warnings were directed to the rulers. If they did not respond to the needs of the people, then revolution was inevitable and, in the language of Thomas Paine, insurrection would find him on the side of the oppressed. When in 1986 I wrote an article on Shelley's *Prometheus Unbound* for the highly respected literary magazine *Weimarer Beiträge,* quoting passages of his *Philosophical View of Reform* to that effect, I was surprised at how strikingly Shelley's words matched the situation in the GDR. Of course, the article was rejected, allegedly because it set *Geist gegen Macht* (mind against power). Though I had nonetheless claimed Shelley for essential appropriation by a socialist society, it was only published after the dissolution of the GDR.

Let us return to Shelley's socialism. As I have already remarked, he was not a socialist in terms of what, in Marxist historiology, was called a social formation, as it was established in the Soviet Union and the other "socialist" countries. They could not be called truly socialist, since the decisive element of the concept of socialism—the free development of the individual in a free association of self-determining human beings—was disastrously lacking. The rights of the individual were eliminated by a new alienation and by the use of oppressive power. However, the seeds of the idea were indeed sown by Shelley and the Romantics: the common demand for bread, shelter, dignified labor, a community of spirits; the absence of war and hierarchies of power as well as of the rule of oppressive ideologies. *Prometheus Unbound* is the vision of this complex liberation of mankind in the figure of Prometheus, a social entity of not merely global but cosmological dimensions symbolizing the unity of man and woman, man/woman and nature, mind and matter. The image is multidimensional; the figures, scenes, and events are always, as Schlegel formulated the essence of Romantic discourse, "alles Bild von allem."[20] When Prometheus and Asia retire to their idyllic cavern, then, this is a metaphor for the ultimate awareness of the highest consciousness of liberated mankind of its ability to withdraw; now mankind can pursue its normal course of fulfillment, represented in the sexual dance of the elements. There is no need to return to allegorical interpretation and split the images of Prometheus and Asia from the totality of the poem.[21] Whether we call Shelley's vision socialist could be an irrelevant question. But it does contain all the elements of a human society that, though it may be unattainable, can at least serve as a corrective to the world of today, which holds the possibilities of global communion and material welfare for all but sadly lacks the element of love that, in Shelley's understanding, aligns the individual with the social potential of the race.

SHELLEY AND CONTEMPORARY THOUGHT

IV

Shelley in Posterity

Andrew Bennett

18

O<small>N</small> D<small>ECEMBER</small> 26, 1811, Shelley ended a letter to Elizabeth Hitchener from Keswick in the Lake District with a one-sentence paragraph, "I *will* live beyond this life," and with a signature, "Yours yours most imperishably Percy S." (*PBSL* 1:214). His next surviving letter, dated January 2, 1812, is also to Hitchener. This letter includes a quotation of seven and a half stanzas from Wordsworth's "A Poet's Epitaph," but most of the letter is taken up with one of Shelley's many attempts to prove to Hitchener the impossibility of the existence of a creative deity. Much of the argument concerns what Shelley sees as the logical contradictions of the Bible and its conflict with modern science: "Moses," says Shelley, "writes the history of his own death whic[h] is almost as extraordinary a thing to do as to describe the creation of the World" (*PBSL* 1:216). The reference to Moses writing the history of his own death seems to refer to the way in which the Book of Deuteronomy opens, in the King James version, with the pronouncement "These be the words which Moses spake" and ends with the narrative of that prophet's death.

In these two letters, Shelley presents early configurations of what I shall term "posthumous writing." His extravagant claim in the December letter that he will live beyond "this life," imperishably, returns a week later, rather differently, in a quotation from Wordsworth's fiction of posthumous poetic address in "A Poet's Epitaph" and in the reference to Moses. In such texts as "Essay on a Future State" and "Essay on the Punishment of Death," Shelley argues against an afterlife or the possibility of our knowing in what such an afterlife might consist: His claim that he will live on after this life would seem to involve the writer living on in his writing in the minds and thoughts of readers—in posterity. But Shelley's configuration of posterity in these letters already involves an unconventional formulation: The idea of Moses writing the history of his own death suggests that posterity might be constituted by the writer *writing* after his own death—posthumous writing.

These two letters are far from isolated occurrences of the notion of posthumous writing in Shelley; in fact, it is suggested in various ways throughout his life. Shelley's first volume of poetry (written with his sister Elizabeth), *Original Poetry; by Victor and Cazire,* for example, includes on its title page an epigraph from Scott's *Lay of the Last Minstrel* that refers to nature mourning the dead poet. His second collection of poems explicitly develops this fiction in its very title: *Posthumous Fragments of Margaret Nicholson.* In an unfinished piece entitled "The Elysian Fields: A Lucianic Fragment," written a few years later, the speaker addresses the living from beyond the grave. Toward the end of his life, Shelley announced in the first sentence of the advertisement to his anonymous *Epipsychidion* that "The Writer of the following Lines died at Florence" (373). Even more curious than this relatively conventional fiction of the poet as editor of posthumous poetry is Shelley's suggestion in a letter to his publisher Charles Ollier that "indeed, in a certain sense, [*Epipsychidion*] is a production of a portion of me already dead; and in this sense the advertisement is no fiction" (*PBSL* 2:262–63). Finally, writing to Byron in July 1821, Shelley comments on his own "public neglect" before expressing his admiration for Byron's poetry, mediated by a hope for the older poet's *future* work: "You say," Shelley continues, "that you feel indifferent to the stimuli of life. But this is a good rather than an evil augury. Long after the *man* is dead, the immortal spirit may survive, and speak like one belonging to a higher world" (*PBSL* 2:309). Once again, Shelley hints at a contemporary posterity: Byron's ennui makes possible a posthumous writing, writing that takes its authority from the poet's death.

These fictions of posthumous writing, then, begin to suggest a radical displacement and disturbance of conventional notions of posterity. If posterity is understood to be constituted by those who come after, those who live on after the poet, the audience for poetry after his death, Shelley's figuration of the poet as already dead warps this temporality, collapsing a posthumous and always anticipated or deferred reception in posterity into the present. By writing after his own death, Shelley can live his own posterity: He can live on or survive himself.

The temporal convulsions presented by such a notion of posterity are suggested most clearly in Shelley's 1819 essay *A Philosophical View of Reform.* Toward the end of this tract Shelley argues for the importance of poets and philosophers, the "unacknowledged legislators of the world" (*Julian* 7:20), as propagandists for reform. He suggests that Godwin, Hazlitt, Bentham, and Hunt should write "memorials" demonstrating "the inevitable connection" between political freedom and the economic health of the country on the one hand, and moral, scientific, and "metaphysical" enquiry on the other. Shelley then explains the potential persuasive force of the arguments of such writers: "These appeals of solemn and emphatic argument from those who have already a predestined existence among posterity, would appal the enemies of mankind by their echoes from every corner of the world in which the majestic literature of England is cultivated; it would be like a voice from beyond the dead of those who will live in the memories of men, when they must be forgotten; it would be Eternity warning Time" (*Julian* 7:52).

The passage is immensely suggestive in what I have called its temporal convulsions: Shelley is attempting to endow living writers with the authority of writing from posterity. These writers, he suggests, are *already* speaking from beyond their own lives. Although the passage appears to present a particularly unusual figuration of posterity, I would suggest that what is being invoked here is, in fact, the very impossibility of the time of posterity itself. Shelley suggests that posterity is a call to the future determined by the past and received in the present. Posterity concerns the possibility that living writers are traversed by their own mortality, that mortality is necessarily inscribed in their writing: Posterity is only possible on condition of the inscription in writing of the writer's death. In this way, posterity is a kind of haunting of the present by the future. As Shelley says in *A Defence of Poetry,* in one of many formulations of the idea, "the future is contained within the present as the plant within the seed" (481). Our first configuration of Shelley in posterity, then, posthumous writing, involves an attempt to fold or collapse the future into the present.

To engage with the subject of Shelley as poet and legislator is, above all, to elaborate questions of reading and the law of reading. "All laws," Paul de Man suggests in *Allegories of Reading,* "are future-oriented and prospective;

their illocutionary mode is that of the promise."[1] Shelley's inscription of the law into the discourse of poetry, not only in the notion of poets as legislators but in various ways and in many different texts, can be read in terms of a projection of poetry into or toward the future. A second, more general, figuration of posterity that I outline involves a future determined by the radical absence of the poet: In this configuration, poetry is future-oriented and proleptic because of its necessary engagement with a reception which can only occur in a time beyond the poet's own death. But as a corollary to this, I shall suggest that posterity is inscribed in Shelley's work, and, indeed, in Romantic writing generally, as a reception in a time not only beyond the death of the poet but also, necessarily and crucially, in a time beyond the death of the reader.[2]

Before attempting to establish this claim, I briefly elaborate a historical context for Shelley's notion of *living on,* of being "imperishable." As Timothy Clark has recently suggested, poetic immortality for Shelley is bound up, in the first place, with technologies of publishing. Clark quotes Trelawny quoting Shelley: "Intelligence should be imperishable; the art of printing has made it so on this planet."[3] The poet, it seems, is made imperishable by print technology. Reading Shelley's letters, we find that, during the twelve years of his publishing career, he became expert in the various technologies that constitute the "art" of publishing—in the knowledge related to such skills as printing, copyediting, binding, and paper selection—and expert in the associated skills of advertising; distribution to reviewers, bookshops, and individuals; and the monitoring of reviews. The "art of printing," then, was a craft that Shelley took pains to learn in order to make himself imperishable in print. This being the case, it is significant that the phrase "the art of printing" itself occurs in Leigh Hunt's review of *The Revolt of Islam.* After registering the urgency of the social and political message of the poem and at the same time its obscurity and inevitable unpopularity, Hunt ends his review with a eulogy on this art: "although the art of printing is not new, yet the Press in any great and true sense of the word is a modern engine in the comparison, and the changeful times of society have never yet been accompanied with so mighty a one. *Books* did what was done before; they have now a million times the range and power."[4]

Hunt explicitly contrasts this potential power and influence of "books" with the inevitable unpopularity of Shelley's poem, which, he says, "cannot possibly become popular." In purely pragmatic terms, then, the "art of printing" is understood to be crucial because of its potential social and political influence. But this potential should be contrasted with the actual neglect of Shelley's works: only one of Shelley's books went into an authorized second edition in his lifetime, and the largest print run of any of his books, 1489, was that of his first volume—it is thought that no more than 100 copies were sold.[5]

The technologies of mass book production and their potential social effects, then, are contrasted explicitly by Hunt, and implicitly for Shelley throughout his career, with his failure to reach a popular audience. This produces a crucial fissure of publication that reminds us, if nothing else, of the necessary prolepsis of Romantic poetic address: It reminds us that, in some sense, Romantic discourse *must* be imperishable precisely because it must perish under contemporary neglect. At least in certain configurations, Romantic discourse is congruent with what comes to be called the avant-garde, with an appeal to a necessarily deferred reception. A number of critics, including P. M. S. Dawson, Stephen Behrendt, and Timothy Clark, have recently commented on the importance of posterity in Shelley's writing toward the end of his life.[6] But I would suggest both that this recognition should be extended back to Shelley's first publications and that critics have yet to register the strange torsions that posterity exerts on his writing.

Behind my argument is a recognition of the work of such critics and historians as Jerome McGann, Alvin Kernan, Lee Erickson, Clifford Siskin, Marilyn Butler, Elizabeth Eisenstein, Jon Klancher, and Tilottama Rajan on a general shift in the relationship between British poets and their readers and audiences in the late eighteenth and early nineteenth centuries, together with significant alterations in conditions and conceptions of reading.[7] A number of factors may account for a necessary reconceptualization of the audience for poetry at this time, including developments in print technology; an increase in the market for books, in literacy, and in the spread of print media generally; and a decline in patronage and a subsequent professionalization of the writer, together with a number of more general socioeconomic, aesthetic, and ideological developments as a result of industrialization, urbanization, and an unprecedented increase in population. At the beginning of the nineteenth century, writers found themselves in the predicament of what Lyotard calls "modernity," a predicament in which the writer "no longer knows for whom he writes."[8] The possibilities and dangers of this situation can be graphically illustrated by referring to a few sales figures: Whereas Byron's *The Corsair* is said to have sold 10,000 copies on the day of publication, a letter written by Keats's publisher delightedly records having sold seven or eight copies of *Endymion*,[12] and the first edition of the *Lyrical Ballads*, despite its eventual relative success, was remaindered. In a letter Shelley himself estimated the total readership for *Prometheus Unbound* to be only five or six (*PBSL* 2:388). Thus, although the Romantics, and Shelley not least, were aware of and eager to exploit the possibilities offered by a vertiginously expanding reading public, at the same time, in the face of these forces, the reception of their poetry by *future* generations of readers became crucial to their writing. Shelley's response to Peacock's *The Four Ages of Poetry* in *A Defence of Poetry* is a response to his friend's claim, baldly summarized in a letter to Shelley of December 1820, that "there is no longer a poetical audience among the higher class of minds" and that "the poetical reading public" is "composed of the mere dregs of the intellectual community" (*PBSL* 2:245). Shelley's argument in *A Defence of Poetry* that "Even in modern times, no living poet ever arrived at the fulness of his fame," together with the concomitant assertion that "the jury which sits in judgement upon a poet . . . must be impanelled by Time from the selectest of the wise of many generations" (486), is a claim, responding to contemporary conditions of publication, that displaces reception from a degenerate present to an eternal future.

A number of historical, technological, and cultural transformations at the end of the eighteenth century, then, may be said to account for the way in which posterity becomes an increasingly important determinant of the Romantic audience. Although the appeal to posterity is undeniably a conventional poetic trope that extends at least as far back as Horace's assertions of poetic immortality in his odes ("*non omnis moriar*") and that receives extensive and even obsessive elaboration in the Renaissance in, for example, Shakespeare's sonnets, I would suggest that in the early nineteenth century there is both an intensification of concentration on poetic afterlife and a radical redescription of that survival. Put very crudely, we can say that during this period the audience for romantic poetry is redescribed and displaced from an empirically constituted presence to an absence deferred to the future. But I would suggest that this deferral becomes an infinite if undecidable deferral to a time beyond the death of the reader. And I would also argue that this paradoxical and impossible death is figured in a variety of ways in early-nineteenth-century texts: Wordsworth's 1815 "Essay, Supplementary to the Preface," for example, writes a reception history of English poetry in which it becomes clear that no great writer has *ever* been properly received; rather differently, the most explicit and powerful figuration of the death of the reader occurs in Keats's poem "This living hand"—a poem that, arguably, suggests that the poet's hand lives because the reader toward whom it is held has given it blood and is dead. William Hazlitt considers the question of posterity in at least two important essays: "On the Living Poets" in his *Lectures on the English Poets* of 1818 and an essay from 1827, "On the Feeling of Immortality in Youth." In these texts, it is Hazlitt, rather than Jacques Derrida, who provides a vocabulary for posterity by referring to the poet as "living on," "outliving himself," or "surviving himself."[10] But in Romantic discourse, such a survival would seem to involve the necessary inscription of the reader's death.

As these texts suggest, figurations of posterity tend, *necessarily,* to be hidden, disguised, distorted, or displaced. Posterity as constituted by the death of the reader must be read but is not, by definition, susceptible to reading. Indeed, if I am right in suggesting that the death of the reader is inscribed in Romantic writing, this causes a fissure or fold in romantic texts, which is a secret or crypt, a haunting, that must remain in some sense unread and unreadable.[11] Such a haunting might be taken to be the singular force of the inscription of posterity in Shelley's writing in particular. Shelley inscribes posterity into his writing as a kind of ghostly spirit haunting or inhabiting the minds of readers. This is most powerfully suggested in *A Defence of Poetry,* in which Shelley states that poetry "acts in a divine and unapprehended manner, beyond and above consciousness" (486) and that its effect is one of what he calls "entrancement" (from the Latin *trans,* across or beyond): Poetry is, precisely, that which is *not* perceived or apprehended and which takes the reading subject *outside* him- or herself. Shelley figures this entrancement in terms of reading as the creation of a "being within our being" (505). Such a being within our being, both inside and outside the reading subject, can never be known: "Veil after veil may be undrawn, and the inmost naked beauty of the meaning never exposed" (500). That poets are "unacknowl-edged" should, then, be understood as part of a larger claim in *A Defence of Poetry* about what cannot be presented: Shelley suggests that reading is haunted by the unreadable, the unspeakable, or the immemorial. Indeed, this very unreadability of posterity, an interdiction of reading, might itself be said to contain the "secret" of Romantic reading: The scandalous but unreadable secret encrypted within the Romantic text is that of posterity, the unspeak-able assertion in Romantic writing of the death of the reader.

Although this inhabitation or haunting is unspeakable and necessarily hidden, we might begin to read it, even—or especially—in its interdictions of reading, within the torsions of rhetoric throughout *A Defence of Poetry.* One formulation occurs in Shelley's well-known description of poetic defamiliarization: "Poetry lifts the veil from the hidden beauty of the world and makes familiar objects be as if they were not familiar; it reproduces all that it represents, and the impersonations clothed in its Elysian light stand thenceforward in the minds of those who have once contemplated them, as memorials of that gentle and exalted content which extends itself over all thoughts and actions with which it coexists." (487).

The light of poetry is Elysian, that of the blessed dead, and the work of reading is inhabited by death as a work of remembering. As Karen Mills-Courts has pointed out in a discussion of this passage, this ghostly impersonation is neither living nor dead but both.[12] But the passage from Shelley's essay makes it clear that there is a metonymic infection of such memorialization, that the haunting or cryptic structure of poetry as memorialization is a structure that not only inhabits the "mind" of the reader but in fact becomes, or impersonates, the reader. At the same time, the reader may be understood to *be* an impersonation, a mask of a person, constructed by the deadly work of reading. Readers then become incarnations of poetry, they are translated into the flesh of language, they *impersonate* language or become embodied, actualized impersonations of language: Readers, in a precise and deadly sense, are figured. Readers are given a face, are subject to an eerie prosopopoeia in which, as Paul de Man suggests in his reading of Wordsworth's *Essays upon Epitaphs,* they speak from beyond the grave.[13]

This reading of posterity in Shelley has significant consequences for his poetry, some of which might be suggested by a very brief enumeration of ways in which a few of Shelley's canonical poems present the death of the reader. In "Ozymandias" Shelley presents monumentalization in terms of the survival of the passions of the King of Kings on the "lifeless" stone, beyond the sculptor who is explicitly described as a *reader* of those passions. Similarly, the ending of the poem presents a scene of devastation from which all living beings, including the traveler who has read the words of Ozymandias written on the pedestal, are excluded. *Alastor* narrates the poet's journey toward death after his meeting with the "veilèd maid" (line 151) who is "Herself a poet" (line 161): The poet is also a reader who dies after engaging with poetry. *Adonais* again presents the poet-as-reader dying into Keats's poetry. The poem also seeks to disrupt the distinction between life and death in order to suggest that "*We* decay"—we readers decay—"Like corpses in a charnel . . . / And cold hopes swarm like worms within our living clay" (lines 348–51).

The opening of "Letter to Maria Gisborne" presents the poet as weaving a "soft cell" round his own "decaying form," "From the fine threads of rare and subtle thought." The poem continues,

> a soft cell, where when that fades away,
> Memory may clothe in wings my living name
> And feed it with the asphodels of fame,
> Which in those hearts which must remember me
> Grow, making love an immortality. (lines 11–14)

In this poem, reading is linked to love, immortality, and death: The asphodels, immortal flowers of the Elysian fields, grow in the hearts of those who remember the poet, a death inhabiting and growing within readers. "The Triumph of Life" once again presents the poet as reader, this time of Rousseau: a poet-reader who thinks and is thought by Rousseau—"the grim Feature, of my thought aware" (line 190)—but thinks him from the regions of the dead. Finally, in "Ode to the West Wind," the poet spreads "dead thoughts" over the world in an equivocal attempt to "quicken a new birth": If the poet's dissemination of thoughts is "like" the West Wind's dissemination of leaves and seeds, the poet is, like that wind, a "Destroyer and preserver" (line 14). The complex dislocations of this poem, presented most compactly in the uncertainty of the poem's closing rhetorical question, may be understood in terms of the possibility that spreading dead thoughts may not revitalize but can only preserve. "Ode to the West Wind" presents a figuration of posthumous writing, the dissemination of dead thoughts. But this posthumous writing also involves the death of the reader, who may be understood to be figured by a burial, the disseminated seed of poetic thoughts lying like "a corpse within its grave" (line 8). In this poem, and repeatedly throughout Shelley's writing, reading is conceived in terms of memorialization, monumentalization, preservation.

In the early nineteenth century, then, posterity not only develops into a crucial determinant of audience for poetry but is itself redescribed. Such a reconfiguration occurs in, and has important implications for the poetry, not least, of, Percy Bysshe Shelley. And such a recognition in turn has significant implications for our very conception of Romantic writing—our conception of a reader-response criticism or a *Rezeptionsästhetik* for Romantic poetry, our conception of the Romantic engagement with the avant-garde and with questions of reading, and, finally, our conception of what it might mean to speak about Shelley in posterity.

Shelley's Ineffable Quotidian

Karen A. Weisman

19

I BEGIN MY reading of Shelley with Wallace Stevens, but with a Shelley-refracted Stevens I wish to appropriate by way of nodding in two directions. In the first instance, I am interested in a particular *poetic* sensibility (a Shelleyan sensibility), one that continues to strike resonant chords in modern and contemporary poetry. I also mark the direction of our *reading* sensibility, indeed the reading sensibility from which a kind of postdeconstructionist Shelley of the "qualified sublime," as it were, has lately come down to us. In Stevens's "The Poem that Took the Place of a Mountain," the persona is reminded "how he had needed / A place to go to in his own direction, / . . . How he had recomposed the pines, / Shifted the rocks and picked his way among clouds."[1] The poem concludes, as all mountain poems of Romantic descent seem to do, with a revelation of a poetic self that has very little to do with lithic structures; recalling also, perhaps, Wordsworth's adventures in the sublime, Stevens situates his reader-cum-mountain gazer on the "exact rock," one "Where he could lie and, gazing down at the sea, / Recognize his unique and solitary home" (374). For Stevens, recomposing the pines and

This chapter is a development of salient points put forth in the author's *Imageless Truths: Shelley's Poetic Fictions* (Philadelphia: Univ. of Pennsylvania Press, 1994). Brief sections of it were first outlined in her article "Shelley's Triumph of Life over Fiction," *Philological Quarterly* 71 (1992): 337–60.

shifting the rocks and picking a way among clouds are offered as a *poetic taking place*, one that displaces both mountain and, perhaps, other mountain-poems. We might pause also to look briefly at Steven's "The American Sublime," which I read not quite as Steven's ironic "answer" to Shelley's "Mont Blanc," but as his reading of Shelley's own ironic skepticism in "Mont Blanc":

> But how does one feel?
> One grows used to the weather,
> The landscape and that;
> And the sublime comes down
> To the spirit itself,
>
> The spirit and space,
> The empty spirit
> In vacant space.
> What wine does one drink?
> What bread does one eat?   (114)

Stevens's answer to "Mont Blanc" as poetic object—to *mountain* as poetic object—inspires no feelings of sustained vertigo. Poems do not really take the place of mountains so much as they place them, and in the Shelleyan world that so affected Stevens (and many other twentieth-century poets), one worries over what bread one eats, what wine one drinks—that is, what quotidian ground of reference one barters to purchase our poems that would take the place of mountains. Still, even bread and wine insistently, obtrusively, remind one of transubstantiation, which could in fact serve as metaphor for all poetic yearning for what metaphors (ideally conceived) might accomplish. But I have begun with Stevens to make a point about *reading* Shelley, and about particular precedents for reading Shelley, to whom I now turn.

In "Mont Blanc," Shelley exclaims, "Mont Blanc yet gleams on high:—the power is there" (line 127). Now power is not exactly there in the mountain, of course, and this has inspired a bevy of important critical and scholarly responses to the problematics of metaphoric predication. But to Shelley's assertion of "there" (i.e., "the power is there"), it might be time for us to start responding with "where?"—on as egregiously obvious a note as I hope I am striking. Asking "where?" brings us back to "there," brings us back, that is, to the elusiveness of the *mountain* "over there" that is being appropriated as the sign of some antecedent reality. But the object that provides the sign itself—the mountain—is already an obtrusive reality, exists well before it becomes part of an equation in a scheme of metaphoric predication.

This issue, I submit, subtly haunts Shelley as an undertone of anxiety throughout his career. Having pondered, in "Mont Blanc," the metaphysical analogies and the epistemological traumas suggested by his look at the great mountain, he finally concludes by addressing at once the mountain and one of the central problematics of his poetry:

> And what were thou, and earth, and stars, and sea,
> If to the human mind's imaginings
> Silence and solitude were vacancy? (lines 142–44)

In her important essay "What the Mountain Said," Frances Ferguson reminds us that whatever the various critical cruxes suggested by the poem, *one* point of agreement that has come down to us, at least, is that the mountain "is repeatedly seen as the ultimate example of materiality, of the "thingness" of things, so that its symbolic significance is quite explicitly treated as something added to that materiality."[2] With this in mind, I read the lines as follows: If Mont Blanc becomes an object only to be troped upon, then what is the mountain qua mountain? If the silence and solitude of Mont Blanc were only vacancy to its percipient, a vehicle looking for a tenor, a gap waiting to be filled by a transcendent presence, would it retain its value as mountain?

Depending on our critical predilections, we might as easily ask, would it matter? Would we care? What I am getting at is an anxiety feature of the Romantic visionary, the anxieties that attend not epistemological uncertainty per se—that we can take as a given—but that attend the inexorable poetic attenuation of the value of the quotidian, precisely when the quotidian is appropriated to serve some symbolic, or metaphoric, or otherwise analogical function. I might add that by quotidian I intend not simply the mundane and trivial, but also the temporal world of time and space, in short, the world of "everydayness," in which objects and events are experienced in their *presymbolic* being (or, at least, as close as we can get to a presymbolic experience). And this is not really a question of the epistemology of the *Ding-an-sich,* for it is a few steps before we might even get to such issues (though *Ding-an-sich* does, to be sure, have its correlative areas of discussion). I would suggest that this is a concern shared by British Romanticism in general, that it is more manifest, more self-conscious, in Shelley's poetry, and that forays into the area of the Romantic sublime necessarily beg the question about the world of quotidian pathos that is being transcended. More important, it questions the status of that very world as it stands to be appropriated in the symbolic scheme of sublime yearning. This position tries to take account of the human predilection for figuration and for formalizing figured expressions and so might be situated somewhere in between David Simpson's "figurings of the real" and Stuart Curran's conceptual structures haunting the human mind.[3]

Under the rubric of these concerns, the reciprocity between experience and its aesthetic renderings does not fully answer the culpability potentially inherent in aesthetic rendering. The beginning trope of "Mont Blanc" is of the universe of things flowing through the mind, and however we decide finally to construe the sense of those difficult opening lines, it is particularly remarkable that the inscrutable universe that flows through a dimly comprehended mind is a universe of *things*. If the poem explores, among other issues, the nuances of deflecting attention away from the mountain and transferring attention instead to a constructed metaphoric equivalent, then the assertion that it is a universe of *things* that flows through the mind is of peculiar significance, especially if we recall the context in which *things* can be understood, one in which to think and to mark things are inextricably related. *Things,* in any case, has always been an immensely shifty word: Kant's "thing-in-itself," of course, has a long progeny, and Horne Tooke, according to a much quoted passage from his *Diversions of Purley,* sees the Latin *res* (thing) as etymologically related to *reor* (I think). He concludes, "Remember, where we now say, *I think,* the antient expression was—*Me thinketh,* i.e. *Me thingeth, It thingeth me.*"[4] The word is used in fascinating ways by Wordsworth, from "rolls through all things" in "Tintern Abbey," to "She was a thing" in the last Lucy poem, and even to his note to "The Thorn," in which, drawing on a long-established philosophical tradition, he insists that words can be viewed *as* things. I do think Shelley would have been counting on the reader's more immediate association of "thing" with the idea of empirical object, but it is important to bear in mind that it can also be set against a more complicated history. Later, in the twentieth century, William Carlos Williams is to insist, "No ideas but in things." In the anxiety scenario I have been outlining, we in fact have a kind of "no things except as they *render* ideas."

But we must recall the inherent abstractness even of the quotidian, and "things" is also a nondefining term, less culpable as a characterization because it does not impose attributes. Even before the poem's fictionmaking really begins, then, even before the mountain or the mountain's function is introduced, the quotidian world briefly, quietly, but nonetheless remarkably counters its inevitable metaphoric displacements; it is a "thing" more than it is a metaphoric equation, at least some sort of thing *before* it is an object to be troped upon in the service of a construction of presumed greater spiritual value.

A Defence of Poetry, then, finally defends the world from which poetry constructs its tropes as much as it valorizes the production of poetry. The "Language of poetry is vitally metaphorical" because it marks "the before unapprehended relations of things" (482). By ensuring that signs remain signs ("pictures of integral thoughts"), instead of lazily allowing them to become signifieds ("signs for portions or classes of thoughts"), we mark relations of things, we synthesize desire with the empirical world, we guarantee self-consciousness in a world defined by Shelley's reading of Berkeley—"All things exist as they are perceived: at least in relation to the percipient" (505, italics mine). Things must be perceived, though the mountain in "Mont Blanc," for example, is a thing that stands as sign for what is not perceived, of course, at least not by the senses.

Shelley's poetry, then, written in the self-consciousness of the necessary qualifications of imaginative vision—and hence written in the self-consciousness that accompanies those of us who do not ascend into the "intense inane" (to use the language of *Prometheus Unbound*)—is a poetry of what I should like to call the *hyperquotidian,* a poetry of the desire for and failure of transcendent vision, a poetry betraying that vision as finally a seeing in terms of the signs of its absence, but in which absence is recognized in the terms of a presented quotidian world. Again, the *Defence* provides the clearest explanation:

> Poetry defeats the curse which binds us to be subjected to the accident of surrounding impressions. And whether it spreads its own figured curtain or withdraws life's dark veil from before the scene of things, it equally creates for us a being within our being. It makes us the inhabitants of a world to which the familiar world is a chaos. It reproduces the common universe of which we are portions and percipient, and it purges from our inward sight the film of familiarity which obscures from us the wonder of our being. It compels us to feel that which we perceive, and to imagine that which we know. It creates anew the universe after it has been annihilated in our minds by the recurrence of impressions blunted by reiteration. (505–6)

If we are consigned to the quotidian, temporal world, then our poetry is a poetry of and for the quotidian; the being created by poetry is one within

the normative quotidian being, and the poetic world as conceived in the
Defence is what I have referred to above as the hyperquotidian, especially
when it strives toward some modulation of the ineffable, and even when it is
in the service of intimating (or, for that matter, deconstructing) some
transcendent order. There is no real ontological status for poetry or for its
tropes. Poetry both spreads and uncovers a curtain, because in a dualistic
universe both processes of embellishment amount to the same thing. When
impressions are no longer blunted by reiteration, when we become attuned
to the wonder of the attributes of the quotidian and the marvels of the
external, empirical world, when we realize that Mont Blanc is actually a
tremendous mountain, then we are also made aware that we have been
conceiving of metaphysical otherness, for example, in terms of unconscious
interpretations of an external world that we no longer even notice. If
mountain does not equal power, then we understand something important
about both the mountain and power. But we also begin to understand the
manifold implications this represents, for metaphysics and for the poetry of
desire—or for poetry *as* desire. That is, since things exist as they are perceived,
at least in relation to the percipient, our truths are truths *to us* when we in
our temporal circumscription actualize them.

    Prometheus Unbound's qualified millennium, then, is qualified in the terms
partly of this dynamic. I quote the famous lines from act 3:

> The loathsome mask has fallen, the man remains
> Sceptreless, free, uncircumscribed—but man:
> Equal, unclassed, tribeless and nationless,
> Exempt from awe, worship, degree,—the King
> Over himself; just, gentle, wise—but man:
> Passionless? no—yet free from guilt or pain
> Which were, for his will made, or suffered them,
> Nor yet exempt, though ruling them like slaves,
> From chance and death and mutability,
> The clogs of that which else might oversoar
> The loftiest star of unascended Heaven
> Pinnacled dim in the intense inane.   (3.4.190–204)

When the fictionality to which we enslave ourselves is acknowledged, it is
torn aside, and the "loathsome mask" falls. But the problematic of identity, of
separating our familiar fictions from the reality of human existence, is never
entirely resolved. The question of this millennium scene, then, is not simply
how to differentiate millennial fictions from "inane" ones, but how to join

them with a new, mutable, everyday, but transformed reality. In moving from an old, negated, quotidian reality to a new quotidian reality, what we find is precisely an ineffable of the quotidian. The syntactical ambiguity of the repeated phrase "but Man" reinforces this sense: The mask has fallen, but man is . . . what? In the postlapsarian world in which poems are written and read, we predicate negative adjectives, not nouns, because a demythologized humanity is—for those of us still speaking the "language of the dead"—a humanity without identifiable attributes. The impulse for metaphoric equations may well have been vanquished (in the millennial world), or at least checked (in the world in which we read the poem), but the point of stasis has no language we yet know of. For the abstract concept of "man" a voice is still very much wanting. We are not enslaved by "chance and death and mutability," but that too is a negation, and even then no one knows what it could possibly mean to be not exempt from, but yet to rule, mutability.

"The Triumph of Life" may be conceived as a reading of these very concerns, as Shelley's quite conscious concession, as it were, to the limits as well as the implications of metaphor, which yet he—and we—cannot do without. The last question with which we are left in the fragment, after all, is not what is transcendence, but what is life, the quotidian existence we continue to inhabit when our visionary quests have failed.

The poem *begins,* though, with a smile: "Swift as a spirit hastening to his task / Of glory and of good, the Sun sprang forth" (lines 1–2). In the first stanza, then, we note that the sun has risen, but we are not actually informed of this until the second line. Primacy is initially given to a conception of a spirit hastening to his task, not to the sun: Perception is hence displaced from sun to the equivalent that Shelley provides. This is a perverse answer to, and virtual parody of, the Berkeleyan assertions he has been making in his later years, that "all things exist as they are perceived." Perverse as it may be, though, it possesses a brutal and unforgiving logic. For if *things* exist only as they are perceived, then the sun Shelley perceives—first as the analogue of something else (a swift spirit), and then as basis for myth (all things "Rise as the Sun their father rose"; line 18) does not exist as sun in the mind of the percipient. Denied its status as *empirical* phenomenon, its light dissipates, and a transparent "shade" is spread over the scene. If troped objects can cease to exist as objects for the mythmaker, and if we remain living anyway in a world progressively robbed by us, through our troping, of its components, then life ultimately overcomes us.

The defeat by life of both the merely literal and the merely metaphoric is the note on which Shelley's life ended, and it is one that continues to resonate within various current critical discourses, in some more obviously than in others. Certainly a political Shelley could share something in common with a Shelley of anxiety over the quotidian, but the quotidian I have been emphasizing is, in a sense, prepolitical (though certainly *not* apolitical). Furthermore, if newly disinterred Romantic women authors describe the world about them in ways that hold the quotidian as absolute—as Stuart Curran has recently suggested[5]—then in fact what is central to much women's writing may be precisely what tugs at the very heart even of the high canon.

The "tug" at the heart, of course, is rarely simply a tug at the heart; what I have called the "prepolitical" is never truly *before* politics, no more so than sexuality, or power, could ever define a temporal boundary whose presumed origins demarcate human experience. Indeed, given the critical currency of the historicity of context, the very term *quotidian* is, perhaps, rhetorically overloaded. And Shelleyans in particular—still in some measure battling against F. R. Leavis's claim that Shelley has a weak "grasp upon the actual"— tend to be uniquely sensitive to the problematizations through which an external reality can be grasped. But I have been trying to identify a hermeneutics of the quotidian, as it were, or a process, more precisely, in which historical contingency is not yet a factor in the individual's conscious interpretive activity. Let us grant as an indisputable fact, then, that Shelley was always intensely interested in the political events of his day, that Peterloo, the ominous effects of Eldonism, widespread famine, the Greek war of independence, and so on, were of the most urgent concern to him. The intimacy of Shelley's relations to such events has been brilliantly documented by various scholars.[6] But this is precisely where we must remember also that, though the mountain in "Mont Blanc" may well have a "voice" that "the wise, and great, and good / Interpret, or make felt, or deeply feel" (lines 82–83), the mountain itself has no say in the matter. The semiotic fractures of the mountain's voice do not break the mountain; the immediate and subtle political resonance of our perceptual mediation of it ought to remind us that what "Flows *through* the mind" (line 2, italics mine) is "everlasting": "The everlasting universe of things" (line 1).

The ineffability of the quotidian is, for Shelley, an affirmation of his felt experience of *being* in the world, the very world of actuality whose grasp he held so tight that words could only glisten with their triumphant qualifications.

"The Empire of Man":
Shelley and Ecology

P. M. S. Dawson

20

I TAKE MY point of departure from a book by Jonathan Bate entitled *Romantic Ecology: Wordsworth and the Environmental Tradition.*[1] In this work, beyond offering a reading of Wordsworth, Bate proposes a new program for literary criticism, one that involves what he calls "the move from red to green" (8–9). He is aware that this proposal might seem merely modish, an attempt to acquire "a 'green' literary criticism to go with our lead-free petrol and our ozone-friendly deodorant" (9), but he is perfectly correct to argue that "The ends of literary critics are not only exegetical but also polemical; consciously or not, critics always read texts selectively in order to make them serve their own purposes" (5). The ability to enlist the past in seeking to achieve an understanding of the present is the main advantage that we living curs have over the dead lions. As we become more preoccupied with the fate of our environment, it is inevitable that we should seek to recycle the canonical writings of our culture to reflect these new concerns.

Some circumspection might, however, be in order. The environmental crisis with which we are confronted is hardly an accidental outcome of the development of our culture, so that to focus our attention on those writers who are what one might call politically correct on this matter might be to misrepresent the whole problem. Bate is only too willing to stroke the past with the grain. His claim that where "the critic's purposes are also the writer's . . . there can be a communion between living reader and dead writer which may bring with it a particular enjoyment and a perception about endurance" (5) proposes an appropriation of the past that sacrifices its potential to provoke in order to derive an illusory reassurance. There is, I would suggest, rather too much sympathy between our modern ecologism and Wordsworth to allow a proper critical distance to be adopted, whether toward the present or toward the past. The Wordsworth who objected to working-class trippers from the new industrial towns intruding into his Lake District serves only too easily to underwrite that NIMBYism that is no small part of the modern middle-class concern for the environment.[2] To hazard a reading of some of Shelley's concerns from an ecological perspective will, perhaps, prove more usefully provocative, and demonstrate that the enduring value of great literature is rather in the way it challenges our beliefs than in an easy confirmation of them.

Bate's neo-Stendhalian counterpoising of the red and the green, of Marxism and environmentalism, reveals clearly enough what he hopes to be saved from by his proposed turn to ecocriticism. One need not share his postcold war disillusion with Marxism (demuralization, one might call it) to recognize here the terms of a real dilemma. In these terms Shelley is certainly more red than green. Like Marx, his hope in human betterment invests heavily in a belief in economic and hence in scientific and technological progress. Again like Marx, he was only too aware that the astonishing economic progress of the preceding half-century had not entirely fulfilled this faith: "The cultivation of those sciences which have enlarged the limits of the empire of man over the external world, has, for want of the poetical faculty, proportionally circumscribed those of the internal world; and man, having enslaved the elements, remains himself a slave. . . . From what other cause has it arisen that the discoveries which should have lightened, have added a weight to the curse imposed on Adam?" (502–3). Where Shelley departs from Marx is in his fundamentally idealist conception of the problem, which he sees as resting on a disproportion between "the selfish and calculating principle" and "the creative faculty." He conceives the crucial opposition less as class struggle than as a psychomachia.

It is hardly surprising that Shelley should posit the problem in these terms, if we consider the nature of the connection that he saw between economic progress and political liberation. It is not so much that the creation of abundance would free man from both the curse of Adam and the competition for scarce resources that is at the root of economic exploitation and hence of political oppression. For Shelley there are additional moral factors that make it imperative that "the limits of the empire of man over the external world" should be extended. In the *Essay on Christianity* he explains why: "Too mean spirited & too feeble in resolve to attempt the conquest of their own evil passions, & of the difficulties of the material world, men sought dominion over their fellow men as an easey method to gain that apparent majesty & power which the instinct of their nature requires."[3]

The fixed point here is that the "instinct of [human] nature" *requires* "majesty & power," which men have erroneously sought by exercising power over their fellows. The true path to human "majesty & power" lies for Shelley in the double conquest over "their own evil passions" on the one hand and over "the difficulties of the material world" on the other. To fail to take this path is fatal; there is an "instinct" at work that will find expression in one way or another. It is an instinct that demands *conquest* and *power*, and this disturbing language saturates Shelley's account of man's relations both with his own nature and with external nature. Man's proper relation with his own nature is described with exemplary clarity in Shelley's "Sonnet: To the Republic of Benevento":

> Man who man would be,
> Must rule the empire of himself; in it
> Must be supreme, establishing his throne
> On vanquished will,—quelling the anarchy
> Of hopes and fears,—being himself alone.—   (lines 10–14)

Richard Cronin sees something self-contradictory in Shelley's language here, observing, "In struggling against the emotive power of language, the poet can succeed only by diverting, not by destroying, that power. So, Shelley must celebrate republicanism in the language of monarchy."[4] But I would argue that Shelley is not struggling as hard against the power of language (or rather the language of power) as one might imagine; in his conception there is a desire—or rather a need—for power that can only be diverted rather than destroyed.

The same language of power and implicit violence recurs in Shelley's account of man's negotiations with the external world (I think it would be misleading to elide the sexism of this language by replacing *man* with *human*).[5] The passage I have in mind is one of the Earth's lyrics in act 4 of *Prometheus Unbound* (lines 370–423), part of Shelley's supreme lyric celebration of liberated human consciousness. A full commentary on this lyric would take us far indeed. For our present purposes it is clear enough that man's liberation is inseparable from his dominion over both himself and the world outside:

> Man, oh, not men! a chain of linked thought,
> Of love and might to be divided not,
> Compelling the elements with adamantine stress—
> As the Sun rules, even with a tyrant's gaze,
> The unquiet Republic of the maze
> Of Planets, struggling fierce towards Heaven's free wilderness.
>
> Man, one harmonious Soul of many a soul
> Whose nature is its own divine controul
> Where all things flow to all, as rivers to the sea;
> Familiar acts are beautiful through love;
> Labour and Pain and Grief in life's green grove
> Sport like tame beasts—none knew how gentle they could be!
>
> His Will, with all mean passions, bad delights,
> And selfish cares, its trembling satellites,
> A spirit ill to guide, but mighty to obey,
> Is as a tempest-winged ship, whose helm
> Love rules, through waves which dare not overwhelm,
> Forcing life's wildest shores to own its sovereign sway.
>
> All things confess his strength. —   (4.394–412)

Shelley here finds himself forced to seek liberation in the exercise of a repressive violence against his own inner impulses and against the natural world outside. But the same lines also show Shelley attempting to sketch at least a conceptual way out of this dilemma. His paralleling of inner and outer in terms of an astronomical metaphor evokes the scientific or parascientific thinking of his time in a way that qualifies somewhat the rigor of the envisaged control. The sun's "rule" of the planets is a function of the gravitational forces in which both ruler and ruled participate. We know that Shelley was attracted to the speculations of animal magnetism, which tended to assimilate the forces of gravity, magnetism, and electricity, both to each other and to some universal force that could be conceived as being as much moral as physical. Shelley draws on magnetic theories when he punningly refers to man "Compelling the elements with adamantine stress." In the language of Shelley's source, Aeschylus, "adamantine" refers to the material from which Prometheus's chains were made and hence to a purely physical compulsion. But the *adamant* is also the lodestone or magnet, the locus of a force that, like gravity, acts at a distance, with no visible physical support. Such forces—particularly for an antidualist skeptic like Shelley—facilitate an assimilation of physical to moral laws. That man's nature should be "its own divine controul" suggests a collapsing of the agent and the action, the law and obedience to it. The human will, too, is "ruled" by Love—the most obvious Shelleyan name for the universal force—but the result is an identity of ruler and ruled that makes references to "compelling" and "ruling" seem in the end rhetorical.

The demand that the human "instinct" for rule be directed inwards, against "their own evil passions" rests, as Shelley's language makes clear, on a view of human nature as inherently divided. This conception is (in Western thought) a highly traditional one, and the two terms across which the human subject was thought to be divided were traditionally referred to as passion and reason.[6] I have already referred to Shelley as "an antidualist skeptic," and we might expect him to have been less than entirely happy with this dualist conception of man's nature. I am not sure that he ever totally rejected it, and his utopian speculations certainly rest to a large extent on his belief in the possibility of transcending it.[7] The climax of book 8 of *Queen Mab* (which anticipates the climax of act 3 of *Prometheus Unbound*) is eloquent on this point:

> All things are void of terror: man has lost
> His terrible prerogative, and stands
> An equal amidst equals: happiness
> And science dawn though late upon the earth;
> Peace cheers the mind, health renovates the frame;
> Disease and pleasure cease to mingle here,
> Reason and passion cease to combat there;
> Whilst each unfettered o'er the earth extend
> Their all-subduing energies, and wield
> The sceptre of a vast dominion there;
> Whilst every shape and mode of matter lends
> Its force to the omnipotence of mind,
> Which from its dark mine drags the gem of truth
> To decorate its paradise of peace.   (8.225–38)

Central to the pathos of Shelley's description in *Queen Mab* of man's present state is the division that exists between "the outcast, man" (*Queen*

Mab, 3.199) and nature. In an ecological perspective this alienation of man from the natural is the root of human violence against the natural. But in the final analysis—and in this I would argue that he is like all the Romantics, Wordsworth included, *pace* Bate—Shelley neither believes it possible nor desires to reconcile the human subject to nature. The division within the subject might seem merely an introjection of the division between man and nature, but in Shelley's formulation the healing of that inner division will only free man to establish "the omnipotence of mind" in the form of a "vast dominion" over the whole world outside himself. The inner division, by which (masculine) reason finds itself grappling with (feminine) passion, will not so much be healed as projected outward. The human "instinct" for dominion shifts but is not to be abolished. Just as my account here is stubbornly reactionary with respect to the inviting green perspectives that Bate holds out, so Shelley repeats an old topos of our culture's ethical thinking. Like Marx an heir of the Enlightenment, he also inherits that murderous dialectic of enlightenment that Adorno and Horkheimer have traced back to the roots of Western culture.[8]

So far I have been at pains not to distinguish Shelley from a tradition of thought, often referred to as Judeo-Christian, that has received a good deal of blame for legitimating Western man's destructive exploitation of the natural environment. A founding text of this tradition speaks as emphatically as does Shelley of human "dominion" over nature: "And God said, Let us make man in our image, after our likeness: and let them have dominion over the fish of the sea, and over the fowl of the air, and over the cattle, and over all the earth, and over every creeping thing that creepeth upon the earth" (Genesis 1:26). A poet whose place in this tradition and whose importance for Shelley are equally indisputable makes significant use of this passage in denouncing what he considered to be the imposture of monarchy.[9] Milton's Adam, seeing in prospect the political sins of his fractious descendants, exclaims:

> O execrable son so to aspire
> Above his brethren, to himself assuming
> Authority usurped, from God not given:
> He gave us only over beast, fish, fowl
> Dominion absolute; that right we hold
> By his donation; but man over men
> He made not lord; such title to himself
> Reserving, human left from human free.
> (*Paradise Lost,* 12.64–71)

Milton, like Shelley, needs urgently to find some explanation of this perversion, and his account is remarkably close to that which we have seen Shelley offering. As Michael explains to Adam, with his fall man lost "true liberty . . . which always with right reason dwells" (12.83–84). When men allow themselves to be enslaved by their own "inordinate desires" and "upstart passions," the consequence and punishment is to be enslaved by other humans:

> since he permits
> Within himself unworthy powers to reign
> Over free reason, God in judgment just
> Subjects him from without to violent lords;
> Who oft as undeservedly enthral
> His outward freedom: tyranny must be,
> Though to the tyrant thereby no excuse.   (12.90–96)

Between them Shelley and Milton articulate a coherent account of political inequality: For Shelley he who shirks the task of self-rule is ripe to become a tyrant, and Milton argues that those who fail in this task are marked out as slaves. And of course neither man's success nor his failure in this respect is likely to free the natural world from human "dominion."

Not only does this tradition not offer a solution to our environmental dilemmas, it mispresents the problem disastrously. Its fundamental ethical bias leads to the conclusion that is reached by Walt Kelly's Pogo, as he gazes over the manmade desolation of the Okefenokee swamp and comments, "We have met the enemy and he is us." As long as we continue to think within the terms that Shelley proposes, this would be an acceptable conclusion. Intellectuals are not averse to this kind of self-culpabilization; if anything they find it somewhat flattering. If, as Walt Kelly himself claimed, "The job of cleaning up the mess starts just behind the nose,"[10] then the professional intellectual has a stake in the solution, since the changing of minds is his or her business. But the problem may not be there. The problem might lie rather with an economic system that makes it possible for private interests to own and exploit without check whole areas of the natural world, and moreover to own other areas within which they can insulate themselves from the consequences of this exploitation. Marx's faith in the unending expansion of the forces of production certainly indicates that he was no more alive to the environmental costs of economic progress than was the bourgeois economic order he attacked. But Marx would never have made the mistake—which some environmentalists seem to have made—of thinking that systems of morality and philosophical traditions could be centrally responsible for material conditions. It is this idealist turn that, as I noted at the outset, distinguishes Shelley from Marx. Shelley certainly fails to be green; but he does so, not by being red, but by not being red enough.

Promethean Narrative:
Overdetermined Form in
Shelley's Gothic Fiction

Tilottama Rajan

21

SHELLEY'S EARLY novel *St. Irvyne* breaks off with a declaration that Ginotti and Nempere are the same character, thus seeming almost to parody the too-convenient tying up of loose ends that had come to characterize the overdetermined genre of Gothic romance. Ginotti is the strange figure who sanctions Wolfstein's poisoning of the bandit Cavigni. Facilitating Wolfstein's tempestuous union with Megalena, he shadows Wolfstein's footsteps until he imparts the secret of the elixir of life to him, just before the plot does away with both of them. Nempere is the casuistical seducer of Eloise, who later settles down with the Shelleyan poet Fitzeustace. Fitzeustace accepts her although she is carrying Nempere's child, and the plot conveniently and predictably disposes of Nempere offstage. Until now the Wolfstein and Eloise stories have seemed completely unconnected, to the point that Shelley actually omits the two chapters (five and six) that might have linked them. The last paragraph merges these plots, announcing that Eloise is Wolfstein's sister and summarily disposing not only of Wolfstein but also of Ginotti and any residues of Nempere.

At the same time, the hastiness of this last paragraph makes conspicuous the fact that the conventionally moral resolution fails to close the gaps opened up by constructing the novel out of semiautonomous pieces. Why, for instance, does Nempere, who has already been killed, return to die in another time and place as Ginotti? And if Ginotti needs to die twice, is he actually dead at the end? Or does he survive as the text's unconscious, its figure for what it has not yet articulated? For although the desired unity of Radcliffe's *Mysteries of Udolpho* is similarly threatened by the semiautonomy of certain recesses and subplots, *St. Irvyne* emphasizes the ways in which it fails to cohere. Its two plots share a character (Ginotti) who performs different functions in each one; likewise they share plot positions that are occupied differently by characters in each story. This shifting of plot positions makes the character of Ginotti unreadable, whereas his return displaces us from any sense that the simple story of Eloise united with Fitzeustace is where the novel ends. As the uncanny link between the two plots, Ginotti's return as a phantasm the text must recall does not simply repeat the death of Nempere so as to confirm it in both narrative sectors. It also inscribes the utopian story of a heroine saved by a Shelleyan poet within another set of signifiers, marking the Gothic plot as the unconscious of the romance story.

The phantasmal repetition of characters in the early novel strikingly anticipates what Shelley will do in *Prometheus Unbound,* where he has a character speak through the phantasm of another character, and where he has Demogorgon occupy roles in the plot that are radically incommensurable. The amorphous and troubling Demogorgon of act 2 is the unconscious of the figure conjured up in the final act by Asia's desire, not in the sense that he or it is the reality behind appearance but in the sense that he is the other within her own language. Shelley's metaphor for this doubling of the self as its other is the underworld visited by the Magus Zoroaster, from where we can speculate that the phantasm Ginotti reappears, as the shadow or un-resolved remainder left after the destruction of Nempere. But this sense of the self as laterally related to a specular image that is not its hidden depth but its other also takes the structural form of an action whose parts exceed the whole one tries to construct out of them. Thus Demogorgon's violently Jovian overthrow of Jove coincides with Prometheus's attempt to recall his curse, as though the public and private sectors have failed to take account of each other.

The form of *Prometheus Unbound* can be approached in terms of Louis Althusser's extension of the Lacanian model of the unconscious to the historical process itself. For Althusser history is made up of semiautonomous parts that move at different speeds and in different directions. In Fredric Jameson's development of Althusser in *The Political Unconscious,* the discrepancies between these parts make history the unconscious of the imaginary resolutions we impose on its real contradictions, through narrativizations that omit intractable material.[1] The story that culminates in the marriage of Prometheus and Asia thus fails to take into account Demogorgon's violent overthrow of Jupiter, which is the site of a discrepancy between the play's base and its superstructure. Likewise the happy ending of the love plot in *St. Irvyne* sidesteps the shadowy presence of Ginotti on the fringes of Eloise's story. This presence can be demystified if we unmask Ginotti as nothing more than Nempere. But the reduction of Ginotti to Nempere works only if we forget that Ginotti is in some sense the phantasm of Zastrozzi, a figure for the haunting of this novel by its more transgressive precursor.

Overdetermined forms are by no means unique to Shelley. We find a similar use of form in Blake's revolutionary prophecies, *Europe* and *America,* in which the illustrations, the main narrative, and the preludium function as interconnecting parts that cannot be synthesized, because they seem to inhabit different spaces and times. Nor is this use of Althusser to read Romantic historicism entirely anachronistic. For one thing, Jameson has already pointed out that Hegelian phenomenology contains elements of what later comes to be called structural causality, within a model of the historical process that is still expressive and teleological.[2] Second, the notion of necessity so crucial to Godwin and Shelley is itself the site of a contradiction between organicist and mechanist explanations of history that provide the historical antecedents for Althusser's distinction between expressive and structural causality. That Demogorgon is amorphous and absent, that he resists representation and yet is a "living Spirit," that spirits nevertheless have "inorganic" voices (1.135; 2.4.7) are all indications that Romantic prometheanism is consciously overdetermined by organicist and mechanist discourses, freedom and determinism.

My argument will be that Shelley's Gothic novels begin an experiment with the pretexts and leitmotifs of prometheanism that is intertextually replayed in *Prometheus Unbound* as part of a self-conscious resumption of the structural and ideological problems in which the early work remains caught. For although these novels are jeux d'esprit whose plots border on the ridiculous, rather than dismissing them as adolescent, we might recall Julia Kristeva's characterization of the novel itself as an adolescent form. Noting that the novel allows for a trying out of roles in which the writer dresses up as his characters, she suggests that it creates a space withdrawn "from reality testing" that the novelist is then free to reorganize "in the time before an ideally postulated maturity." Adolescence provides the writer with metaphors of "what is not yet formed . . . what awaits the writer . . . what calls to him."[3]

That Zastrozzi and Ginotti are adolescent masks for the Promethean transgressor is obvious. Unable to think through the contradictions of the desire figured in Zastrozzi, Shelley destroys his creature according to the conventions of Faustian melodrama, but also undoes this destruction by allowing the first novel a displaced return in the second. The novels are clearly pastiche and refer to other texts—literary, social, and moral—rather than to the real. But they are also attempts to question the cultural semiotypes in which they remain caught. Their seriousness is indicated by the way in which they seem to be in excess of what they are. For both texts are highly melodramatic and correspond to Peter Brooks's characterization of the melodramatic world as overburdened "by a weight of mysterious and grandiose reference beyond itself."[4] The titanic characters seem to be more than what they are, actors in some drama beyond their own. At the same time, this further meaning is never revealed, because the very flatness of melodrama, as a form whose characters have no interiority, impedes the emergence of such meaning. The novels do not so much convey a content as they suggest the *form* that such a content might have. Their rapid pace and sudden reversals project a sense that they are dealing with something momentous. Their grandiose characters locate the intrapsychic conflicts dramatized in these tales of passion and murder within an action of world-historical significance. The characters seem overdetermined, acting in different ways at different times. But instead of working these contradictions out as complexity or ambiguity, the texts leave them in suspension by stagily eliminating characters whose significance they are not ready to think through. In short, the conjunction of psychic turmoil with titanic characters asks us to read these texts in relation to some kind of political unconscious. But the abrupt endings of plots and the rapid accumulation of events unmediated by psychological or intellectual linkage also suggest Shelley's inability at this point to work through the content of history.

The novels do nevertheless introduce two key elements that will return in the later drama. Both novels construct a form of closet literature, in which reality has been replaced by hyperreality, and mimesis by the simulacrum. As examples of hyperrealism the novels are both flamboyantly dramatic and completely unreal. In other words, their theatricality puts their credibility under erasure, detaining whatever designs they have upon us in the realm of writing. But at the same time they have a certain performativity, which is the condition of possibility for our rewriting them in the theater of our own minds. Functioning partly as a metadiscursive return to the first novel, the second one also introduces the form characteristic of the later work: a form composed of semiautonomous parts that do not add up to a whole, even as they remain haunted by the phantasm of an absent synthesis figured in Ginotti. Moreover, if the parts unsettle each other, this is also the relationship that obtains between the novels themselves. *St. Irvyne* is not a sequel, a recantation, or a paler repetition of *Zastrozzi*. Rather the relationship between the texts is lateral and supplementary, with Zastrozzi functioning as the excess that survives his dismantling into his phantasmal remainder Ginotti.

We can begin with the structurally simpler of the two novels, *Zastrozzi*. Although this novel contains only one plot and ends predictably with the defiant defeat of Zastrozzi, its effect upon the reader is overdetermined by the splitting of the villain into a male and a female figure, and by a disconnection between ideas, acts, and agents that allows the novel as writing and hypothesis to survive its dismantling as plot and mimesis. *Zastrozzi* is unusual as an example of feminist Gothic in that its male and female protagonists are allied, while Julia, the equivalent to Radcliffe's Emily, is relegated to the margins. A composite of Faust, the Jacobean revenge hero, and Vathek, Zastrozzi himself embodies a defiance of existing norms that is conflictedly projected as Promethean and destructive.

Zastrozzi's female conspirator, however, is motivated not simply by revenge but also by desire. Shelley's heroine is an intertextual development of a character with the same name, Laurentini, who appears in *Mysteries of Udolpho* as the silenced double of the novel's more conventional heroine. Reduced by Radcliffe to a (his)story told by others, Matilda returns in Shelley's novel to rewrite the patriarchal encoding of women who seek control over their sexual and legal property within narratives that associate good with passivity and female will with evil. Matilda is passionately in love with Verezzi, and the fact that she has a "commanding countenance" whereas her rival Julia has a "mild, heavenly countenance" and "ethereal form" (29, 33)[5] more or less prescribes the hopelessness of her passion. Plotting to have Zastrozzi poison Julia, she replots her life so as to act it out beyond the constraints of a gendered semiotics. At the center of her scheme is her staging of an episode in which she is wounded while saving Verezzi from a pretended attack by a ruffian (presumably Zastrozzi in disguise). In staging this scene,

Matilda constructs a plot that allows Verezzi to see her differently, shifting the actantial positions assigned characters within the narratives into which society writes them. That Verezzi does very soon fall in love with her suggests the arbitrariness of the social script within which his love for Julia has been constructed. Nor is Matilda's replotting of Verezzi's life simply a deception, since on some deeper level she *is* risking her life for him and ultimately dies for the plot she stages. Moreover, this plot, in which she appears as his savior but is actually his seductress, is itself a disguise for the plot she does not know how to write or to act within the narratology available to her.

The splitting of the transgressor into a manipulative male and a vulnerable female lamia, and the resulting introduction of the gender issue, narrate the conflicted nature of the motives and effects surrounding transgression, not all of which are without legitimacy. Equally important, this splitting corresponds to a suspension of the text between acting and action that is characteristic of closet literature. Zastrozzi commits crimes, but until close to the end Matilda only imagines them. We are first introduced to Matilda by way of the escritoire at which she has been writing. For much of the novel, her outrageous violations of morality remain unreal because Julia's death, the event that allows her to replot Verezzi's life, has not really happened. Moreover, when the fictional narrative is finally made real with the deaths of Julia and Verezzi, responsibility is again deferred away from Matilda with the introduction of Zastrozzi as the author of a plot into which she has been fitted. Enacting through Zastrozzi what he only imagines through Matilda, yet finally punishing him while he allows her to recant, Shelley is at once able to write and to withdraw a transgressive narrative, to recant and to withdraw his recantation. For Zastrozzi's heroic defense of his atheism supersedes Matilda's mandatory recantation, and it allows the "idea" he represents to survive its flawed expression in him.[6] At the same time, in rehabilitating Matilda while destroying Zastrozzi, Shelley agrees not to perform his transgressive drama and thus reclaims the right to write it.

The affinity between the novel and writing, and the character of writing as a withholding of presence that is also possessed of performativity, can both be linked to a certain semantic excess characteristic of closet literature. Or, put differently, this excess is what suspends the genre within the realm of writing, if by writing we imply something that is not ready to happen, something that is still being worked through. Characteristic of closet texts is the disconnection between their components and levels. Ideas are voiced by certain characters without being grounded in a personality, so that they function in abstraction both from their context and from the person who is their mouthpiece. Actions happen apart from their agents: Someone is murdered, but the murderer seems more the vehicle than the agent of the crime. Because there is no determinate agency in closet literature, characters act without consequences. Or, to put it differently, the characters produce powerful effects, but are without psychological credibility, because they are signs for ideas melodramatically and unreally staged in the laboratory of a mental theater.

This semiautonomy of actions and ideas has two effects. It gives them a theoretical quality, thus withholding active commitment from them but also suspending their consequences so that the reader can entertain them without being responsible for them. It also inscribes ideas, characters, and actions as signifiers, signs for a drive or desire rather than enactments of a specific ideology. Zastrozzi's atheist materialism, for instance, inscribes Shelley's desire for a contestation of social norms, but as a form for which he has still to find an appropriate content. His atheism is a vehicle with an indeterminate tenor, the form of a content rather than the content itself. Despite their trans-gressiveness, the novels inscribe the desire for an ethical order by construct-ing the conventional plot positions of villain and virtuous innocence and by ending with the restoration of "justice." Characters, however, do not occupy these plot positions with any stability, and an abducted innocent like Megalena in *St. Irvyne* can very quickly become the epitome of evil. The rapidity of these role reversals suggests that although closet Gothic is com-mitted to the triumph of good over evil, there is no clear sense of what constitutes evil or what good really is.

The disconnection of acts, agents, and ideas, in other words, is the narrative expression of a semiotics in which vehicles exist without clear tenors, so that characters and their actions become figures for the form of a content rather than for the content itself. The narrative excess, in turn, reflects the overdetermination of the social and psychic texts in which the narrative has its genesis. Closet writing thus resists closure, or reaches an ending that is always premature. Shelley deals with the resulting sense of a text not yet ready for performance outside the theater of the mind in two ways. Whereas the staginess of the novels prevents what happens in them from really happening, *Prometheus Unbound* acts out a version of history that it recognizes as a performance, and it provides us with the metahistorical tools to call this performance into question.[7] Those tools, however, are ones that Shelley first stumbles across in his second novel. For unlike *Zastrozzi*, *St. Irvyne* is profoundly resistant to being read on a thematic level. Instead it is

Shelley's first metadiscursive text, in that it is about the functioning of the signifier, and it is in that sense a commentary on the form of *Zastrozzi,* on the problems in signification and emplotment that complicate the reading and the writing of the texts we shape out of the political unconscious.

The second novel is more conspicuously disunified than the first one, and this in itself shifts our attention from theme to structure, from the signified to the signifier. That Shelley in returning to the genre of political Gothic now finds himself detained at the level of the signifier is a problem with which he will grapple in *Prometheus Unbound.* For the later text can be read on both a narrative and a metadiscursive level, as staging an action in the form of a world-historical romance, but also giving us a framework within which to critique its emplotment of history. In *St. Irvyne,* by contrast, the narrative level is unreadable. Whatever Shelley is trying to "say" through his characters and the things that happen to them, it seems he must first negotiate the gaps in the unfolding of a plot whose real (as distinct from textual) closure is withheld by these very gaps. In considering the novel at a metadiscursive level, I shall accordingly focus on two things: the functioning of Ginotti as a figure for deferred reference and the double plot as the formal marker of a semantic excess that was still unthematized in the earlier novel. Nevertheless, I suggest that in this early novel Shelley discovered certain semiotic shapes and structures by which he remained haunted, and that he returned to them in *Prometheus Unbound* to make them into consciously metadiscursive signifiers.

The first of these shapes is that of a narrative that works itself out in bits and pieces, such that the closure reached on one level is an imaginary resolution achieved by forgetting something else. Curiously enough, the two plots in *St. Irvyne* are not as disconnected as Shelley makes them seem. In both plots an innocent and recently orphaned virgin is abducted. Megalena's character changes unaccountably, and she and her rescuer seduce each other into evil; in Eloise's story the roles of rescuer and seducer remain separate, as do the boundaries between good and evil, innocence and experience. Moreover, the two plots simplify and separate elements that were condensed into a single plot in *Zastrozzi.* Megalena's degeneration dehumanizes the more ambiguous character of Matilda, whereas on the other hand the Eloise subplot idealizes subversion by constructing its erotic utopia upon the peaceful challenging of marital and other social conventions.

The gaps opened up by the double plot have to do with the relation between romantic love and Gothic power, and between private and public spaces. Like the union of Prometheus and Asia, the love of Fitzeustace and Eloise remains lyrically disconnected from the violence that proliferates in the rest of the novel and that may even be the enabling condition of this love. This disconnection is figured in the later text by the two chariots that Asia sees after her conversation with Demogorgon, one light and one dark, imaging a movement with different centers that, like the gyres of Yeats, may coincide only momentarily. As if to compromise this coincidence, the earlier text effects it not by allowing the comic movement to succeed the anarchic overthrow of tyranny, but by having the darker main plot reoccupy the foreground at the end, closeting the lovers in the narrative's past rather than its present or future. The plot quite literally ends with a revolution, in the double sense of an overthrow and a cyclic return of the past.

In freeing Eloise by a narrative convulsion that overthrows Ginotti by bringing him back, Shelley inscribes the Gothic plot as the unconscious of a romance that is more nostalgic than subversive. For the gap between the plots is also a gap within Eloise's story, which is reopened by the closing paragraph. The cryptic equivalence, "Ginotti is Nempere. Eloise is the sister of Wolfstein" (199), gets rid of Ginotti by allowing him to recede into a story that is already over, but also reopens the question of Eloise by bringing her into a plot that is not yet over. The ending inscribes each plot within the other, reminding us of the kinship of Eloise with Wolfstein, who throughout the novel has been shadowed by a phantasm that De Quincey was later to describe in *Suspiria de Profundis* as the Dark Interpreter. Eloise never meets her darker double, since they are antithetically confined in separate sectors of the action. But by having Eloise transit more rapidly the narrative of kidnapping and seduction that proves Megalena's undoing, Shelley reminds us that her innocence is constituted on the text's forgetting of the jeopardy in which it has so recently placed what it figures through her.

As the uncanny link between two plots in which he has different names and functions, Ginotti/Nempere is the primary signifier of the nonidentity underlying the syntax of identification by which closure is imposed in the last paragraph. Moreover, because of his shadowy presence, he allows us to figure this nonidentity as a textual unconscious rather than a simple gap or aporia. Ginotti is on one level a version of Zastrozzi. Both characters are larger than life and are possessed of unexplained power. Moreover, Ginotti plays the same role in relation to Wolfstein as Zastrozzi does in relation to Matilda, whom he manipulates while forwarding her destructive passion. But unlike his precursor, Ginotti remains shadowy and absent: He seems a key to the plot's meaning that we are never given, a sign rather than a character. Whereas Zastrozzi's crimes are Gidean gratuitous acts that challenge moral absolutes, Ginotti seems to have no motives and does not really do anything, being no more than the condition of possibility for crimes that are actually committed by Wolfstein and Megalena. As a deconstruction of Zastrozzi, Ginotti on one level becomes Nempere, the displaced name of the father from whose incestuous tyranny the young lovers must free themselves. But Ginotti cannot entirely be reduced to Nempere, because Nempere himself seems to be more than or other than what he seems. He seems to be Ginotti rather than the reverse. As a sign that Nempere is more than what he seems, and as the obscure force behind Wolfstein's life, Ginotti is the possibility that the crimes of the text's characters are not ordinary crimes, but metaphysical acts like those of Zastrozzi and Byron's Cain. But since Ginotti never discloses himself as Lucifer, this notion of crime as a signifier in a higher script also remains ungrounded, opening up the further possibility that history is simply a process without a subject, an action that only intermittently signifies.

The point is not to identify Ginotti, but to recognize that as a gap in the plot's construction, he functions as the text's unconscious, inscribing all attempts at interpretation within the language of the other. Moving one step beyond *Zastrozzi,* the second novel discloses the hidden or metaphysical dimension behind surface events as a further text. In *Zastrozzi* the plot constructed by Matilda was written into a further plot designed by Zastrozzi, with the enfolding of plot within plot suggesting a mystery that is finally unfolded. But Ginotti, who seems to know the script that determines Wolfstein's life, is himself inscribed in a further plot he cannot read. As the site of a deferral, Ginotti's abrupt death figures an absence already implicit in the death of his precursor, whose disclosure of his true motives and identity at the end is unsatisfyingly incoherent. For the conclusion that feminist subversion is the dupe of a masculine will to power unravels into the oddly conflicted information that Zastrozzi has made use of another woman to avenge the wrongs done to his mother by the patriarchy. To all this is added a description of Zastrozzi's defiant dignity in the face of death, and a speech on atheism that seems thought up on the spur of the moment.

The semantic overdetermination of the first novel's ending is replayed in the more consciously decentered ending of the second text. The fact that Ginotti dies and thus proves not to be supernatural deconstructs the promise of a hidden meaning, though the fact that he dies twice reconstructs that possibility by allowing him to survive as an uncanny remainder. He seems to be the cause of everything that has happened in the novel, even playing a major role in a plot where he is not named. As the motivating force behind the novel, he is, however, curiously absent. He is absent also from our reading, this very absence being in fact what makes us read.

Ginotti in short functions as a metanarrative figure for the political unconscious, which Shelley will later figure through Demogorgon. If the split structure of the novel expresses a sense that history is made up of parts that do not cohere, the unconscious is the absent cause that constantly promises and withholds coherence. Or, put differently, the unconscious, as a depth that is not a depth, is the ambiguous possibility that overdetermination has some unreadable significance. It is important to recognize in Ginotti not simply absence but also possibility: the sense of something left over at the end of the novel, which is the possibility of the characters being something other than what they seem to be.

That Ginotti figures something unfinished, functioning as remainder or reminder, comes also from the fact that *St. Irvyne* must be read intertextually with Godwin's *St. Leon,* which introduces into it an unfulfilled horizon of expectations. Having received the elixir of life from a mysterious stranger, St. Leon lives twice over and assumes two quite different characters, first as a dissolute gambler and then as a reforming rebel, the failed savior of Hungary. Since Wolfstein receives the formula for the elixir from Ginotti but not its benefits, he never becomes St. Leon and never bridges the gap between what he is and what he could be. However, the concentration of allusions to Godwin at the end of the novel reinscribes Shelley's text within its ideological desire at the moment of its apparent deconstruction. Ginotti's death does not so much end the novel as return it to its cultural unconscious, to a world inhabited by the "shadows of all forms that think and live" (*Prometheus Unbound,* 1.198), the phantasms and traces of other texts.

Returning to this unconscious in *Prometheus Unbound,* Shelley replays *St. Irvyne* so as to emancipate Promethean romance from Jovian power. In so doing he creates a shape all light from something that has neither form nor outline, using language to impose an imaginary resolution on "thoughts and forms, which else senseless and shapeless were" (4.417). *Prometheus,* however, is both a performance of things as they should be and a metanarrative structure that exhibits its narrativization of history as relative to its own historical moment. Crucial to its metanarrative dimension are two elements: a structural disjunction that is the conscious sign of the text's overdetermination, and a textual apparatus that is proto-psychoanalytic. The drama is conspicuously constructed out of parts between which there are significant gaps. Critics have often pointed to the lack of connection between the first three acts and act four. But in fact the previous three acts seem equally unconnected, with the action in each case being dominated by a different character. Act 1 supposedly projects an inner revolution in which Prometheus is victorious over the Jovian elements in himself. Act 3 replays this revolution in the theater of history, the melodramatic flatness of the characters Demogorgon and Jove being a sign that we are dealing with historical forces rather than individuals. Not only is the inner revolution externalized at a historical level solely through the intervention of a deus ex machina, it is also contradicted by the violence Demogorgon uses in his overthrow of Jupiter, a violence that no doubt alludes to the French Revolution. Act 1 is likewise at odds with act 2, opposing to the cooperative, feminist society of the sisters a more agonistic and confrontational psychology in which Prometheus, who proclaims himself "king over myself" (line 492), still has recourse to hierarchical metaphors at odds with Shelley's antimonarchism. In the first three acts the sisters, as vehicles for a dream of which Prometheus is the tenor, remain very much auxiliaries in a revolution still conceived in terms of heroic struggle. But Prometheus's disappearance after the first act and his resulting demotion from agent to symbol allow the fourth act to substitute for a hero-centered drama a lyrical fluidity that some might consider intensely inane. As in Althusser's model of history, which posits the semiautonomy of various sectors within the base and superstructure, ideology and enactment, inside and outside, seem to function somewhat apart from each other. In fact the intermediate fair copy of the play in the Bodleian Library may well recognize the radically overdetermined nature of Shelley's historical moment. This copy scrambles the linear narrativization of the four acts by juxtaposing different sectors of the play's action on facing sides of the page. We read parts of act 4 side by side with act 1. Similarly, the lyrical speeches of the fauns are placed opposite Asia's dialogue with Demogorgon, as if to lay out the unconscious of history on a flat surface, through the lateral exposure of each textual segment to its other.[8]

Equally important is the way in which the scenes that move the action forward double as part of a psychoanalytic apparatus that constantly confronts Promethean desire with its own unconscious. I refer here to Prometheus's recalling and thus repetition of his curse through the summoning up of psychic phantasms, to Asia's and Panthea's recollection of their dreams, and to the Magus Zoroaster's encounter with his own image. Such scenes make us aware that the imaginary selves constructed by Prometheus after his summoning up of the phantasm and by Asia after her cryptic dialogue with Demogorgon may be based upon a (mis)recognition. In Earth's speech on the Magus Zoroaster, the realm of the drama's performance is uncannily underwritten by a realm of phantasms or images, each belonging to a dramatic character, but capable of being summoned into playing the role of a character it is not. Earth's speech links the narratological machinery of the drama to a textual unconscious in which characters have no essential selves and in which the identity between plot positions and the characters who occupy them is unstable. As the words once spoken by Prometheus can now be uttered by the phantasm of Jove, so the position occupied by Demogorgon when he overthrows Jove can also be occupied by the agent of a different kind of revolution.

In this textual unconscious, made up not of archetypes but of phantasms and images that function as floating signifiers, Shelley finds a metanarrative figure for the excessive relationship between acts, agents, and words in his early novels. The phantasm is the possibility of the self and the plot in which it acts being otherwise, the possibility of a self that is different from its Promethean performance, or an image whose Promethean potential survives its Gothic deconstruction. These phantasms, however, are not the hidden depth of the political unconscious. Rather they are narrativizations or images that may produce as much as disclose the tenor of history. Indeed, the radically indeterminate relationship between the tenor and the vehicle of history, and the uncertainty as to whether vehicles produce or convey their tenor, are figured in the chariots that bear the hours of history, and in Asia's doubt as to which chariot she should enter, or which vehicle will provide her history with its tenor. Undecidably tenor or vehicle, the phantasm travels between the text's imaginary and its unconscious, making the text itself a mirror—a mimesis and a specularization—of the giant forms or shadows futurity casts on the present.

Prometheus Unbound and the
Postmodern Political Dilemma

Linda Brigham

22

I CONSIDER SHELLEY´S ambivalence about poetry in the context of a general revolutionary ambivalence toward history. History, after all, subverts revolution; as the Furies remind Prometheus, "In each human heart terror survives / The ravin it has gorged" (1.618–19). The past haunts and possesses the present, captivating the future. But the problem of history in Shelley runs exceptionally deep, even to the level of language, of sign processing. Much has been written, of course, on Shelley's complex view of language, some of it by those represented in this volume. Rather than try to add something new to this already formidable corpus, in this chapter I attempt a deliberate anachronism and put Shelley in the context of contemporary debate on postmodernism, particularly postmodern connections of politics, aesthetics, and economics.

This debate involves a problematic of history, I would claim, in a way that resembles Shelley's setup of the relation between history and mentality. History is a sign construct, subject to revision by sign use. However, postmodernism's problem is to *prevent* history's erasure rather than to accomplish it. The question is how can we *save* history, if we should, rather than how can we *erase* history, if we should.

Postmodernist commentators tend to fall into two camps: those who work to historicize postmodernism's dehistoricizations and those who see the erasure of history as a new epoch that our current sense of history is inadequate to comprehend. I draw on the work of two of postmodernism's more suspicious critics, Fredric Jameson and David Harvey, and one of postmodernism's apocalyptic advocates, Jean Baudrillard, to assess the status of *Prometheus Unbound*. *Prometheus,* thus illuminated, has a deep-structured antihistorical, and, as a result, antipolitical, unconscious.

The erasure of historical time leaves space. Postmodernism became reflexively self-aware in the field of architecture, and critiques of postmodernism are often critiques of a space. The design of the Bonaventure Hotel in Los Angeles, Jameson relates, achieves utopian distinction from its surroundings not by physical barriers, but by a trick of perception: Its reflective surfaces play back the troubled city in which it rests, but in the process distort and aestheticize those reflections. Inside, the Bonaventura substitutes its own engines for the motors of the body: escalators, elevators, and revolving terraces replace the "narrative stroll," as Jameson calls it, that formerly marked any space as space. Jameson concludes that "postmodern hyperspace has finally succeeded in transcending the capacities of the individual human body to locate itself"; in other words, the grounds for distinguishing thought—mental space—from perception—physical space—have disappeared. Machines have made the distinction obsolete.[1]

For historical geographer David Harvey, space—and consequently, aesthetics—provide a kind of seductive shorthand during periods of multifaceted cultural fragmentation. This fragmentation arises from the upheavals in our experience of space and time. Spatial representation, Harvey asserts, "always brokers between Being and Becoming."[2] Harvey portrays aesthetics as a midwife, bringing in a new set of economic relations, defining new deployments of labor, new kinds of commodities.

I would define this shift in emphasis from time to space as a shift away from a certain kind of reference, an *indexical* way of referring to things, adopting the term from the American philosopher C. S. Peirce. Indices are signs that refer to what they themselves are not; they direct the attention away from the sign itself to some absent thing. An index is a trace, a clue, a footprint in the sand. Causes and effects are indices of each other. It might be said that modernity, with its anxious historical self-constitution, regards the present as an index, pointing backward to an absent history and forward to an absent future. Such a technique of reference reinforces the construction and maintenance of historical continuity; continuity becomes necessary for meaning, and the necessity for maintaining continuity consolidates social relations.

Perhaps the most often cited characteristic of postmodernism, however, is its indeterminacy. The signs of the present point nowhere with certainty. As a result, indexical reference ceases to dominate the way in which we obtain meaning. We are thrown back upon synchronic, spatialized relationships. A familiar Shelleyan trope describing the nature of mental life, one both desired and feared, illustrates the displacement of indexical reference by synchronicity; it portrays the destruction of the temporal implications of the present. In *A Defence of Poetry,* like *Prometheus* a prophetic, utopian work, the metaphor is a positive one. Here poetry is a revolutionary constituent; Shelley calls poetry "the interpenetration of a diviner nature through our own; but its footsteps are like those of a wind over a sea, which the coming calm erases, and whose traces remain only as on the wrinkled sand which paves it" (504). In "The Triumph of Life," however, the same image appears in a much more sinister context; the erasure comes as the result of an enchanted liquid:

> And suddenly my brain became as sand
>
> Where the first wave had more than half erased
> The track of deer on desert Labrador,
>   Whilst the fierce wolf from which they fled amazed
>
> Leaves his stamp visibly upon the shore
> Until the second bursts—so on my sight
>   Burst a new Vision never seen before. (2.405–11)

In both these examples, time covers its own tracks, prohibiting an indexical technology of reference. Things *cannot* refer to a temporal beyond. Instead, Shelley foregrounds the arbitrariness of indexical reference, its dependence on an assumed continuity that may well be imaginary. In one case, the *Defence,* Shelley celebrates the process; in "The Triumph" he is suspicious of it.

In *Prometheus Unbound* freeing mental dependence on time proves indispensable to the revolution the drama depicts. This freedom constitutes Prometheus's primary realization. In contemplating revenge against the tyrant Jupiter, Prometheus's attention shifts to the atemporally qualitative character of his own mental image and he recognizes it as an evil and violent one. "Disdain? Ah no! I pity thee," he declares,

What Ruin
Will hunt thee undefended through wide Heaven!
How will thy soul, cloven to its depth with terror,
Gape like a Hell within! I speak in grief,
Not exultation, for I hate no more,
As then, ere misery made me wise.   (1.53–58)

The image of Jupiter's suffering has more power over Prometheus than Jupiter's indexical meaning. The object of indexical reference must be supplied by memory. Prometheus shifts to a picture language, an act of imaginative visualization. And though a masculine, Protestant, and Miltonic discipline would recommend distrust of these mental images, Prometheus in this case fails to overcome an aesthetic and traditionally feminine submission to the dictates of a (possibly) hysterical imagination.

The transition in technology of reference has radical social implications; it occurs not only at the expense of tyranny, but also at the expense of those institutions that purportedly ameliorate tyranny: the rule of law, for example. Prometheus frees himself from the rigidity of justice, which, as a system of compensation, indexes actions against forms of retribution. This system constructs a past made up of the deeds of discrete criminal agents, the chief of whom, in Prometheus's view, has been Jupiter. As a system linked to guilt and personal agency, justice fosters an indexical reference technology; the present remains confined to indicating the past. But by shifting to a synchronic and spatial reference technology, Prometheus flattens Jupiter's agency into the phenomenal present, where definite relations to the past no longer form the chief constituents of individuals.

In *Prometheus Unbound* the new age arrives not primarily because of a change in time, but because of a change in the relation of imagination to representation. A new technology of reference confers an abstract and commutable value on the objects of imagination. They are no longer subordinated to a representational function. Imagination and reference intertwine in a new mental mapping. The recitation of Prometheus's forgotten curse shows the Titan *as* Jupiter, as so many critics have pointed out. Prometheus's vision of the Phantasm of Jupiter becomes necessary to his recall of the curse because past events, like tracks in the sand, have been erased from his mind. The Phantasm restores the "reality" of the curse as a current event, toward which the new Prometheus is a spectator. The indexical signs of the curse's evil—the ruin of the world and of humanity—cannot do this. The new spectacle of the curse and the old historical fact of the curse employ two different technologies of reference. The equation of Jupiter with his indices, pain and sorrow and despair, only makes existing polarities more rigid and self-destructive, as Earth's self-lacerating recital of the effects of her own curse demonstrates (1.176–79). Prometheus's vision of his curse, on the other hand, shows the equivocal nature of the Jupiterian adversary and recasts reaction as repetition and opposition as doubling. Previously, the curse behaved as an outgrowth of the indexical technology of language, a use of words to structure a world that itself became a retribution, a fallen world that has become a punishment for a crime. But Prometheus hears in the words their phenomenal impact, their immediately contagious rage, and it is on this phenomenal level that he recants, with disarming simplicity:

> It doth repent me: words are quick and vain;
> Grief for awhile is blind, and so was mine.
> I wish no living thing to suffer pain   (1.303–5)

Prometheus thus becomes a consumer of his own imaginative products. In the process, he validates the imaginary as a commodity in a new economy.

The second act, dominated by the Asian rather than Promethean consciousness, puts into practice the breakthrough that Prometheus has made in theory. Here Asia's imagination no longer coexists representationally with a present-or-absent external reality; instead, in mapping that reality, she brings it into being. In a flush of positive feedback, reality is no longer separate from mind. Asia's mental state has an a priori complicity with the physical state of the world. They coincide, double. In Baudrillard's words, "Release from the real is achieved *by the very excess of its appearances.* Objects resemble too much what they are, and this resemblance is like a second state, their true depth. It is the irony of excess reality, through *allegorical* resemblance, and diagonal lightning."[3]

This "release from the real" clears the ground for a new relation to the real, very much like the process de Certeau describes in his contemporary critique of the cultural aggression of mapping. Maps eliminate traces—the pasts—of the practices that formerly produced a given space. They provide, paradoxically, a *double* of a new space. Furthermore, as Harvey remarks, "The map is, in effect, a homogenization and reification of the rich diversity of spatial itineraries and spatial stories."[4] Mapping eliminates history from space.

I offer several comments on what Shelley originally planned as the spatial center of the drama, the interchange between Asia and Demogorgon. Where

Prometheus in act I rearranged the concept of historical agency, the focus of Asia's investigation is value—things, commodities, worth. Asia recites a history of technology focusing on the historical moment of alienation—the creation of Jupiter. Symbolically, this is the moment when humankind becomes creatively free. As with Prometheus, this creative freedom means bondage to the objects created. It was Prometheus who created Jupiter as the supreme being. Narrating the progress of human invention and the spread of civilization into unmapped territories, Asia finds that she is talking about a repetitive process, an iterative series. She concludes her account by critiquing the creative subjugation of nature as a whole. It is, she says, because "Man looks on his creation like a God" that "Evil . . . drives him on, / The wreck of his own will" (2.4.101–4). The objectification of the imagination in the products of labor—more precisely, in the ideal form into which productive processes violently transform matter—reinforces a splitting of subject from object and renders them antagonists. History in the drama is synonymous with alienation, a process perpetuated by an indexical reference technology. Creations refer to creators and vice versa by a play of absences, of shadows.

Demogorgon's famous comment on the ultimate source of meaning reinforces the nature of Asia's realization as something quite different from the usual form of conceptualization characterizing understanding in prior ages. Asia requests the name of the "master of the slave," and Demogorgon responds:

> If the Abysm
> Could vomit forth its secrets:—but a voice
> Is wanting, the deep truth is imageless;
> For what would it avail to bid thee gaze
> On the revolving world? what to bid speak
> Fate, Time, Occasion, Chance and Change? To these
> All things are subject but eternal Love   (2.4.114–20)

Demogorgon guides Asia to matter, not form. And redundantly: Asia has already realized that she is talking about the process of the material cosmos itself, not a unified and controlling entity, when she asks for the "master of the slave." The "imagelessness" of the deep truth, so easily mistaken as an exemplary assertion of Romantic iconoclasm, is just the opposite. It is actually the extreme of immanence rather than transcendence. Imagination and physical reality no longer have a barrier between them. In more contemporary terms, imagelessness is the hyperreal loss of the referent that occurs when the imagination becomes a materially productive power. Products, consisting of objects pressed into forms, these shadows of man the creator, give way to a new decentered ontology, a semiotic flux featuring a whole new array of commodities—imaginative ones.

What happens to standards of value? Gold, the controversial center of monetary debate in Shelley's time, is mentioned explicitly only in passing in Asia's theodicy:

> And he tamed fire, which, like some beast of prey
> Most terrible, but lovely, played beneath
> The frown of man, and tortured to his will
> Iron and gold, the slaves and signs of power.   (2.4.66–69)

Michael Scrivener reports that gold in Shelley has almost exclusively negative connotations, and so we should take it here. Yet in *A Philosophical View of Reform* and *The Mask of Anarchy,* both written in an interventionist ardor after the Peterloo Massacre, Shelley recommends a return to gold coinage and opposes paper money. This is the position much of the landed aristocracy took, as Donald H. Reiman points out in his profile of Shelley in this light as an agrarian reactionary.[6] But it is the position of William Cobbett as well, and the money issue also offered socially progressive reasons to insist on wages in gold; ordinary wage earners were most profoundly victimized by the bank failures and currency fluctuations enabled by inconvertible paper. Thus to insist on gold, the real thing, is part of making man "king over himself" (*Prometheus Unbound,* 1.492).

But Scrivener is right about gold in *Prometheus Unbound.* Here Shelley clearly moves away from gold, even from a gold standard. What he moves *toward* emerges in Asia's response to Demogorgon; she expresses the new revolutionary situation by an irreducible image: that of the sun, of absolute visibility, the antitype of gold: "Prometheus shall arise / Henceforth the Sun of this rejoicing world" (2.4.126–27). This sun is no longer a unified solar standard but an internal one, multiplied infinitely in human consciousness. This Asian sun, providing the basis for all other images, is no longer a centrally located totalitarian power; replacing the sun as the gold standard of cognition, it no longer, as an overarching abstraction, hierarchizes what it defines. Human creative power in *Prometheus Unbound* frees itself from the comparative standard of money entirely. In utopia commodity value becomes transparent; things need no longer be evaluated through the abstract index of money.

The removal of commodities from direct indexing by money may perhaps be equally well expressed by what happens when money itself becomes a commodity, a characteristic of both Shelley's age, when the volatility of paper currency facilitated poor credit practices by the banks, and our own period, in which international credit relations become more and more of a determining factor for financial stability, complicating the relationship between production and wealth. Harvey, ascribing this instability to the cyclical nature of capitalism, asserts that "the more flexible motion of capital emphasizes the new, the fleeting, the ephemeral, the fugitive, and the contingent in modern life." The social effects of this system, Harvey claims, despite its radically fluid economic ontology, are probably, even dangerously, reactionary: "as Simmel long ago suggested, it is also at such times of fragmentation and economic insecurity that the desire for stable value leads to a heightened emphasis upon the authority of basic institutions—the family, religion, the state. And there is abundant evidence of a revival of support for such institutions and the values they represent throughout the Western world since about 1970."[7] In short, it may be that Shelley's more superficially conservative stance, his insistence on gold as the medium of exchange, is at least no more politically problematic than his move in the opposite direction in his radical utopia.

After the deindexing of value, the diachronic process of life itself remains the chief barrier to aestheticizing history. In the final act of the drama, Shelley recovers even death for the new pansemiotic utopia. The justification of death for revolution is a familiar Shelleyan assertion; in *Queen Mab* the Fairy Queen tells Ianthe, "Death is no foe to virtue" (9.176); in *Laon and Cythna* the afterlife bestows the honor life itself withholds. But both these cases pertain to prerevolutionary existence. In *Prometheus Unbound,* the postrevolutionary dismissal of death no longer serves the same rhetorical purpose; here its value becomes entirely aesthetic. In act 4 Panthea describes the evolution and revolution of the earth. Geological history once linked the Earth to her "wheel of pain" (1.141) and, more important, created the mechanism of transgression and revenge that drove humanity for so many centuries. These cycles gave death a meaning in martyrdom. But now history becomes, on the revolutionary earth, like language and music, a series of appearances and disappearances. Panthea concludes her long description of the canceled cycles of antediluvian epochs—vegetation, minerals, abandoned cities and civilizations, and monstrous animal forms (4.270–318)—with a terse absence of regret:

> the blue globe
> Wrapt Deluge round it like a cloak, and they
> Yelled, gaspt and were abolished; or some God
> Whose throne was in a Comet, past, and cried—
> "Be not!"—and like my words they were no more.   (4.314–18)

Like her words, the ages of the earth form parts of a system of pure difference. Like the sands of the mind, they disappear with the next epochal wave. Death, in other words, becomes syntagmatic. Its function is informational; it prevents cosmic stasis. Individual death serves the consistency and aesthetic dynamism of the system.

Baudrillard indicts a similar transition in Marx after the failed revolutions of 1848; in his view, *Kapital* moves from an immediate millenarian prospect for renewal to a historical dialectic. Whether or not this is doing justice to Marx, I think his words do apply in a modified way to Shelley's *Prometheus Unbound*. In fact, this criticism is central to the ambivalence in Shelley's shifting and ephemeral images of mentality, in his distrust of language generally. Baudrillard writes, "The Revolution as 'end' is in fact equivalent to the autonomization of the means. What has happened is clear: it has the effect of stifling the current situation, of exorcizing immediate subversion, of diluting (in the chemical sense of the term) explosive reactions in a long term solution."[8] "The autonomization of the means" is both a redundancy and an oxymoron. The phrase refers to the absorption of revolution into a system of deferred gratification; this is in turn the codification of individual life, or individual death. But once the means are autonomized, the *end* disappears; we are no longer agents in history. Deferral paradoxically describes the present; it is an aesthetic combination of differences, like act 4 of *Prometheus Unbound*.

So it seems that Shelley's postmodern utopia raises the same problems for critical consciousness as Jameson's Bonaventure Hotel. The conversion of the object to information annihilates purposive activity in the same way that the antispace of the hotel annihilates the old Euclidean map, the past against which the present can be indexed.

But another reflection: The purported contemporary advantage of spatial reference over indexical reference as described in Baudrillard may ultimately be a response to time, to what Harvey refers to as temporal compression, that is not entirely unhealthy. The revolution in *Prometheus Unbound* happens in a moment, a flash of intuition at the breaking of the dawn. Synchronic mapping employs a mercurial swiftness. Indices, on the other hand, whose nature it is to point toward causes, or toward effects, require a world in which events happen slowly, regularly, and ponderously enough to make tracing their individual sources and destinies worthwhile. It is, after all, reactionaries like Edmund Burke who promote the kind of time in which reference could make sense and depth could have meaning: a time of luxurious contemplation. But the maintenance of such a time requires a denial of phenomena and of phenomenal swiftness, a denial of the overwhelming influx of novelty in the multicultural montage borne of commerce, conquest, and empire. Today, when imaging "the operations of the human mind" (*Prometheus Unbound*, preface) has become technologically routine, and mentality is extended and multiplied by cybernetics, the influx of signifiers and their synergistic interactions may no longer tax the physical abilities of culture. One hopes that critical thinking will be able to keep up the pace, or it will certainly be outrun by the creative destruction of a postmodern economy.

All Shapes of Light:
The Quantum Mechanical Shelley

Arkady Plotnitsky

23

THIS CHAPTER explores the conjunction of two metaphorical models: one is generated by Shelley's usage of figures and theories of light, especially in "The Triumph of Life;" the other is derived from Niels Bohr's interpretation of quantum mechanics, known as complementarity. Both models are defined by the conjunction of two features: the first is the metaphoric duality of light, combining wave and particle imagery; the second is the suspension of classical causality. The theoretical economy based on these features leads to a radical dislocation, or deconstruction, and a reinterpretation of the classical understanding of interpretive and theoretical processes. This reinterpretation has deep-seated affinities with postmodernist theory and in some of its aspects moves beyond it. The chapter thus relates Shelley, postmodernism, and modern or postmodern science. These connections are not surprising given Shelley's interest in science, especially optics and atomic theory, which were brought together by quantum physics a century later. Such interests by themselves, however, can account neither for the complexity of the models at issue nor for their implications. Nor can they encompass the scale of Shelley's achievement. Shelley develops a conceptual and metaphorical economy that gives him a very special place in the intellectual landscape of modernity and postmodernity and their relationships to science. In 1930 Karl Grabo pronounced Shelley "a Newton among poets."[1] By that time, he could have said "Bohr" instead of "Newton" and spoken of quantum mechanical science and the quantum mechanical Shelley.

COMPLEMENTARITY

Complementarity is a representational and theoretical framework developed by Bohr in order to account for what he calls *complementary* features—features that are mutually exclusive but equally necessary for a comprehensive description of quantum phenomena. In this interpretation, quantum mechanics is defined through a conjunction of two forms of complementarity.

The first is wave-particle complementarity, reflecting the duality of the wave and particle behaviors of quantum objects, and relating the continuous and the discontinuous representations of quantum processes. Light, classically only a wave phenomenon, has two shapes: At times it behaves as particles (photons), at times as waves. There have been classical corpuscular theories of light, such as Newton's. Prior to quantum mechanics, however, for light and matter alike, there was always either one form of representation or another, never a complementary combination of both. By contrast, in order to develop a coherent account of their object, quantum theories must employ both representations, without subjecting them to a classical, such as Hegelian, synthesis.

The second complementarity is the complementarity of coordination and causality. It dislocates the causal dynamics by means of which the behavior of physical objects is determined and that allows one to know with certainty their positions and motion. It suspends the *claim* of such causality, grounding all classical physics and, one might add, all classical metaphysics. In Bohr's defining formulation, "The very nature of quantum theory . . . forces us to regard the space-time co-ordination and the claim of causality, the union of which characterizes the classical theories, as complementary but exclusive features of the description, symbolizing the idealization of observation and definition respectively."[2] The term *idealization* is crucial. Both coordination and causality must be seen as idealizations, symbols, or metaphors. This understanding defines Bohr's interpretation and establishes its proximity to postmodern theories, on the one hand, and Shelley's poetic practice, on the other.

The mathematical counterpart of the complementarity of coordination and causality is Werner Heisenberg's uncertainty relations. Disallowing the simultaneous precise measurement of quantum variables, such as position and momentum, uncertainty relations entail an irreducible loss in representation affecting any quantum system.[3] The result of this loss, however, is not the impoverishment but the enrichment of quantum systems, defined by an irreducible, infinite multiplicity and incessant transformations of their elements. These systems are simultaneously both irreducibly incomplete or fragmented and irreducibly rich.

The features just described—indeterminacy, the radical loss in representation, fragmentation, irreducible multiplicity—are related to many by now familiar features of the postmodernist landscape. I shall not elaborate on these connections here any further, for the preceding discussion in effect spells them out and partly depends on them. Complementarity itself can be defined in very general terms, well beyond physics. One may further expand the concept of complementarity, beyond designating only *mutually exclusive* features. Thus understood, complementary relations, which may be paired or multiple, are neither simply mutually exclusive nor simply subjected to a full synthesis. Instead, they manifest at times one of their complementary features, at times another; at times they show these features operating jointly, at times in conflict or inhibiting each other. They may also enter new complementarities at any point.

Shelley's texts offer extraordinarily rich metaphorical models for exploring such complementary economies. Often using light itself as their main figure, they fragment and complementarize all shapes or figures, and all disfigurations, of all light—physical, conceptual, or metaphorical—and all shapes or figures of causality and decausation: in fact, all shapes and figures. Wave and particle imagery can be traced throughout Shelley's works, where it often accompanies the dislocation of causality, on the one hand, and an economy of multiplicity, on the other (although Shelley enacts multiplicities in a great variety of ways). Here I shall restrict myself to "The Triumph of Life," arguably the most quantum mechanical and the most postmodern, or even post-postmodern, of Shelley's works.

THE TRIUMPH OF LIGHT

In "The Triumph of Life" the wave-particle complementarity of light, the radical loss in representation and causality, and the plural character of cognition and interpretation are jointly introduced and made to interact from the outset:

> Swift as a spirit hastening to his task
>> Of glory and of good, the Sun sprang forth
> Rejoicing in his splendour, and the mask
>> Of darkness fell from the awakened Earth
>
> . . . .
>
> and at the birth
> Of light, the Ocean's orison arose   (lines 1–7)

The *inaugural* figure or shape of the poem is the Sun—a shape of light, "a shape all light." Even leaving aside the general suspension of all unconditionally original events and figures in view of Derrida's deconstruction of (the concept of) origin and related developments from Nietzsche on, it would be impossible to speak of the poem's *first* or original figure in view of Shelley's practice of metaphor.[4] Here the physical, material sun is preceded by its metaphorization as "a spirit"—an ideal or idealist figure juxtaposed with "matter." "Swift," however, preceding "spirit" and accompanied by "hastening to his task," reinscribes a certain materiality into the network. This rematerialization is reinforced by the title, "preceding" the opening lines and suggesting the all-conquering material force of life as life-death. With other signifiers grafted into the title and the first lines—"triumph," "try," "lie," "life," "light," "eye," "I"—the picture becomes still more, finally irreducibly, complex and complementary. The inscription thus suspends both the general possibility of absolutely original figures and the possibility of any unconditional claim upon either material or spiritual grounding of the interpretive process. The complementary aspect of Shelley's inaugural figuration has another important, if textually deferred, manifestation. The figure of the Sun as "a shape all light" is parallel-complementary to a female shape all light, encountered by Rousseau later in the poem, but rendered here by its masculine counterpart as a father figure.

If the inaugural figure of the poem is a shape of light—the Sun, its inaugural event is "the birth of light." This "event" is again neither first, absolutely original, nor single or unitary, but is irreducibly disseminated along various gradients. The phrase connotes and connects, without full synthesis, the birth of the day, the birth of modern civilization (after the exile from Paradise), and the physical processes of the birth of light, both to its macroorigins—the light originating within the stars—and to its microorigins—the atomic processes through which physical light is born. "The birth of light" is also the birth of knowledge, for the poem's opening follows the exile from Paradise, prompted by the desire for the excess of knowledge. Later in the poem, the Sun itself, "the true Sun" (line 290), becomes the figure of reason and knowledge, human or divine—the figure of "en-lighten-ment" in its broadest sense, as Shelley problematizes the value and the very possibility of enlightenment in both historicopolitical and theoretical contexts. In its perhaps greatest generality, "the birth of light" is the birth of birth itself—the figure relating to the (im)possibility of origin.

The poem enacts a deconstruction of causality by using, separately or in combination, all three figures—"the birth of light," "birth," and "light." The conjunction is forceful and fitting. The origin of any perceptive and interpretive event depends—conceptually, metaphorically, and physically— on the possibility of light, on one shape of light or another. "Glimmering" light—unsteady, continuous-discontinuous, particlelike and wavelike light— pervades the poem (*glimmer* is one of its key words), suggesting the problematic nature of classical models of origin, causality, and cognition.

In this sense, "the birth of light" might still be the originating or precomprehending "event" and metaphor of the poem insofar as, analogously to the Derridean economy of *différance, trace,* and *writing,* it connotes simultaneously the possibility and necessity of knowledge—en-lighten-ment—and the impossibility of complete knowledge. There is never enough light, as it were, even and particularly when there is too much light, when the light is excessive, as in "The Triumph of Life." In quantum physics, too, or already in relativity, light as a carrier of information and, thus, of a certain (material) en-lighten-ment is a necessary, although not sufficient, condition for all knowledge. We must *see* in one way or another in order to perceive (*produce*) and connect events and establish causal sequences between them, although we have, when we have it at all, only limited power in determining what specific shape these events, connections, and causalities will take. As Einstein's theory of relativity demonstrated, the specific material features of light (whose speed is always constant and limits the transmission of all information) affect all causal relations and demand a different physics and a different philosophy of causality. Quantum physics was to deconstruct causality and, by implication, subjectivity even more radically.

Shelley in fact makes the birth of light—the dawn—a quantum rather than a continuous event, a quantum leap—"the Sun *sprang* forth." The image is analogous to the quantum mechanical picture of light as photons emitted discontinuously and acausally, as, according to the quantum postulate, electrons shift their orbits, or more precisely their levels of energy in the atom. Paul de Man was the first to notice this transformation of dawn in the poem in his "Shelley Disfigured": "The most continuous and gradual event in nature, the subtle gradation of the dawn, is collapsed into the brusque swiftness of a single moment." Shelley institutes a kind of poetic quantum postulate; and, as in quantum mechanics, once the birth of light can be a discontinuous and acausal event, it demands a deconstruction of perceptual and conceptual continuity and causality. This deconstruction, enacted throughout the poem, announces a transformation of all our ideas about nature, representation, perception, light, and finally life. All other events related to vision or light and many other appearances (made possible by one light or another) depicted by the poem obey this acausal quantum law, including the appearance of Shelley's vision itself ("And then a Vision on my brain was rolled"; line 40); the appearance of the chariot and the Shape of life, or life-death; the appearance of Rousseau, who is also introduced as a shape ("the grim Feature"; line 190) without light and without life; and the appearance of a shape all light to Rousseau. All these are "new vision[s], never seen before" (line 411). They may appear to be, in de Man's words, "brusque and unmotivated,"[5] but they may be instead both motivated and unmotivated, discrete and continuous, causal and acausal—in short complementary in all their aspects.

The figure of light may also be read as the figure of the very process of figuration—the figure of the efficacity (to oppose this term to source, origin, or cause) of all possible figurations and causality. According to de Man, the shape is "the figure of the figurality of all signification." From the present perspective, it would be the figure or antifigure—or, like Derrida's *différance,* neither a term nor a concept—of the complementary production and deconstruction, figuration and disfiguration, of all figures. Any given shape or figure of light—or of anything, including figuration itself—can only be an effect of this noncausal efficacity. Shelley's text functions through a complementary process that disfigures a great deal but also produces and transforms figurations, without subjecting them to classical synthesis. In closing his essay, de Man makes the following strong claim: "*The Triumph of Life* warns us that nothing, whether deed, word, thought, or text, ever happens in relation, positive or negative, to anything that precedes, follows or exists elsewhere, but only as a random event whose power, like the power of death, is due to the randomness of its occurrence."[6] Perhaps the poem instead tells us that the power of death—and of life—is always a Democritean play of complementary chance and necessity, multiplicity and oneness, centering and decentering. The disfigurative power of the processes enacted by the poem is, it is true, nothing short of extraordinary. It is equally important, however, to understand the accompanying productive—figuring—aspects and the complementarity of both figuration and disfiguration in these processes. This complementary economy emerges in the most extraordinary way in the central event of the poem, Rousseau's encounter with "a shape all light," which *reflects* and *embodies* (in either sense)—and refracts—all shapes of light:

> there stood
>
> Amid the sun, as *he* amid the blaze
> Of his own glory, on the vibrating
> Floor of the fountain, paved with flashing rays,
>
> A shape all light, which with one hand did fling
> Dew on the earth, as if *she were the Dawn*
> Whose invisible rain forever seemed to sing
>
> A silver music on the mossy lawn,
> And still before her on the dusky grass
> Iris her many coloured scarf had drawn.
>
> (lines 348–57, emphasis added)

"Iris" is the rainbow—the paradigmatic event of physical and poetic optics—that will return with even more power later in the text. The dawn—"the birth of light"—returns now in all its (or her) quantum glory, as Shelley continues the interplay of the masculine and feminine shapes of light. "That light's severe excess" (line 424)—the dose of radiation, as it were—reaches beyond the critical limit, however, leading to a meltdown, a kind of intellectual Chernobyl. It is no longer "the physics of paradise," to borrow Stuart Curran's description of act 4 of *Prometheus Unbound,* rendering a happier moment.[7] The tragic landscape encountered by Rousseau is both *post*lapsarian and *post*modern:

> like day she came,
> Making the night a dream; and ere she ceased
>
> To move, as one between desire and shame
> Suspended, I said—"If, as it doth seem,
> Thou comest from the realm without a name,
> Into this valley of perpetual dream,

> Shew whence I came, and where I am, and why—
>> Pass not away upon the passing stream."   (lines 392–99)

"Like day she came" establishes another brilliant parallel with the opening of the poem. The relationship between, to return to Bohr's phrase, "the space-time co-ordination and the claim of causality" ("whence I came, where I am, and why") is here subjected to the most radical uncertainty relation heretofore seen in Western history. Spinoza, Rousseau, Hume, and other precursors do help Shelley along the way. Shelley's contribution, however, remains unique both in the radical nature of his questioning and in the complexity of the processes and figures he engages. The "event" also enacts a uniquely Shelleyan conjunction of *nous, physis,* and *eros*—mind, matter, and eroticism:

> "Arise and quench thy thirst," was her reply.
> And as a shut lily, stricken by the wand
>> Of dewy morning's vital alchemy,
>
> I rose; and, bending at her sweet command,
>> Touched with faint lips the cup she raised,
> And suddenly my brain became as sand
>
>> Where the first wave had more than half erased
> The track of deer on desert Labrador,
>> Whilst the fierce wolf from which they fled amazed
>
> Leaves his stamp visibly upon the shore
>> Until the second bursts—so on my sight
> Burst a new Vision never seen before.   (lines 400–11)

These images form an immense catachrestic conglomerate, joining the postmodernist and the quantum mechanical Shelley. The metaphors include those borrowed from classical optics, such as the reflection and refraction (as distortion or disfiguration) of light in water. At this point in history, one can also think of the violence of subatomic processes, let us say, the gamma ray (intensified light) bombardment of subatomic particles and the violent interaction of waves and particles. The pictures we have of such processes can only be traces, or traces of traces, of such collisions. But these pictures (one might think of corresponding photographs) are similar to what Shelley's metaphoric technology renders here by way of mixing the traces of ocean waves and the tracks of a pursuit left on the particles, the *grains* of sand, as this interaction of particles and waves induces Rousseau's vision. Shelley offers a strikingly graphic rendition of the process—the waves erasing the traces on the grained surface of the sand, which is in turn inscribed with and refigured by the traces of waves. The image is prepared by an echo metaphor earlier in the poem: "nor other trace I find / But as a foam after the Ocean's wrath / Is spent upon the desert shore" (lines 162–64). The picture looks very much like a photograph of (traces of) subatomic collisions, which appears here as a picture of a human mind subjected to an extraordinarily violent impact— "the light's severe excess." This impact is multiplied by Shelley's picture of an equally violent pursuit, of which we again encounter only traces and traces of traces—traces of recollection and traces of forgetting, traces of pain and traces of pleasure.

Shelley closes with a rainbow—the arch of victory for the chariot of life or life-death, overarching and en-closing the landscape of the poem: "A moving arch of victory the vermilion / And green and azure plumes of Iris had / Built high over her wind-winged pavilion" (lines 439–41). The rainbow is preceded by the figure of a "star" (line 438)—a macrosource of light—and followed by micro-, atomic, images: "the crew / Seemed in that *light* like *atomies* that dance / Within a sunbeam" (lines 445–47). The word *atomies* may (very appropriately) *refer* to particles of dust, but the signifier also inscribes "atoms" and the play of atoms and light—a kind of proto–quantum mechanical metaphorical model. Shelley uses similar "atomic" imagery in the "Ode to Heaven" (line 38). An allusion to Lucretius later in "The Triumph of Life" (lines 481–83) establishes another link to atomic theory.

Shelley continues to extend his quantum poetics, as Rousseau's encounter with the shape, life's triumphant chariot, and the textual chariot of the poem itself move "onward" to their closure, or their suspension of closure. The wave and particle imagery continue to play their role, as in a turbulence metaphor, reminiscent of modern-day chaos theory:

> The chariot and the captives fettered there,
>   But all like bubbles on an eddying flood
> Fell into the same track at last and were
>   Borne *onward*.—I among the multitude
> Was swept.   (lines 457–61, emphasis added)

The press "onward" of the procession will actually close the text (line 546), which closure, or un-closure, may signal the birth "onward" of the life—or life-death—and of the poem itself and its future history. Again repeating and parodying the sunrise of the opening lines—"the mask / of darkness fell from the awakened Earth" (lines 3–4)—the figuration by means of light is converted into metaphoric disfiguration by the next wave—or particle-wave—of the poem's textual drift:

> As the sun *shapes* the clouds—thus, on the way
>   Mask after mask fell from the countenance
> And form of all, and long before the day
>
>   Was old, the joy which waked like Heaven's glance
> The sleepers in the *oblivious* valley, died,
>   And some grew weary of the ghastly dance
>
> And fell, as I have fallen by the way side,
>   Those soonest from whose forms most shadows past
> And least of strength and beauty did abide.
>
>   (lines 535–43, emphasis added)

Even here, however, alongside oblivion and obliteration, the sun still *shapes* the clouds. All Shelley's signifiers—shape, sun, light, clouds—also inscribe productive metaphoric play enabled by and enacting manifold shapes of light. This complementary conjunction of production, preservation, and obliteration—rendered earlier by the West Wind, "Destroyer and preserver"—structures Shelley's textual field. The indeterminacy and complementarity of this field continuously make us return to the questions asked by "The Triumph of Life:" What is knowledge? What is interpretation? What is reading? What is anything? Who are we, and whence did we come and why? In order to ask these questions or in order to reask them after postmodernism and other postisms and afterisms, one must write something like "The Triumph of Life," or perhaps create a textual field still more radical than Shelley's poem or such paradigmatic (post)modernist textual machines as those of Joyce or Blanchot. Reading, even a work as great as "The Triumph of Life," may not be enough; and this insufficiency of reading is among the many great lessons of the poem.

Would the poem also imply the insufficiency of writing, and, in a kind of counterargument to the *Defence,* specifically of poetry, either as literature or as the extended field so designated by Shelley? Would this insufficiency of all writing—oral or written, or painted, sculpted, danced, musically performed or composed, all of which are enacted in the course of the poem—be a great lesson of life, in whose history writing, even in Derrida's sense (arguably the broadest sense available for now), is only a small episode? The radical uncertainty enacted by the poem also suggests the possibility of its death for material, intellectual, cultural, and political reasons. For all we *know,* the poem's existence, particularly in its present form, is a complex interplay of chance and necessity that could have led to its "death" at many points in its history. Life conquers all—all shapes of light and enlightenment, or anti-enlightenment, all modernisms and postmodernisms, or all archaisms or prearchaisms—all reading and all writing. But then, "What is life?":

> "Then, what is Life?" I said . . . the cripple cast
> His eye upon the car which now had rolled
> *Onward,* as if that look must be the last,
>
> And answered . . . "Happy those for whom the fold
> Of   (lines 544–48, emphasis added)

I break off here, as Shelley does, finish or leave it unfinished, as Rousseau or Shelley casts his eye (or I) upon life-death, rolling onward. Rousseau's or Shelley's eye—or die—is cast, perhaps, since this event too is subject to the incalculable Democritean play of chance and necessity. The signifier "die" also inscribes death, as perhaps it must—"as if that look must be *the last,*" the poem says. "Happy" somehow manages to get in, even if only as a signifier left suspended without its signified: "Happy those." "The fold of . . . " is another signifier that would need a long analysis. One cannot perhaps finish or, complementarily, finish-*un*finish, any text, at least for now, better than with this question: "Then, what is life?" "The Triumph of Life" continues to be read and will continue to be read, at least for a while, even though and because it inscribes the death of reading and the death of writing, and thus its own death. Some indeterminate quantum-like force continues to move it *onward,* as it continues to invoke "happy those for whom the fold of. . . . " But happy, who?

Notes

Chapter 1:   SHELLEY AND THE HUMAN CONDITION

1. *PBSL* 2:699. For Godwin's ideas, see *Enquiry Concerning Political Justice,* ed. F. E. L. Priestley (Toronto: Univ. of Toronto Press, 1946), 1:283–84, 2:369.

2. Edited from the diplomatic text in *SC* 6:980–81.

3. For Shelley's perspective on the pressures of society, see my essay "Wordsworth, Shelley, and the Romantic Inheritance" in Reiman, *Romantic Texts and Contexts* (Columbia: Univ. of Missouri Press, 1987), especially 350.

4. Julian Edition (Ingpen and Peck), 5:229.

5. Ibid., 254.

6. See especially Stuart Curran's *Shelley's* Cenci: *Scorpions Ringed with Fire* (Princeton: Princeton Univ. Press, 1970) and *Shelley's Annus Mirabilis: The Maturing of an Epic Vision* (San Marino, Calif.: Huntington Library, 1975), 120–37.

7. Page 473; for the textual history of the essay and discussion of its significance in Shelley's thinking, see *SC* 6:633–47.

8. An essay reexamining the evidence on the parentage of Elena Adelaide Shelley will appear in *SC* 10.

9. "Shelley, Dryden, and Mr. Eliot" in Lewis's *Rehabilitations and Other Essays* (London: Oxford Univ. Press, 1939; as rpt. in M. H. Abrams, ed., *English Romantic Poets: Modern Essays in Criticism,* New York: Oxford Univ. Press, 1960), 256.

10. Note to line 197 of *Hellas*.

11. For my view of Byron's personal and poetic development, see Chapter 7, "Byron and the 'Other,'" in Reiman, *Intervals of Inspiration: The Skeptical Tradition and the Psychology of Romanticism* (Greenwood, Fla.: Penkevill, 1988).

Chapter 2:   ETERNITY AND THE RUINS OF TIME

1. Terence Hoagwood, *Shelley and Ideology: Shelley's Political Prose and Its Philosophical Context from Bacon to Marx* (Iowa City: Univ. of Iowa Press, 1988); Jerrold Hogle, *Shelley's Process: Radical Transference and the Development of His Major Works* (Oxford: Oxford Univ. Press, 1988); G. Kim Blank, ed., *The New Shelley* (New York: St. Martin's Press, 1991).

2. Blank, *New Shelley*, 2–5.

3. Lawrence Lipking, *The Ordering of the Arts in Eighteenth-Century England* (Princeton, N.J.: Princeton Univ. Press, 1970), 10.

4. Kenneth Neil Cameron, "The Social Philosophy of Shelley," *Sewanee Review* 50 (1942): 458.

5. Earl Wasserman, *Shelley: A Critical Reading* (Baltimore: The Johns Hopkins Univ. Press, 1971); William Royce Campbell, "Shelley's Philosophy of History: A Reconsideration," *Keats-Shelley Journal* 21–22 (1972–73): 43–63; Betty T. Bennett, "The Political Philosophy of Mary Shelley's Historical Novels: *Valperga* and *Perkin Warbeck*," in *The Evidence of the Imagination*, ed. Donald H. Reiman, Michael C. Jaye, and Betty T. Bennett (New York: New York Univ. Press, 1978); Daniel Stemple, "'A Rude Idealism': Models of Nature and History in Shelley's *Prometheus Unbound*," *Mosaic* 21 (1978): 105–21; Bruce Haley, "Shelley, Peacock, and the Reading of History," *Studies in Romanticism* 29(1990):439–61; Mark Kipperman, "History and Ideality: The Politics of Shelley's *Hellas*," *Studies in Romanticism* 30 (1991): 147–68; Stuart Curran, "Shelley," in *The English Romantic Poets*, ed. Frank Jordan (New York: Modern Language Association, 1985), 624.

6. Campbell, "Shelly's Philosophy of History," 63.

7. James Granger, *A Biographical History of England* (London: T. Davies, 1769), 1:v.

8. René Wellek, *The Rise of English Literary History* (New York: McGraw-Hill, 1966), 72–81.

9. Horace Walpole, *Anecdotes of Painting in England* (London: T. Farmer, 1762), 1:ix.

10. David Hume, *The History of England* (New York: Harper, 1851), 2:508.

11. Oliver Goldsmith, *An History of the Earth* (London: J. Nourse, 1774), 1:4.

12. Thomas Warton, *The History of English Poetry* (London: T. Tegg, 1824) 1:4.

13. Thomas Warton, *An Enquiry into the Authenticity of the Poems Attributed to Thomas Rowley* (London: J. Dodsley, 1782), 7–8.

14. Warton, *History of English Poetry,* 4:321.

15. Nathan Drake, *Literary Hours* (London: T. Cadell, 1804), 2:159.

16. Henry Headley, *Select Beauties of Ancient English Poetry* (London: T. Cadell, 1787), xiv.

17. Robert Southey, *Sir Thomas More: or, Colloquies on the Progress and Prospects of Society* (London: John Murray, 1829), 1:30, 36; 2:387.

18. Thomas Malthus, *An Essay on the Principle of Population* (London: J. Johnson, 1798), 13.

19. Stuart Curran, *Shelley's Annus Mirabilis: The Maturing of an Epic Vision* (San Marino, Calif.: Huntington Library, 1975), 40.

20. Marie Jean Antoine Nicolas Caritat, Marquis de Condorcet, *Sketch for a Historical Picture of the Progress of the Human Mind,* trans. June Barraclough (London: Weidenfield and Nicolson, 1955), 10.

21. Wasserman, *Shelley,* 376.

Chapter 3:   LITERARY ART AND POLITICAL JUSTICE

1. [Paul Henri Thiry, Baron d'Holbach], *The System of Nature; or The Laws of the Moral and Physical World. Translated from the French of M. Mirabaud* (London: G. Kearsley, 1797); *Christianity Unveiled; Being an Examination of the Principles and Effects of the Christian Religion. Translated from the French of Boulanger, by W. M. Johnson* (London: Richard Carlile, 1819).

2. William Godwin, *Cursory Strictures on the Charge Delivered by Lord Chief Justice Eyre* (London: Daniel Isaac Eaton, 1794) (first published in the *Morning Chronicle,* October 21, 1794; *Considerations on Lord Grenville's and Mr. Pitt's Bills* (London: Joseph Johnson, 1795).

3. Godwin to Thelwall, September 18, 1794, quoted by William St Clair, *The Godwins and the Shelleys: A Biography of a Family* (1989; Baltimore: The Johns Hopkins Univ. Press, 1991), 127.

4. For accounts of Mary Hays, see Gina Luria's introduction to Hays's *Appeal* (New York: Garland, 1974); Jane Spencer, "Mary Hays," in *British Women Writers: A Critical Reference Guide,* ed. Janet Todd (New York: Continuum [Frederick Ungar], 1989); and Terence Allan Hoagwood's introduction to Hays's *The Victim of Prejudice* (Delmar, N.Y.: Scholars' Facsimiles, 1990). Gary Kelly, *Woman, Writing, and Revolution* 1790–1827 (Oxford: Clarendon Press, 1993) appeared after the present essay was written, and discusses Hays in Chapter 3.

5. Mary Hays, *Letters and Essays, Moral and Miscellaneous* (1793; rpt. New York: Garland, 1974), 19–20.

6. Mary Wollstonecraft, *A Vindication of the Rights of Men* (London: Joseph Johnson, 1790), 19.

7. Paul Henri Thiry, Baron d'Holbach, *The System of Nature; or, Laws of the Moral and Physical World,* trans. H. D. Robinson (Boston: J. P. Mendum, 1853), 13–14.

8. William Godwin, *Enquiry Concerning Political Justice and Its Influence on Morals and Happiness,* ed. F. E. L. Priestley (Toronto: Univ. of Toronto Press, 1946), 1:26.

9. *Political Justice,* 1:vi–vii.

10. Ibid., 1:4–5, 5–6.

11. Marie Jean Antoine Nicolas Caritat, Marquis de Condorcet, *Outlines of an Historical View of the Progress of the Human Mind,* translator anonymous (London: Joseph Johnson, 1795), 3, 4.

12. *Political Justice,* 1:450–51.

13. Plotinus, in *The Essential Plotinus,* trans. Elmer O'Brien (Indianapolis, Ind.: Hackett, 1964), 48–49.

14. I quote Holbach's *System of Nature,* as quoted in Shelley's note to *Queen Mab,* from the translation by E. F. Bennett that is reproduced in *Shelley's Prose; or, The Trumpet of a Prophecy,* ed. David Lee Clark (Albuquerque: Univ. of New Mexico Press, 1954), 354.

15. Doris Lessing, *Prisons We Choose to Live Inside* (Montreal: CBC Enterprises, 1986), 23.

Chapter 4: SHELLEY AND THE CONSTITUTION OF
POLITICAL AUTHORITY

1. Timothy Webb, "The Unascended Heaven: Negatives in *Prometheus Unbound,*" in *Shelley Revalued: Essays from the Gregynog Conference,* ed. Kelvin Everest (Totowa, N.J.: Barnes and Noble, 1983), 37–62; P. M. S. Dawson, *The Unacknowledged Legislator: Shelley and Politics* (Oxford: Clarendon Press, 1980), 118–22.

2. William Godwin, *Enquiry Concerning Political Justice and Its Influence on Morals and Happiness,* ed. Isaac Kramnick (Harmondsworth, U.K.: Penguin, 1985), 604.

3. Thomas Paine, *The Rights of Man,* ed. Eric Foner (Harmondsworth, U.K.: Penguin, 1984), 71.

4. Dawson, *Unacknowledged Legislator,* 59.

5. Godwin, *Political Justice,* 606.

6. Dawson, *Unacknowledged Legislator,* 61.

7. Edmund Burke, *Reflections on the Revolution in France,* ed. Conor Cruise O'Brien (Harmondsworth, U.K.: Penguin, 1982), 120.

8. Edmund Burke, *On a Motion Made in the House of Commons . . . for a Committee to Enquire into the State of the Representation of the Commons in Parliament* (1782), quoted in J. G. A. Pocock, "Burke and the Ancient Constitution: A Problem in the History of Ideas," in *Politics, Language, and Time: Essays on Political Thought and History* (Chicago: Univ. of Chicago Press, 1989), 225–27.

9. Jerrold Hogle, *Shelley's Process: Radical Transference and the Development of His Major Works* (New York: Oxford Univ. Press, 1988), 247.

Chapter 5:   SHELLEY AND THE IDEOLOGY OF THE NATION

1. Michael Scammel, "Slovenia and Its Poet," *New York Review of Books* (October 24, 1991): 60.   •

2. José Ortega y Gasset, *The Revolt of the Masses* (1932; rpt. New York: Norton, 1957), 174n., 183.

3. See William St Clair, *That Greece Might Still Be Free: The Philhellenes in the War of Independence* (London: Oxford Univ. Press, 1972).

4. Hans Kohn, *Pan Slavism: Its History and Ideology* (Notre Dame, Ind.: Univ. of Notre Dame Press, 1953), 13.

5. Eric Hobsbawm, *Nations and Nationalism Since 1790: Programme, Myth, Reality* (Cambridge: Cambridge Univ. Press, 1990), 19–22; see also the discussion of nationalism and language, 51–63. Hobsbawm shows that a national language was more a cultural and a psychological force confined to literate elites; it was rarely sufficient to mobilize masses of people speaking many dialects into feeling a common national interest.

6. Timothy Webb, *Shelley: A Voice Not Understood* (Atlantic Highlands, N.J.: Humanities Press, 1977), 196, 214.

7. *The Journals of Mary Shelley:* 1814–1844, ed. Paula Feldman and Diana Scott Kilvert, 2 vols. (Oxford: Oxford Univ. Press, 1987), 1:352.

8. Shelley and Mary Shelley read avidly in J. C. L. de Sismondi's *Histoire des républiques italiennes au moyen âge,* which appeared in sixteen volumes from 1807 to 1818. "We are all very studious here," wrote Mary Shelley to Maria Gisborne from Naples on January 22, 1819, "and we are all reading 'Sismondi's Histoire'"; *MWSL* 1:85.

9. Hans Kohn, *Nationalism: Its Meaning and History,* rev. ed. (Princeton, N.J.: Van Nostrand, 1965), 15; Hobsbawm, *Nations and Nationalism,* 33.

10. "Parmi les divers développements de l'esprit humain, c'est la littérature philosophique, c'est l'éloquence et le raisonnement que je considère comme la véritable garantie de la liberté. . . . La poésie a été plus souvent consacrée à louer qu'à censurer le pouvoir despotique. Les beaux arts, en général, peuvent quelquefois contribuer, par leurs jouissances mêmes, à former des sujets tels que les tyrans les désirent." *De la littérature, considérée dans ses rapports avec les institutions sociales,* ed. Paul van Tieghem, 2 vols. (Geneva: Librairie Droz, 1959) 1:32–35. The English translation is *Madame de Staël on Politics, Literature, and National Character,* trans. and ed. Morroe Berger (Garden City, N.Y.: Doubleday, 1964), 148–49. On the date of Shelley's reading, see Mary Shelley's reading list in Newman Ivy White, *Shelley,* 2 vols. (New York: Knopf, 1940), 2:541.

11. James Chandler, "Representative Men, Spirits of the Age, and Other Romantic Types," in *Romantic Revolutions: Criticism and Theory,* ed. Kenneth Johnston et al. (Bloomington: Univ. of Indiana Press, 1990), 126–27.

12. Kenneth Cameron, *Shelley: The Golden Years* (Cambridge: Harvard Univ. Press, 1974), 370. On the date of the poem's composition, see 365, 630–31n.5.

13. Bertolt Brecht, "Against Georg Lukács" (trans. Stuart Hood, 1938), in *Aesthetics and Politics* (London: Verso, 1980), 81–82.

Chapter 6: UNACKNOWLEDGED LEGISLATION

1. Charles E. Robinson reported his discovery of the poem's publication in the *Morning Chronicle* in 1981; "Shelley to the Editor of the *Morning Chronicle:* A Second New Letter of 5 April 1821," *Keats-Shelley Memorial Bulletin* 32 (1981):57. Newman Ivey White reported its publication in the *Military Register* much earlier. But, unlike Robinson, White speculates that "the publication could hardly have been authorized by Shelley or his publisher, because four months later (February 22, 1822 [*sic*]) Shelley offered it to Ollier for publication in his *Literary Miscellany*"; *Shelley* (New York: Knopf, 1940), 2:223. White's presentation of the facts hardly suggests that Shelley, having written the ode in August but supposedly seeking publication only in February, was urgently hoping to influence public events. In any case, little notice appears to have been taken of White's discovery. Thomas Hutchinson's Oxford edition, "corrected" by G. M. Matthews long after White's *Shelley,* continues to list the *Posthumous Poems* of 1824 as the publication in which the ode first appeared; (*OSA* 616). The fact that Shelley offered the poem to Ollier in February 1821 perhaps shows less that Shelley failed to authorize its original publication than that he had no knowledge of its original publication. The editors of the *Morning Chronicle* and the *Military Register* may never have acknowledged their receipt and publication

of the poem and Shelley may never have received copies of these newspapers. (I am indebted for this suggestion to Carlene Adamson.) When in February Austrian pressure, having subsided somewhat, was again mounting on the government in Naples, Shelley attempted to reach his public a second time. If anything, the offer to Ollier reflects Shelley's anxiety to comment publicly on the course of events.

2. Irene H. Chayes, "Rhetoric as Drama: An Approach to the Romantic Ode." *Publications of the Modern Language Association of America* 79 (1964): 67–79.

3. In the text that Shelley sent to Ollier in February 1821, he dropped these headings as well as the opening two epodes. Shelley clearly sought to suppress the ode's Pindaric associations. If he was indeed under the mistaken impression that his first attempt to publish the ode had failed, he probably reasoned that a less learned and complex version was likely to meet with more success. Clearly, publishing any kind of attempt at influencing events was better than publishing none at all.

4. All quotations from the "Ode to Naples" are from the text published in the *Morning Chronicle* (September 26, 1820):3.

5. Frank J. Nisetich, "Introduction," in *Pindar's Victory Songs* (Baltimore: The Johns Hopkins Univ. Press, 1980), 24.

6. George T. Romani, *The Neapolitan Revolution of 1820–1821* (Evanston, Ill.: Northwestern Univ. Press, 1950), 115.

7. Leigh Hunt, *Examiner* 660 (August 20, 1820): 538.

8. Shelley's claim here is not entirely fanciful. In March of 1821, just when the Austrians began moving against Naples, a revolution broke out in Piedmont. The revolutionaries proclaimed the same Spanish constitution as had the Neapolitans; Harry Hearder, *Italy in the Age of the Risorgimento* (London: Longman, 1983), 55.

9. Marcel Brion, *Pompeii and Herculaneum: The Glory and the Grief,* 2nd ed. (London: Cardinal, 1973), 44.

10. John Buxton, *The Grecian Taste: Literature in the Age of Neo-classicism, 1740–1820* (London: Macmillan, 1978), 10–11.

11. John Chetwode Eustace, *A Classical Tour through Italy: An. MDCCCII,* 6th ed., 3 vols. (London: J. Mawman, 1821), 2:334, 107.

12. C. J. Bartlett, *Castlereagh* (New York: Charles Scribner's Sons, 1966), 218.

13. Leigh Hunt, *Examiner* 641 (April 9, 1820): 234.

14. Bartlett, *Castlereagh,* 215–16.

15. Romani, *Neapolitan Revolution,* 113.

16. Ibid.

17. John Gillies, *The History of Ancient Greece* (London, 1786; rpt. Philadelphia: Thomas Wardle, 1843), 145, 141, 143.

18. Ibid., n.p.

282 / Notes to Pages 73–78

Chapter 7:   FROM AVANT-GARDE TO VANGUARDISM

1. Philip Corrigan and Derek Sayer, *The Great Arch: English State Formation as Cultural Revolution* (Oxford: Basil Blackwell, 1985).

2. Renato Poggioli, *The Theory of the Avant-Garde,* trans. Gerald Fitzgerald (Cambridge, Mass.: Harvard Univ. Press, 1968); Peter Bürger, *Theory of the Avant-Garde,* trans. Michael Shaw (Minneapolis: Univ. of Minnesota Press, 1984).

3. Pierre Bourdieu, Le Marché des biens symboliques, *L'Année sociologique* 22 (1971): 49–126.

4. Nancy Armstrong, "The Rise of Domestic Woman," in *The Ideology of Conduct: Essays in Literature and the History of Sexuality,* ed. Nancy Armstrong and Leonard Tennenhouse (New York: Methuen, 1987), 96–141.

5. Gary Kelly, *Revolutionary Feminism: The Mind and Career of Mary Wollstonecraft* (London: Macmillan, 1992), chap. 6 and 8.

6. Joan B. Landes, *Women and the Public Sphere in the Age of the French Revolution* (Ithaca, N.Y.: Cornell Univ. Press, 1988).

7. Gary Kelly, *Women, Writing, and Revolution 1790 to 1827* (Oxford: Clarendon Press, 1993), chap. 2 and 6.

8. Londa Schiebinger, "Skeletons in the Closet: The First Illustrations of the Female Skeleton in Eighteenth-Century Anatomy," in *The Making of the Modern Body: Sexuality and Society in the Nineteenth Century,* ed. Catherine Gallagher and Thomas Laqueur (Berkeley: Univ. of California Press, 1987), 42–82.

9. Robert M. Maniquis, "Holy Savagery and Wild Justice: English Romanticism and the Terror," *Studies in Romanticism* 28 (1989): 365–94; Peter L. Thorslev, Jr., "Post-Waterloo Liberalism: The Second Generation," *Studies in Romanticism* 28 (1989): 437–61.

10. Martin J Wiener, *English Culture and the Decline of the Industrial Spirit 1850–1980* (Cambridge: Cambridge Univ. Press, 1981).

11. For other accounts of Romanticism and feminism, see Anne K. Mellor, "On Romanticism and Feminism," in *Romanticism and Feminism,* ed. Anne K. Mellor (Bloomington: Indiana Univ. Press, 1988), 3–9, and Meena Alexander, *Women in Romanticism* (London: Macmillan, 1989).

12. Marilyn Butler, "Telling It Like a Story: The French Revolution as Narrative," *Studies in Romanticism* 28 (1989): 345–64; Gerald McNiece, *Shelley and the Revolutionary Idea* (Cambridge, Mass.: Harvard Univ. Press, 1969), 190–217; Carl Woodring, *Politics in English Romantic Poetry* (Cambridge, Mass.: Harvard Univ. Press, 1970), 254–58; Michael H Scrivener, *Radical Shelley: The Philosophical Anarchism and Utopian Thought of Percy Bysshe Shelley* (Princeton, N.J.: Princeton Univ. Press, 1982),

119–33; Lee Sterrenburg, "Mary Shelley's Monster: Politics and Psyche in *Frankenstein*," in *The Endurance of Frankenstein: Essays on Mary Shelley's Novel*, ed. George Levine and U. C. Knoepflmacher (Berkeley: Univ. of California Press, 1979).

13. Anne K. Mellor, *Mary Shelley: Her Life, Her Fiction, Her Monsters* (New York: Routledge, 1989); Nathaniel Brown, *Sexuality and Feminism in Shelley* (Cambridge, Mass.: Harvard Univ. Press, 1979); E. Douka Kabitoglou, "Shelley's (Feminist) Discourse on the Female: *The Revolt of Islam*," *Arbeiten aus Anglistik und Amerikanistik* 15 (1990): 139–50.

14. Scrivener, *Radical Shelley*.

15. Greg Kucich, *Keats, Shelley, and Romantic Spenserianism* (University Park, Pa.: Pennsylvania State Univ. Press, 1991), pt. 3.

16. Joseph W. Lew, "The Deceptive Other: Mary Shelley's Critique of Orientalism in *Frankenstein*," *Studies in Romanticism* 30 (1991): 255–83.

17. John McManners, *Death and the Enlightenment: Changing Attitudes to Death in Eighteenth-Century France* (Oxford: Oxford Univ. Press, 1985), 417–18; Philippe Ariès, *The Hour of Our Death*, trans. by Helen Weaver (Harmondsworth, U.K.: Penguin, 1983), chap. 10.

18. Dorinda Outram, *The Body and the French Revolution: Sex, Class and Political Culture* (New Haven, Conn.: Yale Univ. Press, 1989), chap. 5.

19. Laura Claridge, "The Bifurcated Female Space of Desire," in *Out of Bounds: Male Writers and Gender(ed) Criticism*, ed. Laura Claridge and Elizabeth Langland (Amherst: Univ. of Massachusetts Press, 1989), 109n.15.

20. Mellor, *Mary Shelley*, chap. 5; Fred V. Randel, "*Frankenstein*, Feminism, and the Intertextuality of Mountains," *Studies in Romanticism* 23 (1984): 515–33.

21. Peter Finch, "Shelley's *Laon and Cythna*: The Bride Stripped Bare . . . Almost," *Keats-Shelley Review* 3 (1988): 23–46.

22. John Donovan, "Incest in *Laon and Cythna*: Nature, Custom, Desire," *Keats-Shelley Review* 2 (1987): 49–90.

23. Marilyn Butler, *Romantics, Rebels and Reactionaries: English Literature and Its Background 1760–1830* (Oxford: Oxford Univ. Press, 1981).

Chapter 8:   THE TRANSGRESSIVE DOUBLE STANDARD

1. Lawrence Stone, *The Family, Sex and Marriage in England* (New York: Harper, 1977), 229–39, 532–34, 607–15, 629–44; Edward Shorter, "Illegitimacy, Sexual Revolution, and Social Change in Modern Europe," *Journal of Interdisciplinary History* 2 (1971): 236–72; P. E. H. Hair, "Bridal Pregnancy in Rural England in Earlier Centuries," *Population Studies* 20 (1966): 233–43.

2. James Lackington, *Memoirs of the Forty-Five First Years of the Life of James Lackington* (1791; revised London: Lackington, 1794), 133–34; *Letters of Robert Burns,* ed. J. DeLancey Ferguson and G. Ross Roy (Oxford: Clarendon Press, 1985), 1:24, 34–37, 39; John Gibson Lockhart, *Life of Robert Burns* (Edinburgh: Constable, 1828), 107–12; Samuel Bamford, *Early Days* (London: Simpkin, Marshall, 1849), 229–30, 291; on parish officials' eagerness to discourage settlement of expectant unmarried mothers, see Ivy Pinchbeck, *Women Workers and the Industrial Revolution* (1930; rpt. New York: Kelley, 1969), 79–83, and C. M. L. Bouch and G. P. Jones, *A Short Economic and Social History of the Lake Counties* (Manchester: Manchester Univ. Press, 1965), 295–96.

3. Pinchbeck, *Women Workers,* 81; Louis A. Tilly, Joan W. Scott, and Miriam Cohen, "Women's Work and European Fertility Patterns," *Journal of Interdisciplinary History* 6 (1976): 464–66; Angus McLaren, *Birth Control in Nineteenth-Century England* (New York: Holmes and Meier, 1978), 45–47.

4. Stone, *The Family,* 640; Shorter, "Illegitimacy," 250; Neil J. Smelser, *Social Change in the Industrial Revolution* (Chicago: Univ. of Chicago Press, 1959), 250, 282–84.

5. For example, Smelser, *Social Change;* E. P. Thompson, *The Making of the English Working Class* (New York: Vintage, 1966), 340, 416.

6. On professional prostitution, see Stone, *The Family,* 615–19; but the term was broadly used to refer to all sexually transgressive women.

7. See the divorce and adultery debates, *Parliamentary History of England* 17 (1771): 185–86; 20 (1779): 592–601; 34 (1800): 1552–62; 35 (1800): 225–326; *Parliamentary Debates* 13 (1809): 321–22, 326–35; 14 (1809): 326–35, 612–15.

8. *Parliament* 35 (1800): 235.

9. Lawrence Stone, *The Road to Divorce* (Oxford: Oxford Univ. Press, 1990), 121–346; Keith Thomas, "The Double Standard," *Journal of the History of Ideas* 20 (1959): 201–2, 212.

10. *Parliament* 35 (1800): 231, 233, 236, 324.

11. Ibid., 261.

12. Ibid., 228.

13. William Godwin, *Enquiry Concerning Political Justice* (London: Robinson, 1793); modern readers tend to rely on the revised third edition of 1798, in which the section on marriage appears as the book 8 chapter 8 appendix; see the collated edition edited by F. E. L. Priestley (Toronto: Univ. of Toronto Press, 1946–48), 2:499–514, 3:218–23.

14. The second edition (1796) was the most radical on the issue of illegitimacy; the first edition (1793) simply stated, "It cannot be definitely affirmed whether it be

known in such a state of society who is the father of each individual child. But it may be affirmed that such knowledge will be of no importance."

15. Godwin, *Memoirs of the Author of a Vindication of the Rights of Woman* (London: Johnson, 1798) (the revised edition published later that year deleted some details of the liaisons); rpt. Mary Wollstonecraft and William Godwin, *A Short Residence in Sweden* and *Memoirs of the Author of 'The Rights of Woman,'* ed. Richard Holmes (Harmondsworth, U.K.: Penguin, 1987), 258–60; Cecilia Lucy Brightwell, *Memorials of the Life of Amelia Opie* (Norwich: Fletcher and Alexander, 1854), 141; Thomas James Mathias, *The Shade of Alexander Pope* (London: Becket, 1798) *Anti-Jacobin Review and Magazine* 1 (1798): 859; Peter H. Marshall, *William Godwin* (New Haven, Yale Univ. Press, 1984), 194, 215, 284.

16. Alaric Alexander Watts wrote the *Blackwood's* editors on September 7, 1822, recounting London gossip that "there was so little certainty as to the father of [Claire's] child that Shelley and his Lordship threw dice for the honor of providing for it"; the "league of incest" rumors began with the trip to Geneva in 1816, resurfaced in 1820 following the episode of Elena the Neapolitan foundling, and, as Mary Shelley discovered, persisted after she returned alone to England. See Alan Lang Strout, "Knights of the Burning Epistle: The *Blackwood* Papers in the National Library of Scotland," *Studia Neophilologica* 26 (1954): 90.

17. Emily W. Sunstein, *Mary Shelley: Romance and Reality* (Boston: Little, Brown, 1989), 27, 35; Marshall, *William Godwin* 249–51; Mary Wollstonecraft Godwin Shelley was herself legitimated at birth though not at conception.

18. Mary Shelley retrospectively described her elopement journey in *History of A Six Weeks' Tour* (London: Hookham and Ollier, 1817), iii–iv, as the excursion of "a party of young people. . . . the author, with her husband and sister."

19. Claire Clairmont's September 16, 1834, and June 2, 1835, letters to Mary Shelley are quoted by courtesy of Marion Kingston Stocking from her edition of *The Clairmont Correspondence.* (Baltimore: Johns Hopkins University Press, 1995).

20. Godwin to Hull Godwin, February 21, 1817; Godwin to John Taylor, August 27, 1814, *PBSL* 1:390–92, 525.

21. Robinson, December 16, 1816, and November 2, 1817, *On Books and Their Writers,* ed. Edith J. Morley (1938; rpt. New York: AMS Press, 1967), 1:199, 211.

22. Shelley to Godwin, June 3, 1812, *PBSL* 1:303; Harriet Shelley, to Catherine Nugent, November 20, 1814, *Harriet Shelley's Letters to Catherine Nugent* (London: privately printed, 1889), 57–9.

23. Shelley to Mary Shelley, January 11, 1816; Godwin to John Taylor, August 27, 1814, *PBSL* 1:390–392, 527.

24. Entry for May 27, 1816, *The Diary of Dr. John William Polidori,* ed. William Michael Rossetti (London: Elkin Mathews, 1911), 101.

25. Shelley's "Even love is sold" note to *Queen Mab* (1813) called "chastity" a "monkish and evangelical superstition"; his September 26, 1814, letter to Harriet Shelley said, "The pure & liberal principles of which you used to boast you were a disciple, served only for display. In your heart it seems you were always enslaved to the vilest superstitions"; his October 4, 1814, letter to T. J. Hogg called marriage one of the "vulgar superstitions," *PBSL* 1:377, 403.

26. James Lawrence, *Das Paradies der Liebe* (1801); *L'Empire des Nairs;* (1803); *The Empire of the Nairs; or, the Rights of Women, an Utopian Romance* (London: Hookham, 1811); the original 1793 essay, "Nair System of Gallantry and Inheritance," was published four months after *Political Justice;* see Walter Graham, "Shelley and the Empire of the Nairs," *Publications of the Modern Language Association of America* 50 (1925): 881.

27. Shelley, to Hogg, July 15, 1811, *PBSL* 1:122; on Harriet's reading of the *Nairs,* see Boas, *Harriet Shelley: Five Long Years* (London: Oxford Univ. Press, 1962) 227; from the September 26, 1814, *Journals of Mary Shelley,* ed. Paula R. Feldman and Diana Scott-Kilvert (Oxford: Clarendon, 1987), 1: 29, and *Journals of Claire Clairmont,* ed. Marion Kingston Stocking (Cambridge, Mass.: Harvard Univ. Press, 1968), 46, it appears neither expended much time on this four-volume tome.

28. If male successors were likely to get Godwin wrong, they were even more likely to misappropriate Wollstonecraft's use of the expression "legal prostitution" to describe marriage; *A Vindication of the Rights of Woman* (London: Johnson, 1792); rpt. *Works of Mary Wollstonecraft,* ed. Janet Todd and Marilyn Butler (New York: New York Univ. Press, 1989), 5:129, 218.

29. *Queen Mab* (London: for the author, 1813), 144–52; *PBSL* 2:298–302, 350, 355; Mary's 1839 note on *Queen Mab* says that "it is doubtful whether he would himself have admitted it into a collection of his works"; but Thomas Medwin, *Life of Percy Bysshe Shelley,* ed. H. Buxton Forman (1824; rpt. Oxford: Oxford Univ. Press, 1913), 186, said of the poem, "however he might have modified, and did modify his opinions, he was the last man to have recanted them."

30. Shelley's fragment "On Marriage" (circa 1817) developed Godwin's concept of "the female the possession . . . the property of men. . . . Those laws or opinions which defend the security of property suggested also the institution of marriage."

31. "Love is free: to promise for ever to love the same woman, is not less absurd than to promise to believe the same creed: such a vow, in both cases, excludes us from all inquiry."

32. Even Shelley, angry that the birth of William (named after Mary Shelley's father) did not bring reconciliation with Godwin, invoked the popular dichotomy: "a young family, innocent and benevolent and united, should not be confounded with prostitutes and seducers"; March 6, 1816, letter to Godwin, *PBSL* 1:459.

33. Wollstonecraft, *Vindication,* 5:140.

34. Leigh Hunt, *Lord Byron and Some of his Contemporaries* (London: Colburn, 1828), 1:308–12.

35. Shelley to Hogg, August 3, 1811, *PBSL* 1:131.

36. *Laon and Cythna* (2:xliii); on the popularity of this phrase among the Owenites, see Paul Foot, *Red Shelley* (London: Sidgwick and Jackson, 1980), 153, and M. Siddiq Kalim, *The Social Orpheus: Shelley and the Owenites* (Lahore: Research Council, 1973), 108–12.

37. Frank Podmore, *Robert Owen* (1907; rpt. New York: Haskell, 1971), 2:647; Medwin, *Life of Shelley,* 97–98, refers to the John Brooks edition of *Queen Mab,* which, if reliable, would date the episode as 1829 or later.

38. "Whether the marriage contract shall be dissolved if agreeable to one or both parties, and many other circumstances, are not yet determined," Poole to Mr. Haskins, March 24, 1820; Margaret E. Sandford, *Thomas Poole and His Friends* (London: Macmillan, 1888), 1:95–98.

39. On female Owenites, see Barbara Taylor, *Eve and the New Jerusalem* (London: Virago, 1983), xv, 40–43, 69, 213–16; Carol A. Kolmerten, *Women in Utopia* (Bloomington: Indiana Univ. Press, 1990), 10, 25–27, 79–85, 133–35. Jeremy Bentham mentioned a contraceptive sponge in print as early as 1797, but contraception did not become a public advocacy issue until the 1820s and 1830s with publications by Francis Place, Richard Carlile, and Robert Dale Owen. Midwifery techniques and abortifacients were privately circulated, however; see McLaren, *Birth Control,* 51ff. Wollstonecraft alluded to the use of lactation to widen birth intervals, *Vindication* 5:263. Godwin and Shelley had vague notions about contraception; on Godwin's "chance-medley system," see Marshall, *William Godwin,* 185; on Shelley's note (circa 1819–20) on the "small and almost imperceptible precaution," see Foot, *Red Shelley,* 113. Mary Shelley counseled Marianne Hunt, in a letter of March 24, 1820, that "a woman is not a field to be continually employed either in bringing forth or enlarging grain"; *MWSL* 1:136.

40. "Mr Bentham and other writers have urged the admission of females to the right of suffrage; this attempt seems somewhat immature"; Wollstonecraft, *Vindication,* 5: 217. On early suffrage initiatives, see Miriam Williford, "Bentham on the

Rights of Women," *Journal of the History of Ideas* 36 (1975): 134, 167–76; Claire Tomalin, *The Life and Death of Mary Wollstonecraft* (London: Penguin, 1992), 341–43.

41. Edward Royce and James Walvin, *English Radicals and Reformers* (Brighton, U.K.: Harvester Press, 1987), 134, 186; Smelser, *Social Change,* 236, 306; Taylor, *Eve,* 98; K. D. M. Snell, *Annals of the Labouring Poor* (Cambridge: Cambridge Univ. Press, 1985), 313–17; Anna Clark, "The Politics of Seduction in English Popular Culture," in *The Progress of Romance,* ed. Jean Radford (London: Routledge, 1986), 59–62.

42. Shelley to Godwin, July 29, 1813, *PBSL* 1:318.

43. *Queen Mab* (London: W. Clarke, 1821); *Reply to the Anti-Matrimonial Hypothesis and Supposed Atheism of Percy Byssche* [sic] *Shelley, as laid down in* Queen Mab (London: W. Clark, 1821), 11, 19, 33–37. Newman Ivey White slightly conjectures William Johnson Fox as its author; see *Shelley* (New York: Knopf, 1940): 2:304–5, 405–6, and *The Unextinguished Hearth* (1938; rpt. New York: Octagon, 1966), 63, 95–97, 370–73.

44. Laetitia Pilkington, *Memoirs,* ed. Iris Barry (New York: Dodd, Mead, 1928), 103, 221; Alice Browne, *The Eighteenth-Century Feminist Mind* (Detroit: Wayne State Univ. Press, 1987), 134, 204; Wollstonecraft, *Vindication,* 5:139–40, 209.

45. On nuptiality trends and surplus women, see Taylor, *Eve,* 192–93, 203–6, 334; Ian Watt, *The Rise of the Novel* (Berkeley: Univ. of California Press, 1959), 142–48; E. A. Wrigley and R. S. Schofield, *The Population History of England* (Cambridge, Mass.: Harvard Univ. Press, 1981), 262; E. A. Wrigley, "The Growth of Population in Eighteenth-Century England," *Past and Present* 98 (1983): 123–24.

46. Wollstonecraft, *Thoughts on the Education of Daughters* (London: Johnson, 1787), *Works,* 4:25–27; *Vindication,* 5:134, 218–19; Clara Reeve, *Plans of Education* (London: Hookham and Carpenter, 1792), 119–25; Mary Hays, *Letters and Essays* (London: Knott, 1793), 84–85; Mary Ann Radcliffe, *The Female Advocate* (1799), rpt. *Memoirs of Mrs. Mary Ann Radcliffe* (Edinburgh: Manners and Miller, 1810), 419, 431; anonymous, *Appeal to the Men of Great Britain* (London: Johnson, 1798), 195, 201; Priscilla Wakefield, *Reflections on the Present Condition of the Female Sex* (London: Johnson, 1798), 71–72, 150–54, 164; Mary Brunton to Mrs. Balfour, January 17, 1818, *Emmeline* (London: Murray, 1819), xcvi–xcvii; Jane Austen, to Fanny Knight, March 13, 1817, *Jane Austen's Letters,* ed. R. W. Chapman and D. LeFaye, 3rd ed. (New York: Oxford Univ. Press, 1995), 332.

47. On rumors about Harriet Shelley, see *PBSL* 1:521, 525, 527–28; Strout, "Knights," 89. Mary Shelley also came to sympathize with Harriet Shelley on some level, according to the February 12, 1839, journal entry excised by Lady Jane Gibson Shelley from most copies of *Shelley and Mary* (London: privately printed, 1882), 1222: "[T. J.] Hogg has written me an insulting letter because I left out the dedication to

Harriet [prefacing *Queen Mab*]. Poor Harriet, to whose sad fate I attribute so many of my own heavy sorrows as the atonement claimed by fate for her death." Claire Clairmont, to Mary Shelley, April 29, 1825, *Journals*, 298, 401–5; R. Glynn Grylls, *Claire Clairmont* (London: Murray, 1939), 199, 201; Medwin, *Life of Shelley*, 176.

48. Grylls, *Claire Clairmont*, 38.

49. Clairmont, *Journals*, 294–96; Edward C. McAleer, *The Sensitive Plant: A Life of Lady Mount Cashell* (Chapel Hill: Univ. of North Carolina Press, 1958), 119, 174–76; *MWSL* 1:306–7, 312, 437.

50. Shelley to Byron, May 26, 1820, *PBSL* 1:199.

51. Longdill's document emphasized "being very circumspect (particularly as far as respects Girls) in the Books which are permitted to be brought before them"; Leslie Hotson, *Shelley's Lost Letters to Harriet* (London: Faber and Faber, 1980), 66–67, 70–71.

52. Polidori, April 26, 1816, *Diary*, 32–33.

53. Marchand, *BLJ* 6:278.

54. Edward Dowden, *Life of Percy Bysshe Shelley* (London: Kegan Paul, 1886), 286.

Chapter 9: SHELLEY LEFT AND RIGHT

1. See especially "Shelley Disfigured," in Paul de Man, *The Rhetoric of Romanticism* (New York: Columbia Univ. Press, 1984), 93–123.

2. See McGann, *The Textual Condition* (Princeton, N.J.: Princeton Univ. Press, 1991), 12–13, which includes a discussion of Genette.

3. I have commented in much greater detail on Mary Shelley's construction of Shelley through her editions in "'I Hate to Mutilate': Mary Shelley and the Transmission of Shelley's Textual Corpus," a lecture delivered at the CUNY Graduate Center in November 1990. This subject is also well developed, as I have recently discovered, in an essay by Susan Wolfson, "Editorial Privilege: Mary Shelley and Percy Shelley's Audiences," in *The Other Mary Shelley*, ed. Audrey Fisch, Anne K. Mellor, and Esther Schor (New York: Oxford Univ. Press, 1993):39–72. Wolfson's essay also considers how Mary Shelley's editions of Shelley's works function to construct Mary Shelley herself.

4. *Literary Gazette and Journal of Belles Lettres* 226 (May 19, 1821): 305.

5. Robert Durling, *Petrarch's Lyric Poems: The "Rime Sparse" and Other Lyrics* (Cambridge, Mass.: Harvard Univ. Press, 1976), 370. For a second epigraph from Petrarch that Mary Shelley ultimately decided not to print in *Posthumous Poems*, see Emily W. Sunstein, *Mary Shelley: Romance and Reality* (Boston: Little, Brown, 1989),

235. For Mary Shelley's continued use of untranslated epigraphs from Petrarch in her 1839 edition, see Wolfson, "Editorial Privilege."

6. *Posthumous Poems of Percy Bysshe Shelley,* ed. Mary Wollstonecraft Shelley (London: John and Henry L. Hunt, 1824), vii. All quotations of *Posthumous Poems* are from this edition.

7. The obituary appears in the *Paris Monthly Review* 2, no. 7 (August 1822): 392–96. I quote from Stuart Curran, "Horace Smith's Obituary Panegyric on Shelley," *Keats-Shelley Journal* 37 (1988): 31.

8. For the reception and reproduction of Shelley's lyrics, see, for instance, Karsten Klejs Engelberg, *The Making of the Shelley Myth: An Annotated Bibliography of Criticism of Percy Bysshe Shelley 1822–1860* (London: Mansell, 1988), 78–82. Two other essential sources are Sylva Norman, *Flight of the Skylark: The Development of Shelley's Reputation* (Norman: Univ. of Oklahoma Press, 1954), and "Shelley's Posthumous Reputation," the penultimate chapter of Newman Ivey White, *Shelley* (1940; rpt. New York: Octagon, 1972), 2:389–418.

9. Engelberg, *Making of the Shelley Myth,* 78.

10. For a recent discussion of Mary Shelley's plans for publishing Shelley's works, see Neil Fraistat, ed., *The "Prometheus Unbound Notebooks,"* The Bodleian Shelley Manuscripts, vol. 9 (New York: Garland, 1991), xxxiv–xxxv.

11. These numbers are given in White, *Shelley,* 2:398, 397.

12. William St Clair contends that one reason *Queen Mab* "caused such deep hatred was that it was published by the author of this book [i.e., *Every Woman's Book; or What is Love,* Richard Carlile's pamphlet on contraception] and sold in his shop." See *The Godwins and the Shelleys: A Biography of a Family* (New York: W. W. Norton, 1989), 479.

13. The most extensive studies of the literary pirates' modes of production as well as their cultural contexts are Iain McCalman's *Radical Underworld: Prophets, Revolutionaries and Pornographers in London, 1795–1840* (Cambridge: Cambridge Univ. Press, 1988), and Hugh J. Luke's dissertation, "'Drams for the Vulgar': A Study of Some Radical Publishers and Publications in Early Nineteenth-Century London" (Univ. of Texas, 1963). More specifically for the pirating of Shelley, see Charles H. Taylor, Jr., *The Early Collected Editions of Shelley's Poems* (New Haven, Conn.: Yale Univ. Press, 1958); and appendix 3, "Shelley and the Pirates" in St Clair, *The Godwins and the Shelleys,* 512–18.

14. I cite the account of the case in J. H. Merivale, *Reports of Cases Argued and Determined in the High Court of Chancery from the Commencement of Michaelmas Term, 1815 to the End of the Sittings after Michaelmas Term, 1817* (London: Joseph Butterworth and Son, 1818), 2:439.

15. This point is well made by Peter Manning, "The Hone-ing of Byron's *Corsair*," in *Textual Criticism and Literary Interpretation,* ed. Jerome McGann (Chicago: Univ. of Chicago Press, 1985), 124.

16. In *Walcot* [*sic* for Wolcot, i.e., "Peter Pindar"] v. *Walker* (1802), Eldon first cites the precedent set by Eyre, which he repeats in *Southey* v. *Sherwood.* For Eldon's opinion in *Walcott* v. *Walker,* see Francis Vesey, *Reports of Cases Argued and Determined in the High Court of Chancery during the Time of Lord Chancellor Eldon. Containing from Easter Term to the Sittings after Trinity Term Inclusive,* 42, Geo. III (London: Brooke and Clarke, 1804), 7:1–2. For Eldon's opinion in *Murray* v. *Benbow,* see *Quarterly Review* 27, no. 54 (April 1822): 130.

17. *Rambler's Magazine; or, Fashionable Emporium of Polite Literature . . . and All the Gay Variety of Supreme Bon Ton* 1, no. 3 (March 1822): 119.

18. For general background on Benbow's career, see *The Biographical Dictionary of Modern British Radicals,* ed. Joseph O. Baylen and Norbert Grossman (Sussex, U.K.: Harvester Press, 1979), 1:35–36, and especially Luke, "Drams for the Vulgar," 25–77.

19. *Rambler's Magazine* 1, no. 9 (September 1822): 396.

20. Quoted from *The Works of Lord Byron,* ed. Rowland E. Prothero (London: John Murray, 1901), 6:399.

21. Derwent Coleridge, "An Essay on the Poetic Character of Percy Bysshe Shelley, And on the Probable Tendency of his Writings," *Metropolitan Quarterly Magazine* 2, no. 3 (September 1826): 197.

22. Gareth Stedman Jones, *Languages of Class: Studies in English Working Class History,* 1832–1982 (Cambridge: Cambridge Univ. Press, 1983), 106–7. Jones is specifically referring here to *political* representation. I am following Jon Klancher in extending the implications of Jones's comment to encompass a broader notion of representation within the semiotics of the culture itself. See Klancher, *The Making of English Reading Audiences,* 1790–1832 (Madison: Univ. of Wisconsin Press, 1987), 102.

23. De Man, *Rhetoric of Romanticism,* 120.

Chapter 10: SHELLEY AND THE CHARTISTS

1. Shelley's presence in the Chartist press was the subject of my "Shelley in the Chartist Press," *Keats-Shelley Memorial Bulletin* (now *Keats-Shelley Review*) 34 (1983): 41–60. His reception by the Christian Democrats is the subject of my "Shelley and the Barmbys," *Keats-Shelley Journal* 41 (1992): 122–138. My study of Shelley items in Owenite journals, particularly in the Owenites' major literary organ, the *New Moral World,* is still in progress.

2. See vol. 5, no. 6 (December 1, 1838), 83–85; vol. 5, no. 7 (December 8, 1838), 103; vol. 5, no. 9 (December 22, 1838), 134–36; vol. 5, no. 11 (January 5, 1839), 166–68; and vol. 5, no. 17 (February 16, 1839), 262–64.

3. *Athenaeum* 262 (November 3, 1832), [705].

4. *People's Paper* (September 17, 1853). Also see September 24, 185.

5. H. Buxton Forman, *Vicissitudes of Shelley's* Queen Mab: *A Chapter in the History of Reform* (London: privately published, 1887), 21.

6. See Bouthaina Shaaban, "Shelley in the Chartist Press," *Keats-Shelley Memorial Bulletin* 34 (1983), 41.

7. See, for example, vol. 16 (1854), 221; vol. 18 (1855), 123; no. 3, 24; no. 4, 32; no. 5, 40; no. 6, 48; and nos. 7, 8, 9, and 10. Also see vol. 19 (1855), vol. 20 (1856), vols. 21 and 22 (1857), vol. 23 (1858), and vol. 24 (1859).

8. *Studies of Sensation and Event, Poems by Ebenezer Jones* (London 1879), ed. by Richard Herne Shepherd with memorial notices of the author by Sumner Jones and William James Linton (1843; London: privately published, 1879), xxxix, xliv. In the same footnote the editor further explains that this letter to M. Considerant by Ebenezer Jones also appeared in the first number (January, 1842) of the *Promethean, or Communitarian Apostle,* a monthly magazine edited by Goodwyn Barmby.

9. Dante G. Rossetti, *Notes and Queries* 5, no. 110, 4th series (February 5, 1870), 154.

10. T. Mardy Rees, *Ebenezer Jones, the Neglected Poet* (1820–1860) (Chelsea: privately published, n.d.), 1.

11. Thomas Cooper, *Eight Letters to the Young Men of the Working Classes* (London: privately published, 1851).

12. Thomas Cooper, *The Belief in a Personal God and a Future Life* (London: Holyoake, 1860) and *A Calm Inquiry into the Nature of Deity* (London: privately published, 1864).

13. See Jones's introduction to his important poem *My Life* (London: privately published, 1846).

14. Yuri B. Kovalev, ed., *An Anthology of the Chartist Literature* (Moscow: privately published, 1956), preface.

15. Martha Vicinus, *The Industrial Muse: A Study of Nineteenth Century British-Class Literature* (London: Croom Helm, 1974), 100.

16. Diary of Ernest Charles Jones, 1839–1847, 2 vols. Manchester Public Library, England. MS. 923.2J18.

17. Jones, *Studies of Sensation and Event,* 106.

18. "Literary Review," *Labourer* 2 (1847): 239–40, 96.

19. *Plain Speaker* 1, no. 2 (1849), [9], no. 8 (1849), 57–58.

20. George Lukács, *Goethe and his Age,* trans. Robert Anchor (London: Merlin Press, 1979), 153.

21. "Politics of Poets," *Chartist Circular* 42 (July 11, 1840), 170.

22. "P. B. Shelley," *Chartist Circular* 4 (October 19, 1839), 16. For a similar evaluation of Shelley's poetry, see the *Times,* January 28, 1869.

23. Diary of Ernest Charles Jones, 1839–1847, vol. 1.

24. Ernest Charles Jones, "Literature and Reviews," *People's Paper* (September 9, 1854), 5.

25. Ernest Charles Jones, *Notes to the People* (London: privately published, 1851), 1:4.

26. *People's Paper* (March 28, 1857), [4].

27. MS. F. 923.2J8 (italics are in the original). These pages carry no date, but the epigraph suggests that the poet is not alive. Both the fact that Jones died in 1869 and the use of the word *socialists* indicate that this plan might have been written in the 1870s or 1880s.

28. In *The Battle Day and Other Poems* (London, New York: privately published, 1855), 125–27.

29. In *Songs of Democracy* (London: privately published, 1856–57), [1].

30. The edition I used for this study is the first edition of *The Purgatory of Suicides* (London: privately published, 1845).

Chapter 11: "THE NAME OF FREEDOM"

1. "My Queen, some destructive power or evil spirit, that appeared I know not whence, caused the beginning of our utter route"; Aeschylus, *The Persians,* Loeb Classical Library, trans. H. Weir Smyth (London: Heinemann; Cambridge: Harvard Univ. Press, 1922), lines 353–54. It was Aeschylus who revived the world of the daemons, Dodds informs us, emphasizing that it was through the *alastor* or evil spirit that the *phthonos* (envy) of the gods worked; E. R. Dodds, *The Greeks and the Irrational* (Berkeley: Univ. of California Press, 1951), 31–40.

2. Timothy Webb points out that "Shelley's admiration for Greece was balanced by an understanding of its weaknesses," for instance, the dependence of Athenian society upon a slave class, or the "system of revenge and retribution against which Aeschylus had warned his countrymen so often"; *Shelley: A Voice Not Understood* (Manchester: Manchester Univ. Press, 1977), 194.

3. "Ancient Greece is indeed an enduring, atemporal ideal for Shelley and his circle, but one that can speak to the present era . . . [which Shelley] portrays as emerging from authoritarian Christianity to a new pagan-inspired liberality, egalitar-

ianism, and harmony"; Mark Kipperman, "History and Ideality: The Politics of Shelley's *Hellas,*" *Studies in Romanticism* 30 (1991): 154.

4. "Shelley uses the word 'legislator' with an exact sense of its contemporary meaning," Stuart Curran remarks, "signifying not a parliamentarian disputing over the methods of rule, but a law giver, like Zoroaster or Moses"; *Shelley's Annus Mirabilis: The Maturing of an Epic Vision* (San Marino, Calif.: Huntington Library, 1975), 199. Conversely, Timothy Clark indicates that "the conception of poets as legislators becomes, tragically, their implication in the chain of tyrannies constituting the greater part of history"; *Embodying Revolution: The Figure of the Poet in Shelley* (Oxford: Clarendon Press, 1989), 227–28.

5. References to Plato's text are to *The Collected Dialogues of Plato,* ed. Edith Hamilton and Huntington Cairns (Princeton, N.J.: Princeton Univ. Press, 1963). William Keach believes that it is useful to look at Monboddo's commentary on the *Cratylus,* which "suggests a basis for Shelley's positive ideal of linguistic arbitrariness," adding that it is "certainly consistent with Shelley's idea of poets as 'unacknowledged legislators' to think of words as originally produced by the imagination of *arbiters,* 'lawgivers' of language"; *Shelley's Style* (New York: Methuen, 1984), 17–18.

6. For Heidegger's discussion of history, language, and freedom, see especially "Hölderlin and the Essence of Poetry" and "What is Metaphysics?" in *Existence and Being,* ed. Werner Brock (Chicago: Henry Regnery, 1949); also "On the Essence of Truth," in *Basic Writings,* ed. David Farrell Krell (New York: Harper and Rowe, 1977). Heidegger does not only homologize the openness of "truth" to "freedom," but also to "conflict": "Truth is the primal conflict in which, always in some particular way, the Open is won"; *Poetry, Language, Thought,* trans. Albert Hofstadter (New York: Harper and Row, 1971), 60.

7. "Shelley's structural solution in *Hellas* is a combination of the perspectives that each genre provides. . . . [in a play of] generic opposites against one another" to heighten the "contrast of the contradictory forms and of the inimical mental attitudes that they express," Constance Walker maintains. I am in total agreement, although, as the development of my argument will show, I would not subscribe to the proposition that follows, namely that the "dynamics" of drama must be overcome before the paradise of Hellas may be regained—"opposition," as I see it, being precisely the metaphysical structure of Hellenism that is not then the "antithesis of antitheses"; "The Urn of Bitter Prophecy: Antithetical Patterns in *Hellas,*" *Keats-Shelley Memorial Bulletin* 33 (1982): 37, 39.

8. Besides Heidegger's well-known position on freedom as open receptivity, Ricoeur also sees the ultimate state of freedom as that which "passes over into necessity, becoming subordinate to the initiative of things"; this freedom, he points

out, "no longer dares: it consents, it yields"; Paul Ricoeur, *Freedom and Nature: The Voluntary and the Involuntary,* trans. Erazim V. Kohak (Evanston, Ill.: Northwestern Univ. Press, 1966), 482.

9. "If Shelley sees the imagination as freedom, he also conceives of it as order . . . [which makes] true order and true liberty . . . [the] result of imaginative activity"; (P. M. S. Dawson, *The Unacknowledged Legislator: Shelley and Politics* (Oxford: Clarendon Press, 1980), 244–45).

10. Martin Heidegger, *Early Greek Thinking,* trans. David Farrell Krell and Frank A. Capuzzi (New York: Harper and Row, 1975), 13. In his commentary Heidegger states that the fragment is essentially "tragic," that we discover in it "a trace of the essence of tragedy" (44).

11. Fragments 83, 82, and 75, in *The Art and Thought of Heraclitus: An Edition of the Fragments with Translation and Commentary,* ed. Charles H. Kahn (Cambridge: Cambridge Univ. Press, 1979).

12. Defined by Ricoeur as "the tragic theology of the god who tempts, blinds, leads astray," "the scandalous theology of predestination to evil"; *The Symbolism of Evil,* trans. Emerson Buchanan (Boston: Beacon Press, 1967), 173, 212.

13. *Schelling's Treatise on the Essence of Human Freedom,* trans. Joan Stambaugh (Athens: Ohio Univ. Press, 1985). Curran, discussing Shelley's conception of freedom, emphasizes that "Failure to discriminate between free will and will is finally responsible for all the tyrannies of the world. . . . [because] the former is predicated on the liberty of all beings, the latter only on that of oneself"; *Shelley's Annus Mirabilis,* 200.

14. Ricoeur, *The Symbolism of Evil,* 312, 326. "Without the dialectics of fate and freedom," Ricoeur observes, "there would be no tragedy. Tragedy requires, on the one hand, transcendence and, more precisely, hostile transcendence. . . . [and on the other] the upsurge of a freedom that *delays* the fulfillment of fate" (220).

15. Richard Cronin, *Shelley's Poetic Thoughts* (London: Macmillan, 1981), 136, and Milton Wilson, *Shelley's Later Poetry: A Study of his Prophetic Imagination* (New York: Columbia Univ. Press, 1957), 195, also perceive this sinister undertone.

16. René Girard, *Violence and the Sacred,* trans. Patrick Gregory (Baltimore: The Johns Hopkins Univ. Press, 1977), 307.

17. Jerrold E. Hogle also focuses on the "female" nature of the chorus, pointing toward the subversive role played by nonmilitaristic, marginalized women in a patriarchal society; *Shelley's Process: Radical Transference and the Development of his Major Works* (New York: Oxford Univ. Press, 1988), 293.

18. W. B. Yeats, "The Second Coming,"; *The Collected Poems of W. B. Yeats* (New York: Macmillan, 1956), 185. This argument appropriately closes with Yeats because

of his interest in Shelley's work and perceptive discussion of "The Philosophy of Shelley's Poetry," incorporated in his *Ideas of Good and Evil;* his own reading of history in terms of a very strict system of historical cycles; and his virtual copying in the poem "Two Songs from a Play" of the final stanza of *Hellas* in a context that brings together "holy Dionysus," "God's death," "darkening thought," "formless darkness," "odour of blood," and the failure of "Platonic tolerance"—all pointing toward the futility of hoping "Another Troy must rise and set, / Another lineage feed the crow, / Another Argo's painted prow / Drive to a flashier bauble yet" (210). Northrop Frye points out both similarities and differences in the Shelleyan and Yeatsian visions: "Here we touch on the feature of Shelley's thought that so delights Yeats, the prophesy of a new religion 'antithetical' to Christianity and reverting to many features of Greek thought and culture. . . . Shelley's version of this new culture is," the critic admits, "much less vulgar than Yeats's: it does not rest on a facile cyclism or rationalize everything brutal and degenerate in both Greek and modern culture as part of a 'tragic' or 'heroic' way of life"; *A Study of English Romanticism* (New York: Random House, 1968), 101.

Chapter 12:   SHELLEY'S IMPACT ON ITALIAN LITERATURE

1. Giacomo Zanella, "Paralleli Letterari. P.B. Shelley e G. Leopardi," *Nuova Antologia* (January 8, 1883).

2. *The Romantics' Reviewers* 1802–1824, ed. John O. Hayden (Chicago: Univ. of Chicago Press, 1968), 124.

3. Giuseppe Nicolini, *Vita di Giorgio Lord Byron* (1834; Milan: Lombardi, 1855), Books 3–4.

4. Giambattista Niccolini, "Beatrice Cenci. Discorso intorno all'antica e moderna tragedia," in *Opere edite e inedite di Giovanni Battista Niccolini,* ed. Corrado Gargiolli, vol. 3: *Tragedie Varie* (Turin: M. Guidoni, 1862).

5. The article appeared in the Neapolitan Magazine *Il Museo.* In the same year, however, Marcello Mazzoni published his *Fiori* and *Glorie della letteratura Italiana,* in which a translation by Blennio of *Alastor* also appeared; this issue helped to spread Shelley's name and work among Italian critics.

6. *Byron: A Self-Portrait, Letters and Diaries,* ed. Peter Quennell (London: John Murray, 1950), 2:399.

7. Ibid., 480–81.

8. Zanella, "Paralleli Letterari," 412, 425–26, 428.

9. Federico Olivero, "Percy Bysshe Shelley e il paesaggio italico," *Nuova Antologia* 941 (March 1, 1911): 90.

10. *The Journals of Mary Shelley*, 1814–1844, ed. Paula R. Feldman and Diana Scott-Kilvert (Oxford: Clarendon Press, 1987), 1:226. It is true, however, that Mary Shelley would return to Monti as well as to Alfieri when writing her *Lives of the Most Eminent Literary and Scientific Men of Italy, Spain and Portugal* (London: Longman, 1835). See also her letters to Gabriele Rossetti sent on April 3 and 20, 1835.

11. *Byron*, 2:479–86.

12. Alfieri must have remained important for Mary Shelley until at least March 1819, when she was still translating his *Mirra*. See *MWSJ* 1:226–27, 253.

13. Alan M. Weinberg, *Shelley's Italian Experience* (London: Macmillan, 1991), 23.

14. Giovanni Caldana, "Giudizi di Percy Bysshe Shelley sui poeti italiani," *Nuova Antologia* (May–June 1907): 672.

15. See, for instance, the letter Shelley sent to Peacock on April 20, 1818, expressing his intention to write a tragedy on Tasso's madness, and also his letter to the Gisbornes on July 11, 1818. See also his visit to Ferrara on November 7, 1818, described in detail in a letter to Peacock (*PBSL* 2:45–48). Shelley enclosed in this letter a piece of wood from the door of Tasso's cell.

16. Emilio Cecchi, "La Difesa della Poesia," *Nuova Antologia*, 228 (September 1, 1909), 57. Benedetto Croce, *Ultimi Saggi* (Bari: Laterza, 1935), 59–78.

17. Giosuè Carducci, "Introduzione," in *Prometeo Liberato*, trans. Ettore Sanfelice (Turin: L. Roux, 1894), xiv.

18. Ibid., xv–xvii.

19. Walter Binni, *La Poetica del decadentismo* (Florence: Sansoni, 1936), 107–9.

20. Ibid., 109.

21. See Carla Chiummo, *Shelley nella bottega di Pascoli* (Fasano: Schena, 1992).

22. Ibid., 21.

23. Binni, *La Poetica del decadentismo*, 22.

24. For a further discussion of Shelley's critical heritage in Italy, see L. M. Crisafulli Jones, *Shelley fra Ottocento e Novecento* (Bologna: CLUEB, 1990).

25. Gabriele D'Annunzio, "Commemorazione di Percy Bysshe Shelley," in *Opere di Gabriele D'Annunzio* (Milan: Mondadori, 1950, rpt. 1962), 370.

26. D'Annunzio will come back again to Shelley in 1925 in Mario Praz's early appreciation of the Romantic poet. Praz notes how two dominant themes prevail in Shelley's poetry: the platonic conception of cosmos and a deep attraction toward magic and the occult. Praz shows how these two elements make possible the birth of a new religion in which the primordial elements of the earth become myths once again, while nature herself turns into a human being or, better into a freer and more spiritual sort of mankind. See Mario Praz, "Percy Bysshe Shelley," in *Poeti Inglesi*

dell'Ottocento (Florence: Bemporad, 1925), 190–91, and also "Gabriele D'Annunzio e la letteratura anglosassone," in *G. D'Annunzio nel primo centenario della nascita* (Rome: Centro di Vita Italiana, 1963), 95–113.

27. See also Gabriele D'Annunzio, "Commemorazione di P. B. Shelley", in *Prose di Ricerca*, ed. E. Bianchetti (Milan: Mondadori, 1968), 3:366.

Chapter 13: SHELLEY AND THE EMPIRE IN THE EAST

1. Constantin Volney, *The Ruins; or a Survey of the Revolutions of Empires*, trans. unknown (London: Edward Edwards, 1822), 148–49.

2. Quoted by Kelvin Everest, headnote to *Queen Mab*, in *Poems of Shelley* (London: Longman, 1989), 1:268.

3. Volney, *Ruins*, 124–25.

4. Ibid., 282ff.

5. Ibid., 399–400n.106.

6. As writers who shaped history, both Shelley and Volney benefited from the pirating of their work from the 1820s. See E. P. Thompson, *The Making of the English Working Class* (London: Penguin, 1964), 107–8, and Iain McCalman, *Radical Underworld* (Cambridge: Cambridge Univ. Press, 1988), 79–82. Richard Carlile (who issued several editions of *Queen Mab*) championed French materialism and particularly science.

7. Robert Southey to William Taylor, September 1798, quoted in Elisabeth Schneider, *Coleridge, Opium and "Kubla Khan"* (Chicago: Chicago Univ. Press, 1953), 134.

8. Priestley's polemical *History of the Corruptions of Humanity* (Birmingham: Joseph Johnson, 1782) discussed the theological "corruptions" introduced into the early church, for example from the East, including the divinity of Christ. Southey borrowed it from the Bristol Lending Library, on March 27, 1795, while preparing his twelve historical lectures, designed to complement Coleridge's series on modern politics and religion. He began serious work on *Thalaba* between August and the autumn of the same year.

9. A scholastic, fully documented approach to medieval texts and oral materials, such as that of Joseph Ritson in the 1780s and 1790s (and in the 1790s of Southey's Norwich friends, the Germanists Frank Sayers and William Taylor) implied sympathy with the popular cause, or resentment at appropriation of the popular style by gentrifiers. See Ritson's truculent criticisms of Thomas Percy's ballad editing and courtly theories of ballad origins: "Historical Essay on National Songs," in *Select Collection of English Songs* (London: Joseph Johnson, 1783).

10. *Collected Letters of Samuel Taylor Coleridge,* ed. Earl Leslie Griggs (Oxford: Clarendon Press, 1956), 1:121.

11. Nigel Leask, *British Romantic Writers and the East: Anxieties of Empire* (Cambridge: Cambridge Univ. Press, 1993), 141–54.

12. For a development of this point, see Marilyn Butler, "Orientalism," in *Sphere History of English Literature: the Romantic Period,* ed. David Pirie (London: Penguin, 1993).

13. The symbolic language and furniture of the poem belong generically to late-Enlightenment syncretic religion, so that to look for sources is strictly redundant. But for many of the poem's better-documented passages on, for instance, symbolic animals, nature gods, the Egyptian bull, and the hermaphrodite, compare discussions in the first forty pages of Richard Payne Knight's *An Inquiry into the Symbolic Language of Ancient Art and Mythology* (London: A. J. Valpy, 1818).

Chapter 14:   SHELLEY'S INDIA

1. "Instructions by Major General Sir John Malcolm, To Officers Acting Under his Orders in Central India in 1812," in Sir John Malcolm, *The Political History of India from 1784 to 1823* (London, 1826), app. 8, cclxiii–cclxiv.

2. Bernard Cohn, "The Command of Language and the Language of Command," *Subaltern Studies IV: Writings on South Asian History and Society,* ed. Ranajit Guha (New Delhi: Oxford Univ. Press, 1985), 276, 283.

3. William Jones, *Asiatic Miscellany,* 2 vols., ed. Francis Gladwin (Calcutta, 1785–86) 1:22.

4. Edward Said, *Orientalism* (New York: Vintage, 1979), 115.

5. Raymond Schwab, *The Oriental Renaissance: Europe's Rediscovery of India and the East,* 1680–1880, trans. G. Patterson-Black and V. Reinking (New York: Columbia Univ. Press, 1984), 63.

6. For an elaboration of Owenson's influence, see John Drew, *India and the Romantic Imagination* (New Delhi: Oxford Univ. Press, 1987), 241–58.

7. In his essay "The Intentional Structure of the Romantic Image," Paul de Man argues that poetic language is "unable to give a foundation to what it posits except as an intention of consciousness"; in *Romanticism and Consciousness,* ed. Harold Bloom (New York: Norton, 1970), 69.

8. M. K. Gandhi, *Collected Works* (New Delhi: Publications Division of the Government of India), 1:289.

9. M. K. Gandhi, *Satyagraha in South Africa: The Selected Works of Mahatma Gandhi* (Ahmedabad, India: Navjivan Trust, 1986), 3:150–51.

10. For an elaboration, see Gauri Viswanathan, *The Masks of Conquest: Literary Study and British Rule in India* (New York: Columbia Univ. Press, 1989), 142–65.

11. Quoted in Tapan Raychaudhuri, *Europe Reconsidered: Perceptions of the West in Nineteenth Century Bengal* (New Delhi: Oxford Univ. Press, 1988), 14.

12. Thomas Babington Macaulay, *Selected Poetry and Prose,* ed. G. M. Young (Cambridge, Mass.: Harvard Univ. Press, 1967), 729.

13. Benedict Anderson, *Imagined Communities* (London: Verso, 1991), 9.

14. Gandhi, *Collected Works,* 68:202–4.

15. *Young India,* 13, no. 8 (New Series) (February 23, 1921): 57, 59, 61.

Chapter 15:   SHELLEY'S HUMANE CONCERN
AND THE DEMISE OF APARTHEID

1. Shelley's pointed reference to the negro implies his condemnation of the system of slave labor that in the colonies was justified on grounds of racial superiority. He also understands that the concept of race is underpinned by a struggle for power based on wealth. Thus the peasantry are the class of poor, who "rose against their natural enemies, the rich, and repaid with bloody interest the tyranny of ages"; ibid.

2. F. R. Leavis, *Revaluations* (London: Chatto and Windus, 1949), 206.

3. At the time this essay was written, South Africa was still governed by the white minority class. Since then, free elections have been successfully held in April 1994, following a period of complex negotiations; Nelson Mandela—after 27 years of imprisonment—is the new President; and a government of national unity has been instituted for a period of five years, to oversee the transition to full majority rule. In his inaugural speech on May 10, 1994, Nelson Mandela declared, "The time for the healing of the wounds has come. The moment to bridge the chasms that divide us has come. The time to build is upon us" (*Star,* May 11, 1994).

4. I refer, in particular, to the historic meeting in Dakar in 1987 between Afrikaans dissidents and the African National Congress (ANC). This meeting took place in spite of the government's refusal to talk to the ANC and the continuance of its fierce propaganda campaign against the organization. Commenting on the Dakar meeting, the organizer, former opposition leader of the Progressive Party Frederick van Zyl Slabbert, said that "an 'extraordinary meeting of minds' occurred there. 'We found that we have a great deal in common . . . and although there are some differences we found that there is a great deal of flexibility and negotiability'"; Allister Sparks, *The Mind of South Africa: The Story of the Rise and Fall of Apartheid* (London: Heinemann, 1990), 384.

5. As a political ideology, apartheid originates in the segregationist policy formulated at the beginning of the twentieth century; Saul Dubow, *Racial Segregation and the Origins of Apartheid in South Africa, 1919–36* (London: Macmillan, 1989). As a concept, it came into being from the moment the first traders settled at the Cape and planted what Sparks calls "A Hedge of Bitter Almonds"; *Mind of South Africa,* 15–18.

6. Frantz Fanon, *The Wretched of the Earth,* trans. Constance Farrington (Harmondsworth, U.K.: Penguin, 1963; rpt. 1990).

7. J. M. Coetzee, *White Writing: On the Culture of Letters in South Africa* (New Haven, Conn.: Yale Univ. Press, 1988), 12–35.

8. Njabulo S. Ndebele, "The English Language and Social Change in South Africa," *TriQuarterly* 69 (Spring-Summer 1987): 224.

9. Sartre writes: "Our soldiers overseas, rejecting the universalism of the mother country, apply the 'numerus clausus' to the human race: since none may enslave, rob or kill his fellowman without committing a crime, they lay down the principle that the native is not one of our fellow-men. . . . the order is given to reduce the inhabitants of the annexed country to the level of superior monkeys in order to justify the settler's treatment of them as beasts of burden. Violence in the colonies does not only have for its aim the keeping of these enslaved men at arm's length; it seeks to dehumanize them"; preface to *The Wretched of the Earth,* 13.

10. Sartre, preface, 21.

11. Sparks, *Mind of South Africa,* 11.

12. Clause (c) of section 47(2) of the Publications Act indicates the very broad terms of the censorship code: any "publication or object, film, public entertainment or intended public entertainment. . . . [is] undesirable if it or any part of it is prejudicial to the safety of the State, the general welfare or the peace and good order"; Publications Act No. 42, *Statutes of the Republic of South Africa* (Pretoria: Butterworths, 1974), 117.

13. Frantz Fanon, *Black Skin, White Masks,* trans. Charles Lam Markmann (London: Pluto Press, 1967; rpt. 1991), 231.

14. "8,967 people are said to have died in violence since the new reforms were announced in 1990"; *Sunday Times* (Johannesburg), August 22, 1993, 5. In 1993 some 4,398 died in a frenzied outburst of enmity and lawlessness; *Human Rights Commission Human Rights Review: South Africa* 1993 (Johannesburg: Braamfontein, 1994), 15.

15. Fanon, *Black Skin, White Masks,* 192.

16. Rian Malan, *My Traitor's Heart* (London: Bodley Head, 1990), 344. For the moment, reason has prevailed and that is why the election in South Africa has been

called a "small miracle." It remains to be seen whether reason is assured and whether love can indeed triumph. In pledging his country to a new order—a "golden age"—Mandela believes that the conditions for future success have indeed been met: "We have triumphed in the effort to implant hope in the breasts of the millions of our people. We enter into a covenant that we shall build the society in which all South Africans, both black and white, will be able to walk tall, without any fear in their hearts, assured of their inalienable right to human dignity—a rainbow nation at peace with itself and the world" (inaugural speech, *Star,* May 11, 1994). While acknowledging that there is much to be done, Mandela has more recently remarked in an interview " . . . You could not have expected that the transition would have been so smooth—that the population would respond so impressively, so remarkably. That is why I say this transition has gone better than my wildest dreams" (*Saturday Star,* May 20, 1995).

Chapter 16: SHELLEY AND BRECHT

1. The fullest comparison of the two works is in Richard Cronin, *Shelley's Poetic Thoughts* (New York: St. Martin's Press, 1981), 39–55; see also S. S. Prawer, *Comparative Literary Studies: An Introduction* (New York: Barnes and Noble, 1973), 92–96.

2. This is the argument both of the Marxist reading of events by E. P. Thompson, *The Making of the English Working Class* (New York: Vintage, 1966), 682–84, and of a typical revisionist reading, Donald Read, *Peterloo: The "Massacre" and Its Background* (Manchester: Manchester Univ. Press, 1958), 113–22. For an overview of the historiographic issues, see Philip Lawson, "Reassessing Peterloo," *History Today* 38 (March 1988): 24–29.

3. P. M. S. Dawson, *The Unacknowledged Legislator: Shelley and Politics* (Oxford: Clarendon Press, 1980), 222, suggests that Shelley's concept of "legislator" should be defined in the context of the practical politics of the Reform movement.

4. Stuart Curran, *Shelley's Annus Mirabilis: The Maturing of an Epic Vision* (San Marino, Calif.: Huntington Library, 1975), 190–91.

5. David Mayer, *Harlequin in His Element: The English Pantomime, 1806–1836* (Cambridge, Mass.: Harvard Univ. Press, 1969), 23–31. The sources for pantomime figures—as found in the commedia dell'arte—were much in vogue among twentieth-century European artists; Brecht was greatly interested in this and other popular theatrical traditions.

6. On the poem's strange asymmetries, see Morton Paley, "Apocapolitics: Allusion and Structure in Shelley's *Mask of Anarchy*," *Huntington Library Quarterly* 54, no. 2 (Spring 1991): 91–109.

7. The German text of Brecht's *Der anachronistiche Zug oder Freiheit und Democracy* is from *Gedichte 3, Gesammelte Werke* (Frankfurt am Main: Suhrkamp Verlag, 1967), 10:943–49. I quote from the English translation in *Bertolt Brecht Poems 1913–1956,* ed. John Willett and Ralph Manheim (New York: Methuen, 1979), 409–14. The ballad is cited hereafter in the text by line number; the Willett-Manheim text is cited as *Poems.*

8. Frederic Ewen, *Bertolt Brecht: His Life, His Art, His Times* (1967; rpt. New York: Citadel, 1992) 390 (page citation is to the reprint edition).

9. Prawer, *Comparative Literary Studies,* 95.

10. Walter Benjamin, "Brecht's Threepenny Novel," in *Reflections,* ed. Peter Demetz, trans. Edmund Jephcott (New York: Schocken, 1986), 201–2.

11. For an openly interested discussion of these exchanges, see Terry Eagleton, *Marxism and Literary Criticism* (Berkeley: Univ. of California Press, 1976), 63–67.

12. Brecht, "Weite und Vielfalt der realistischen Schreibweise," *Schriften zur Literatur und Kunst 2, Gesammelte Werke,* 19:340–49. Translations of Brecht's prose are my own, but various competing translations of his key critical terms are by now conventional.

13. Brecht, "Über experimentelles Theater," *Schriften zum Theater 1, Gesammelte Werke* 15:285–305.

14. Brecht, *Weite und Vielfalt,* 348.

15. Brecht, "Volkstümlichkeit und Realismus," *Schriften zur Literatur und Kunst 2, Gesammelte Werke,* 19–326.

16. Ewen, *Bertolt Brecht,* 415–42.

17. *Poems,* 593n.

18. Ewen, *Bertolt Brecht,* 443.

19. See William Blackstone, *Commentaries on the Laws of England,* 4 vols. (Oxford: Clarendon Press, 1773), 1:194–95, and the influential political application by Edmund Burke, *Reflections on the Revolution in France,* ed. Conor Cruise O'Brien (Harmondsworth, U.K.: Penguin, 1986), 103–5.

20. Bodleian MS. Shelley adds. e. 18, Bodleian Library, Oxford University.

21. As reported in *Communications from the International Brecht Society* 19, no. 1 (November 1990): 80, 86.

Chapter 17:   SHELLEY'S "SOCIALISM" REVISITED

1. William Keach, *Shelley's Style* (New York: Methuen, 1984). See my review in *Zeitschrift für Anglistik und Amerikanistik* 37 (1989): 174.

2. Newman Ivey White, *Shelley,* 2 vols. (New York: Knopf, 1940), 2:406.

3. Friedrich Engels, *Die Lage der arbeitenden Klasse in England* (1845), in Marx Engels, *Werke* (Berlin: Dietz Verlag, 1956–68) 2:455. Hereafter cited as *MEW.*

4. Edward Aveling and Eleanor Marx Aveling, *Shelley's Socialism* (1888; rpt. London: Journeyman Press, 1979), 16 (page citation is to the reprint edition).

5. *Die Neue Zeit* (Stuttgart) 6 (1888).

6. Georg Herwegh, "Sonnet 11: Shelley" (1840) in *Gedichte eines Legendigen* (1841; Stuttgart:: Göschen, 1847), 101.

7. Cited in Solomon Liptzin, *Shelley in Germany* (New York: Columbia Univ. Press, 1924), 57–58.

8. Gustav Kühne, "Shelley," in *Weibliche und männliche Charaktere* (Leipzig: Engelmann, 1838), 116.

9. "Feuerbach löst das religiöse Wesen in das *menschliche* Wesen auf. Aber das menschliche Wesen ist kein dem einzelnen innewohnendes Abstraktum. In seiner Wirklichkeit ist es das Ensemble der gesellschaftlichen Verhältnisse. Feuerbach, mit dem *abstrakten Denken* nicht zufrieden, appelliert an die *sinnliche Anschauung;* aber er faßt die Sinnlichkeit nicht als *praktische* menschlichsinnliche Tätigkeit." (Feuerbach dissolves religious essence into *human* essence. But human essence is not an abstraction inherent to the individual. In its reality it is the ensemble of social relations. Feuerbach, not satisfied with *abstract thinking,* appeals to *sensual perception;* but he does not conceive of sensuality as *practical* human sensuality.) *MEW* 2:534.

10. *MEW* 4:482. Engels: "Die Gesellschaft kann sich selbstredend nicht befreien, ohne daß jeder einzelne befreit wird." (It goes without saying that society cannot liberate itself as long as each individual is not liberated.) *MEW* 20:273.

11. "Daß von den Jüngeren zuweilen mehr Gewicht auf die ökonomische Seite gelegt wird, als ihr zukommt, haben Marx und ich teilweise selbst verschulden müssen. Wir hatten den Gegnern gegenüber das von diesen geleugnete Hauptprinzip zu betonen, und das war nicht immer Gelegenheit, die übrigen an der Wechselwirkung beteiligten Momente zu ihrem Recht kommen zu lassen. . . . Und diesen Vorwurf kann ich manchen der neueren 'Marxisten' nicht ersparen, und es ist dann wunderbares Zeug geleistet worden." (To a certain extent, Marx and I had to be guilty of the fact that the younger ones have sometimes put more emphasis on the economic side than is due to it. We had to stress this main principle against opponents who denied it, and there was not always room for doing justice to those factors which have a share in the interrelations. . . . And I cannot exempt certain later "Marxists" of this reproach, and so a lot of miraculous stuff has been produced.) Engels to Conrad Schmidt, August 5, 1890, *MEW* 37:234.

12. Anatoly Lunacharsky, *Die Revolution und die Kunst* (Dresden: Verlag der Kunst, 1964); Walter Benjamin, *Der Begriff der Kunstkritik in der deutschen Romantik* (Bern: Francke, 1920).

13. "Am deutschen Wesen soll die Welt genesen" (The world should be cured by regarding the German character) is a line from a poem by the nineteenth-century German poet Emmanuel Geibel.

14. Bertolt Brecht, *Über Lyrik* (Frankfurt am Main: Suhrkamp, 1964).

15. Johann Wolfgang von Goethe, *Über Kunst und Literatur*, ed. Wilhelm Girnus (Berlin: Aufbau-Verlag, 1953), 95.

16. W. Winogradow, "Zu den Diskussionen um Wort und Bild," *Kunst und Literatur* 8 (1960): 892–917.

17. Anna Arkadevna Elistratova, *Nasledie angliiskogo romantizma i sovremennost* (Moscow: Izdatelstvo Akademiia Nauk SSSR, 1960), 13.

18. See also the significant work by I. N. Neupokoyeva and N. J. Diakonova.

19. Elistratova, *Nasledie*, 14, 15.

20. August Wilhelm Schlegel, *Vorlesungen über schöne Literatur und Kunst* (Heilbronn: Henninger, 1884), 279.

21. Horst Höhne, "Shelleys 'Der entfesselte Prometheus,'" *Weimarer Beiträge* 35 (1989): 2007–26.

Chapter 18: SHELLEY IN POSTERITY

1. Paul de Man, *Allegories of Reading: Figural Language in Rousseau, Nietzsche, Rilke, and Proust* (New Haven, Conn.: Yale Univ. Press, 1979), 273.

2. Compare Jacques Derrida's more general comments on writing and the death of the addressee in, for example, "Signature, Event, Context," in *Margins of Philosophy*, trans. Alan Bass (Brighton, U.K.: Harvester, 1982), 315–16.

3. Timothy Clark, *Embodying Revolution: The Figure of the Poet in Shelley* (Oxford: Oxford Univ. Press, 1989), 222.

4. *Shelley: The Critical Heritage*, ed. James E. Barcus (London: Routledge and Kegan Paul, 1975), 114.

5. For a useful summary of Shelley's print runs and sales figures, see Barcus, *Critical Heritage*, 3–4.

6. See P. M. S. Dawson, *The Unacknowledged Legislator: Shelley and Politics* (Oxford: Oxford Univ. Press, 1980), 252–54; Stephen C. Behrendt, *Shelley and His Audiences* (Lincoln: Univ. of Nebraska Press, 1989), 233–34; Clark, *Embodying Revolution*, 212–23.

7. See, for example, Jerome McGann, *Social Values and Poetic Acts: The Historical Judgment of Literary Work* (Cambridge, Mass.: Harvard Univ. Press, 1988); Alvin Kernan, *Printing, Technology, Letters and Samuel Johnson* (Princeton, N.J.: Princeton Univ. Press, 1987); Lee Erickson, "The Poet's Corner: The Impact of Technological Changes in Printing on English Poetry, 1800–1850," *ELH* 52 (1985): 893–911; Clifford Siskin, *The Historicity of Romantic Discourse* (New York: Oxford Univ. Press, 1988); Marilyn Butler, *Romantics, Rebels and Reactionaries: English Literature and its Background, 1760–1830* (Oxford: Oxford Univ. Press, 1981); Elizabeth L. Eisenstein, *The Printing Press as an Agent of Change: Communications and Cultural Transformations in Early-Modern Europe,* 2 vols. (Cambridge: Cambridge Univ. Press, 1979); Jon P. Klancher, *The Making of English Reading Audiences, 1790–1832* (Madison: Univ. of Wisconsin Press, 1987); Tilottama Rajan, *The Supplement of Reading: Figures of Understanding in Romantic Theory and Practice* (Ithaca: Cornell Univ. Press, 1990).

8. Jean-François Lyotard and Jean-Loup Thébaud, *Just Gaming,* trans. Wlad Godzich (Manchester: Manchester Univ. Press, 1985) 9. In a comment that cannot but be read in the context of Shelley's political messages in bottles, homemade boats, and balloons (see Richard Holmes, *Shelley: The Pursuit* [London: Weidenfeld and Nicolson, 1974], 148–50), Lyotard says that "I believe that it is important that there be no addressee. When you cast bottles to the water, you don't know to whom they are going, and that is all to the good. That must be part of modernity, I think."

9. See Philip W. Martin, *Byron: A Poet Before His Public* (Cambridge: Cambridge Univ. Press, 1982), 38; Hyder Edward Rollins, *The Keats Circle: Letters and Papers 1816–1878,* 2 vols. (Cambridge, Mass.: Harvard Univ. Press, 1948) 1:52–53.

10. See Jacques Derrida, "Living On: Border Lines," in *Deconstruction and Criticism,* ed. Harold Bloom et al. (New York: Seabury Press, 1979).

11. This vocabulary of "crypts" and "haunting" is taken from the psychoanalysis of Nicolas Abraham and Maria Torok; see *The Wolf Man's Magic Word: A Cryptonymy,* trans. Nicholas Rand (Minneapolis: Univ. of Minnesota Press, 1986). See also Esther Rashkin, "Tools for a New Psychoanalytic Literary Criticism: The Work of Abraham and Torok," *Diacritics* 18 (1988): 31–52.

12. Karen Mills-Courts, *Poetry as Epitaph: Representation and Poetic Language* (Baton Rouge: Louisiana State Univ. Press, 1990) 37.

13. Paul de Man, "Autobiography as De-Facement," in *The Rhetoric of Romanticism* (New York: Columbia Univ. Press, 1984), 78: "'Doth make us marble,' in the *Essays upon Epitaphs,* cannot fail to evoke the latent threat that inhabits prosopopoeia, namely that by making death speak, the symmetrical structure of the trope implies, by the same token, that the living are struck dumb, frozen in their own death. The

surmise of the 'Pause, Traveller!' thus acquires a sinister connotation that is not only the prefiguration of one's own mortality but our actual entry into the frozen world of the dead."

Chapter 19: SHELLEY'S INEFFABLE QUOTIDIAN

1. I quote Stevens from *The Palm at the End of the Mind,* ed. Holly Stevens (New York: Vintage–Random House, 1972), 374.

2. Frances Ferguson, "What the Mountain Said," in *Romanticism and Language,* ed. Arden Reed (Ithaca: Cornell Univ. Press, 1984), 202.

3. I refer, respectively, to David Simpson, *Wordsworth and the Figurings of the Real* (London: Macmillan, 1982), and Stuart Curran, *Poetic Form and British Romanticism* (New York: Oxford Univ. Press, 1986).

4. John Horne-Tooke, *Diversions of Purley,* 2 vols. (Menston, U.K.: Scolar Press, 1968), 2:406.

5. See Stuart Curran, "The I Altered," in *Romanticism and Feminism,* ed. Anne Mellor (Bloomington: Indiana Univ. Press, 1988), 185–207.

6. See, for example, P. M. S. Dawson, *The Unacknowledged Legislator: Shelley and Politics* (Oxford: Clarendon Press, 1980); Terence Allan Hoagwood, *Skepticism and Ideology: Shelley's Political Prose and Its Philosophical Context from Bacon to Marx* (Iowa City: Univ. of Iowa Press, 1988); and Michael Henry Scrivener, *Radical Shelley: The Philosophical Anarchism and Utopian Thought of Percy Bysshe Shelley* (Princeton, N.J.: Princeton Univ. Press, 1982). The *Shelley and His Circle* volumes also provide excellent political and social contexts for Shelley's thought.

Chapter 20: "THE EMPIRE OF MAN"

1. Jonathan Bate, *Romantic Ecology: Wordsworth and the Environmental Tradition* (London: Routledge, 1991).

2. NIMBY: an acronym for Not In My Back Yard, coined in Britain as a satirical description for those who object to developments that have an adverse affect on their own local environment.

3. *Bodleian MS Shelley e. 4: A Facsimile Edition with Full Transcription and Textual Notes,* ed. P. M. S. Dawson (New York: Garland Publishing, 1987), 101; also in *Shelley's Prose; or, The Trumpet of a Prophecy,* ed. D. L. Clark (Albuquerque: Univ. of New Mexico Press, 1954), 207–8.

4. Richard Cronin, "Shelley's Language of Dissent," *Essays in Criticism* 28 (1977): 214.

5. Cf. "The concordance between the mind of man and the nature of things that he [Bacon] had in mind is patriarchal: the human mind, which overcomes superstition, is to hold sway over a disenchanted nature"; Theodor Adorno and Max Horkheimer, *Dialectic of Enlightenment,* trans. John Cumming (1944; rpt. London: Verso, 1979), 4 (page citation is to the reprint edition).

6. Passion particularly is seen with some ambivalence; an early poem stresses this in addressing the woody nightshade, *Solanum dulcamara,* known also as the bittersweet; see *The Poems of Shelley,* vol. 1, ed. Geoffrey Matthews and Kelvin Everest (London: Longman, 1989), 189–91. This plant remains a stable code in Shelley's work, losing its poisonous nature in his utopian passages in order to figure a passion no longer destructive and thus no longer needing to be repressed (see *Queen Mab,* 8:129–30, *Prometheus Unbound,* 3.2.78–83).

7. In *Queen Mab* he suggests that the "war" between "judgment" and "passion's unsubduable array" is "unnatural" and will cease when once "suicidal selfishness" has withered away (5:16–21). The early poem cited in note 6 blames the destructive effects of passion on "Custom's chains" (line 46), and *Queen Mab* sees the two as having been equally oppressed by "falsehood"; with the latter's disappearance they are imaged as loving "sisters" (9:43–56).

8. Cf. "Man's domination over himself, which grounds his selfhood, is almost always the destruction of the subject in whose service it is undertaken; for the substance which is dominated, suppressed, and dissolved by virtue of self-preservation is none other than that very life as functions of which the achievements of self-preservation find their sole definition and determination: it is, in fact, what is to be preserved"; Adorno and Horkheimer, *Dialectic of Enlightenment,* 54–55.

9. Shelley's atheism is no real obstacle to inscribing him within the Judeo-Christian tradition, as he himself as good as acknowledges when he refers to labor as "the curse imposed on Adam." Milton would consider his account of liberty and tyranny as biblical, but it proves easy to secularize for Shelley's purposes, and it may not be irrelevant that Shelley's basic exposition of this account is offered in the context of an attempt to recuperate Christ's teaching.

10. Walt Kelly, *The Best of Pogo,* ed. Mrs. Walter Kelly and Bill Crouch, Jr. (New York: Simon and Schuster, 1982), 163, 224.

Chapter 21: PROMETHEAN NARRATIVE

1. Fredric Jameson, *The Political Unconscious: Narrative as a Socially Symbolic Act* (Ithaca, N.Y.: Cornell Univ. Press, 1981), 41.

2. Ibid., 50–52.

3. Julia Kristeva, "The Adolescent Novel," in *Abjection, Melancholia and Love: The Work of Julia Kristeva,* ed. John Fletcher and Andrew Benjamin (London: Routledge, 1990), 10, 21.

4. Peter Brooks, *The Melodramatic Imagination: Balzac, Henry James, Melodrama, and the Mode of Excess* (New Haven, Conn.: Yale Univ. Press, 1976), 105.

5. All page references to Shelley's novels are to Percy Bysshe Shelley, *Zastrozzi and St. Irvyne,* ed. Stephen C. Behrendt (Oxford: Oxford Univ. Press, 1986).

6. I use the word *"idea"* in its Hegelian sense, in which it functions as an empty category or signifier variously filled in the course of the world-historical process, in accordance with the current narrativization of the political unconscious.

7. For further elaboration, see my chapter on *Prometheus Unbound* in *The Supplement of Reading: Figures of Understanding in Romantic Theory and Practice* (Ithaca, N.Y.: Cornell Univ. Press, 1990), 298–322.

8. For further discussion of the Bodleian manuscript, see *The Supplement of Reading,* 319–21.

Chapter 22:   PROMETHEUS UNBOUND

1. Fredric Jameson, "Postmodernism, or the Cultural Logic of Late Capitalism," *New Left Review* 146 (1984): 80–84.

2. David Harvey, *The Condition of Postmodernity* (Oxford: Basil Blackwell, 1989), 273.

3. Jean Baudrillard, *Selected Writings,* ed. Mark Poster (Stanford, Calif.: Stanford Univ. Press, 1988), 156–57 (italics in original).

4. Harvey, *Condition of Postmodernity,* 253.

5. Michael Henry Scrivener, *Radical Shelley: The Philosophical Anarchism and Utopian Thought of Percy Bysshe Shelley* (Princeton, N.J.: Princeton Univ. Press, 1982), 160.

7. Donald H. Reiman, "Shelley as Agrarian Reactionary," *Keats-Shelley Memorial Bulletin* 30 (1979): 5–15.

7. Jean, Baudrillard, *Mirror of Production,* trans. Mark Poster (St. Louis: Telos Press, 1975), 162.

Chapter 23:   ALL SHAPES OF LIGHT

1. Karl H. Grabo, *A Newton among Poets: Shelley's Use of Science in* Prometheus Unbound (Chapel Hill: Univ. of North Carolina Press, 1930).

2. *The Philosophical Writings of Niels Bohr* (Woodbridge, Conn.: Ox Bow Press, 1987), 1:54–55. The literature on the subject is by now enormous. I have considered

the relationships between modern physics and critical theory in detail in *Complementarity: Anti-Epistemology After Bohr and Derrida* (Durham, N.C.: Duke Univ. Press, 1994).

3. These measurements can be mathematically represented and are often interpreted in terms of probability or statistics. As Bohr warns, however, conceptually this language can be misleading.

4. See especially Jacques Derrida's "White Mythology: Metaphor in the Text of Philosophy," in *Margins of Philosophy,* trans. Alan Bass (Chicago: Univ. of Chicago Press, 1982), 207–71.

5. Paul de Man, "Shelley Disfigured," in *The Rhetoric of Romanticism* (New York: Columbia Univ. Press, 1984), 117.

6. Ibid., 117, 122.

7. Stuart Curran, *Shelley's Annus Mirabilis: The Maturing of an Epic Vision* (San Marino, Calif.: Huntington Library, 1975).

Shelley : poet and legislator of the world / edited by Betty T. Bennett and
    Stuart Curran
        p.   cm.
    Includes bibliographical references (p.   )
    ISBN 0-8018-5175-0 (cloth : alk. paper).—ISBN 0-8018-5176-9 (pbk. : alk.
paper)
    1. Shelley, Percy Bysshe, 1792–1822—Political and social views—
Congresses.   2. Politics and literature—Great Britain—History—19th century
—Congresses.   3. Literature and society—England—History—19th century—
Congresses.   4. Romanticism—Great Britain—Congresses.   I. Bennett,
Betty T.   II. Curran, Stuart.
PR5442.S58S48   1995
821'.7—dc20   95-21793
                                                              CIP